The *Legendary*
MODEL T
FORD

The Ultimate History of America's First Great Automobile

Tom Collins

©2007 Krause Publications

Published by

krause publications
An Imprint of F+W Publications

700 East State Street • Iola, WI 54990-0001
715-445-2214 • 888-457-2873
www.krausebooks.com

Our toll-free number to place an order or obtain
a free catalog is (800) 258-0929.

Library of Congress Control Number: 2007924548
ISBN-13: 978-0-89689-560-7
ISBN-10: 0-89689-560-2

Designed by Kara Grundman
Edited by Tom Collins

Printed in China

Dedication

Dedicated to Grandpa Ralph Becker, especially for his memories of "Model T Days."

Ralph Becker, with his wife Lucille, worked on Model T Fords with his step-dad, John Becker beginning in his teens. He retired as a respected auto mechanic from Cuene Buick, Green Bay, Wisconsin, in 1972.

You can be sure this Model T Fordor on the Becker's Garage lot was in top condition. "Drive with certainty" was their slogan. Their word was a bond Model T and other drivers trusted.

Introduction

Imagine a scene in the summer of 1961. A dad and his son are touring the Henry Ford Museum in Dearborn, Michigan. Spotting a 1926 Model T, the dad points out that it was the first year for an opening door on the driver's side. The dad was just 20 years old when that change was made on Model Ts made in the U.S.

And the son remembered.

The dad was Charlie Collins, my dad, who was born in 1906 and grew up with Model Ts around his rural neighborhood near Montello, Wisconsin, as well as a Dort and an Oakland. But most people drove or learned to drive on the Model T Ford.

My mother, Helen Hemmy Collins, learned to drive a Model T at age 12 in 1924, helping her father, Dr. Christian Hemmy, on his rounds as a veterinarian based in New London, Wisconsin.

Growing up in the late 1950s and 1960s, I learned about demountable rims, retarding the spark, attending to the throttle and all the rest.

From stories about my grandfather, I knew the T could kick if not properly treated. But Grandpa had treated some of the best horses in Wisconsin and he knew how to treat his Model T properly. He was strong enough and it was light enough that he could lift the front end, if needed.

Model T stories also flowed from another person who had grown up with them, my grandfather-in-law, Ralph Becker. Grandpa Ralph was just a teenager when he began working with his step-dad, John, at Becker's Garage in De Pere, Wisconsin. Grandpa Ralph used to take the train to Milwaukee and sit on a box placed over the gas tank driving a Model T chassis to De Pere or Green Bay where bodies were put on the cars. All of us enjoyed hearing about "Model T days."

On one of my birthdays in grade school, I was given an AMT-sized 1/25th scale Model T kit. It came with parts to make a scale version of a Model T—roadster or coupe—and also parts for a hot rod. I chose the roadster with the pickup box and used the hot rod parts to make another car.

In black plastic form the Model T seemed rather fragile but I learned along the way that these cars were pretty tough and often survived some incredible circumstances and came back for more.

These were cars that changed North America and the world. Everyone could afford one and could find a way to keep them running in all kinds of weather and in the most primitive road conditions.

Some thought the Model Ts were gawky, perhaps even ugly. I've always thought they had a friendly look to them. They gave people around the world a chance to get behind the wheel, many for the first time. I'd say they must have looked pretty handsome to many of those drivers!

It's an honor to be able to chronicle their history for Krause Publications and to learn more about these wonderful cars. They were simple and straightforward. They changed the way all of us live today. Anyone who gets behind the wheel of a car or truck today owes something to the Model T. Its legend endures.

I'd like to thank Keith Mathiowetz, Bruce McCalley and especially Don Chandler for their technical advice and information. Many have contributed photos, including pros like Tom Glatch, Bob Harrington, Doug Mitchel, Tom Myers, Mike Mueller, Robin Salmon and Don Voelker.

And dedicated people like Jerry Banks, Dr. Herb Bloom, David Lyon, David Nolting, Don Radbruch and others offered their photos and valuable information. There were many people who offered their stories—readers who sent dozens of letters and shared incredible memories. They're all in the book, though edited for space.

Some special thanks to my former supervisor, Brian Earnest and my current "coach," John Gunnell for trusting me with this project while I still was balancing a typical workload. I'm also very grateful for the Krause Publications archives for all their well-preserved materials and for the generosity of librarians at the Clintonville, Wisconsin, Public Library.

My friend and fellow writer Mary Thoele helped with

some editing advice along the way and my constant friend and spouse, Kathy, took time from her always-busy schedule to do some editing as well.

Thanks for thinking outside of the box to Henry Ford and his dedicated associates. They produced a car that continues to be a favorite of people around the world.

"Déan aon uair is beidh sé déanta faoi dheoidh," they would say in Irish Gaelic, "Do it right once and it will be done forever."

I hope you will enjoy this look at Model T Days.

Tom Collins.
Mar. 17, 2007

CONTENTS

CHAPTER 1

HENRY FORD & HIS EDUCATION IN CAR MAKING

Henry Ford's vision of a car that most people could afford put North America and the world in motion.   *Robin Heil-Kern*

Young Henry Ford was like many people of his era. He was inventive, handy and intrigued by machines.

Some say the Model T was an extension of Henry Ford's inner self. When one begins to probe the man, one begins to understand his thinking about the car. And the Model T and the man have been forever linked in history. Yet, Ford didn't begin with the Model T. He didn't just open a garage door one day and drive out into the world with his car that transformed the automotive world.

His was a long process of learning filled with many tangents, twists and even setbacks, all of which molded him into the man he eventually became. Ford's education and experience was largely by doing. Formal education always was a struggle for him, but when he could put his hands on something, often tinkering with it, he began to absorb and dream.

When a child of friend Harvey Firestone, the tire maker, proudly explained that he'd saved some money, Ford told the boy to buy a set of tools with his savings.

"Make something. Create something." [1]

Ford's advice revealed his path to success. He had experimented and created, learning along the way by doing. Yet there was a time when those in his family, especially his father, William, wondered what would become of Henry in life.

Ford definitely took a circuitous route from his childhood on a farm near Dearborn, Michigan, to his international fame as an automotive tycoon. At several points along the way, Ford might have spent his career as a talented machinist. He may have settled into his role as supervisor at Edison Illuminating Company in Detroit. Even his early steps with automobiles might easily have been lost to history along with such cars as the Crawford, Grout, Bliss, Lambert and Gale.

Perhaps if William Ford and others who doubted Henry could have obtained a list of leadership traits, they may have understood that young Ford was on his way to being someone special. Comparing Henry Ford's talents with a list provided in *Leadership Journal* is revealing. 2

Of the dozen traits listed, Ford would excel at each one by the time he and his team produced the first Model T Ford late in 1908.

Among those traits that stood out during Ford's "education by doing" years are these:

1. Creating or catching a vision.

(Just imagine Ford tinkering with his first engines or assembling his Quadricycle in 1896.)

2. Accepting the thrill of a challenge.

(Ford constantly took on work that allowed him to learn about portable steam traction engines, the intricacies of watches, gasoline engines and electricity.)

3. Using a spirit of discontent.

(Early in life, Ford knew he wanted to find ways to apply machinery to take away the drudgery of farm work.

Like the creations of several early inventors, the Ford Quadricycle was part bicycle, part coach and part futuristic invention.

Henry Ford was a tough-minded visionary whose way of thinking was different from others. Many times he kept his principles in the face of convention.

His displeasure with something often motivated him to create something new.)

4. Not being locked in the status quo.

(Ford had several chances to earn money and a comfortable living through farm work and in various machine trade jobs but always had his mind on inventions and learning new skills.)

5. Forming practical ideas.

(Ford liked to simplify technology. Whether it was mechanizing farm chores or tinkering with a steam engine, Ford enjoyed making things as practical as possible.)

6. Choosing good ideas.

(Early in life, Ford was known for sharing ideas and listening to fellow workers. He could sift through a number of ideas and pick those that would keep a project moving forward.)

7. Gaining peer respect.

(As Ford gained work experiences, he attracted loyal associates including Childe Harold Wills and "Spider" Huff, friends like Thomas Alva Edison and also a number of wealthy investors.)

8. Making others listen.

(Time and again, even when he was a struggling machinist, Ford had the almost charmed ability to have others listen, believe and follow his ideas.)

By the time the Model T appeared in 1908, Ford had proven his excellence in all 12 of the traits listed for dynamic leaders in the *Leadership Journal*.

In his book *The Reckoning* author David Halberstam described Ford in this manner:

"Henry Ford was an odd, somewhat cantankerous Michigan farmer whose mechanical skills had catapulted him far above the place in society where he felt comfortable. He was also perhaps the greatest celebrity of his time." [3]

Some of that quote probably would also describe the Model T! Ford did have several flaws, especially apparent as he aged, and some of his beliefs were rather odd.

He thought people with poor eyesight should exercise their eyes more and throw away their glasses. And he'd once observed people who worked in oil fields had healthy-looking hair so he applied kerosene to his hair daily and asked his personal secretary to keep a kersosene can in their office. [4]

For those who enjoy cars, Ford's pursuit of a practical and affordable vehicle for the masses, his support for a network of dealerships, his experiments with mass production, work time studies, worker compensation and education, and reinvesting profits in the business all exhibited the best of Ford's talents.

Following the first 45 years of Ford's life, before the Model T began production in 1908, also reveals that he was a very fortunate man in addition to being very talented. Time and again, people came into his life who influenced him, beginning with his mother, Mary, to men who guided him in his early work, like Frank Kirby, to friends he met like Charles B. King. Ford seemed to attract moneyed men who patiently supported him, including William Murphy and John S. Gray. Others close to him offered inspiration including Edison and Ford's wife, Clara.

Henry Ford was very much a young man of his era, someone who easily adapted to all things mechanical and learned on the fly by doing, absorbing, observing and experimenting. But one might also can say that Ford was not unique, even in that era.

There are long lists of people who built early self-propelled vehicles. Still others formed early car-building companies. A few carmakers earned success in the marketplace. A handful of those early names have survived in North America in addition to Ford including Dodge and Buick.

The 1909 Zimmerman resembled early Ford cars but this Indiana car company fell by the wayside of history. Ford Motor Co. cars survived and prospered.   Don Voelker

The 1901 Haynes-Apperson was an automotive partnership of early American car pioneers Elwood Haynes with Edgar and Elmer Apperson.   *Don Voelker*

Henry Ford knew cars had to go beyond the powered-buggy era. Cars like the 1908 Kiblinger were firmly entrenched in the power-buggy style.   *Don Voelker*

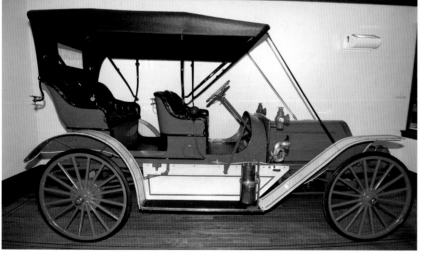

The 1909 McIntyre seemed on the fence retaining carriage-like high top and seats plus large artillery-style wooden wheels. It also had hints of modern touring cars of the day. *Don Voelker*

While Henry Ford had a dream, so did many others. One similar example is the Apperson Brothers, Elmer and Edgar, who built a gasoline-powered car with Elwood P. Haynes at Kokomo, Indiana, in 1894. Later, both Apperson and Haynes offered their own vehicles to the early automotive public.

Ford believed in proving cars through racing, but that was quite common in the early days of automaking. It helped draw attention to the cars as well as show people how tough and reliable the vehicle was that won the competition. Alexander Winton was just one prominent example of an early car racer who also built automobiles.

Ford was a Michigan boy who was thrilled with anything mechanical and shared tools with his father, yet Ransom E. Olds had a remarkably similar upbringing. And Olds built his first gasoline-powered vehicle the same year that Ford brought his Quadricycle to the streets of Detroit.

Ford eventually focused on bringing a practical, affordable car to the public, yet Olds had the same concept. His early curved dash Olds runabout was popular, practical, relatively inexpensive and a durable vehicle that led the nation in sales in 1903 and was written about in songs.

Ford earned a reputation as a talented machinist who attracted attention through his skills but so did Walter P. Chrysler, a mechanic who also gained vast amount of knowledge through experience in the railroad industry. Both Ford and Chrysler adapted those experiences, offered new possibilities and changed facets of automaking.

Ford was heavily influenced by the bicycle fad that dominated Europe and North America in the 1880s and 1890s and his Quadricycle had several bicycle influences. Yet Thomas Jeffery was also heavily involved in the wave of bicycle popularity. Jeffery brought out a screw-type device to attach tires to bicycle rims. When he saw his first automotive race, Jeffery built a car named after his popular Rambler bicycle. [5]

Certainly some who knew the Dodge Brothers, John and Horace, might have predicted they would succeed on a grander scale than young Henry Ford. Accomplished

The 1899 Locomobile borrowed heavily from bicycle technology. This restored example has a fire extinguisher and whitewall tires—no, they weren't period accessories!

machinists, tool makers and early automotive component makers, the Dodge Brothers had been involved in bicycle making in Canada, then turned to operating a machine works in Detroit. Later, they brought out a line of cars in their name.

At least twice, decisions by the Dodge Brothers would hold the fate of Henry Ford's future in their hands. Decisions they made helped Ford ventures make it through some tough times at critical points, but more on that to come in later chapters. Suffice it to say, the Dodge Brothers were important in Henry Ford's rise in the automaking world. 6

When the Ford Motor Company began production in 1903, another Detroit-area company was underway. It was a partnership that included one of Ford's friends who had filled his eyes with wonder at the sight of his motorized wagon rumbling down the street.

Today, little is said about pioneer automaker Charles B. King and his Northern. It was a practical, affordable car that was very similar in looks, price, engine size and innovations to the early Olds cars—and the cars that Henry Ford would produce. The Ford succeeded while the Northern fell by the side of the road.

This depiction of Henry Ford's workshop shows that it was a crucible of thought and invention.

Another contemporary of Henry Ford, David Buick, had the nation's leading car in 1908. But writers Terry B. Dunham and Lawrence Gustin said Buick was no longer with the company.

"David Buick has often been described as a tinkerer, dreamer [and] poor businessman." 7

Had his fate not taken other directions or had investors, suppliers and associates lost faith in him, Henry Ford and his early automotive pursuits might be recalled in a similar manner as David Buick.

Many people shared similar accomplishments as Henry Ford. Henry Leland was a master of precision. Alexander Winton and Louis Chevrolet were accomplished racers. The Duryea Brothers were the first in America with their 1893 automobile. The Olds was out in front in the sales race by 1903.

We know the outcome. Destiny took Henry Ford by the hand, guided him through some rough times and failures, mostly unscathed. Ford succeeded, continued to learn and focus and eventually surpassed them all. His life was like a Model T on a country road—he just kept plugging on. Ford was remarkably resilient.

When the Model T was at its most popular there were many jokes and stories about the car. "Is there anything a Model T Ford can't do?" one farmer asked another. The proud owner thought for a moment and answered, "Well, sir, she can't vote." [8]

Like his Model T, when Henry Ford decided he could do something, especially his concept of building practical cars, one like the other, there was no stopping him. Perhaps one thing that made Ford overcome everything was a sheer determination that never failed him.

On one occasion late in life, Ford was discussing education with a younger man named John Dahlinger, whom some say was Ford's illegitimate son. When Ford talked about his education, young Dahlinger tried to deflect the conversation and said he was talking about the present world.

"Young man," said Ford. "I invented the modern age." [9]

In some way, Ford had an inner confidence or a moral compass that kept him pointed in the proper direction and helped him keep moving forward. In his mind and soul, he knew that his work would change the world around him. In February 1900, he took a reporter for a ride in one of his early cars. Passing a blacksmith shop, Ford said: "His trade is doomed." [10]

ABOVE: *Clara Ford deeply influenced and supported her husband, Henry. Her patience helped him perfect his automotive dreams.*

CENTER: *In the mind of young Henry Ford, machines and mechanization meant a much better life for farm families.*

LEFT: *Farming in the 19th century often meant long hours of hard work, often by hand. Henry Ford thought that there should be a better way.*

That expression is remarkable. He understood that automobiles would become commonplace, that they would offer a new method of transportation and that their use would change the world. He hadn't worked all the bugs out of his early vehicle, yet he already had an innate understanding of the world he would play a part in creating. It was very simple to him—the sputtering, unreliable and intolerable automobile would overcome and replace the popular, conventional and dominant form of transportation, the horse.

Ford's firm will to win was as tough and flexible as vanadium steel. His wit disarmed the unsuspecting. His practical nature struck a chord with people everywhere. His rebellious streak found a way to overcome rules and never accepted conventional answers. His ability to think "out of the box" would have amazed those of today's computer generation. His visions of the future took him and his loyal associates to extraordinary levels.

Destiny's guide took Henry Ford through a meandering school of hard knocks, experimentation and hard work that wasn't so different from any of his contemporaries but in Ford's case, it helped him prepare for his future, from his boyhood ideas in rural Michigan through the machine shops, farms and plants where he worked in the first 40-plus years of his life.

At age 45, Ford caught lighting in a bottle in a way that can only be compared to the impact of Coca-Cola, the Beatles, color television and the personal computer, all rolled into one.

Henry Ford and his Model T literally moved society

From the Bagley Avenue workshop came Henry Ford's vision of what a car should be—light but strong, practical and versatile. That vision eventually became the Model T.

forward and in the process, changed the lives of carmakers, workers in car factories, people who owned the cars and people who learned to drive one of them. Cow paths and ruts that hadn't changed since the first horse and wagon churned them up were never the same again after the Model T Fords rolled over them.

By the time the Ford grew old and the T was outdated, America and the world started moving in a way nobody, even Ford, had ever imagined. The man and the car were superstars on a stage they had created. It had been a long journey for Henry Ford to that point.

Born near Dearborn, Michigan, in 1863, Henry Ford grew up in rural America at a time when the nation was on the move from its heavily rural past to something new, a country that was influenced by machines and industry. Nobody knew what direction the nation was headed but they knew that everything was in an upheaval.

Resourceful Americans were tinkering and dreaming in every conceivable way, it seemed, to make machines that would change the way they worked and lived. Young Henry Ford would be swept up in that tidal wave of change and experimentation, following the crowd and exploring the span of possibilities as he grew into adulthood.

"He was born with wheels in his head," said his father, William. 11

The elder Ford was an immigrant from the southern Irish coastal town of Clonakilty, County Cork. A carpenter, it was said William arrived in the United States nearly penniless but carrying a small tool box. He worked as a carpenter for railroads, traveling around the new land building train stations until he earned enough money to fulfill his dream, buying 120 acres of land near Dearborn, Michigan, in 1864.

William Ford was a presence in his rural Dearborn community serving as the local road commissioner and as a member of the school board. He took a term as Justice of the Peace and enjoyed reading sociology and philosophy. William attended the Philadelphia Exposition of Progress in 1876, a melting pot of new ideas at the time.

His oldest son, Henry, had a hard time in school. In fact, Henry Ford never really was at ease with reading or writing. Tools were another matter. With them, young Ford could express himself and be creative. William Ford was proud to see that his oldest son Henry could work with his hands.

"My toys were all tools," Henry once remarked. 12

"Father was quick to recognize Henry's ability in making new things," recalled Henry's sister, Margaret Ford Ruddiman. "…the shop was one of the best equipped in the neighborhood." 13

Yet William Ford's ideal was that Henry would apply his knowledge to farming and settle on the land. Henry disliked 19th century farm work and had a broader vision of the world in mind. He was much more of a dreamer than his father. It was a difference that would be a tug between father and son for many years.

Author Robert Lacey says the parent Henry adored was his mother, Mary Litogot O'Hern Ford, the adopted daughter of Patrick O'Hern. Her death at 37, when Henry was just 13, had a profound influence on him.

"I have tried to live my life as my mother would have wished," Ford recalled later in life. "She taught me that disagreeable jobs call for courage and patience, and she taught me …you may have pity on others, but you must not pity yourself." 14

One moment from his childhood that Henry Ford remembered vividly, even as an elderly man as his mind was failing him at times, was his first encounter with a Nichols and Shepard steam traction engine, rumbling down a rural road near his home. It was the first vehicle he'd ever seen not pulled by a horse.

"I was off the wagon and talking to the engineer before my father…knew what I was up to," Ford recalled. "…this one had a chain that made a connection between the engine and the rear wheels of the wagon-like frame in which the boiler was mounted." 15

Automobile historian Beverly Rae Kimes says young Henry began experimenting at his local school where an early steam turbine created some extra energy, and certainly must have drawn a crowd of youthful admirers, as it exploded and then set fire to a fence at the school! [16]

Another school boy experiment was designed to bring water to a farmer's field. It worked so well that the parched field became flooded! Ford always was thinking about some ways to alleviate farm drudgery. It was one pursuit he would follow most of his life. One of Ford's devices was applied to his father's farm, a mechanism that could close a farm gate from a wagon.

Kimes wrote that young Henry had a brief taste of the working world with the Michigan Car Company of Grand Truck Junction, a company that built and repaired streetcars. Henry Ford recalled that lesson of his six days of work at the Michigan Car shops.

"I learned not to tell all you know," said Ford. "I made repairs in about 10 percent of the time it took my cohorts." [17]

William Ford helped his son get his next job, with the James Flowers and Brothers Machine Shop. David Dunbar Buick also worked there early in his career. Henry earned $2.50 a week and also took a job repairing clocks and watches for the McGill Jewelry store at night.

A man named Fred Strauss offered a unique view of Ford, having worked with him at Flowers and Brothers and in later ventures.

"It was a great old shop," recalled Flowers. "They manufactured everything in the line of brass and iron—globe and gate valves, steam whistles, fire hydrants and valves for water pipes. They had all kinds of machinery, large and small lathes and drill presses..." [18]

After nine months with Flowers and Brothers, Ford moved on to Detroit Dry Dock Company, another step in his learning curve. Detroit Dry Dock made and repaired boats including some of the Great Lakes cargo carrying vessels of the day. Young Ford was exposed to various engines at the shops and also was guided by a creative and supportive engineer named Frank Kirby.

"Stick in your toe-nails, boy and you will make it," Ford recalled Kirby saying. He was impressed that the successful engineer would favor him. [19]

After gaining valuable information learning about the importance of the right tools at Flowers and Brothers, his vast experience as a young machinist with Detroit Dry Dock and his extra work repairing watches for McGill Jewelry, the tug of expanding his dreams versus the practicality of earning a living welled again within Ford. Already, Ford had a direction in mind, according to Halberstam.

"...Ford was sure a new world of efficient gasoline-powered machines was about to arrive. He wanted to be a part of it." [20]

His father encouraged him to return back to the land. To the Irish-born William Ford, the land was something substantial he and his fellow Irish immigrants often had been deprived of owning. Dreams were fine but the land offered stability and a living. The land was something tangible that could offer an income and respect.

For a brief time, Henry Ford did return to the land, harvesting timber from a plot that his father helped him own. Yet it was only an interlude for Henry. What it did offer him was a savings account for times ahead when his focus on experimentation outstripped his income.

In the summer of 1882, Henry took another step on his journey to making cars. He had a chance to demonstrate Westinghouse portable steam engines to farming communities in southeastern Michigan. For 83 days, Ford went from place to place firing up the steamer's boiler and showing farmers how it could be used for threshing, cutting corn, sawing wood and grinding feed. [21]

"I have never been more satisfied in my life," Ford once recalled. "For a day or so the wandering mechanic was the focus of interest in the community, welcomed into its homes, and sharing in its rituals, especially at harvest time." [22]

This experience underlined Ford's boyhood experiences about farm drudgery. It galvanized his feelings that machines could make life easier for people. He knew from his experiences growing up on a farm that the chores and tasks were back breaking and time consuming. Machines could free these people from such a daily burden and begin to help farmers connect with the world around them. Machines that did the work could change the lives of those in rural areas.

He also respected the politics prevalent among the people in rural areas of this era. While farmers were able to produce more, it seemed their lives were getting harder because they weren't getting good prices for their crops. Among the forces that were blamed were the powerful railroads, the bankers and others.

Agrarian populism would form a lot of the thinking that Henry Ford carried with him for the rest of his life. The formal political movement called Populism would call for help for farmers, regulation for railroads and a graduated income tax. 23

His work for Westinghouse that Michigan summer took him farther along his path of interest in machines and he would fondly remember the people he met and their lifestyles.

On April 11, 1888, Henry Ford married Clara Bryant. It was still another step in his formation. In Clara, Henry found a person who supported his dreams and suffered through his unconventional notions. While some spouses may have wanted a husband with his feet on the ground, Clara Ford knew that someone with "wheels in his head" would one day make that dream come true.

"Clara acceded unflinchingly," noted author Kimes. "She had unwavering faith in her husband and was convinced that if such an unlikely vehicle could be built, Henry could build it." 24

Early in his marriage, Ford had another opportunity to delve into things mechanical. His reputation as a machinist offered part-time work for at least two summers with the Buckeye Harvester Co. repairing their "Eclipse" portable farm engines. Once again he traveled to parts of southeastern Michigan, absorbing more about self-propelled machinery and appreciating rural life. 25

Ford's time on the land soon came to an end when he decided take a job with the Edison Illuminating Company in

imagination at work GE

This GE magazine ad shows the friendship between two legends. Thomas A. Edison inspired Henry Ford to continue inventing and dreaming.

1891. That meant that Clara and Henry left their early home on the timber land and moved into the city. It was a major shift for the young couple but there Henry eventually worked his way up to a supervisory role and had many chances to tinker and dream.

Remarkably, Fred Strauss was there once again at the same time and witnessed Ford's work and the joy of his experiments.

"Henry had a little lathe," said Strauss. "He had the idea of making a little gasoline engine out of scrap. We would just joke away. Sometimes we would work and sometimes not. It took us about six weeks to get this little engine built." 26

One engine that attracted Ford's attention was being

used at a Detroit bottling plant. The Otto Cycle Engine, nicknamed the "silent Otto," was perfected by German Nikolaus August Otto and was an early example of the four-stroke method of intake and combustion. Ford was reportedly so fascinated by the Silent Otto that he came home and began drawing it for Clara on a back of her piano sheet music. 27

Ford received even more exposure teaching machinist classes at the Detroit Y.M.C.A. at night.

Legend has it that on Christmas Eve 1893, shortly after their son Edsel's birth that November, Henry interrupted Clara's work preparing the next day's Christmas dinner and asked her to help him start his experimental engine. Henry decided to mount the engine on the kitchen sink and instructed Clara to dribble gasoline to the intake valve.

"...a reamed out one-inch gas pipe [served] as the cylinder into which fitted a homemade piston carrying a rod to the crankshaft with a five-inch stroke," noted Kimes. "An old lathe supplied the flywheel, and the engine was equipped with a gear to activate a cam, opening the exhaust valve and timing the spark." 28

One can imagine the Christmas Eve scene, almost like something out of a Frank Capra movie, when Henry spun the flywheel, exhaust and fumes filling the tiny kitchen and the Fords laughing and crying with joy. The first Ford engine was brought to life in their version of a Christmas miracle of invention.

Kimes says Ford quickly perfected a larger, more complex engine, especially after seeing information about the Kane-Pennington power plant in a publication called *American Machinist*.

Soon Ford had a four-cylinder engine that displaced 59 cubic inches with a three to one compression and was estimated to produce about four hp. It used a needle valve for carburetion and a low-tension coil for ignition. When he found air cooling wasn't good enough, Ford added water jackets. He expected to use leather belts and pulleys to transmit power.

Work at Edison Illuminating also meant Ford was able to increase his circle of friends. One was Charles Brady King, who had been an engineer for the Michigan Car Co.

Ford and King shared a desire to bring a self-propelled vehicle to reality. The Massachusetts bicycle makers, the Duryea Brothers, had been first in America with a horseless carriage in 1893 and the Apperson brothers and associate Haynes had followed quickly on their heels in Indiana. Now King would be the first person to drive his self-propelled vehicle in Detroit, on May 6, 1896.

Just one month later, on June 4, 1896, Ford's Quadricycle hit the streets.

Kimes says William Ford was embarrassed when his son visited in the contraption. He still thought of his 33-year-old son as much more of a dreamer than a solid man who was making something of himself.

"He doesn't settle down. I don't know what will become of him," the elder Ford said. 29

Henry didn't worry about his father's view of his tinkering. He was too busy thinking what possibilities existed for a self-propelled vehicle. With his Quadricycle and some other examples that followed, he was beginning to show the world that he thought speed, reliability and lightness were important to an automobile. Clara Ford was patient and appreciative of his efforts.

"It was very great thing to have my wife even more confident than I was," Ford noted later. 30

Ford also would receive advice and friendship from an unlikely source at nearly the same time. It was a profound moment in the young inventor's life. Attending a conference of all the Edison Illuminating Companies in New York City as a representative of the Detroit operation, Henry Ford encountered Thomas Alva Edison.

In 21st century terms, it was similar to Steven Jobs and Bill Gates coming together to share computer stories. When the young Ford shared his automotive experiment and was able to sketch some further ideas for Edison, the famed inventor of electricity profusely encouraged Ford.

"Young man...you have it!" Edison exclaimed. "Keep at it!" 31

Even in the beginning of his automotive career, Ford was thinking beyond the realm of fellow early automobile enthusiasts and was wondering what such a vehicle could do in terms of work potential.

"The idea of a horseless carriage at first did not seem so practical to me as the idea of an engine to do the harder farm work," said Ford. "To lift farm drudgery off flesh and blood and lay it on steel and motors was my most constant ambition." [32]

By 1898, Ford's work had attracted the interest of Detroit mayor William C. Marbury, who not only offered Ford official permission to run his vehicles on the city's streets, he gathered some wealthy investors to further endow the tinkering car maker. [33]

Some time in late 1897 or early 1898, a second Ford car was made and it brought Ford a small degree of notoriety from an engineer who had worked with Charles Duryea. R. W. Hanington, was impressed that Ford had come up with

The attention given to the Quadricycle in 1896 gave Henry Ford confidence that he was headed in the right direction in terms of a self-propelled vehicle.

a cooling system, something the Duryea car had lacked. He also liked the Ford "sparker" and carburetor.

"The whole design strikes me as being very complete, the carriage should equal any that has been built in this country." 34

Hanington's comments helped support Ford's feelings that his experience and experimentation were bringing positive results. While others, like William C. Murphy, who structured Detroit Auto Company around Ford in 1899, believed in young Henry, Ford was immersed in a long period where he was focused on perfecting rather than producing an automobile.

"Henry wasn't ready. He didn't have an automobile design," recalled Strauss. "Henry gave me some sketches to turn up some axle shaftings. It was just a stall until Henry got a little longer into it." 35

The Detroit Automobile had been advertised as "Swifter Than a Race Horse," but turned out to be less than a stable nag. The automobile producer in Henry wasn't ready in 1899—nor would it be in at least two other ventures that came his way. Ford was following his steady pace, following his inner compass, though to others, he seemed frustrating and unpredictable. But Ford's course would lead him in the right direction in the long run.

It was the difficult path that all dreamers take, not measurable by conventional means nor in rigid profit and loss lines on an accounting sheet. Ford was thinking as a machinist and was focused on the invention, not someone's expectations of him.

One tangent that motivated Ford was his understanding that a dependable car needed to be perfected and proven before people would buy it. Racing and competition were the ways to prove an auto's worthiness.

"My company will kick about me following racing but they will get the advertising and I expect to make dollars where I can't make cents in manufacturing," Ford said. 36

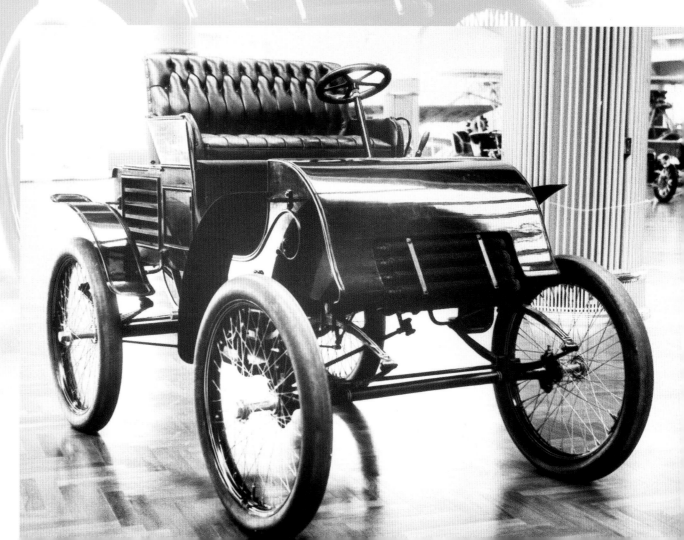

The second Ford car, built in late 1898 or early 1899, was another version of the Ford concept—a lightweight car that was simple and practical. This time it had a steering wheel, not a tiller.

When racing came between him and having the Henry Ford Company in his name, he continued in the racing venture, hoping to learn more about proving the dependability of an automobile. Down the road, Ford would be ready to produce cars but it was as if he needed to complete his courses and graduate before he could focus in that direction.

All of the steps along the way, even the failures and missteps, would be folded into the first Ford Motor Company cars, and would soon form thinking that led to the Model T.

Ford had been brought along by investors and, when their expectations did not work out and they had gone their separate ways, Ford had lived on his timber-cutting savings. Earning an income or making a profit were not his primary driving forces. Remarkably, compared to his contemporaries, little or none of his money had been involved in the ventures. All the lessons he had learned and concepts he had formed had not mired him in debt.

By the time coal dealer Alexander Malcomson approached him about another automotive venture in August 1902, Ford was just about ready to use his lessons from all his experiences up to that time and apply them to his vision of making a car.

It was nearly time for Ford to take another step, changing from the pure dreamer and inventor to the automaker. At the time Malcomson came along, Ford still was involved in racing but was almost ready to make his own cars. His energies were beginning to move from perfecting his skills to applying them along with talented and trusted associates he had gathered around him. He was at the doorstep of focusing on making automobiles with the lessons he had learned.

He described his experiences in his first 40 years in a 1928 interview.

"I feel I have never done anything by my own volition," said Ford. "I was always pushed by invisible forces within and without me. But all the time I was getting ready." [37]

While early autos came in all forms and sizes, the majority were made with techniques used for decades in the buggy and carriage industry, largely made of wood on wood or some metal pieces in the frames. They were powered by large, often complex engines and were following a trend toward being heavier and larger by 1903, when Ford Motor Company was formed from the shaky foundations of Ford-Malcomson Ltd.

Attorney John Anderson explained that he was going to invest in the new venture in a letter to his father and mentioned Henry Ford.

"Mr. Ford…is recognized throughout the country as one of the best automobile mechanical experts in the U.S. From the very beginning he has been interested in their construction and development. Years ago he constructed a racing machine which was a wonder." [38]

One of Ford's beliefs, underlined in his racing experiences, was making a lighter vehicle.

"I cannot imagine where the delusion that weight means strength came from," he said. "Saving even a few pounds… could reduce the strain on them and that meant they would break down less frequently. They would also go faster and consume less fuel." [39]

He also thought automobile makers should focus on fewer models, even just one version, but should produce it well.

"More of them, better and cheaper," Ford said to attorney John Anderson in 1903. "Shoemakers ought to settle on one shoe, stovemakers on one stove. Me, I like specialists." [40]

While many early vehicles were assembled by hand, like carriages or farm wagons, Ford already was moving against the status quo that existed.

"It was not my idea to make cars in any such petty fashion," he recalled later in life. [41]

In a roundabout way, Ford also was on a par with Henry Leland, who believed that precision parts should be interchangeable, something that was a real problem with early automobiles. Early on, parts came from many suppliers and were formed in lots. Differences were frustratingly common between one car and the next. Parts often were anything but similar. Leland thought precision craftsmanship would

The Line is Drawn

in Northern Automobiles. between Touring Car and Runabout. A Tonneau on a Runabout does not make a "Touring Car."

The Northern Runabout

Pivotal Body Bearings
6½ Horse Power, $750

NORTHERN

The Northern Touring Car

Double Opposed Cyl- inder Motor. Direct Gear Drive. 15 Horse Power, $1500

Write for Catalogue and name of nearest Agent.

NORTHERN MANUFACTURING COMPANY, DETROIT, MICH.
Member National Association Licensed Automobile Manufacturers.

Ford's friend Charles B. King was involved in making Northern cars in 1904. Ford Motor Co. cars would provide competition

solve the problem of part and component consistency. Ford's idea was making great quantities of parts and pieces exactly the same.

"Each piece is machined in a jig, so that every one is absolutely interchangeable," said Ford. "No filing, grinding, sawing or hammering of parts to make them fit." [42]

Ford also envisioned that cars would differ entirely from the traditional carriage-making days of one vehicle up on supports with many workers hovering around it until it took shape. Early on, Ford envisioned what would become known as mass production.

"The way to make automobiles," he told attorney Anderson, one of the first Ford Motor Company investors, "is to make one automobile just like another, to make them all alike, to make them come through the factory just alike." [43]

In 1908, the same year that the new Model T would begin to be produced, Henry Ford hired an efficiency expert named Walter Flanders to help the young company try to improve its manufacturing process. Once again, Ford was thinking out of the box.

"Henceforth, the history of the industry will be the history of the conflict of giants," Ford told a Detroit newspaper reporter as early automobile makers were struggling to make a profit. [44]

Perhaps his inner compass was offering some inner confidence again and somehow Ford knew that he would be one of the giants involved in forging that history.

In 1901, Ford read a book by a writer named Oliver Barthels. Ford said up to that time, even he hadn't understood his meanderings from one interest to another but reading Barthels' work helped him put his life in focus.

"It was as if I had found a universal plan," Ford recalled. "I was no longer a slave to the hands of the clock. There was time enough to plan and create." [45]

The mechanically-adept farm boy with "wheels in his head" had come a long way from the exploding steam turbine at his school and the tools on his father's farm. He had taken a remarkable journey through machine shops and factories of his time, learning and absorbing and being encouraged.

He'd earned a degree of success and had known failures as well but he had arrived at a place where he could almost touch the visions he had dreamed about and lessons he had absorbed.

Now the pieces were all coming together for him and it was all beginning to make sense.

Ford was ready to take his place in the automotive world.

By 1903, 40-year-old Henry Ford had become a man with his feet on the ground in a new industry with his name on a new company, reformed from quicksand of the Ford-Malcomson Ltd.

This time he was ready.

His father may never have envisioned that experimenting with wheels would lead to business success. Yet Henry already was thinking ahead to an entirely new direction that, with a few more lessons from the world of car making, would draw on all of his earlier experiences, pool them with the skills of others and produce a remarkable automobile

Engine of the Dawson Gasoline Car.

LEFT: *Ford understood that complexity was never an asset in producing a reliable automobile engine. His thinking was the opposite of a creation like this 1904 Dawson engine.*

RIGHT: *By the time Ford Motor Co. was formed in June 1903, Henry Ford was a man who was confident about his dreams and ideas. His thinking was reinforced by positive racing experiences.*

that would fill a void in the marketplace while creating niches other early car makers had not envisioned. Ford's destiny with the Model T was just ahead by 1903.

In 1963, a Canadian leader remembered Henry Ford quite succinctly:

"...a profound belief in mechanical organization, boundless energy and eager curiosity, combined with quick judgment and not very profound thinking when out of his field..." [46]

Ford had survived his "coursework" and now was ready to graduate and become a leader in the automotive world. His vision and his foibles would often combine in the products he produced.

Yet Ford was a driven man in terms of his ideas about what an automobile should be. Soon he would drive into the lead among all automobile makers in a vehicle even his father, William, admired.

Part of the reason he succeeded was that he never forgot the audience he was trying to serve, people like those he had grown up with in rural Michigan, whom he remembered in a 1924 interview.

"The world is held together by the mass of honest folk who do their daily tasks, tend to their own spot in the world, and have faith that at last the right will come fully to its own. These are the salt of the earth...forever reviving a moribund world. They believe...that if their faces are turned toward the light they cannot miss the road, and all right minded men desire to see this true faith of the people vindicated. This is our truest basis of prosperity. It is the essence of all our security. It is the promise of all our progress." [47]

He had followed the advice he'd given to young Firestone. He had used tools to create something. Even more importantly, experience with those tools had forged another set of inner tools Ford could rely on. The world was about to understand the promise so many had seen in Henry Ford.

*Another version of the same story was related by David Halberstam in his automotive history "The Reckoning." In it Ford alluded to the way other products were made when he talked to Anderson. "The way to make automobiles is to make one automobile just like another automobile, just as one pin is like another pin or one match is like another match when it comes from the match factory." [48]

Chapter 2

AMERICAN CAR CULTURE BEFORE THE MODEL T

"Progress consists in a number of related things changing together for the future."
Henry Ford

The Ford Model A entered the early automotive field in 1903. It could be purchased as a two person runabout or with the deck-mounted, rear-entrance tonneau shown here.

In 21st-century hindsight, one has to wonder why anyone would have plunged into the eclectic, wide-open world that was the North American automobile manufacturing industry in the early 1900s.

Yet, we know the automobile is a tantalizing machine today and it was an equally tantalizing dream more than 100 years ago. People like Henry Ford felt compelled that their idea would be different. Investors, with visions of dollar signs, were only too eager to slap backs, offer a handshake and agree to hand over money today hoping to see it multiply in days ahead.

Automobiles were far from a necessity for North Americans in the new century. They were just one more in a flurry of inventions that included dozens of machines and gadgets. Some of the inventions would grow to change

society like the telephone, Edison's electric lights, and motion pictures.

The horse was a common sight across North America and was used to power many forms of work and transportation. And from villages to large cities, the blacksmith's shop and the veterinarian were accepted as vital members of community life. Horses were vital to daily life and work.

Catalogs were available that showed the handiwork of artisans who trimmed and shaped wood into bright varnished buggies and surreys as well as workaday wagons. The horse-drawn vehicle makers were found in many locations across North American with brand names that literally went from A to Z.

People did make their way without horses but there were limited choices. Walking for miles was a common practice, not a burden or done merely for exercise. In urbanized areas, trolley cars were means of public transportation. Trains had established their ribbons of steel across the United States and Canada to carry passengers and freight. Ships, with sails or with steam power, were used in commerce and transit over larger bodies of water while riverboats, ferries, barges and water taxis also were used regionally.

Roads were almost universally unpaved. In some places, stone paths or timber-lined roadways had been built, but in most places roads were rutted and dusty, often bogged down by rain and frozen over by winter storms. Streams and small rivers often went without bridges and had to be forded.

By the 1880s, the two-wheeled bicycle fad had swept across North America. Many greeted the bicycles as challenging fun. Making bicycles taught many to master the machining of parts, bearings and gears and they also learned about freight, export and shipping. Unwittingly, many would apply those lessons in the automotive world that would come in years ahead.

Horace and John Dodge had joined forces with Fred Evans to make bicycles in Windsor, Ontario, across the river from Detroit. Orville and Wilbur Wright, Thomas Jeffery and the Duryea Brothers made them in the United States. When Henry Ford watched Charles B. King drive the first car in Detroit, Ford was following close behind on the seat of his bicycle. 1

The 1903 Model A fit Henry Ford's vision of a light but dependable automobile that could be purchased for a fair price.

Roads were poor, rutted by wagon wheels and often grew muddy and often impassible due to rain. Travel was slow at best.

For all the mastery of skills and excitement for those who made and used them, there was an almost opposite emotion from the keepers of the status quo in society. They often saw bicycles as a threat, a scenario author David Roberts portrayed in his book "In the Shadow of Detroit."

"Speeding, often abusive cyclists, popularly known as scorchers, added a mild element of danger and excitement to the streetscapes; some wondered about the propriety of female riders; cycling shaped sermons and adages. ('He that rideth with wise men shall be safe; but a companion of scorchers shall be destroyed!')" 2

With the advent of the automobile, there was a natural progression in the outrage to people who liked noisy autos even less than bicycles. The same fury that was spent on bicycle owners was vented even more on those interested in automobiles, especially those powered by internal

combustion gasoline engines.

When observers experienced early examples of these self-propelled noisemakers, they often were horrified. Some thought that humane societies across the country should get involved. In 1906, the *North American Review* reported that cars killed more people than perished in the Spanish-American War. 3

Even as late as 1908, the New Glasgow, Nova Scotia, *Eastern Chronicle* in its July 28 edition: "...cheered the temporary absence of the 'stink wagon' from the town's streets..." 4

There were no gasoline stations, repair centers or even organized dealerships when automobiles began to gain a foothold in North America. Those who could afford to purchase an early auto were heading into the world alone and often were going against society's grain.

In 1924, a *Motor World* ad called attention to those early days.

"Back in the days, farmers shied rocks at any driver with the hardihood to venture outside the city limits. They called them 'horseless carriages' and joshers cried 'Get a horse!' [and] sent the village into gales of laughter." 5

Even during the bicycle fad of the 1880s and 1890s, some had turned to making smaller versions of the gigantic steam traction engines. Others were thinking about electric-powered vehicles. And still others, including Henry Ford, worked on gasoline-powered engines.

In 1885, Gottlieb Daimler and Wilhelm Maybach perfected a new gas engine in their spare time at Nicholas Otto's Deutz Gasmotorenfabrik. The light, small Daimler-Maybach engine had a vertical cylinder and a carburetor. Daimler made a bicycle with an engine, then a self-propelled wagon.

At the same time, in 1886, Karl Benz received a patent for a three-wheeler powered by a gas engine. Daimler was building four-wheeled vehicles and licensing engines to others in 1891. Karl Benz made his Vicktoria in 1893, then by 1896 had the Benz Velo in production.

From Germany, the interest in the new vehicles swept through France. There, in 1900, Louis Renault made his voiturette, a dead ringer for the early Cadillac and Ford Model As. Armand Peugeot, René Panhard and Emile Levassor, the Comte de Dion and his partner, Georges Bouton, former bellmaker and steam carriage experimenter Amédee Bollée and Alexander Darracq all got into making cars and making progress with them.

Panhard and Levassor set a standard for others by taking a Daimler engine and crafted a vehicle with a front-mounted engine, a gearbox and rear-wheel drive—a layout that would be copied by many companies.

Many French terms also were applied to early autos. A "voiturette" was literally a "small car" with two seats and a minimum of coach work. "Vis-à-vis" and "dos-a-dos" applied the French words for seating arrangements—face to face and back to back. Such terms as garage, chauffeur and

Today Ford is a lot more than cars...
it's a Control Center for astronauts circling
the earth...an electronic machine
that reads 36,000 zip-coded addresses an hour.
The Mariner IV antenna sending back
the first pictures from Mars...
a laser beam that creates 10 million volts
out of thin air...Philco refrigerators...
medical research...guided missiles.
It's a company that goes where good ideas take it.

"And to think I started all that."

While we look back on Ford history with a 21st century view of a success story that began with the 1903 Model A, it was a tough and competitive world back then.

automobile all were words originated in French.

The 1865 Red Flag Act prohibited much progress in England. John Henry Knight was arrested after testing an early automobile in 1896. Interested nobles could sputter around their own grounds but were penalized on public roads. The speed limit was set at 4 mph and a flag bearing person had to walk in front of the vehicle. Horse owners were heavily favored.

It took entrepreneur H. J. Lawson with the influence of royalty to get the law changed and to encourage the first London to Brighton rally in November 1896. Once the laws were loosened in England, people like Frederick Lanchester, Herbert Austin, Frederick Wolseley, Thomas Humber and John Marston would propel the British auto industry forward.

It didn't take long for interest to pick up in Canada and the United States by the early 1890s. In 1893, Charles and Frank Duryea set their bicycles aside to build a small gasoline-powered buggy in Massachusetts while the Apperson Brothers with Elwood Haynes built a gas-powered carriage in Indiana that same year. All that was known about steam, electric and gasoline engines was being blended in a frenzy of invention and adaptation across Europe and throughout North America.

When Charles B. King, famed for his creation of that dubious noisemaker and body-rattler, the pneumatic hammer, took his gas-powered wagon onto the streets of Detroit on May 6, 1896, Henry Ford was close behind drinking in the scene. Undoubtedly, Ford was eager to complete work he'd begun on his own vehicle. 6

ABOVE: *German automotive visionaries like Gottlieb Daimler had pioneered gasoline-powered vehicles in 1886. Their ideas influenced Henry Ford and many others.*

RIGHT: *Horseless carriages and their drivers often drew jeers from the locals. The horse still was mandatory, especially when their was trouble, as the Horseless Carriage Gazette portrayed.*

HORSELESS CARRIAGE GAZETTE

Vol. 52, No. 4 • July–August, 1990

In 1896, Henry Ford was 33-years-old and still very young at heart. He wasn't at all concerned about any scorn for motorized vehicles. He was too passionate about them to care what others thought. As long as his beloved wife, Clara, supported his early efforts, he went forward.

On the morning of June 4, 1896, Ford was ready to axe open a portion of his rented shed on Bagley Avenue to free his Quadricycle, part slender bicycle and part lightweight, motor-powered vehicle. Originally equipped with a bicycle seat, it weighed just 500 lbs. [7]

Ford had gained a world of experience as a mechanic, watch repairer, electric company engineer and portable steam engine repairer. Ford had dreamed and watched and asked and done things and had formed many ideas about what a self-propelled vehicle should be.

One influence from the bicycle fad was his conviction about lightness. Unlike King's rather ponderous wagon, Ford's Quadricycle was almost fragile looking. But its two-cylinder, four-cycle engine could push it to 20 mph at high speed or up to 10 mph at lower speed. Transmitting power to the wheels was accomplished with a bicycle-like chain drive. The Ford Quadricycle had a 49-inch wheelbase and a 38.5-inch tread with 26-inch wheels.

While lawyers already were setting their attentions on finding ways to get rid of "the beasts," men like Henry Ford and legions of others were preparing to add to what they saw as the future, the self-propelled vehicle that soon was known everywhere by its French name, automobile.

Ford soon made two changes to the Quadricycle—a buggy type seat so Clara and young son Edsel could come along for the ride and he added about 175 lbs. of steel replacing the earlier wooden pieces. [8]

Ford moved ahead and soon the Quadricycle was sold to a man named Charles Ainsley. [9]

Later, another owner, A. W. Hall of Detroit, wrote to Ford, praising the vehicle, in what must be considered the first endorsement of a Ford-made car.

"You will be surprised when I tell you that this little carriage is still doing its usual duty," Hall wrote. "...the little

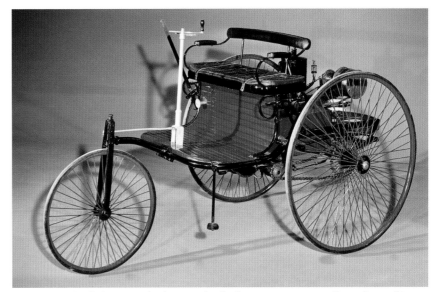

The three-wheeled Benz vehicle was also built in 1886. It was still another influence on those interested in self-propelled vehicles like Henry Ford.

The Daimler Motor Works "Motorkutsche" was essentially a four-place carriage with a gasoline engine. And it was a pioneer vehicle in 1886.

rig was still in fair shape after all the banging around that it has had. I was out in Chicago all last fall and looked over the few horseless carriages there. Among them all I did not see one I would of rather had then that little rig..." [10]

Americans who got into the automotive fray included Haynes with Elmer and Edgar Apperson, Jonathan D. Maxwell, Ford racing rival Alexander Winton, Ransom E. Olds and Ford's Detroit friend King. Europeans like Daimler,

Benz, August Horch, Renault, Panhard and Levassor and many others already were setting the pace.

While his personal savings usually weren't risked, unlike many early car makers, Ford rode a roller coaster of innovation and was involved in at least five ventures between the time he drove his Quadricycle in 1896 and when the day the Ford Motor Co. was incorporated in June 1903.

By the time Ford began working on making his second auto a reality, sometime late in 1897 or early in 1898, friend and Detroit mayor William C. Maybury, who had allowed Ford carte blanche use of city streets, also pulled together financial backing for Ford's second car from investors Ellery L. Garfield, E. A. Leonard and Benjamin Hoyt. 11

The national magazine *Horseless Age* offered Ford his first publicity, according to historian Kimes, although Ford apparently wasn't as adept at publicity in 1898 as he would be later.

"From Mr. Ford himself no information can be gleaned regarding his vehicles or his plans for their manufacture," said the magazine. 12

Ford's official plunge into automaking came from another wealthy Detroit businessman. William H. Murphy asked Ford to take him on a run from Detroit to Farmington and back through Pontiac, a healthy day's journey on early roads. Murphy was enthused and on July 24, 1899, Detroit Automobile Co. was formed.

Murphy's partners included Clarence Black, Albert E. F. White, Frank Alderman, Mark Hopkins, William C. McMillan, Lem Bowen and F. W. Eddy. Ford was committed enough to the venture that he resigned from the Edison Illuminating Company and went to work as superintendent at Detroit Auto's facilities on Cass Avenue. 13

The vision at that time was an 800-lb. vehicle but the reality was a 1,200-lb. delivery wagon that historian Kimes called "...a rather breakable toy." 14

Even though the Detroit Auto Co. would fall short of

Cars like the 1901 Mercedes by Benz offered race-proven practicality, sturdiness and versatility. Those who cared about cars, like Henry Ford, were watching.

expectations, the company did receive a favorable comment from the Detroit *News-Tribune* whose poetic writer attempted to describe the car's engine.

"…a long, quick, mellow gurgling sound, not harsh, not unmusical, not distressing; a note that falls with pleasure on the ear." [15]

Ford soon soured on the manufacturing end. He was both distracted by proving his concepts of automobiles in racing competition, and in testing and rethinking what an automobile should be like. Ford wasn't ready to concentrate on demands of manufacturing autos at this time. His mind still was on dreaming, perfecting and proving his ideas through racing.

And the Detroit Auto Co. was also plagued by two curses of early auto manufacturing: inferior parts and components combined with an inexperienced work force. In just one year, $86,000 had been expended, several of the original investors were discouraged and few of the Detroit Auto Co. products rolled out the factory doors to buyers.

"You would be surprised at the amount of detail about an automobile," investor Ackerman said in frustration, according to historian Kimes. [16]

Undaunted by the losses and still believing in Ford's potential, Murphy and four of the original Detroit Auto backers regrouped and decided to back Ford in a second venture. The investors kept the Cass Avenue facilities and its assets and went forward late in 1899. Focused on racing, Ford was preoccupied with proving and perfecting his automotive concepts.

One thing racing did as Ford progressed to his destiny with the Model T was to allow him to bring together one of his Edison Illuminating associates, Edward "Spider" Huff with the talented young Childe Harold Wills, himself a future car maker, and Ed Ver Linden. All investments in this second venture ended up in racing. [17]

By 1900, fledgling automakers had popped up like dandelions offering cars in many sizes and forms of technology from both sides of the Atlantic Ocean. Some vehicles were barely removed from coaches and even included seats for footmen and racks for outmoded apparel cases. It seemed a wide open frontier where all ideas and all comers were welcomed on the journey.

By 1901, Henry Ford had become well known for taking on speed demons who came his way and that fame brought a third auto venture his way, called the Henry Ford Company. It was formed on Nov. 30, 1901. This time, investors were more demanding. They quickly grew tired of Ford's penchant for racing competition and attempted to put him on a short leash under the supervision of precision engineer Henry M. Leland. They wanted results from both Ford and the Henry Ford Company.

Their company was advertised as "Builders of High-Grade Automobiles and Touring Cars" and the "Makers of Automobile Specialties" and they wanted some progress as well as profits. [18]

When investors demanded that Ford concentrate on making cars and spend his free time on racing interests, he rebelled. The stubborn nature of Ford emerged. He was determined to continue to focus on racing, not manufacturing, at this stage. Ford left the company and took his name, a $900 settlement and plans for another racing car with him. Leland and the financiers decided to rename their venture the Cadillac Motor Car Company and moved forward. [19]

Ford went headlong into racing at this point, in a partnership with bicycle racer Tom Cooper. The race cars they built, named after famed express trains of the time, were the 999 and the Arrow. While the cars were formidable, their partnership soon cooled and their egos clashed. In 1902, in the midst of his partnership with Cooper, Ford was presented with plans for a fourth automotive venture. [20]

While working at the Edison Illuminating Company, Ford had gotten to know entrepreneur Alexander Malcomson. The "Hotter than Sunshine" coal products dealer was well known around the Detroit area—sometimes for the way he threw good money at ill-conceived investments and the way he often overextended himself in business ventures other than coal supplying. Ford soon learned that Malcomson had a torrid passion about getting into automaking. [21]

During his racing partnership with Cooper, Ford was in a rare period when he was putting up some of his own money. He was drawing from his timber-cutting savings plus his settlement from the Henry Ford Company.

He decided to listen to Malcomson, understanding that his relationship with Cooper would be short-lived. While still linked in his partnership with Cooper, Ford-Malcolmson Ltd. was formed in June 1902. Their car was to be called the Fordmobile. [22]

"Ford brought his patents, tools, models, drawings and a promise of both a racing car and work on a passenger car," said writer Robert Lacey. [23]

Automobiles available to buyers in North America at that time nearly filled the alphabet with choices that ranged from the four-cylinder Apperson touring car to the Waltham Orient, the latter cars available in buckboard or surrey, and each weighing only about 500 lbs. The Waltham Orient models were priced at an entry level $450 to $475, with tops.

The upper end of the price scale included the German-made, 2,300-lb. Mercedes, available in horsepower ranges from 28 to 90. A popular touring version was advertised for $12,450. Karl Benz was working to conquer a temporarily poor reputation from a previous model and his Benz Parsifahl, a practical touring car, was helping. For those with racing in mind, the 1,100-lb. Packard Grey Wolf could be had for $10,000. French, British, German, Canadian and American makers all competed for business.

There was little or no competition in the Waltham Orient's price range, but a sea of automobiles were priced in the $2,500 to $3,500 ranges and upward. In many cases, there was little to differentiate from one maker to the other except some name recognition and reliability.

Certainly new automobile ventures of the time were a tenuous proposition at best but Ford investor and attorney John Anderson saw automobiles as the potential for profit.

"The demand of automobiles is a perfect craze," Anderson wrote to his father in June 1903, "Every factory here [Detroit] has its entire output sold and cannot begin to fill its orders." [24]

Certainly John and Horace Dodge saw a business opportunity with the Ford-Malcomson Ltd. venture they were not able to get from the Olds Motor Works.

Malcomson had plenty of ideas about investments but he had spread himself thin in terms of his credit rating. Instead of the accepted standard 45 to 60 days payment for work they did for the Olds Motor Works, the Dodge Brothers would get a 15-day turnaround from Ford-Malcomson with the guarantee of the new company's machinery if they failed to come through on their payments.

It was a $162,500 commitment by Ford-Malcomson and close to a no-lose prospect for the Dodge Brothers. They decided to drop their profitable work with the Olds Motor Works and turn their attention to making components for the Ford-Malcomson venture, with the prospect of a higher yield, whether the Ford-Malcomson venture succeeded or not. [25]

"Dodge Bros. are the largest and best equipped machine plant in the city," Anderson noted. "They have a new factory, just completed and it is not excelled anywhere as an up-to-date and thoroughly equipped machine shop." [26]

The Dodge Brothers supplied running gear and various chassis parts while the C. R. Wilson Carriage Co. made wooden bodies at $68 each. Hartford Rubber supplied tires and the Lansing, Michigan-based Pruden Co. sold Ford and Malcolmson wooden wheels.

Malcomson arranged to get the new venture a shop on what was then called Mack Street (now Mack Avenue), thanks to Albert Strehlow, the contractor who built several of Malcomson's coal yards. It took just five months, from June to November 1902, for debt to mount and for the fourth Ford-related automaking venture to be on the ropes. One of the biggest bills was owed to the Dodge Brothers. [27]

"They were only paid $10,000 on account and they had to take all the rest of the risk themselves," explained Anderson. "They had to borrow $40,000, place orders for castings all over the country, pay their men from last October…and do everything necessary to manufacture all the machines before they could hope to get a cent back." 28

The fascinating Anderson letter to his father also described the Mack Street plant and the assembly processes Ford-Malcomson Ltd. were using.

"It is large, light and airy, about 250 feet long by fifty feet wide," wrote Anderson. "To this assembly plant are shipped the bodies, wheels, tires and the machines from Dodge Bros., and here the workmen, ten to a dozen boys at $1.50 a day, and a foreman fit the bodies on the machine, put the cushions in place, put the tires on the wheels, the wheels on the machine and paint it and test it to see that it runs o.k." 29

There was a real possibility that Ford-Malcomson Ltd. would have slid into bankruptcy and failure. Had the Dodge Brothers been as adamant about pressing for payments due at this time as they were about 15 years later in demanding stock dividends, the Ford-Malcomson Ltd. venture may have become a footnote in history.

Fortunately, the idea-rich but cash-flow poor Malcomson had one more ace up his sleeve. His uncle, John S. Gray, was a successful Detroit banker with a strong reputation among

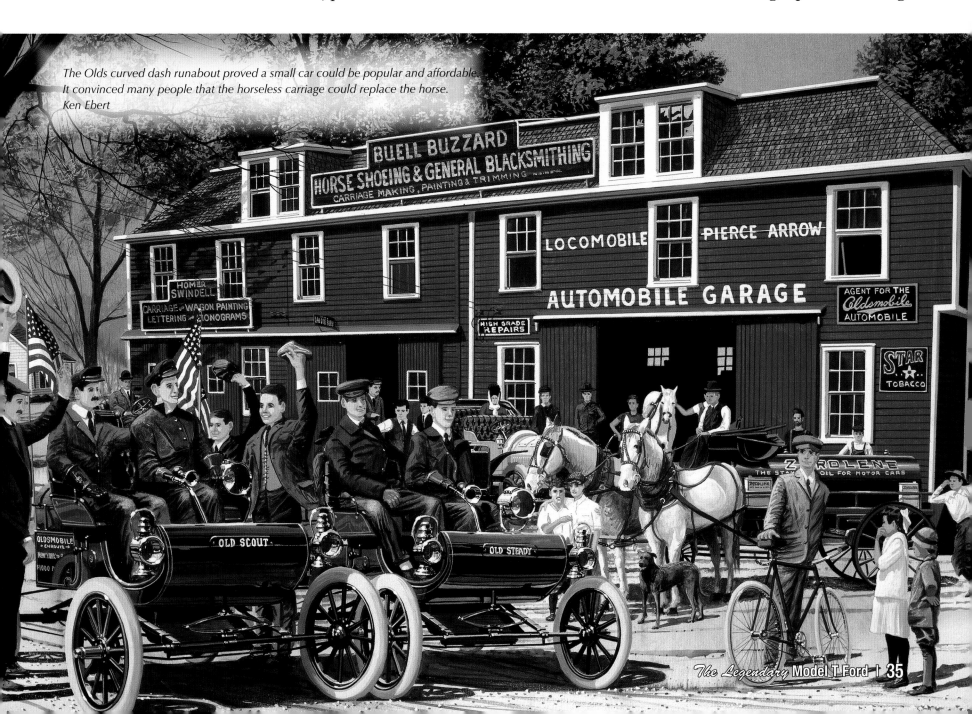

The Olds curved dash runabout proved a small car could be popular and affordable. It convinced many people that the horseless carriage could replace the horse.
Ken Ebert

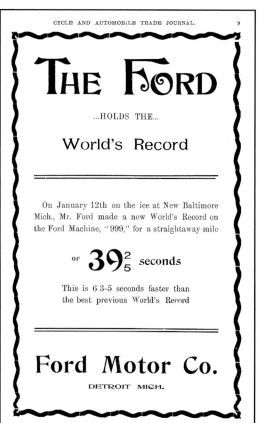

ABOVE LEFT: *The Ford Model A was the first Ford Motor Co. product to be promoted by the company. It was center stage at a 1904 auto show.*

ABOVE CENTER: *Ford Motor Co. had entered the automotive marketplace with a solid racing reputation in place.*

ABOVE RIGHT: *The competitive-minded Winton was a car that gained a lot of attention thanks to racing. It was a popular choice when Ford Motor Co. was in its infancy.*

investor circles. And while historian Kimes says Gray went to his death just three years later constantly expressing the opinion to anyone who would listen that the business would not last, Gray worked to support his nephew Malcomson and Ford.

Investors were solicited and the venture was restarted, this time as the Ford Motor Company. Some historians saw it as the fifth automaking venture that Henry Ford was involved in. Others saw it as a morphing of Ford-Malcomson Ltd. into the Ford Motor Company.

Whatever your point of view, this time Henry Ford would find both sound financial backing and a taste of success in the business. Now in his 40th year, Ford was beginning to

seriously focus on what it took to succeed as an automaker, a few steps beyond what he had accomplished as a recognized inventor and a champion racer.

Ransom E. Olds had made those steps up as had Ford's racing rival Alexander Winton and inventors like Benz and Daimler in Germany. Even Detroit friend King had moved on to being an active leader in the Northern car line.

While it was a very wide-open and wild-eyed time to manufacturer cars, many found it also was a crude way to do business. As always, Ford's inner confidence guided him and he was confident that he was doing the right thing just as he felt he was hitting his stride and had plenty of time to be a success.

His expert "Ford team" that included Wills, Ver Linden, "Spider" Huff and other bright minds now added a cashier from the Malcomson side who would make vital contributions as a stockholder and business manager. The new face was Chatham, Ontario, native James Couzens, whose father was a soap maker. 30

"Mr. Couzens...is going to leave the coal business, for the present at least, and devote his entire time to the office and management of the automobile business—and he is a crackerjack." 31

Because of the ample debt to the Dodge Brothers, they were brought into the venture and credited with 100 shares of stock. Gray pledged $10,500 and was credited with 105 shares of the company. He was also elected president. Couzens, and his sister Rosetta, invested what they could, including some of Rosetta's meager savings as a teacher.

Contractor Albert Strehlow, who had built several Malcomson coal yards, also was in as were lawyers John Anderson and Horace Rackham. Even air gun maker Charles Bennett invested in the new company that was incorporated on Saturday June 13, 1903. 32

In one tense month, the new company had spent more than $19,000 before the first Ford was sold. Then on July 15, 1903, a Chicago dentist named Pfennig purchased the first Model A for $850. Couzens had been able to determine that the new company could make approximately $150 per car, based on costs of $554 and a sales price of $750 for the basic Model A. 33

Between July and the following March, Ford Motor Co. sold 658 cars and made more than $98,000. Investors realized a profit and the company began to realize its place in a crowded market.

Even as Ford Motor Co. was beginning to take its first steps, admirers were watching. One was Gordon McGregor, who was managing the Walker Wagon Works in nearby Windsor, Ontario and was searching for business possibilities.

"There are men in Detroit, like Henry Ford, who say every farmer will soon be using an automobile. I don't see why we can't build autos right here." 34

The first Ford Motor Co. product, the 1903 Model A, was based on concepts worked on at the Henry Ford Co. In fact, there was a striking resemblance between the car that was developed at the Henry Ford Company and became the first one-cylinder and the Model A Ford of 1903.

The new thinking was in the Ford Model A engine. It was a compact power plant that featured two opposed cylinders and was located under the two-place seat. The engine was water-cooled and power was transmitted via chain drive to the rear wheels.

While the first Model A prototype was wrecked, a potentially bad omen, any misfortune was overcome by a second version that went into production. Along the way, Ford and his associates soon learned producing a successful car meant even more growing pains than they'd experienced in racing.

"Flywheels came loose, water boiled in the radiator under the best of conditions, the chains wore quickly, the oiling system was more flood than splash, bands slipped in the transmission." 35

Ford and his team worked to solve problems with the A, a 1,250-lb. car that had a 72-inch wheelbase and was powered by an 8 hp, 100.4 cid, two-cylinder engine with horizontally opposed cylinders, each with a 4 x 4 in. bore and stroke. The Model A was advertised in *Colliers Weekly* as the "Boss of the Road," a familiar moniker Ford would use again some 65 years later on a Mustang. *Frank Leslie's Popular Monthly* observed: "...a boy of 15 can run it." 36

Other ads promoted the Model A engine. "The Heart of the Ford is the Motor," said a Valentine-shaped image of the engine imposed over the car. "The popularity of the Ford is due to the power, simplicity and correct mechanical design of its opposed motor." In another ad, the Model A was focused in a flashlight beam: "The Ford Stands Against the Searchlight of Criticism," the Model A headline read.

Fred Rockelman, then a young mechanic barely out of his teens, gave a remarkable interview to Springfield *Sunday Republican* writer Carl Stender in 1964 that was reprinted

FORD FIRSTS

FIRST OF ALL

The FORD is FIRST in everything that constitutes a first-class automobile.

The FORD was the FIRST American-made automobile to clip seconds off the mile record.

The FORD was the FIRST automobile of moderate size, price and horse power to defeat large American and foreign cars in races on the track.

The FORD was the FIRST practical two-cylinder opposed touring car to sell at a moderate price.

The FORD was the FIRST easy and quiet-running gasoline touring car made in America.

The FORD was the FIRST automobile to be shipped in train lots to one dealer.

The FORD was the FIRST American automobile popular enough to warrant the establishing of a factory in Canada.

The four-cylinder FORD was the FIRST $2000 automobile made which, in speed, endurance and quality equaled cars in the $3000 class.

There are many other FORD FIRSTS, which collectively make the FORD FIRST in quality, FIRST in service, and FIRST in the hearts of the automobilists.

FORD FACTS

MODEL F, $1200.00

This popular car, at a popular price, has behind it the prestige of FORD success, and before it the record of satisfied automobilists. If the price you wish to pay is about $1200.00, look no further, but make sure of the wisdom of your investment by buying the FORD Model F. Weight, 1400 lbs. Motor, FORD two-cylinder, horizontal opposed. Maximum speed, 35 miles an hour.

FORD Model B, $2000.00, is the car about which there was much favorable comment at the Automobile Shows, because it combines all the advantages of the most expensive four-cylinder cars, with the additional advantage of minimum weight, 1700 lbs., which fact is made possible on account of its simplicity and scientific construction. An investigation and demonstration will result in your being convinced that it is a superior car for the price. Circulars sent on request.

FORD MODEL B, PRICE $2000

FORD Model C, Price $950.00, 10 H. P., double opposed motor; rear entrance, detachable body. Light and simple in construction; guaranteed economy of maintenance.

Ford Motor Co.
DETROIT, MICH.
Canadian Trade supplied by Ford Motor Company of Canada, Ltd., Walkerville, Ont.

Ford Motor Co.
DETROIT, MICH.
Canadian Trade supplied by Ford Motor Co. of Canada, Ltd., Walkerville, Ont.

FORD MODEL C, PRICE $950

This 1905 Ford reflected the growing struggle between Henry Ford and Alex Malcomson. The C and F Fords were lighter and less expensive while the B was larger and pricier.

in 1984 in *Model T Times*. Rockelman says the early cars had to be thoroughly road tested at the factory.

"…each driver took the new car, drove it over the road, made repairs as necessary, adjusted valves, carburetor, resetting the timing," he recalled. "Many dealers knew nothing about the cars they sold. Buyers knew even less." [37]

While Ford Motor Company was in its infancy, at least two steps taken would have a profound effect on the future of the automobile industry.

The first involved Couzens who worked to establish Ford agencies across the country. At that time, cars were sold in a rather haphazard manner by businesses ranging from blacksmiths and bicycle shops to dry goods stores. Couzens began to create a network of dealers who would be responsive to Ford Motor Company's main office. The dealers would be relied on for parts and service, not merely sales.

The second step involved Henry Ford, who wanted to take the proper steps for the new company and asked Fred Smith of Olds Motor Works how to approach the Association of Licensed Manufacturers (ALAM), the keepers of the

Selden Patent, to which all early automakers had to pay rights in order to manufacture cars in the United States.

Essentially, Ford was given the back of the hand by Fred Smith, son of Olds Motor Works owner Solomon Smith. The reaction of Fred Smith, speaking for ALAM members, shocked Ford. He said that in their estimation, the new Ford Motor Company was an "assemblage plant," not a true automobile manufacturer. [38]

It's been said that Irish people never forget a wrong and this son of an immigrant from Clonakilty, County Cork, was not about to let ALAM slight go quietly. The company's board of directors agreed the ALAM decision was unfair and that the idea of collecting rights fees under the Selden Patent was outmoded. They decided to make public their choice not to attempt to pay the rights fees. While that transgressed legal lines, and was considered suicidal for an automaking venture of the time, the Ford Motor Company decided to fight for their viewpoint.

A prized possession today, the 1904 Ford Model C runabout with top had a slightly larger, more powerful engine than the A version.

Soon a Ford Motor Co. ad in the Detroit *Free-Press* stated the company's firm position.

"We are pioneers of the Gasoline Automobile. Our Mr. Ford made the first Gasoline Automobile in Detroit and third in the United States. The machine made in 1896 is still in use." 39

It took several years but by the time the legal fur stopped flying, the Selden patent was judged to be worthless and manufacturers no longer had to pay its holders to make their cars. In the mean time, Ford and Ford agencies often promised to protect everyone associated with the Ford cars, including their buyers. The lawsuit earned Ford and Ford Motor Company a great deal of positive attention.

Reliability, a problem with many early cars, still continued to be a problem with Ford cars, among others. The Windsor, Ontario, *Evening-Record* reported one example in its Dec. 17, 1904 edition.

"The 1904 Ford of Oliver Hezzlewood, a bookkeeper of the McLaughlin Carriage Company in Oshawa, sounded like a threshing machine...[and] 'stopped about every 5 minutes for repairs.'" 40

Yet even in the midst of Ford Motor Company's growing pains, Henry Ford was dreaming about both a concept of standardized automobiles, one like the other, and to make a car that was available and practical for a larger market.

In 1903, the automobile still was a convenience or a hobby, out of reach at most income levels. Most of the time, the autos sold were sprinkled across a limited spectrum of middle and upper income buyers. The 1903 Olds was the notable exception. It sold 5,000 cars led by its 1,100-lb. curved and straight dash two-passenger runabouts.

Ford had retained his deeply held belief that an automobile could work and change the lives of rural customers. Ford and his associates were determined to broaden the marketplace with a car that more people would buy and continued to explore ways of accomplishing their goal.

The Ford Motor Co. introduced variations of the A with the AC, then the C. The C offered a cone clutch, a slightly larger 10 hp engine, a 78-inch wheelbase and a top speed of 30 mph. The C offered what turned out to be a faux engine covering with a 9-gallon gas tank underneath. The power plant still was mounted under the driver's seat.

MODEL A 1903-DEC. 1904	
Body	Runabout or tonneau*
Color	Carmine body and gearing
Engine	8 hp, two cylinders—opposed
Bore and stroke	4 x 4 in.
Differential	2 large, 2 small bevel gears
Fuel	5 gallons, tank under seat
Brakes	External contracting
Wheelbase	78 in.
Price	$800
Options	Leather top: $50, Rubber top: $30, *Tonneau body: $100

Note: The Model AC was a 10 hp version of the A.

MODEL C NOV. 1904 - DEC. 1905	
Body	Runabout or tonneau*
Color	Dark green body, red gearing
Engine	10 hp, two cylinders—opposed
Bore and stroke	4 ¼ x 4 ¼ in.
Differential	2 large, 2 small bevel gears
Fuel	9 gallons, tank under faux hood
Brakes	External expanding
Wheelbase	78 in.
Price	$950
Weight	1,250 lbs.
Top speed	30 mph
Options	Top: $30, *Tonneau body: $100

Ford Motor Company was presented with an opportunity during this period to reach across the Detroit River and into a potentially larger marketplace. The Walkerville Wagon Works Ltd. was seeking to differentiate its business and to find a new way to make a profit. Manager Gordon McGregor had been charged with making the Wagon Works a success and he wanted to get into automaking. He had admired the

The 1904 Model B version of the Ford was a pretty car, in hindsight, but was a poor seller when it was new.   Dr. Herb Bloom

MODEL B 1904-1905	
Body	Tonneau, side entrance
Color	Dark green body, yellow gearing
Engine	20 hp, four cylinder
Bore and stroke	4 ¼ x 4 ¼ in.
Fuel	15 gallons
Brakes	External expanding
Wheelbase	92 in.
Price	$2,000
Weight	1,750 lbs.
Top speed	40 mph

Ford Motor Company efforts and decided to approach Ford.

It would become a good match with Ford Motor Company—to spend a minimal amount to circumvent the high Canadian tariff and to gain access to export markets throughout the vast British Empire. Ford Motor Co. of Canada was formed in 1904. Some differences were noted, such as side entrances on the dominion version of the C instead of the American Ford's rear entrance design. [41]

Back in Detroit, Ford Motor Company produced a show car that soon would be another product of the company's lines. The Model B show car had shaft drive rather than chain drive and rear hub drum brakes in place of differential brakes. Spokes were built into the flywheel that provided air cooling for the engine.

When the B entered production, the four-cylinder engine was water cooled and had a separate fan but at 20 hp it was the most powerful Ford to date and rode on a 92-in. wheelbase. It weighed 1,700 lbs. and was priced at $2,000.

While Ford liked some of the mechanics, the high price bothered him and other members of the team around Ford. Ford and Malcomson began to have a fundamental difference in their vision of what cars to make. Malcomson's more conventional thinking followed the prevailing flow of selling larger, ever more expensive cars to established audiences. Ford wanted to go another way. His ideas began to spill out in public.

"That guy has a bird in his head," said an ex-Ford worker of the era explained later. "The bird in Henry's brain…was the cheap car, one that everyone could afford, and the notion had been flittering around his head for some time." [42]

"The engines must be simplified to get them within the comprehension of the ordinary owner," Ford observed. [43]

In 1905, Ford also expressed another view of making cars that appeared in a Detroit *Journal* headline: "Ten Thousand Autos at $400 Apiece." [44]

It would be a tug of war played out in the cars Ford produced from the B in 1904 through the S in 1907. Ford and his team continued to refine smaller, lighter and more durable cars for the masses while Malcomson envisioned a larger, more impressive Ford, something he wanted to own.

Ford wasn't alone in battling others to produce his vision of what an automobile should be. At Olds Motor Works, Fred Smith, acting as president for his investor father, Solomon, kept pushing the conventional wisdom of the day—a larger, more upscale car at a higher price. Smith ignored the nugget that should have been before his eyes, the popularity of the early Olds curved dash and straight dash runabouts, two-cylinder cars that sold for $675 to $750 in 1904, with a top.

Ransom E. Olds lost his place at the Olds Motor Works over the issue and the bright young Roy Chapin also was forced to move on. Each formed a new automobile venture with Olds forming Reo, using his initials, and Chapin getting involved in making Hudson cars, named for prime investor and Detroit merchant J. L. Hudson. [45]

The tug of vehicle direction continued at Ford Motor Company. In 1904, the two-cylinder Model F was introduced. At $1,000 it offered a two-cylinder, 12-hp engine, up-to-date side entrance doors and running boards. To Ford, it was a step in the right direction. Rockelman says a Model G also was developed but the four-cylinder car was never put into production. [46]

MODEL F NOV. 1905 – MAY 1906	
Body	Detachable tonneau, side entrance
Color	Dark green body, yellow gearing
Engine	12 hp, two cylinders—opposed
Bore and stroke	4 ¼ x 4 in.
Differential	3 large, 2 small bevel gears
Fuel	9 gallons, tank under faux hood
Brakes	External expanding
Wheelbase	84 in.
Price	$950-$1,000
Weight	1,400 lbs.
Top speed	35 mph
Options	Top: $30, *Tonneau body: $100

Malcomson pushed for his vision that became the 40 hp, six-cylinder Model K with its 114-in. wheelbase and $2,500 price tag. Rockelman says Malcomson put some of his own money behind the K's development, a total of $28,000. [47]

The Ford Model K was expensive and Henry Ford also disliked its six cylinder engine. The Model K rankled Ford for years to come. It turned him against Malcomson and he avoided producing another six-cylinder engine for decades. To make matters worse, the car gave Ford Motor Company a potentially bad reputation.

"Mechanically this behemoth was sound, but the transmission was open-faced and required regular lubrication, which many owners neglected..." [48]

Ford was ready for a fight and the Model K was the last straw. He was growing restless with having to take a back seat to the wishes of other investors and was determined to gain more control of the company.

MODEL K 1906 – 1907	
Body	Five-passenger touring or runabout
Color	Royal blue
Engine	40 hp, six cylinder
Bore and stroke	4 ½ x 4 ¼ in.
Transmission	Planetary, two speed
Fuel	15 gallons, tank under seat
Brakes	Internal expanding
Wheelbase	114 in.
Price	$2,500
Weight	2,400 lbs.
Top speed	50 mph

The K did have some features owners would become familiar with on the Model T, including the spark and throttle levels on the steering column, a two-speed planetary transmission, a drop-forged crankshaft, floor-mounted pedals for reverse and brake, as well as a magneto.

The K also was a lesson in some elements Henry Ford and his associates wanted to stay away from including cylinders that were cast separately, elliptical springs mounted parallel to the frame, a right-side steering wheel and especially the six cylinder engine.

Rockelman says about this time the Model N was being developed with a new planetary transmission developed by Wills. He demonstrated the unit to Henry Ford.

"He was so pleased with it that he wanted to show Mr.

This image of a 1905 Ford dealership, found on the back cover of the Model T Times in 2003, shows the transition from the horse-powered culture to the newer automotive culture.   *Courtesy Model T Times*

Malcomson what a $500 car could do so we drove it past... Mr. Malcomson's place of business." [49]

Ford and Couzens had discussed the need to move beyond their reliance on component makers, especially the Dodge Brothers, who still were making a profit on engines, chassis, gears and axles while collecting Ford stock dividends. Ford wanted to plow profits back into making more of their own components as a way to both curb production costs and to reach higher output and offer lower-priced cars. [50]

A positive step had been made with the expansion into a new plant at Piquette and Beaubien Avenues and the next step came on Nov. 22, 1905, when Ford Manufacturing

Company. was incorporated, nominally to make engines, parts and more. Of course, Ford knew that when Malcomson was not included, it would bring differences between them to a head.

In turn, Malcomson pledged to form another company called Aerocar with a goal of making 500 large touring cars a year. But that made Malcomson officially a rival and even his uncle, John S. Gray, sided with Ford. On Dec. 6, 1905, Malcomson was asked to resign and Ford Motor Company stock was consolidated. Couzens and his sister, Gray, the Dodge Brothers and attorneys Anderson and Rackham now had 415 shares of stock. Henry Ford owned 585 shares. [51]

Also, the young Ford Motor Company was thinking about a different way to make their cars. In the Jan. 1, 1906, edition of *Cycle and Automotive Trade Journal* James Couzens had bragged about Ford's ability to be productive on a mass scale.

"We are making 40,000 cylinders, 10,000 engines, 40,000 wheels, 20,000 axles, 10,000 bodies, 10,000 of every part that goes into the car. Such quantities were never heard of..." [52]

Soon, those generous numbers would seem pedestrian to Couzens and everyone in the automotive industry as Ford Motor Company's efforts at producing cars became more and more prolific.

Along with the new Model K in 1906, Ford Motor Company launched what many would later consider as the precursor to the Model T, the Ford Model N. The four-cylinder, 18-hp N had an 84-in. wheelbase and a base price of just $500.

"The Model N had embodied Henry Ford's persistent call, fully outlined in *Automobile* in January 1906, for a 'light, low-priced car' of ample horsepower that could go anywhere." [53]

Some compared the Ford N to the reliable Benz Parsifahl, a car with a positive reputation in both Europe and among select circles who knew cars well in North America. The N also expressed at least two iterations of the Ford team's advanced thinking about making cars.

MODEL N 1906 – 1907	
Body	Runabout
Color	Maroon
Engine	18 hp, four cylinder
Bore and stroke	3 ¾ x 3 3/8 in.
Transmission	Planetary, two speed
Fuel	10 gallons, tank under seat
Brakes	Internal expanding
Wheelbase	114 in.
Price	$500
Weight	800 lbs.
Top speed	40 mph

Note: R and S models offered improvements in the N.

It was the first Ford to use tough but light vanadium steel. The N also was the car that strived to reach the realm of mass production, though it was still assembled at Piquette with engines and chassis made at other shops.

The N was aimed at a new audience, a wider group of people whom Ford Motor Company saw as having great potential for buying an affordable vehicle. Today's Model T owners would recognize the transverse front spring and three-point suspension with strut rods.

Ford, though delighted with the direction of the N, saw room for improvement in many ways that included casting cylinders in pairs.

Still, the publication *Cycle and Automobile Trade Journal* called the N "...distinctly the most important mechanical traction event of 1906." [54]

Demand for the N model was high with reportedly 10 Model Ns sold for every Model K. In 1906 and 1907, Ford Motor Company sold 8,423 cars. In 1907, the fancier Model R was introduced, a car with more brass trim and frills, but basically an N. Ford Motor Company built 2,500 Rs by September 1907 and sold them all. In 1908, the N continued along with an upgraded Model S, still a refinement of the N, and 6,398 cars were sold.

Even with the advances made in the Model N, there were problems. In a letter from a Model N owner named F. N.

Briggs, a list of problems were reported within the first 500 miles including massive oil leaks from the crankcase, short circuiting problems and a commutator that was too close to the transmission to easily service, nuts that didn't hold and a faulty emergency brake. Briggs also reported that his engine was loosened from the frame. 55

The Ford Motor Company used these and other problems with the Model N to make improvements in the series, as reflected in the Model R and Model S variations produced in 1907.

The young Ford Motor Company had come a long way, entering the automotive fray at a time of frenetic, creative and unbridled energy. Henry Ford had held onto his ideas and had taken his team along with him, emerging as more than a racer, an inventor and a dreamer. He had become a presence in the ever-growing automotive industry.

Even Ford probably didn't realize what would happen in the next few years, though he was determined to continue working on a car that would be purchased by the great masses of people.

A series of excerpts from trade show publications of 1904 through 1906 show how the Ford car's pre-Model T rise was dramatic. "The Ford Motor Car Has the Center Stage" announced a 1904 ad.

The 1908 Model S version of the Ford previewed what soon would come to the marketplace. It was sturdy but light and was practical, yet within the price range of many buyers.

As if to support and answer those statements, Ford listed a number of "firsts" in 1905 including:

—"The Ford was the *first* practical two-cylinder opposed touring car to sell at a moderate price."

—"The Ford was the *first* easy and quiet-running gasoline touring car in America."

—"The Ford was the *first* American automobile popular enough to warrant establishing a factory in Canada."

The 1906 headline simply said: "The Successful Ford." "The whole thing is very simple when you go about it right," added the copy.

Ford continued to be successful in 1907 and into 1908 and by that time, Henry Ford was gathering his team again, this time in a special room on the third floor corner of the Piquette Ave. plant. Today we might call it a "design center."

"There was a rocking chair in the room in which he used to sit for hours and hours, discussing and following out the development of the design." recalled Joseph Galamb, an early Ford engineer. That rocking chair had belonged to Ford's mother, Mary. And the symbolism of birth and nurturing was strong. 56

From the give and take in that room, a new car would be born that the world would soon come to know. Presciently, Ford hadn't forgotten about getting the vehicle out, as he had with the Quadricycle in his rented backyard shed in 1896. This time, a garage door had been added. Ford Motor Company's best people were preparing to roll the new car out to the world.

And by 1908, the world was quickly preparing to accept those cars. Each year of the Ford Motor Company's existence, the number of autos on city streets and country roads had multiplied. Those trying to deny the existence of the automobile were burying their heads in the sand. Laws were passed and early motoring was difficult, especially before roads began to be improved, but the vehicles were here to stay.

Author Roberts describes a scene from Canada that probably was duplicated all over North America as more

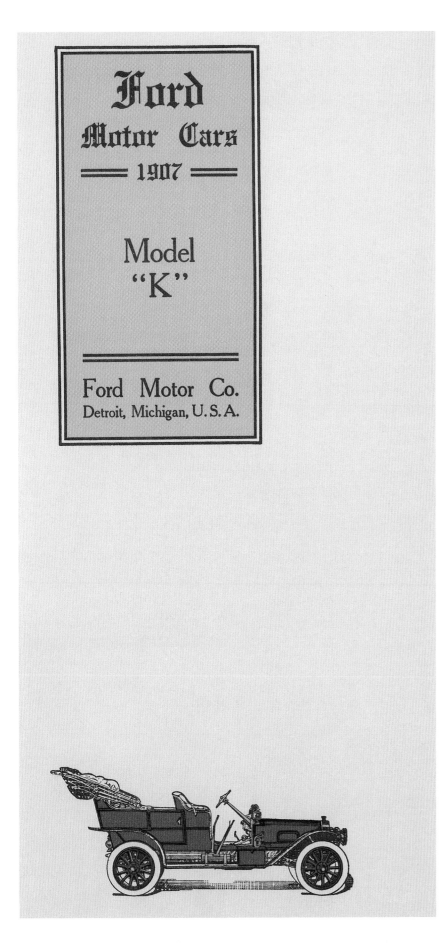

ABOVE: *The 1906 Ford Model N runabout seemed almost toy-like but it was a sturdy car that was popularly priced. Some of its basic technology influenced the Model T design.*

LEFT: *The 1907 Model K brochure cover shows this was a terrific-looking car in either touring car or roadster form. It was also larger and more expensive than other Ford products.*   Tom Collins

and more people learned firsthand about the freedom and possibilities they would find from the automobile.

"In Moose Jaw, Saskatchewan, Fred Hawkins bought a 1903 Model A Ford which he sold in 1906 to Fred W. Green, a progressive farmer who promptly took it apart and reassembled it to learn the mechanics of the internal combustion engine, a response repeated untold times throughout the dominion." [57]

Alone on the rolling prairies of Saskatchewan, Green probably didn't realize he was connecting to something more than the inner workings of the 1903 Ford A. He was joining a North American community that was willingly jumping headlong into the world of automobiles.

Why would anyone plunge into the wide-open world that was early auto making and auto ownership?

The answer was it was very much like a love affair, not really something people could explain, but something they were drawn to with an irresistible impulse. The coming of the Model T Ford would be a tidal wave that sent that love affair around the world.

The world of automobiles in 1906 included the well-constructed Cadillac touring car that reflected Henry Leland's penchant for precision.

> *"The man who will use his skill and constructive imagination to see how much he can give for a dollar... is bound to succeed."*
>
> *Henry Ford*

Chapter 3

THE BIRTH OF THE UNIVERSAL CAR

Early in 1906, the Ford Motor Company was settling in as a recognized player in the automobile industry. That world was beginning to change as the day of idealistic dreamers and dedicated inventors was fading. Making automobiles was beginning to be much more of a serious business that involved sound production techniques, professional sales methods and the ability to prove reliability and call attention to it.

During that year, the original Ford company president, John S. Gray, died. Reportedly, Gray always lacked the belief that the Ford Motor Company would succeed, even though the company continued to make a profit, unlike countless automotive ventures of the time. Henry Ford had been voted into the top spot after Gray's death.

Ford was making a transition from his early days as a dreamer, an inventor and a racer into his role as an automaker and leader. It was still another in the many steps in his remarkable personal growth.

By 1906, the Ford Model N pointed the way to a new generation of affordable and dependable cars targeted to a wider audience of potential buyers.

ABOVE: *In 1909, one of the few cars that offered a low price was the Brush, a United Motors Co. product. It was labeled "Everyman's Car" and was priced at just $485.*

BELOW: *The 1909 Chalmers-Detroit was an example of the industry's conventional thinking about larger, more expensive cars. Cars like this ignored a larger audience the Model T would tap.*

In July 1906, Ford predicted what he thought would soon happen at Ford Motor Company to a young driver and mechanic named Fred Rockelman.

"We're going to expand this company, and you will see that it will grow by leaps and bounds. The proper system, as I have it in mind, is to get the car to the multitude." 1

Ford intuitively felt the era of turning out a car at the highest possible price to limited audiences of wealthy or near wealthy drivers was changing. That upper end was becoming a crowded marketplace. He thought there were potential buyers who had read about or seen automobiles and might be persuaded to buy one if they could find a vehicle at a reasonable price. A few automakers realized they needed to reach out to these growing numbers of potential auto buyers.

Meanwhile, the automobile industry was just old enough to undergo some changes in structure. Several smaller independent auto companies were beginning to bet their futures on consolidation under common management systems.

One of those efforts was the young General Motors under the direction of William C. "Billy" Durant, a strong example of many free-wheeling entrepreneurs in the early world of automaking. Durant, who had been part of the Durant-Dort Carriage Company, took over Buick in 1904. Unlike Ford, Durant's unquenchable business spirit was constantly conceiving a wider spectrum of economic possibilities and searching for new ways of making a deal.

At one point, Durant even approached Henry Ford about bringing the Ford Motor Company under the General Motors umbrella. The negotiation with General Motors was never seriously considered by Henry Ford. He intentionally set a high price and discouraged any offers of stock. An unreformed Populist, Ford wanted what he called "...gold on the table. I want cash." 2

Durant's General Motors began to take shape in 1908 when Olds joined Buick. The next year, the Oakland car was absorbed after owner/builder Edward Murphy died. Then the former Henry Ford Company, re-formed as the Cadillac Motor Car Company, was sold to GM for $5.5 million. Henry Leland and his son, Wilfred, soldiered on at Cadillac. The busy new General Motors also bought the Rapid Truck Company in 1909.

"Billy bought catchy billboards and a song," was one view of the Olds purchase, according to historian William Pelfry. 3

Another Ford Motor Company suitor was the United Motor Company's organizer Benjamin Briscoe. The United umbrella was an amalgamation of early carmakers that included the lower-priced Brush, the Columbia, the Maxwell, the Courier and the Stoddard-Dayton as well as Alden Sampson trucks and Gray Marine.

While GM was an example of the bravado of early business mergers, United Motors was an example of the insecurity of smaller makers coming together, hoping for survival. In 1910, Briscoe was promising a bright future but his empire was built on quicksand. By 1912, United Motor Company was in receivership and only Maxwell would move on.

Ford rebuffed Briscoe with his cash-not-stock demands. Needless to say, Ford Motor Company kept running at its own pace and growing while United Motors fell by the wayside. As usual, Henry Ford was content to go his own way.

Unlike modern corporate marriages, the merging of one automobile company with another didn't often shake foundations in those early days. Durant's purchase of the Olds Motor Works was seen as a footnote to fading glory rather than the trumpeting that modern mergers receive.

Poor product decisions have always hurt automakers. Olds Motor Works president Fred Smith's decision to follow the crowd and make larger cars rather than listen to Ransom E. Olds' insistence on building smaller, more practical cars was a poor one. Smith's stubborn direction eventually withered the sales lead the small Olds had built in the early 1900s. The poor decision would be underlined when Olds left the company in January 1904 to go his own way.

By 1906 and soon after, R. E. Olds was happily building his Reo vehicle line, about the same time the new Ford Motor Co. was growing. The larger Olds was nearly invisible in the teaming marketplace of pricey, large cars—a victim of Smith's lack of vision and unwillingness to listen to Olds. Henry Ford noted the lesson that came from the Olds Works.

Pure business savvy wasn't the formula for automotive success either. The man who had consolidated 45 bicycle companies in 1899, Albert Pope, had purchased a number of auto companies and created the Pope "hyphenated" cars in the early 1900s in the hopes of repeating his bicycle empire. But the magic didn't happen in the automotive world and the Pope-hyphened cars weren't selling.

By the time Ford Motor Company was formed, Pope-Robinson of Massachusetts was on its last legs. By 1908, Pope-Tribune of Maryland would die and be sold to the Montrose Metal Casket Company. That same year, the Pope-Waverly Electric Company in Indiana was sold. The Pope-Toledo would last just one more year, until 1909, leaving the Pope-Hartford the lone survivor of Pope's hoped-for automobile empire.

As Ford Motor Company began to take shape, Henry Ford had continued to assess the market and, along with his associates, was convinced more than ever that a practical car was overdue, a vehicle that would serve the needs of a much wider and largely untapped audience.

Ford and others noted that progress was occurring in American automotive circles. Americans were going their own way, losing the wagon and bicycle-inspired styles and creating vehicles with a touch of practicality. Ford Motor Co. would soon lead the way in spreading this trend.

Henry Ford also was impatient about the way everyone was making their cars—not much differently than carriages had been assembled for hundreds of years. It was a slow, often inexact process. He also disliked the scattered offerings of so many models. Ford, who had expressed to company attorney and investor John Anderson that a shoemaker or a stove maker should concentrate on a single product, wanted to focus on applying that kind of specialization to building a car.

He had no use for buying up someone else's mistakes and trying to re-shape them. Nor was he interested in building several car lines in the vain hope of trying to catch buyer attention. When Ford told young associate Fred Rockelman he was expanding, he meant breaking into a much larger audience that had been overlooked. They would be the people who would buy Ford cars.

In doing that, Ford and Ford Motor Company were

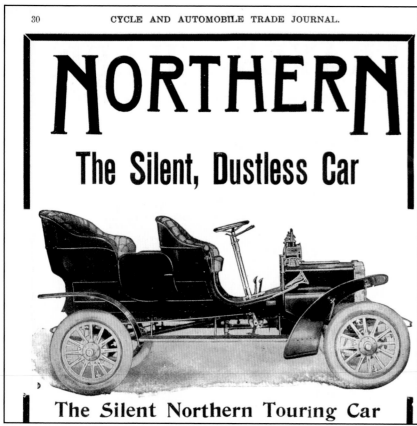

NORTHERN
The Silent, Dustless Car

The Silent Northern Touring Car

One car company that had some of the virtues Henry Ford was pursuing was the "Silent Dustless" Northern, produced by Ford's early inventor friend Charles B. King in Detroit.

heading into new territory, well beyond the prevailing wisdom of making large, fancy cars for a few. Ford's dream, which had been foreshadowed with the Model N, was thousands of people buying smaller and simpler cars, all bearing the Ford name.

There were certainly more and more people willing to buy automobiles, with up to 140,000 registrations in 1907, up from just 8,000 in 1900 according to automotive historian Beverly Rae Kimes. 4

Henry Ford was ready to explore the potential outside the box that had been the early automotive world. The men and women who worked at the Ford Motor Co. also were eager to begin that adventure.

Those people often were talented and young. They complemented one another quite well in terms of their skills. Some had worked with Ford at the Edison Illuminating plant. Others had come into the Ford racing ventures. They were eager to make a mark in the world.

One was Childe Harold Wills, who hated the "Childe" appellation his mother had found in a Lord Byron poem and always went by "C.H." or "C. Harold." Wills was a brilliant and creative mechanical engineer and designer. His father had been a mechanical engineer as well. Early on, Wills had been involved in Ford's many racing ventures and would contribute much to the Ford Motor Company.

Men like Charles Sorenson and C. J. "Jimmy" Smith would make valuable contributions in fabrication and assembly. Efficiency expert Walter Flanders became the Ford Motor Company production manager. James Couzens continued to offer sound financial advice and to build the early Ford dealer network.

Of Sorenson it was said: "…simply hearing an idea from Henry was sufficient go-ahead from him to make a pattern and cast it." 5

Others made vital contributions. Joseph Galamb, an engineer from Hungary, had been trained at the Royal Institute of Technology in Budapest. He was joined by the man who was considered the main draftsman for Henry Ford, Charles Balough Sr., also a Hungarian immigrant and also a graduate of the Royal Institute in Budapest. Another Ford employee was Julies Haltenberger.

Rockelman was just 20 years old and already a talented driver and mechanic. He was able to observe the period of great energy and creation at Ford.

Wills helped develop the Model A, worked on the Model N and other early Ford models as well as pre-Ford Motor Co. race cars. His vision, as well as the ideas and input of others, would blend with Henry Ford's vision and create a new car. Beginning in about 1906, Wills, Ford and the eager employees who formed that first Ford Motor Co. team of innovators were going forward to create a new car from a clean sheet of paper.

The Ford Motor Co. people were taking a broad step. They were counting that there were many more people like themselves in the United States and beyond who had been largely ignored by the automotive industry in its formative years. Now they were venturing into that unexplored territory. Historian Kimes defined the climate for the new car spearheaded by Henry Ford in this way:

"He was providing America with an automobile he knew it wanted, even if America itself wasn't altogether sure." 6

A special room was set aside on the third floor of the Piquette Avenue plant, a place that would become a creative center, something we might call an "innovation center" today. A dedicated sub-team including Galamb, Balough and Haltenberger worked with Ford directly on the new car project with his constant input and contributions from other key Ford Motor Company players including Sorenson, Wills and others. Using the next available letter in the Ford alphabet of development, the new project was called the Model T.

While many people inside the Ford Motor Company contributed to the design of the Model T as it was being developed, at least one outside organization played an important role. The John R. Keim Mills of Buffalo, New York, worked closely with Ford employees to make the axle housings, crankcases and transmission covers. The Keim Mills were eventually absorbed by the Ford Motor Co.

Look at the rear axle of any early Model T and you will see something special, the long housings for the differential gears and the axle shafts, designed to cover and protect them from road dirt, dust and water.

"These housings were the deepest drawing from one piece ever made to that date," wrote Model T expert Bruce McCalley. 7

One other form of technology convinced Ford he was on the right track toward producing a popular-priced car that many could afford. At a race at Palm Beach, Florida, in 1905, Ford picked up a piece of metal from a wrecked French racer. The metal was light, but strong. It impressed Ford and he had the metal studied.

Wills was in charge of that assignment, based on his training in metallurgy, and he worked with a knowledgeable British metallurgist named J. Kent-Smith on the project. 8 Eventually a foundry in Canton, Ohio, was found that could

forge the vanadium steel product.

"Until then we had been forced to be satisfied with a steel running between 60,000 and 70,000 pounds tensile strength," Ford recalled. "With vanadium, the strength went up to 170,000 pounds." 9

In the 1907 model year, some vanadium steel began to appear on the market, especially with the Ford Models N, R and S.

"Vanadium steel resists shock—either one blow or a series of lighter ones, or minute vibrations…to a greater extent than any other metal," reported the Detroit News that year. 10

Strong but lightweight steel was an important ingredient in the formula for making a lower priced quality car that would be adaptable for many uses.

A few years later, early Ford Motor Company sales literature from the Krause Publications archives reveals they even had a section on vanadium steel in a Model T booklet that showed picture of a connecting rod twisted like a licorice stick and a curving crankshaft that appeared to be the handiwork of a balloon maker.

Ford was very happy to report the results of a French testing lab that subjected Model T components to rigorous testing and found it stronger than any other competitor, "… a striking testimonial to Ford quality." Vanadium steel in Fords would definitely be a sales asset.

Meanwhile, even though Ford Motor Co. was still involved in the long and drawn out legal fight to do away with the expensive burden of the Selden patent and its fee collecting ALAM arm, the Ford team was primarily focused on perfecting the new Model T.

The third-floor innovation corner of the Piquette plant was enclosed and even had garage door opening. It was a place where ideas could be shared and the best thinking developed. Henry Ford and team members actively shared ideas.

"He'd never say 'I want this done.' He'd say, 'I wonder if we can do it? I wonder?'" recalled George Brown, then a Ford Motor Company employee. "Well, the men would just

break their necks to see if they could do it. They knew what he wanted." 11

Balough was another player and observer who wrote a letter in 1955, recently excerpted in an article by his grandson, Bruce, in the January-February 1907 edition of Model T Times. Charles Balough recalled the four blackboards in the Model T development room.

"Mr. Ford brought his suggestions and ideas and it was our job to sketch and develop these ideas, first by chalk sketches [that] established the practicality of his ideas, [then] the details were worked out in drawings." 12

Wills had worked on the planetary transmission used in earlier Ford Motor Company cars. He was said to have come up with the Model T's shared engine and transmission lubrication system while taking a bath! 13

According to Balough, the planetary transmission may not have been used, save for the fate of an accident when a prototype Model T was being tested.

LEFT: *Something new was on the horizon. Already in extensive testing by 1906, the new Ford car would change the automotive marketplace.* Tom Glatch

BELOW: *By the Fall of 1908, the potential buyers were aware of something new from the Ford Motor Co. The new Model T was announced to the public in national magazine ads.*

Model T

Ford Motor Company

Detroit, U. S. A.

Souvenir Booklet

"This model incorporated a sliding gear transmission in place of the standard planetary transmission in the earlier Ford cars," Balough recalled. "Mr. Ford wasn't sold on this type. It fell to my lot to take the car on a trial run." [14]

Balough's test run ended in disaster. It was a busy time of day as three street cars converged near the Ford plant taking workers home. One of the street cars turned just as he was trying to pass it.

"The experimental model was completely wrecked, crushed between the street car and a telegraph pole," said Balough. "Naturally I was worried about what Mr. Ford's reaction would be. He said: 'Charley, that's the best job you ever did for this company.'" [15]

Balough recalled that the sliding gear transmission was abandoned but that the team then turned to the possibility of a three-speed planetary transmission as their next step. When that transmission proved problematic, Balough said Ford's reaction was philosophical.

"...the gear that gives you no trouble is the one you never use." [16]

Eventually, the two-speed planetary transmission developed by Wills and used on earlier Fords was retained but improvements were made. The transmissions in the N, R and S versions had only a shroud covering that was susceptible to elements. Plans for the T called for the planetary transmission to be covered and to share oil with the engine, with the Wills brainstorm that constantly bathed the unit in oil.

Model T prototypes borrowed more from the Model N and S Fords. Those cars had three floor pedals and two levers. One of the levers controlled low, neutral and high gears in the transmission. The second was an emergency brake. The floor pedals were for reverse, the transmission brake and for the rear wheel brakes. [17]

There was no textbook or script available for any carmaker in 1907, including the Ford Motor Company development team. There was no proven way to make a successful car. Those who had new ideas and the right financial backers were trying their cars on the public. Many carmakers were following the crowd, trying to get an ever-thinner slice of the automotive sales pie.

There were gearless and sliding gear transmissions available. Both Lambert and Cartercar were proponents of the clever friction disk transmission with its endless possibilities. There were water- and air-cooled engines in the marketplace. Some cars had vertical cylinders and some cylinders were horizontally opposed. Buyers could find cars with one, two, four and eight cylinders. The Iroquois truck claimed it was "built like a locomotive," the Corbin played up its Annular ball bearings and the Autocar claimed to be "modern-to-the-minute." Almost anything seemed possible.

As the Model T project moved along, many Ford Motor Company employees offered opinions. Years later, Rockelman explained that the best knowledge of how to understand and improve automobiles came from having a chance to drive them. So his driving expertise often was valued along with those who had advanced engineering theories or sophisticated training in design.

"The auto industry had not progressed far enough to have experienced, school trained engineers so it depended on personal know-how gained in the hard school of experience. Only by driving the car could the feel of the car be determined." [18]

The new Ford Model T began to take shape. One of the most notable ideas was used in its engine. Henry Ford disliked the separate casting of cylinders—both in manufacture and in operation. The Ford team came up with something new—casting the engine en bloc, in one piece, with only the cylinder head cast separately. That meant the cylinder head could easily be detached for maintenance.

Other experiences with the N, R and S series helped the Ford team focus on some other trouble-free oiling methods. The new car's oiling was accomplished by splash feed and letting gravity have its way.

Springs front and rear were semi-elliptical, mounted cross-wise like those found on many wagons and carriages. This was seen as an advantage, along with a wide enough track, to deal with the tough, wagon-rutted roads, found especially in rural areas. The high stance of the T also gave the car's chassis and drive train clearance to avoid much of the potentially rough terrain it would encounter. The new Ford had a 100-in. wheelbase and was 128 inches long.

An ingenious magneto, attached to the car's flywheel, reportedly developed by "Spider" Huff and Wills, made the car as self-sufficient as possible, doing away with the nuisance of the early dry cell batteries that constantly lost power and had to be replaced. Once cranked and running, the Ford's magneto provided the self-generated current that could be delivered via a coil box "vibrator" to offer ignition.

When some dealers mistakenly put out the advanced information sent from the Ford Motor Company headquarters in March 1908, they reportedly had a tough time selling the remaining 1907 S series Fords. In hindsight, that dilemma probably predicted success for the new car.[19]

Author Lacey says the Ford team gained a great deal of confidence in the car and its then modern technology in several steps including one test with the crankshaft.

"When the team looked at the crankshaft made of the new alloy, they could not believe it would work. It seemed so frail and small compared to any other crankshaft they had seen. When they gave it a shock test, it easily withstood double the load that it would get in the actual operation of the engine." [20]

Earlier in the year, orders were already coming in but Ford Motor Co. had to work hard to prepare to make the new T series, according to a remarkable memo, excerpted here, from James Couzens to Henry Ford sent in February 1908.

"...we received orders for forty-eight from London this morning and have orders for about twenty-five from Paris, to say nothing of the orders for domestic shipments which are coming in quite rapidly," Couzens wrote. "One of the things that contributed to my illness...was the pessimistic view taken by Mr. Flanders as to the outlook for producing Model Ts. I authorized him yesterday to go ahead and run night and day...to put through both [S and T] models at the same time." [21]

On Sept. 1, 1908, the Ford Model T went into production, debuting for dealers at the Sept. 14 through 17 branch meetings. Just like many modern cars, the new Model Ts began as 1909 models, even though early cars were produced in 1908.

The early results caught even the confident Ford team off guard. The new Model T was first officially described for the public in the Friday Oct. 3, 1908, edition of the *Saturday Evening Post*. The *Ford Times* later reported the results:

"Saturday's mail brought nearly 1,000 inquiries. Monday's response swamped our mail clerks and by Tuesday night, the office was well nigh inundated." [22]

If this was an election, the results were showing early indications of being a landslide. As the mail flooded in, so did the cash. Ford Motor Co. not only had to cap production in the winter of 1909 but continue at high production levels through August of that year to keep up with the flood of orders.

Henry Ford and the Ford team involved in bringing out the Model T had produced a car the public had not seen before, a car with the combination of value, practicality and modern technology, yet still within reach for many early car buyers.

For those used to spending a lot of money and getting a very formal look in their automobiles, Ford offered the landaulet—open air for the driver and closed-body styling for the passengers.

The new Ford Motor Co. product, the Model T, was available in several body styles including this very upright coupe version.

In addition to using vanadium steel, casting the cylinders in the engine block and the attention paid to covering and providing oil for the transmission, the Model T offered at least two more advantages, pointed out by Model T expert McCalley.

One was the advanced use of pressed steel in the engine, transmission and rear axle, something that the Ford Motor Company had perfected for the T with the partnership of the Keim Mills foundry experts. Another advantage was the three-point or triangular suspension system in the Model T. While it had been used on some earlier Ford models, the T version was improved. It didn't suffer from the damaging twists and strains inflicted by primitive roads of the time. [23]

Ford team member Rockelman says it was well known that the Model K Ford, for one example, had difficulty with any kind of twists and flexing.

"The workers used to like to get a strong man to try to crank the K, betting him he couldn't do so," recalled Rockelman. "He couldn't, for one of them had jacked up one of the rear wheels, twisting the car and engine enough to cramp the crankshaft." [24]

Original Ford literature for the earliest Model T also showed one very practical advantage. It was called "Left Side Control." While most cars had continued the practice from horse and buggy days of keeping the steering on the right side, the Ford team saw the practicality of mounting the steering on the left-hand side. It meant passengers didn't have to exit in the streets and roads, a point underlined in the Model T-shaped Ford sales brochure.

"…note the pleasure of getting in and out of the car dry shod, of being able to see where you are going, of being in a position to know what the approaching car is doing, and you will wonder how with American road laws, the European idea of right side control gained a hold in this country." [25]

That simple exchange of steering gear placement was just a small way that the Ford Model T would change American life. Soon most U.S. and Canadian automakers copied the Model T and offered left-side drive.

Overall simplicity also was a strong point the public quickly found about the Model T. Its straightforward, self-contained systems reached a wide range of men and women, many of whom had not only been priced out of owning a car but who probably had been intimidated by the technology and sheer size of many early cars.

"In 1909, most Americans had never driven a car," noted McCalley. "Here was a low priced one that almost anyone could learn to drive in a very short time, and without

The new Model T, introduced late in 1908 as a 1909 model, could be as fancy as any town car on the market.

ABOVE: *The Model T continued the pioneering use of the tough but light vanadium steel construction. It was seen in earlier Fords but the Model T used it from the ground up.* Tom Glatch

BELOW: *One of the secrets to the Model T's success was that it would interest people in buying a car who had never thought about owning one—or even considered driving a car before.* Mike Mueller

worrying about clashing gears, grabbing clutches and so on." [26]

After the first 800 Model Ts were produced, Ford Motor Company introduced a change that would almost be a trademark and certainly was a memorable feature of the Model T. Early on, the Model T was a bit of hybrid of the N,

R and S that had used a hand lever for the forward gears and a pedal for reverse.

At first, the T had two levers—one for reverse and the second as an emergency brake. The two floor pedals were for the high and low gears (left) and brake (right). Ford soon eliminated the second lever and used three pedals, with the center pedal now applying the reverse action. Ford's three floor pedals would become famous and also memorable for many first-time drivers.

The beloved Irish poet John Keats once wrote about learning to drive using the three pedals of the Model T saying he would:

"…get into high without bounding down the road, looking like a frog with St. Vitus dance and sounding like a canning factory with something wrong with it." [27]

A Ford ad soon captured what the Model T meant to the public that had been used to riding and driving horses.

"Drive a horse ten-thousand miles day in and day out and you'll need a new horse. The Ford will need but new tires." [28]

There was something special about the Model T that the public quickly latched on to. Farmers liked the fact that it could go through their rough and muddy access roads and fields and still take the family to church on Sunday in style. The early Model T had some sophistication a modern Lexus owner would appreciate, leather seats, but it was also a tough, simple car that could be adapted for almost any use imaginable.

In small towns and county squares, places for horses were now filled with Model Ts. Early on Ford Motor Company found that a remarkable one in five cars sold was a Model T. By 1914, that was one in three cars sold and the success of the car would continue.

Perhaps there were cars that were cheaper—certainly the Waltham Orient buckboard was still available in the $500 neighborhood. But people didn't flock to Waltham. Americans, then Canadians, and then much of the world took to the Model T because it was inexpensive, innovative and reliable.

If repairs were needed, owners could work on the car easily or hand it over to a local mechanic who would be able to quickly get the job done. It was a car that was easy to understand. One could almost say it became part of the family, that Henry Ford and his crew had made the automotive version of the golden retriever.

Even the art and architectural communities were attracted to the T. The architectural community, an often tough crowd to please explained the Model T as:

"Modernism on wheels...the greatest creation in automobiles ever placed before a people." [29]

Ford Motor Co. got so busy with Model T orders that they sent out a memo telling dealers, in Ford mandate fashion, not to take any more orders. William S. Knudsen was hired from the Keim Mills to coordinate the process of getting the cars out. Production would continue to lag behind demand for several years, not something the young auto industry had ever experienced.

When Ford Motor Co. found it was too expensive to ship out completed Ts, they began to learn how to knock them down and ship them to dealers with tires and fenders removed. Seven chassis would be stacked at a 45-degree angle in one half of the box car while the bodies and fenders for seven Ts filled the other half side. [30]

Soon the company literature would explain the importance of these "pack and ship" Model Ts and they're steady impact around the globe. Ford Motor Co. explained exporting as follows:

"Many Fords are shipped abroad each day from the big Ford factories at Detroit, Mich., and Ford, Ont. Most of the foreign shipments from Detroit are to France, Germany and Russia while the majority of the foreign shipments from the Ford, Ont., factory are to Australia, New Zealand, India, South Africa, Straits Settlements [today's Singapore] and other British Colonies." [31]

It wasn't long before shipping Fords by rail, freighter and ferry wouldn't be enough to handle the demand as more branch plants were needed in North America and in several locations around the world.

More than 10,000 Model Ts were produced in 1909.* Not only did that number best the Buick production of 8,820 in the 1908 model year, it renewed the vigor that Henry Ford and Couzens had applied to their unique ideas about manufacturing and pricing a car to reach the masses. As the Model T took off like wild fire, Ford and Couzens took a step back and thought about the consequences of what they were doing.

Soon they would understand that their direction in trying to produce a car for a mass audience had cracked open an entirely different way of conducting the automotive business and automotive production, as Couzens explained with hindsight in a 1921 interview.

"In effect, we standardized the customer," Couzens, who went on to become a U.S. Senator from Michigan, explained in *Lessons Learned at Ford*. "We set the price of the car as a goal to reach and depended for profit upon the economics that we might effect in volume manufacturing." [32]

While many people think of the Model Ts as plain black cars, the first year Model Ts were Carmine Red, Brewster Green and Gray with shiny brass trim. The early 1908 prototypes came only in a touring car body style but the 1909 production versions expanded on that to also include a roadster, a "high boy" coupe, a seven-passenger town car and even a luxurious Model T, the rakish landaulet with its closed-bodied passenger area and open compartment for the driver.

The first Model Ts to reach the public had memorable visible features that included a brass tank mounted on the left-side running board. Carbide crystals were in the bottom portion and water in the top. When the water trickled down, a gas was formed that was piped through tubing to the headlights and to a single rear lamp.

On touring models with an optional top, long straps came forward at a 45-degree angle and hooked into large eyelets fixed into the front axle area of the car. An optional, two-piece windshield brought a varnished wooden board to add a spacer to the cowl between the optional windshield and the lower cowl top. Brass-trimmed supports also ran forward from the top of the windshield down to their body mounts. The look was quite distinctive, especially in profile.

The touring version had doors for the rear section but no doors in front. The town car, like the landaulet, featured a closed rear section but had a flatter "breezeway" top and no front doors. The roadster and coupe were distinctive two-passenger Model Ts in that first year. The roadster came with an opening top, and the coupe, later caricatured in cartoons like "Scrooge McDuck," had an extremely high profile, almost like a telephone booth. Another noticeable coupe feature was its rear-hinged, front-opening doors.

The first 800 Model Ts featured the two-pedal, two-lever setup. There were numerous changes in the first 2,500 Model Ts as well before the cars hit their stride for the remainder of the production year, which lasted well into August of 1909, almost a year since Model Ts first came through assembly at the Piquette plant in September 1908.

The Ford Motor Co. would use many component makers through the Model T's production history. There would be additions and deletions during model year production runs and new items would replace older ones in succeeding model years. Some design changes would produce slightly different body styles through the years and the Model Ts would be offered in a number of body styles from 1909 through 1927. Yet, the car was readily identifiable from its earliest assemblies in 1908 through the final editions that came off the assembly line in May 1927.

Brass, black and nickel plate would almost define T eras as did carbide gas and electric lights. One could see that some Ts had doors while some did not. And the experts would be able to tell an endless array of differences from the tip of the radiator to the end of the tailpipe and at every point in between as the years passed.

The Model Ts would soon fascinate people around the world and when they experienced one, they remembered the car the rest of their lives.

In a booklet sent to dealers to explain selling points of the Model T, as if that was really needed, the T was defined in the following manner:

"It's the one reliable car that does not require a $10,000 income to buy, a $5,000 bank account to run and a college course in engineering to keep in order." [33]

One of the first Model T brochures, later reproduced by Krause Publications, was designed in the silhouette of the first 800 Model T touring cars, complete with double levers and pedals. Inside, the 20 horsepower, four-cylinder engine was coupled with what the Ford writers described as "...the silent, velvety, planetary transmission [and] the new Ford magneto generator..."

In addition to describing the engine and transmission, the early brochure also noted the vanadium steel springs. "Because of the steel used and the method of construction, a strain that would put the ordinary spring on the junk pile will have no effect on these springs."

In terms of the magneto, the Ford writers emphasized simplicity as they noted : "...there are no belts, brushes, contact points, moving wires or commutator."

If all that wasn't enough, Ford mentioned that bodies were interchangeable and offered a guarantee many would depend on. "...the only car manufactured that the average man can afford, yet a car that looks well in the handsome garage of the millionaire, alongside the highest priced car. The imprint 'Ford' is a guaranty of quality wherever it appears." [34]

Finally, the Ford brochure focused on price:

"We make no apologies for the price. Any car now selling for several hundred dollars more could, if built in the Ford shops, from Ford design, by Ford methods, and in Ford quantities, be sold at the Ford price if the makers would be satisfied with the Ford profit per car." [35]

Game, set and match to Ford. There was little to question about the new Model T when it appeared in 1909 and many learned that this faithful companion that had come into their lives would soon change their world and their habits.

"Lean, rangy and occasionally fairly cussed, the Model T was rather like Henry Ford," wrote biographer Lacey. "The Model T converted a plaything of the European rich into the birthright of the American masses." [36]

Early in production, Model Ts like this one were changed. If you look carefully, you'll see two levers and two floor pedals. One of the levers became a floor pedal.

Owning a Model T became an unusual dance between the owner and the car, offering an unlimited independence many had never experienced before but also new forms of responsibility that they'd never experienced. While not as needy as some earlier cars had been with their constant thirst for oil and lubrication or other unyielding details, the Model T still needed attention. And owners found it offered a swift kick to those who didn't treat it with care! Many owners swore the car almost seemed to have a personality.

Humor was one way that Model T owners learned to cope in their tango with the T. One story revolved around the speedometer, often a Stewart unit found on the early Ts.

"When I go five miles an hour, the fenders rattle; when I go 15 miles an hour, my false teeth drop out; and when I go 25 miles an hour, the transmission drops off." [37]

Floyd Clymer, who had a remarkable career that included selling other cars as a boy, said he soon latched on to driving and selling the Model Ts and later chronicled the early world of automobiles.

"...the man who owned a Ford often did most of his mechanical work himself. The motorist accepted his roadside grief with his joy." [38]

And Clymer noted: "The Ford owner swore by his car as well as at it." [39]

"A Model T brought out the ingenuity of its owner as much as crossing the Plains in a Conestoga wagon had taxed the resourcefulness of the homesteader," wrote historian Kimes. [40]

For example, in colder climates, owners learned ways to keep their Model Ts from freezing such as pouring hot water in the radiator, keeping hot plates under the engine or finding ways to heat garages or areas of a barn where the T was stored. Some aftermarket companies specialized in gadgets that would help T owners warm the manifold to get their cold Ts started and running. Others had success jacking up a rear wheel.

"Once the engine had run for a few minutes and the crankcase oil was warmed up," recalled Clymer, "the T settled down...as dependable as a pack mule if you carried a tool kit and checked your gas regularly." [41]

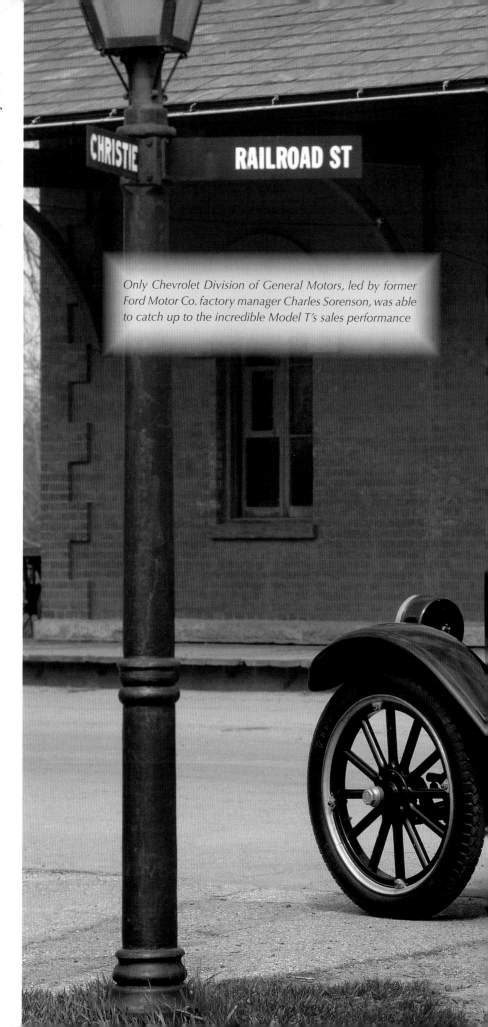

Only Chevrolet Division of General Motors, led by former Ford Motor Co. factory manager Charles Sorenson, was able to catch up to the incredible Model T's sales performance

Many owners experienced what some called "T creep," that the car would begin moving as they were starting it. They learned to brace themselves as the car would begin to roll forward. Some even said it was rather comforting, reminding them of a nudge from a horse. Author E. B. White described that feeling.

"I can still feel my old Ford nuzzling me at the curb, as though looking for an apple in my pocket." [42]

The Model T gas tank was fed by gravity always was mounted on a higher plane than the carburetor it fed. On some versions, like early roadsters, the tank was mounted behind the front seats, out back. On many Model Ts, the front seat was mounted over the gas tank. That meant drivers and passengers had to get out and pull up the seat cushion when it was time for gas.

On Canadian-built Model Ts, the seat cushions were sectioned for easier removal but on the American version, the seat cushion was one piece with a wooden frame door underneath, over the tank.

Gravity feed also meant that on severe uphill grades, the T might begin to starve for fuel. Ts were remarkably agile on most kinds of terrain and in many kinds of situations. Practical owners soon learned to back their way up such grades. Clymer remembers a farmer who lived on such a hill and always was seen backing his way up on the last portion of his journey home.

Model T drivers were responsible for checking their own fuel and oil levels. There were no gauges unless one could be found in the aftermarket. Clymer says he often supplied owners with a black stick like a ruler to help them check their fuel levels. But the sticks often were lost.

Checking the oil was another matter. The Ford team had developed sort of a "feast or famine" ritual that involved two pet cocks. Clymer described the method:

"I got on my knees, and, with a pair of pliers, turned one of the two petcocks located in the lower half of the flywheel housing. If oil ran out of the top petcock onto the ground, the oil supply was OK. If no oil came out of the lower petcock, we were head straight for bearing trouble if oil was not added." [43]

Ford let the new owner know that checking the oil on their Model T was important. The first-time owner was given guidelines to not drive their car faster than 20 mph the first 500 miles and to change their oil after the first 450 miles, then at intervals of 750 miles.

The Model T gained a loyal following in the United States. Across the river, through Gordon McGregor's management of Ford of Canada the former Walkerville Wagon Works was growing. Located in an area of Windsor, Ontario, that would eventually be known as "Ford City," the Canadian Ford operation found many new markets for the Model T. One market that quickly latched onto the Model T was the continent of Australia.

"...[the Model T] was more than capable of withstanding the pounding from the dirt tracks that passed for roads in the Outback. Australians took to it with enthusiasm..." [44]

Through its Canadian operation, the Model T reached such far corners of the British Colonies as Singapore, Ceylon, Java, Sumatra, Burma, Malaya, India and into Africa. New Zealand was another nation where the Model T was popular.

Canadian automobile development had been a bit slower than in the United States but the Model T helped interest first-time car buyers. In Quebec where cities and towns were closer together, people appreciated the T's modern design and dependable technology. Ford writers suggested the advantages of the Model T in snowy weather. In Canada's western provinces, the Model T was a leader in convincing people that they were no longer isolated.

"In one community after another, the automobile, usually a Ford, broadened horizons by breaking down the limits of time and distance associated with the horse-drawn wagon." [45]

Henry Ford biographer Keith Sward used a wonderful phrase to describe the Model T. He said it was "...all bone and muscle with no fat." [46]

The Model T Ford definitely was a hit with everyone who encountered it and eventually, more than 15 million Ts were made over a span of 19 years.

Writer Les Henry describes the place of honor the Model T attained.

"In its day, it commanded honest respect for the service it rendered and for the revolution it wrought, and in our day, it commands a place of honor in our museums, and private collections of venerable motor cars." [47]

Kimes said the Model T brought freedom to everyone who owned one:

"She was the Great Liberator, freeing rural America from the monotony and isolation of geography. The Model T brought Americans closer together." [48]

One might add that the car not only brought Americans closer together but people in every nation where it was sold.

In 1924, an ad for the Moon Motor Car Company of St. Louis proudly showed a list of automotive registrations for Hennepin County, Minnesota, the Minneapolis area. While the Moon ad boasted of having 18 of its cars on the list, at the top were 472 Model Ts, almost four times the number of Buicks sold, its nearest competitor. It was one small example of the way The Model T dominated all competition for many years.

The Model T changed in many small ways through its long production run, yet it always had its four-cylinder engine, the planetary transmission and remained the same size, especially in terms of its wheelbase. In Canada, parts of the south and elsewhere the Model T often was sold with a wider track but that was one of the few exceptions to the formula.

In 1912, engineers presented a new vision of what they thought could be a few modernizations in the Model T and presented the concepts to Henry Ford. The reaction was captured by both Lacey and Halberstam in their accounts.

"[Ford] walked around it several times. Finally he approached the left hand door and ripped it off. Then he ripped off the other door. Then he smashed the windshield. He threw out the back seat and bashed in the roof of the car with his shoe. During all this he said nothing." [49]

Those inside the Ford Motor Co. got a dual message that they should not do anything to change the Model T unless they were told to do so and they were not to challenge Henry Ford. The incredible success of the Model T continued unabated and by 1914, even formal company advertising was discontinued since Ford and the Ford Motor Co. got so much free attention from the media of that time.

One thing that had begun to die away was the close-knit spirit that had sparked the creativity of those who worked to develop the Model T. One by one, many of those men left the company during the first 10 years after the car was introduced. Increasingly, Henry Ford was alone at the top and grew more resistant to changes. The fire that had burned in the younger inventor, racer and tinkerer had largely died out. He was now often taking a defensive posture about the Ford Motor Co. and the Model T.

"I built it and, as long as I live, I propose to run it the way I want it run," Ford told a journalist. [50]

But others were building automotive companies differently. General Motors would become the prototypical corporate structure under Alfred P. Sloan, who avoided personal references and always insisted any communications to the public bear the corporate name, not his. Sloan and his minions were also running counter to Ford's thinking about his Model T. They were actually planning to have model changes, making older versions outdated. A new term was coined called "planned obsolescence." Once again, Ford resisted and told everyone what he thought about it.

"Our principle of business is precisely the contrary," said Ford. "We cannot conceive how to serve the customer unless we make him something…that will last forever. We want the man who buys one of our products never to have to buy another." [51]

Henry Ford and the Model T were linked, and some people thought that wasn't always such a healthy bond. Yet Ford had become part of the prevailing wisdom, what others were running hard to catch up to. Some one in three cars produced was a Model T by 1919. In 1923, Ford produced 57 percent of all cars in the United States. But market share began to diminish in a rapid spiral, down to 45 percent in 1925 and 11 percent lower in 1926. There was no sign of an upswing.

Ford Motor Co. clung to the success of the Model T because Henry Ford wanted it that way but there came a

In 1924, toward the end of the Model T's incredible run, Henry Ford posed with the Quadricycle as well as the "Universal Car." This one was edition number 10,000,000.

time when each needed to retire. Ford the man was judged in history and, like many famous men, was celebrated for his inspiring qualities. Unlike many with so much fame, he often revealed his own weaknesses and flaws quite publicly.

The Model T proved that Henry Ford and his creative team had been correct during the development stages in 1906 through 1908 and their dream car had succeeded beyond all expectations. It was a car that had reached both urban and rural citizens of the world and had changed their lives.

In 1927, shortly after the 15-millionth Model T was celebrated, including a photo opportunity of Henry Ford, the marquee Model T and the Ford Quadricycle together, Ford Motor Co. announced that the Model T production would end. A new car would succeed it. On May 27, 1927, production of the Model T officially ended.

Henry Ford explained it well as relayed by *Automobile Topics* on May 28, 1927:

"The Model T Ford was a pioneer," said Ford. "There was no conscious public need of motor cars when we first made it. This car blazed the way for the motor industry and started the movement for good roads everywhere. It is still the pioneer in many parts of the world. The Model T had stamina and power. It broke down the barriers of distance in rural sections, brought people of those sections closer together and placed education within the reach of everyone. We are still proud of the Model T car." [52]

The little Model T had many miles to go when the first one rolled off the assembly line at the Piquette plant in 1908. By the time the last T came off the assembly line in May 1927, the dependable car had truly become the "universal" machine. It popularized automobiles wherever it went around the globe. Its presence encouraged the need for better roads wherever it traveled. The success of the Model T influenced others to invent new products to care for it. The Model T turned heads wherever it went. Some laughed, some jeered and millions of owners enjoyed it. The Model T stirred the imaginations of people who had places to go and goals to accomplish because of it.

Technology had given birth to the Model T and a new generation of technology eventually passed it by, but not without a tip of the cap and a royal bow for all it had done. Today, the Model T is still admired and studied in each version from its beginnings to its last offerings, as this book will do in year by year form in Chapter 4.

Henry Ford had a motto for the core creative team that worked on the Model T: "Keep it simple and trouble free." [53]

While the Model T wasn't perfect, it was a huge step up in both simplicity and reliability in the early automotive world. The inner team had succeeded in its task—beyond everyone's expectations.

For those who love Model Ts, the production line may have ended but the car is still with us. The venerable Clymer summed up the beloved Model T this way:

"No automobile can ever take the place in the hearts of so many motorists…in the generations to come the legend of Henry Ford and his famous Tin Lizzie will never die." [54]

*The Krause Publications' *Standard Catalog of Ford 3rd edition* and *Standard Catalog of American Cars 1805-1942* each list a production figure of 10,660 Model Ts for 1909 with 1,000 Model Ts produced late in calendar year 1908. The McCalley figures, based on engine production, show 320 produced late in 1908 and 10,839 produced through September, 1909. McCalley also lists a third, but uncredited source of records that offered a total of 11,100 engines produced from Oct. 1 1908 through Sept. 30, 1909, according to *Vintage Ford*, Vol. 21, number 3, May-June 1986.

Chapter 4

THEY WEREN'T ALL ALIKE OR BLACK: A YEAR-BY-YEAR LOOK AT THE MODEL T

"It could almost be written down as a formula, that when a man begins to think that he has at last found his method, he had better begin a most searching examination of himself to see whether some part of his brain has gone to sleep."
Henry Ford

The Model T: Understanding the Model Years

The era of the Model T was much like modern car introduction practices. A new model year often debuted during the previous calendar year. Ford Motor Company began this practice with its new 1909 Model T, premiering the car in October 1908.

In the years that followed, Ford often made production changeovers to new model years during the summer months. Some experts, like Bruce McCalley, refer to the Model Ts in terms of "style years," since some changes were quite subtle from one year to the next.

Ford Motor Company also made new additions and deletions of equipment and components during a production run. That sometimes clouds the differences or similarities between one model year and another. In this chapter, we've tried hard to highlight major differences and distinctions. We understand that Model T aficionados probably will be able to find even more of them.

About sources for the 1908-1927 section:

Ford news notes were pulled from resources footnoted elsewhere in this book and included several articles from the 1910s and 1920s found in vintage magazines in the Krause Publications archives. Production figures were extracted from *Standard Catalog of Ford 1903-2003, 3rd edition* by John Gunnell. Commentary about individual Model Ts was taken from technical articles by Bruce McCalley in a number of issues of Vintage Ford magazine as well as *Model T Times* and the book *Henry's Wonderful Model T* by Floyd Clymer. World and United States historical notes were gathered from Infoplease.com plus other historical sources.

1908: The Earliest Model Ts

Ford Motor Company news:

In 1908, the large six-cylinder Ford Model K continued to be sold at $2,800. The Ford smaller Model N, Model R and Model S were also available. The Model N was priced at $600 while the Models R and S were listed at $750. Buick had taken the baton from the early 1900s success of the small two-passenger Oldsmobile in production and sales. Buick became the leader to catch having nearly doubled its production of 4,641 cars in 1907 to 8,820 in 1908. Buick would continue to grow with more than 14,000 cars produced in 1909 but the Ford Motor Company was about ready to change the playing field. A national ad appeared in magazines like the *Saturday Evening Post* in October announcing the new Ford four-cylinder touring car. "Here is the first and only chance ever offered to secure a touring car at a reasonable price..." began the ad. The Model T name wasn't mentioned until the fourth paragraph of the 13-paragraph ad. Ironically, Ford's ad tag at the bottom of the ad was "Ford—The Car That Lasts Longest." The Model T would propel Ford into the sales lead and catch the attention of everyone in the automotive world.

United States news:

President William Howard Taft was inaugurated. He was considered the heaviest President up to that time. Taft was credited with including automobiles in the White House fleet. One year after a street car strike and just two years after the Great Earthquake of 1906, San Francisco's first taxi company begins with 25 cabs. Cellophane was invented.

1909 Ford (The earliest Model Ts were considered 1909 models. See 1909 for specifications.)

Early T-spotting:
— The earliest 1908-built Model Ts had two foot pedals and two floor-mounted levers. One of the levers was for reverse gear.
— The Model T offered more body types than the Models N, R and S including the touring, town car and landaulet versions in addition to the runabout style.
— The transmission was enclosed and not exposed to dirt, dust, rocks, etc. It shared lubrication with the engine.
— The earliest Model Ts used small timers (commutators) than subsequent editions of the car.

Technical-i-T:
The new Model T, introduced in 1908, was the first Ford with torque tube drive.

Trivial-i-T:
Ford Motor Company offered a $15 three-pedal option retroactively for the earliest two pedal and two lever Model Ts if those owners wanted to convert their cars to the three floor pedals.

The rear view of the 1910 Model T touring car shows a certain simplicity of elegance, enhanced by the tall top and windshield that rose to match the top's height.
Doug Mitchel

1909: The First Full Production Year

Ford Motor Company news:

The success of the Model T drew attention to the company and to Henry Ford. Billy Durant of the rising General Motors saw the potential at Ford Motor Company and sought to buy them out. Henry Ford's suspicion of stock offers dissuaded the suitors with his demand for cash instead of stock deals. Ford reportedly told Durant, who had made an $8 million stock offer that he wanted "…gold on the table." 1 When Durant asked Ford what he meant, Henry made it even plainer saying he wanted cash.

United States news:

Baseball was very popular and Americans were buying sheet music for the new song "Take Me Out to the Ball Game." They also were enjoying Broadway-based songs by Irving Berlin, George M. Cohan and Jerome Kern as well as the voice of Italian opera star Enrico Caruso. Admiral Robert Perry and his team that included Matthew Henson conquered the North Pole. In grocery stores, Americans bought a new product called instant coffee.

1909 Model T:

In production since Sept. 1, 1908 and introduced in October 1908, the Model T went through a number of production changes, especially early on. This would be Ford Motor Company practice with the Model T, especially in the early years, depending on the available components as well as improvements made during the production runs. One of the most visible changes to the 1909

Model Ts came after the first 800 were produced. The two pedals and two levers became one lever and three pedals—clutch, reverse and brake, from left to right. After April 1909, more Model Ts came with tops, windshields and gas headlights, which had been considered accessories. Thermosyphon cooling replaced the water pump used on early production Model Ts.

1909 MODEL T			
Body Type and Seating	Factory Price	Shipping Weight	Production Total
Touring-5p	$850	1,200 lbs.	7,728
Runabout-2p	$825	—	2,351
Town Car-7p	$1,000	—	236
Landaulet-7p	$950	—	298
Coupe-2p	$950	—	47

Prices noted were effective on Oct. 1, 1909. Production totals were based on the fiscal year, from Oct. 1, 1909 to Sept. 30, 1910. Some accounts insist even more cars were built in this time.

Engines:

First 2,500: L-head. Four cylinder. Cast-iron block. B&S: 3 ¾ x 4 in. Displacement: 176.7 cid. Compression: 4.5:1 Horsepower: 22 at 1,600 rpm. Three main bearings. Solid valve lifters. Kingston five ball or Buffalo carburetors. Torque: 83 lbs.-ft. @ 900 rpm.

Note: The first 2,500 engines had an integral gear-driven water pump and a gear driven fan. There was no inspection plate in the crankcase. Valve stems and lifters were exposed with no cover door.

After 2,500: L-head. Four cylinder. Cast-iron block. B&S: 3 ¾ x 4 in. Displacement: 176.7 cid. Compression: 4.5:1 Horsepower: 22 at 1,600 rpm. Three main bearings. Solid valve lifters. Kingston five ball, Buffalo or Holley carburetors. Torque: 83 lbs.-ft. @ 900 rpm.

Note: The engine was now cooled by the thermosyphon method. There was no inspection plate in the crankcase.
Valve stems and lifters were exposed with no cover door.

Chassis:

100 in. wheelbase. Length: 11 feet, 2-1/2 in. (car with body). Front and rear tread: 56 in. (60 in. optional). Tires: 30 x 3 (front) and 30 x 3-1/2 (rear).

Standard equipment:

Two speed planetary transmission with two foot pedals plus brake and reverse levers, first 2,500 cars. April 1909 on: Three foot pedals and one brake lever. Three oil lamps, two side and one tail. Early Model Ts were painted red, green and gray until June 1909 when Brewster Green became the main color.

Options:

Windshield. Carbide gas headlamps. Tops. Bulb horn. Prest-o-lite tank or carbide tank. Robe rail. Tire chains. Top boots. Foot rests. Spare tire carriers. Speedometers. Bumpers.

1909 T-spotting:

—Early Model Ts used rubber/linoleum-covered running boards trimmed with brass moldings.
—Early Ts had wooden bodies over wooden frames. Some were aluminum over wood.
—The 1909 Model Ts had a "no rivet" rear axle housing.
—The "Ford" name had "wings"—a wavy script line was added before and after the Ford name.

Technical-i-T:

Ford's block cast engine and drawn steel rear axle structure were considered technological marvels in 1909.

Trivial-i-T:

Early Model Ts used a hubcap with the Ford name in large block letters rather than the familiar script style.

1 David Halberstam, *The Reckoning*, (New York: 1986), p. 74.

Many people remember the Model Ts as plain black cars but the early versions, like this 1909 touring car, had plenty of color as well as colorful brass trim.   Tom Glatch

The ornate-looking brass spyder portion enhanced the 1909 Model T steering wheel. The Ford Motor Co. decision to place it on the left side revolutionized driving and roads in North America. Mike Mueller

A familiar-looking Model T from 1909 has something missing we take for granted. These cars were produced without doors and the car was called the tourabout.   David Lyon

This 1909 Model T touring car has something missing—a windshield. The windshield was an option at that time and not everyone bought one.   David Lyon

The 1909 Model T appealed to wealthier tastes with this landaulet. Ford literature of the time also called it the "taximeter cab," for those who liked working titles.   David Lyon

1910: Brewster Green Model Ts

Ford Motor Company news:

In 1910, Ford Motor Company continued to work hard to find ways to improve production and meet the demand for the Model Ts. Ford advertising in 1910 suggested that "Buying a Ford is automobile buying with the risk cut out." It was one of the first times that Ford Motor Company used the line, "Buy a Ford car because it is a better car, not because it is cheaper."

United States news:

The Boy Scouts of America was incorporated. The introduction of a device called the kinetophone makes it possible to produce early movies with a form of sound. Scientists were able to capture Halley's Comet photographically. In baseball, the Philadelphia As defeated the Chicago Cubs four games to one to win the World Series.

The 1910 Model T:

In 1910, Model Ts came in Brewster Green, a very dark green that appeared to be black under some lighting conditions. Earlier 1909 Model Ts also came in Carmine Red and Gray. One of the most visible changes in 1910 was the "dash" style running board strip. There were a series of overlapping dashes with no Ford logo. The 14-inch steering wheel, added late in the 1909 production run, continued in Model Ts this year.

1910 MODEL T			
Body Type and Seating	Factory Price	Shipping Weight	Production Totals
Touring-5p	$950	1,200 lbs.	16,890*
Tourabout-4p	$950	—	—
Runabout-2p	$900	—	1,486
Town car-7p	$1,200	—	377
Landaulet-7p	$1,100	—	2
Coupe-2p	$1,050	—	187
Chassis	—	900 lbs.	108

Touring and tourabout production figures were grouped together.

Engine:

L-head. Four cylinder. Cast-iron block. B&S: 3 ¾ x 4 in. Displacement: 176.7 cid. Compression: 4.5:1 Horsepower: 22 at 1,600 rpm. Three main bearings. Solid valve lifters. Kingston five ball, or Holley carburetors were used and occasionally a Buffalo. Torque: 83 lbs.-ft. @ 900 rpm.

Note: The valve stems and lifters were exposed with no cover door. There was no inspection plate in the upper half of the crankcase.

Chassis:

100 in. wheelbase. Length: 11 feet, 2-1/2 in. (car with body). Front and rear tread: 56 in. (60 in. optional). Tires: 30 x 3 (front) and 30 x 3-1/2 (rear).

Standard equipment:

Two-speed planetary transmission with three foot pedals. Three brass oil lamps, two side-mounted and one as a tail lamp. (Open cars:) Windshield. Brass headlamps with a carbide generator. Speedometer. Top with side curtains. (Closed cars had the horn and oil lamps only. The headlamps and speedometer were extra.)

Options:

A Prest-o-lite tank was an optional choice to fuel the gas headlamps. It was longer and mounted horizontally on the left-side running board. The carbide unit was mounted vertically on that side.

1910 T-spotting:

—The cylinder head now had the Ford name on it.
—The hood former had a notch above the steering column.
—Hard rubber crank handles were used in 1910.
—Kingston, Heinze and Jacobson-Brandon coil boxes were used.
—The three pedals had the letters C, R and B on them (clutch, reverse and brake).

Technical-i-T:

The inspection hole cover for the transmission was square during 1910.

Trivial-i-T:

After the first 2,500 Model Ts were produced, the cars used Stewart speedometers. Headlamp makers included E & J (Edmond and Jones), John Brown and Atwood-Castle.

BELOW: *The 1910 Model T interior included a wooden coil box plus a speedometer mounted on the right side and angled upward for better viewing. Doug Mitchel*

If you've ever wondered why a certain group of cars were called the "brass era," just look at this oil lamp. We seem them on homes now. They once offered drivers light in the darkness .   Doug Mitchel

There is something classic and quite memorable about the stance of the 1910 Model T touring car, its top up and posed along a street.   Doug Mitchel

Here's a shot of the unique oil tail lamp with a white lens to illuminate the license plate and a red lens for people following the car.   Doug Mitchel

We think of leather seating as a luxury today but automobile buyers in 1910 thought of it more as a practical, durable upholstery in addition to its level of riding comfort.   Doug Mitchel

1911 Torpedo Runabouts and Other Model Ts

Ford Motor Company news:

Two big events marked another successful year for the overall company and the Model T Fords. On Jan. 9, 1911, the Selden patent lawsuit was settled. Ford Motor Company essentially won the dispute and that freed Ford and other carmakers from paying restrictive fees for automotive production. The second positive event came on June 22, 1911, when Ford Motor Company bought the John R. Keim Mills, the company that had been so successful in producing many of the Model T's key stampings. The Buffalo, New York, plant would soon become a Ford assembly plant and the company gained the services of talented Keim employees including William Knudsen.

United States news:

A tragic fire at the Triangle Shirtwaist Factory in New York City claimed the lives of 146 people, most of them young women. The fire influenced both labor laws and fire codes. The Supreme Court found both Standard Oil Company and the American Tobacco Company in violation of the Sherman Anti-Trust Act. The Princeton University Tigers and the Penn State Nitany Lions were co champions of the college football world.

1911 Ford Model T:

The rakish torpedo and open runabouts appeared. The torpedo had low doors, a 16-gallon fuel tank mounted behind the seat and a small toolbox on the rear deck. The windshield was slightly angled or sloped at the bottom, suggesting speed. The torpedo and roadster had a longer hood and long fenders with shorter running boards. In 1911, more Model T bodies were made of metal over wood frames rather than wood bodies over wooden frames.

1911 MODEL T			
Body Type and Seating	Factory Price	Shipping Weight	Production Totals
Touring-5p	$780	1,200 lbs.	26,405
Runabout-2p	$680	—	—
Torpedo runabout-2p	$725	—	—
Open runabout-2p	$680	—	—
Town car-7p	$960	—	315
Chassis	—	900 lbs.	248

Note: The coupe, runabout and landaulet were originally included in the 1911 model lineup but were deleted before the calendar year 1911.

Engine:

L-head. Four cylinder. Cast-iron block. B&S: 3 ¾ x 4 in. Displacement: 176.7 cid. Compression: 4.5:1 Horsepower: 22 at 1,600 rpm. Three main bearings. Solid valve lifters. Kingston five ball, or Holley carburetors. Torque: 83 lbs.-ft. @ 900 rpm.

Chassis:

100 in. wheelbase. Length: 11 feet, 2-1/2 in. (car with body). Front and rear tread: 56 in. (60 in. optional). Tires: 30 x 3 (front) and 30 x 3-1/2 (rear).

Standard equipment:

Two gas-powered headlamps plus two oil side lamps and an oil-fueled taillight were standard along with a side-mounted bulb air horn. Kerosene, often called coal, was used to fuel the oil lamps.

Options:

Officially, Ford Motor Company offered no options. The company warned that owner warranties would be stripped if non-Ford items were installed. Yet a huge aftermarket that focused on the Model T flourished and included everything from shock absorbers to replacement bodies.

1911 T-spotting:

—The 1911 Model T had more sheet metal for its body than previous years.

—A new rear axle assembly showed tapered ends and a 12-rivet center casting after July 1911.

—The horn had a distinctive double twist in its brass bulb end.

—There were no longer wings in the Ford name and there was a higher filler neck on the radiator.

—The transmission cover opening was changed from a rectangular to a trapezoidal shape. Technical-i-T:

The two valve chambers were enclosed behind steel doors at about car 50,000. An inspection plate now was included in the crankcase as well.

Trivial-i-T:

A company called Kales-Haskell offered the "Hind-View Auto Reflector" for Model T owners just three months after Ray Harroun innovated the rear-view mirror at the 1911 Indianapolis 500.

He was the driver of the Marmon "Wasp."

One of the few Model T editions that wasn't an overwhelming success story was the delivery car, a sculpted and artistic looking version that is prized by today's collectors, like this 1911 edition.   David Lyon

While Ford Motor Co. of the U. S. and Ford Motor Co. of Canada had exported cars from the beginning, the Model T really caught on around the world, like this 1911 version from Holland.   Andrew Morland

This 1911 Model T torpedo runabout shines brightly in the sun, sporting its blue ribbon. It shows us another angle of this two-seat version of the Model T. David Lyon

Ready for rain or snow is this 1911 Model T that demonstrates how side curtains were mounted and did their best to keep the driver and passengers as dry and cozy as possible.   David Lyon

1912: Smooth-sided Model Ts

Ford Motor Company news:

Ford Motor Company continued building the Highland Park plant, specifically designed for automobile assembly. Highland Park, built on old horse racing track grounds, would become the first U. S. plant specifically designed for making cars and offered more space than the Piquette facility.

The Model T continued to be a runaway success story and was beginning to be known around the world. Ford advertising included a novel brochure called "26 Reasons Why" with alphabetical reasons from "Axles of vanadium" to "Zeal of workmen, zest of owner" encouraging more people to buy a Model T. It included such phrases as "Fordcrafter-built," "Joyance of speed," "Natty, neat and nobby" and "X-ceptional they all agree." "These make the Ford all-dominant, supreme at home and o'er the seas!"

United States news:

Once a leader in opposition to the earliest automobiles while a professor at Princeton University, Democrat Woodrow Wilson was elected President. During his second term, Wilson became a Model T owner. States 47 and 48 were admitted to the Union with New Mexico and Arizona earning their statehood. The Radio Act of 1912 assigned three-and four-letter codes.

1912 Model T:

The 1912 touring sedan got what was called the "foredoor" look. Front or "fore" doors were added to a slightly altered body styling to give a smoother look. The "foredoors" were reportedly offered retroactively to 1911 Model T owners as well. An interesting choice was offered in 1912, a removable rumble seat on the commercial roadster. The back deck-mounted open seat quickly earned the nickname "mother-in-law seat." Sans seat, the deck was available for hauling cargo.

1912 MODEL T			
Body Type and Seating	Factory Price	Shipping Weight	Production Totals
Touring-5p	$690	1,200 lbs.	50, 598
Torpedo runabout-2p	$590	—	13,376
Commercial roadster-2p	$590	—	—
Town car-7p	$900	—	802
Delivery car-2p	$700	—	1,845
Coupe-2p	—	—	19
Chassis	—	—	2,133

RIGHT: *A 1912 Model T torpedo runabout has its top open on a sunny day. Many Model Ts could be found filled with people taking a pleasure drive on a sunny Sunday afternoon. David Lyon*

Engine:

L-head. Four cylinder. Cast-iron block. B&S: 3 ¾ x 4 in. Displacement: 176.7 cid. Compression: 4.5:1 Horsepower: 22 at 1,600 rpm. Three main bearings. Solid valve lifters. Holley H-1 and some Kingston "six-ball" carburetors. Torque: 83 lbs.-ft. @ 900 rpm.

Chassis:

100 in. wheelbase. Length: 11 feet, 2-1/2 in. (car with body). Front and rear tread: 56 in. (60 in. optional). Tires: 30 x 3 (front) and 30 x 3-1/2 (rear).

Standard equipment:

Two gas-powered headlamps plus two oil-fired sidelights and an oil-fueled taillight were standard along with a side-mounted bulb horn.

Options:

Officially, Ford Motor Company again warned that owner warranties would be stripped if non-Ford options were added. Yet, a huge aftermarket focusing on the Model T continued to flourish.

1912 T-spotting:

—The 1912 rear axle was changed late in the production year to a larger differential casting. It was actually part of the changes that would mark the 1913 Model Ts.

—Both Kingston and Heinze coil boxes were used in this year's Model Ts.

—It was the final year for the hard-rubber bulbs on the end of the spark and throttle knobs.

—The 1912 Model T had the final brass spiders, the metal portion of the steering wheels.

—The horn now had a single twist.

Technical-i-T:

The horn tubing, that had previously snaked under the left front door opening, now was placed inside the driver's compartment.

Trivial-i-T:

The 1912 Model Ts were produced in a mix of blue and black bodies and fenders. Some were all blue or all black and some mixed the two colors with blue bodies and black fenders.

Without the mother in law seat out back, the 1912 Model T torpedo runabouts often were fitted with a large trunk-like box. It's a rather upright-looking car with the top up. David Lyon

A restored Model T roadster was photographed at Greenfield Village, the living museum that Henry Ford wanted to show everyone the rural way of life. Andrew Morland

This well-preserved 1912 Model T torpedo roadster posed in profile to show off its lines—the lower hood, the tall passenger compartment and the flat deck out back.

ABOVE: This 1912 Model T touring car almost seems ghost-like in its modern shade of white with the contrasting tall black top. Is it ready for a journey into the past?

RIGHT: Many Model Ts traveled on gravel or heavily rutted country roads as they journeyed from one place to another. This is a rear view of the 1912 Model T torpedo runabout. David Lyon

1913 The Assembly Line Model Ts Begin

Ford Motor Company news:

Concentration was given to assembly line techniques during the 1913 model year. Ford Motor Company focused on increasing efficiency and production while cutting costs. Their goal was lower prices and more sales. Older methods were studied and times for assembly processes were shortened. Ford Motor Company used a moving line method borrowed from the meat processing industry. Eventually, Ford's intensive manner of assembly would slash the time needed to make cars and would inspire a new term—mass production, as well as a new verb "to fordize." Ford advertising compared the Model T with "Old Dobbin." "He has only one-twentieth the strength of a Ford car, cannot go as fast or as far, costs more to maintain and almost as much to acquire."

U. S. news:

The 16th Amendment introduced change as it began the income tax. The Federal Reserve System also was created this year. Garment workers struck in New York City and Boston. Democrat Woodrow Wilson became the 28th President. A modern art show debuted the style in America. The undefeated Harvard Crimson were college football's top team.

1913 Ford:

Cost cutting meant that use of brass for lamps and hard rubber knobs were cut back or eliminated. Oil lamps now had black-painted steel drums with brass trim, including the chimneys. The 1913 Model T began to take on the familiar look that would be used well into the 1920s. The touring car, runabout and town car become the three primary Model T styles. The touring car had no door on the driver's side, only a door outline, also known as a "dummy" door. Sales of the distinctive delivery car were disappointing and the style was discontinued after the 1913 model year.

1913 MODEL T			
Body Type and Seating	Factory Price	Shipping Weight	Production Totals
3-door Touring-5p	$600	1,200 lbs.	126,715
2-door Runabout-2p	$525	—	33,129
4-door Town Car-7p	$800	—	1,415
Delivery car-2p	$625	—	513
Chassis	—	—	8,438

Engine:

L-head. Four cylinder. Cast-iron block. B & S: 3 ¾ x 4 in. Displacement: 176.7 cid. Compression: 4.0:1 Horsepower: 20 at 1,600 rpm. Three main bearings. Solid valve lifters. Holley S and Kingston Y carburetors. Torque: 83 lbs.-ft. @ 900 rpm.

* The camshaft was modified for less power and the cylinder head was modified for slightly lower compression.

Chassis:

100 in. wheelbase. Length: 11 feet, 2-1/2 in. (car with body). Front and rear tread: 56 in. (60 in. optional). Tires: 30 x 3 (front) and 30 x 3-1/2 (rear).

Standard Equipment:

Two gas-powered headlamps plus two oil side lamps and an oil-fueled taillight were standard along with a side-mounted bulb horn.

Options:

During this period, Ford Motor Company offered no official options. Buyers often approached the aftermarket for optional equipment.

1913 T-spotting:

—The standard color was now dark blue with black fenders.

—More leatherette was used on door panels while leather still was used for car seats.

—The spider, or steering wheel interior surface, now was cast steel.

—A cocoa mat was used for the rear floor covering.

—More black appeared—on the horn twist, the gas generator and on the headlamps.

—The Model T had a two-piece drive shaft housing—using a universal joint for the first time.

—The "sharp cornered" turtledeck appeared.

Technical-i-T:

Many Model Ts produced after January 1913 used a longer cross member, common in the 1914 Model Ts. The cross member replaced forged body brackets used on earlier Model Ts.

Trivial-i-T:

Model T hubcaps now had "Made in USA" below the Ford script. Some Dodge Brothers parts still were used.

This ¾-angle shows off some of the lines of the 1913 Model T runabout well. The windshield now was canted slightly. Note the correct 1913 New York license plate up front.   David Lyon

In 1913, the Model T began to be assembled via mass-production techniques. The famous black paint began to be the dominant color of paint offered. David Lyon

Ford Motor Co. did its best to promote this pleasing design at a modest price, as seen in this 1912 Ford ad, but there weren't enough takers. The 1913 model year was the last for the delivery car.

The 1913 Model T touring car began a trend that continued through the 1925 model year. It was the so called "dummy door," a non-opening door pressing on the driver's side of U. S.-made Ts.

1914 Any Color As Long As It's Black

Ford Motor Company news:

Profit sharing was the word from Ford Motor Company in 1914. It was the manner that the company used to describe its attention-getting $5 day wage for employees and its sales campaign for buyers, a rebate-style program based on total company sales. The Ford profit sharing plan for employees factored in a profit sharing portion plus a minimum wage to reach the $5 per day wage. Both higher and lower wages also were offered but the $5 per day wage resonated in an era when many automakers were offering from $2.30 to $2.50 per day. A New Year-themed ad showed a smiling globe sitting in the back seat of a Model T touring car with a very young driver. It was headlined "The New Chauffeur" and indicated Ford's growing dominance in the world.

U. S. news:

Actor Charlie Chaplin played the "Little Tramp" for the first time in a movie. American troops occupied Veracruz, Mexico, to protect American business interests. The first red and green traffic lights were used in Cleveland, Ohio. George Washington Carver began his experiments with peanuts to help farming. The Kentucky Derby-winning horse was named Old Rosebud.

1914 Ford:

The styling used in 1913 Model Ts continued in 1914. The period of the all-black Model Ts began. A one-piece driveshaft replaced the two-piece unit. As costs continued to be cut, more leatherette material was used—this year for seat backs. Leather still was used for the seats. The speedometer was discontinued on Model Ts. The deletion was caused by a

shortage. Some joked that they knew how fast a Model T was going by how many bones were vibrating in their bodies!

1914 MODEL T			
Body Type and Seating	Factory Price	Shipping Weight	Production Totals
3-door Touring-5p	$550	1,200 lbs.	165,832
2-door Runabout-2p	$500	—	35,017
4-door Town Car-7p	$750	—	1,699
Chassis	$480	960 lbs.	119

Engine:

L-head. Four cylinder. Cast-iron block. B & S: 3 ¾ x 4 in. Displacement: 176.7 cid. Compression: 4.0:1 Horsepower: 20 at 1,600 rpm. Three main bearings. Solid valve lifters. Holley G (brass body) and Kingston Y carburetors. Torque: 83 lbs.-ft. @ 900 rpm.

Chassis:

100 in. wheelbase. Length: 11 feet, 2-1/2 in. (car with body). Front and rear tread: 56 in. (60 in. optional). Tires: 30 x 3 (front) and 30 x 3-1/2 (rear).

Standard Equipment:

Two gas-powered headlamps plus two oil-fired sidelights and an oil-fueled taillight were standard along with a side-mounted air horn with a bulb.

Options:

During this period, Ford Motor Company offered no official options. Buyers continued to search the aftermarket for optional equipment.

1914 T-spotting:

—Doors had rounded bottoms and were set into the body.
—A reinforcing rib appeared in the center of the fenders and the fender-tip bill was added.
—Victor, Corcoran and E & J provided gas headlamps. Corcoran and E & J also supplied side and taillights.
—The 1914 Model Ts had a slightly sloping windshield that folded toward the driver.
—Windshields were supplied by the Diamond Mfg. Co., the Vanguard Mfg. Co. and Rand Mfg. Co.

Technical-i-T:

On 1914 models, the intake manifolds were made of cast iron instead of aluminum.

Trivial-i-T:

Metal coil boxes appeared on Model Ts in 1914 replacing the former wooden box units.

Coming at you is this 1914 Model T touring car on a country road. Over the course of the 15-million plus Model Ts sold, how many people saw this view of the popular cars? Andrew Morland

By 1914, the Model T was beginning its famed run as a massed produced car and the familiar look of the all-black car became common, like this 1914 touring car on a country road.　Andrew Morland

A restored 1914 Model T touring car shows some popular aftermarket items including the rear view mirror and the accordion-shaped running board cargo container. David Lyon

This 1914 Model T touring offers a terrific chance for enthusiasts to see what an unrestored version of their car of interest looks like after years of service and aging.

This restored 1914 Model T touring car has a prized spot in an owner's garage. Note that the wooden cowling and some brass was still being used at this time. David Lyon

1915 Magneto-Powered Electric Headlamps and Horn

Ford Motor Company news:

The one-millionth Model T was produced in the 1915 model year. The new style in the Model T stable for the 1915 model year was the coupélet, feted in Ford advertising intended for localized markets as "A car of style, beautiful in design, rich in detail of appointments." The coupélet top could be lowered and was similar to a modern convertible. The unique coupélet also had doors that were rear-hinged and opened forward.

U.S. news:

As the United States attempted to stay out of the war in Europe, the Superior Court at Fulton County, Georgia, accepted a charter that allowed the new Ku Klux Klan to be established. Happier moments occurred when the Boston Red Sox won the World Series, Cornell was the undefeated champion of college football and the Vancouver Millionaires won the Stanley Cup.

1915 Ford:

While the 1915 edition of the Model T first appeared at the new Highland Park plant in January 1915, some older 1914-style Model Ts continued to be made at Ford branch assembly plants. Changes included a sloping cowl that replaced the cherry wood version formally used. Magneto-powered electric headlights were available on some models. The windshield was straight but the rear fenders received more curves. Hoods now had six louvers per side. The bulb horn was used in base Model Ts until October 1915, when the magneto-powered horn replaced it as standard equipment.

1915 MODEL T			
Body Type and Seating	Factory Price	Shipping Weight	Production Totals
3-door Touring-5p	$490	1,500 lbs.	244,181
2-door Runabout-2p	$440	1,380 lbs.	47,116
4-door Town Car-7p	$690	—	—
2-door sedan-5p	$975	1,730 lbs.	989
2-door coupe-2p	$750	1,540 lbs.	2,417
Chassis	$410	960 lbs.	119

Engine:

L-head. Four cylinder. Cast-iron block. B & S: 3 ¾ x 4 in. Displacement: 176.7 cid. Compression: 4.0:1 Horsepower: 20 at 1,600 rpm. Three main bearings. Solid valve lifters. Holley G and Kingston L carburetors. Torque: 83 lbs.-ft. @ 900 rpm.

Chassis:

100 in. wheelbase. Length: 11 feet, 2-1/2 in. (car with body). Front and rear tread: 56 in. (60 in. optional). Tires: 30 x 3 (front) and 30 x 3-1/2 (rear).

Standard Equipment:

Two gas-powered headlamps plus two oil sidelights and an oil-fueled taillight were standard along with an under hood-mounted air horn with a bulb, later replaced by magneto-powered horn.

Options:

Magneto-powered electric lights were offered as an option for the first time on a Model T.

1915 T-spotting:

—Headlamp buckets now were painted black and were made of steel. Brass rims were still used on the headlamps and brass chimney tops and rims still were used on the oil lamps in 1915.

—Ribs replaced the familiar C, R and B letters on the three foot pedals.

—The magneto horn was gradually phased in on cars with magneto-powered headlights. The horn button was placed on top of the steering column.

—Non-skid tires with a tread appeared on the 1915 Fords.

Technical-i-T:

Special aluminum panels were used to make the unique splash apron and rear fenders on the 1915 Model T center door sedan.

Trivial-i-T:

Early 1915 cars without electric lights used a bulb-type horn, mounted under the hood. During this period, aftermarket hand-powered klaxon-style horns often appeared on many cars, including Model Ts. Experts say these never were installed at the Ford factories nor offered as Ford-endorsed options. The klaxon-style horns were popular aftermarket additions.

There was room for some cargo—either inside the small door of the 1915 Model T roadster's turtledeck or on top of its flat surface.   *David Lyon*

As this 1915 Model T roadster reveals, very little was still brass on the car beyond the radiator. There was some brass trim on the lights and the small hub caps.
David Lyon

A 1915 Model T touring car is displayed on a sunny day. This is a British version. Model Ts were made for the local market in England but offered the British tradition of right-hand drive.   *Andrew Morland*

Something new by 1915 was Model T center door sedan. The doors were located midway on the body on either side and opened to a plush interior.
David Lyon

1916 Model T in Transition

Ford Motor Company news:

There wasn't a lot of change between the 1915 and 1916 Ford model runs. Ford Motor Company concentrated on improving output and refining mass assembly techniques. While Henry Ford downplayed any chance of American involvement in World War I, he did support the efforts made by Ford of Canada, already involved in the war as an ally of Great Britain. In fact, Ford of Canada boosted its national advertising and film producing budgets. National advertising had been downplayed in the United States since 1914. American Ford dealers advertised locally with Ford Motor Company prepared ads. Dealers had their names and address information inserted.

U. S. news:

Republican Jeannette Rankin was elected from Montana to serve as the first woman in Congress.

The U. S. National Park Service was created. The Boston Red Sox repeated as World Series champions while Pittsburgh University was the undefeated champion of college football. One of the greatest sports dynasties began when the Montreal Canadiens won the Stanley Cup.

1916 Model T:

Now in their second model year, the exotic (by Model T standards!) coupélet and the plush center door Model T sedan created interest among Ford buyers. The center door sedan was like the 1960s LTD with its upscale, plush interiors. Because of two-place seats used in earlier version, the gas tank had originally been placed under the rear seat. That proved too troublesome for gravity-based fuel flow. By 1916, the tank had been relocated under the driver's seat to eliminate fuel flow problems.

Chassis:

100 in. wheelbase. Length: 11 feet, 2-1/2 in. (car with body). Front and rear tread: 56 in. (60 in. optional). Tires: 30 x 3 (front) and 30 x 3-1/2 (rear).

Standard Equipment:

The magneto-powered horn uses a button mounted atop the steering column this year. The speedometer no longer was standard equipment. The early placement of gas tanks on center door sedans is under the rear seat. This causes problems due to the Model T's gravity fuel-feed system and the tank mounting is moved under the driver's seat later in production.

Options:

It was the final year for the 60-inch wide wheelbase option in the United States. Various aftermarket shock absorbers and dampers are popular additions in this era.

1916 T-spotting:

—Oval-shaped windows were added to the coupelet in an attempt to make it easier for drivers to see when the top was up.

—A steel oil cap replaced the former brass oil cap.

—Bodies were numbered and dated and were supplied by more than one supplier.

Technical-i-T:

The center door sedan used a smooth rear body panel without a seam.

Trivial-i-T:

Ford Motor Company made 20,700 ambulances to help the World War I effort, even though Henry Ford personally opposed American involvement in the European car.

1916 Model T			
Body Type and Seating	Factory Price	Shipping Weight	Production Totals
3-door Touring-5p	$440	1,510 lbs.	363,024
2-door Runabout-2p	$390	1,395 lbs.	98,633
4-door Town Car-7p	$640	—	1,972
2-door sedan-5p	$740	1,730 lbs.	1,859
2-door coupe-2p	$590	1,540 lbs.	3,532
Chassis	$360	1,060 lbs.	1,174

Another view of the 1916 Model T coupélet shows its coupe-like stance. Note the landau bars and the rakish angle of the tiny side windows.

Engine:

L-head. Four cylinder. Cast-iron block. B & S: 3 ¾ x 4 in. Displacement: 176.7 cid. Compression: 4.0:1 Horsepower: 20 at 1,600 rpm. Three main bearings. Solid valve lifters. Holley G and Kingston L carburetors. Torque: 83 lbs.-ft. @ 900 rpm.

There were few exterior changes on this edition of the 1916 Model T roadster. The Model Ts still had their traditional brass radiators but more of the car was painted black.   David Lyon

Whether you called it coupe-lette or the more continental pronunciation, coupe-ay-lay, the 1916 Model T coupélet was sporty with its top down and rakish front opening doors.

ABOVE: *Formality by Model T standards continued in 1916 with the center door sedan. Its conservative exterior belied its plush upholstery and appointments inside.*

LEFT: *A common scene of the Model T era could have been from 1916. A rural family was out for a ride in their Model T touring car and stopped along the way for a cool drink from a friendly host.*

1917 Black Paint and Nickel-Plated Trim

Ford Motor Company news:

As American became involved in World War I, Henry Ford at first resisted calls to become involved in wartime production, then yielded. His American operations turned to some war effort. By this time, Ford also was involved in a lawsuit with the Dodge Brothers over his views of which direction the company would take. Ford wanted to plow as much of the company's profits back into the company as possible. The Dodge Brothers insisted they had the right to be paid shareholder dividends. Since they had been long-time component suppliers as well, Henry Ford thought they were "double dipping." Also in 1917, Ford and his son, Edsel, were involved in producing tractors.

U. S. news:

In April, President Wilson declared war on Germany and American troops soon arrived in France.

A poster appears with the image of Uncle Sam, based on a similar British recruiting poster with Lord Kitchener. The slogan "I Want You" and image galvanize American spirit about the war effort. The Yellow Jackets of Georgia Tech were undefeated champions of college football.

1917 Model T:

The brass radiator used on earlier Model Ts was redesigned for the 1917 model year. The new design was higher, rounded at the top and came with a removable steel shell. The new radiator design also was painted black. Nickel plating was used on the steering gear box, hubcaps and radiator filler neck. It was the final year for both the coupelet and the town car. The town car was discontinued during the 1917 production run. Crowned fenders were used this model year. Once again, Ford Motor Company produced ambulances, a total of 1,452 in the 1917 model year.

1917 MODEL T			
Body Type and Seating	Factory Price	Shipping Weight	Production Totals
3-door Touring-5p	$360	1,480 lbs.	568,128
2-door Runabout-2p	$345	1,385 lbs.	107,240
4-door Town Car-7p	$595	—	2,328
2-door sedan-5p	$645	1,745 lbs.	7,361
2-door coupe-2p	$505	1,580 lbs.	7,343
Chassis	$360	1,060 lbs.	1,174

Engine:

L-head. Four cylinder. Cast-iron block. B & S: 3 ¾ x 4 in. Displacement: 176.7 cid. Compression: 3.98:1 Horsepower: 20 at 1,600 rpm. Three main bearings. Solid valve lifters. Holley G and Kingston L2 carburetors. Torque: 83 lbs.-ft. @ 900 rpm.

Chassis:

100 in. wheelbase. Length: 11 feet, 2-1/2 in. (car with body). Front and rear tread: 56 in. Tires: 30 x 3 (front) and 30 x 3-1/2 (rear).

Standard Equipment:

The Model T used a light switch and horn button combination switch, mounted on the left side of the steering column this year. The horn was sounded by pushing the switch while the headlights were activated by turning the switch.

Options:

The hand-powered klaxon horn and shock absorbers continued to be popular aftermarket options.

Some speed and racing equipment began to appear for the Model T's four-cylinder engine in the aftermarket arena.

1917 T-spotting:

—The windshield frame and mounting brackets now were bolted instead of being riveted.

—The three floor pedals now had smooth surfaces.

—The tail pipe was eliminated this year and a hole was left at the end of the muffler.

—Three rectangular windows, size 3.5 x 9.5 inches, were used in the touring car's restyled top.

Technical-i-T:

A new engine pan appeared with a larger section that could hold a larger fan pulley.

Trivial-i-T:

The convertible-top coupelet was replaced by a coupe with a hard top but with removable side window posts that could be stored under the seat. It was an early version of the famed hardtop.

Here's an original press photo of the 1917 Model T touring car arranged on a studio drape to present a neutral background. The higher hoodline blended well with the cowl area.

A proud owner poses next to his restored 1917 Model T, complete with extra tires and accordion cargo carrier. By this model year, the radiator had become a black shell, not brass.   David Lyon

In 1917, Ford Motor Co. began making something new—the Model TT truck chassis. Bodies were prepared by local and regional specialty companies. David Lyon

1918 Model Ts Go "Over There" To War

Ford Motor Company news:

With America's involvement in World War I entering a second year, the Ford Motor Company's production of Model Ts was cut back in order to put more effort into steel helmets, ammunition boxes, armor, airplane engines, tractors, gas masks, the Model T ambulance and Eagle submarine chasing boats. All but the Eagle boats were made at Highland Park. The Model TT, made available in the 1917 model year, now was made available to the public. Unlike the earlier delivery wagon, the truck chassis was an immediate success with more than 41,105 produced. Once again, more than 2,100 ambulances were built, primarily for military service. Ford Motor Company recorded $78 million income at the end of the year from both military and civilian production.

U.S. news:

Americans enjoyed their first experiences with daylight savings time. A subway train jumped a track in Brooklyn, New York, killing 92 people and injuring 100 more. The Boston Red Sox won the World Series for the second time in three seasons. World War I ended on November 11, 1918 and Americans began coming back from France and other parts of Europe.

1918 Model T:

With much effort directed in other ways, the Model T changes introduced in the 1917 model year continued into the 1918 model year. The hard-top coupe was transformed when its window posts were removed. This unique model had a very brief run. Prices remained the same on all models except the chassis-only version that was cut by $35 per unit.

1918 MODEL T			
Body Type and Seating	Factory Price	Shipping Weight	Production Totals
3-door Touring-5p	$360	1,480 lbs.	432,519
2-door Runabout-2p	$345	1,385 lbs.	73,559
4-door town car 7-p	$595	—	2,142
2-door sedan-5p	$645	1,745 lbs.	35,697
2-door coupe-2p	$505	1,580 lbs.	14,771
Chassis	$325	1,060 lbs.	37,648

Engine:

L-head. Four cylinder. Cast-iron block. B & S: 3 ¾ x 4 in. Displacement: 176.7 cid. Compression: 3.98:1 Horsepower: 20 at 1,600 rpm. Three main bearings. Solid valve lifters. Holley G and Kingston L2 carburetors. Torque: 83 lbs.-ft. @ 900 rpm.

Chassis:

100 in. wheelbase. Length: 11 feet, 2-1/2 in. (car with body). Front and rear tread: 56 in. Tires: 30 x 3 (front) and 30 x 3-1/2 (rear).

Standard Equipment:

The Model T was largely unchanged from the 1917 edition.

Options:

Aftermarket options continued to be offered for the Model Ts. New cars had a relatively limited production run due to World War I.

1918 T-spotting:

Refer to the 1917 Model T for styling cues. The 1917 and '18 cars are very similar.

Technical-i-T:

The sedan entered its second model year as a steel-bodied vehicle, replacing the former aluminum body.

Trivial-i-T:

During 1918, Model T production was robust but still was the lowest it would be for several years.

Not as many Model Ts were produced or sold in 1918 because America was involved in World War I and production was diverted. This is one 1918 model, the "hardtop" coupe.   David Lyon

LEFT: *By 1918, nearly half of the cars on the road were Model T Fords and scenes like this one were becoming more common. The number of Model Ts sold grew after World War I.* Robin Heil-Kern

BELOW: *A similar shot of the 1918 Model T coupe shows its most famous feature. The center posts were removable and turned the coupe into an early version of the popular hardtop.* David Lyon

1919 You Don't Have to Crank It

Ford Motor Company news:

Henry Ford resigned as company president at the end of 1918 and his son, Edsel, assumed the leadership role. Still, Henry Ford was firmly in charge. There were some in the Ford Motor Co., including Edsel Ford, who wanted to replace or restyle the Model T. It was the cause of tension for several years and convinced several long-time Ford employees to leave. On Feb. 7, 1919, Henry Ford was ordered to pay more than $19.25 million in stock dividends to the Dodge Brothers following an intense lawsuit. Instead, Ford bought up the stock of John and Horace Dodge, John Anderson, the heirs to John Gray, Horace Rackham and James and Rosetta Couzens for slightly more than $105.8 million. The Ford Motor Company was reorganized as a Delaware Corporation with Henry, Edsel and Clara Ford as the sole stockholders. Long-time Ford Motor Co. associate C. Harold Wills left the company and eventually built the upscale Wills-Sainte Claire car line.

U. S. news:

The 18th Amendment went into effect, curbing manufacture or sale of alcoholic beverages in the United States. Race riots erupted in 26 American cities including Chicago and Washington, D. C.

Actors Charlie Chaplin, Mary Pickford, Douglas Fairbanks and director D. W. Griffith formed United Artists. Dial telephones were introduced by American Telephone and Telegraph Co.

The Indian Packing Co. of Green Bay, Wisconsin sponsored a football team. In future years, that team would grow to become the legendary champions of pro football, the Green Bay Packers.

1919 Model T:

In 1919, Model Ts received electric starters, first in the closed cars, then later available in all models. Cars equipped with the starter received something new for a Model T, a dashboard. It held the ammeter and an ignition/light switch. The electric-starting versions also had electric headlights and a single electric taillight. There was no dashboard in Model Ts without the electric starter. Coupes now had front-mounted door hinges and doors that opened from the rear.

Engine:

L-head. Four cylinder. Cast-iron block. B & S: 3 ¾ x 4 in. Displacement: 176.7 cid. Compression: 3.98:1 Horsepower: 20 at 1,600 rpm. Three main bearings. Solid valve lifters. Holley NH and Kingston L4 carburetors. Torque: 83 lbs.-ft. @ 900 rpm.

Chassis:

100 in. wheelbase. Length: 11 feet, 2-1/2 in. (car with body). Front and rear tread: 56 in. Tires: 30 x 3 (front) and 30 x 3-1/2 (rear). With demountable rims, tires were 30 x 3 ½ all around.

Standard Equipment:

The steering wheel diameter was increased to 16 inches and was made of pressed steel. A new pressed steel muffler also was used.

Options:

An electric starter was available as an option for the first time. The option cost $75 and included the battery, 6-volt headlights and an electric taillight plus an ammeter inside the car. Speedometers were dealer-installed options. Demountable rims were now available for $25 on open Model Ts.

1919 T-spotting:

—Headlights with bright and dim bulbs plus an electric taillight were on cars with electric starters.

—A dash-mounted choke pull was mounted in cars with the electric start option

—Optional demountable wheel rims were manufactured by the Hayes or Kelsey wheel companies.

—The starter switch was located to the left of the driver's heel.

—The battery mount in 1919 was between the frame rails, to the rear of the fuel tank.

Technical-i-T:

To make room for the electric starting equipment, a new cylinder block was designed to make room for the generator, new spiral-cut timing gears were used and the flywheel was modified

with a starter ring gear. A notch also was added to the magneto field coil ring. This allowed free passage of the starter drive shaft.

Trivial-i-T:

The electric starting additions added 95 pounds to the basic weight of Model T cars so equipped.

1919 MODEL T			
Body Type and Seating	Factory Price	Shipping Weight	Production Totals
3-door Touring-5p	$525	1,500 lbs.	289,935
2-door Runabout-2p	$500	1,390 lbs.	48,867
2-door sedan-5p	$875	1,875 lbs.	24,980
2-door coupe-2p	$750	1,685 lbs.	11,528
Chassis	$475	1,060 lbs.	47,125

This 1919 Model T roadster is prepared for bad weather. Note the side curtains are in place. The practical owner had a popular option—a toolbox—on the running board. *David Lyon*

A spotlight, rear view mirror, Moto-Meter and crank handle cradle are among the additions to this 1919 Model T roadster. It was a practical, very affordable car. *David Lyon*

A French-built 1919 Model T sedan was restored with British colors in mind. Model Ts were produced in a factory near Paris. *Andrew Morland*

The rarest 1919 Model T was the coupe with its high-crowned top and its front opening doors. Just over 11,500 of these cars were built. *David Lyon*

1920 Surviving the Recession

Ford Motor Company news:

Henry Ford began to move into some new businesses beyond automobiles in 1920. One of his efforts was the Dearborn *Independent* newspaper where, unfortunately, he vented his anti-Semitic views to the public through writers and editors he employed. Ford also railed against the financial structure of the United States and Europe, alcoholic drinks, munitions makers and textbooks. A major recession in 1920 plus debts caused by buying up company stock, investing in the new River Rouge plant and in coal mines meant Ford Motor Company had some heavy debts. The Ford plan was to again cut Model T costs, ship cars and parts packages to dealers and make them absorb the costs. The plan got the company out of debt and eventually Model T sales rebounded.

U. S. news:

The implementation of the 19th Amendment guaranteed women the right to vote. A bomb explosion at the Morgan Bank in New York City killed 30 people and injured 200 more. Station KDKA of Pittsburgh transmitted the first commercial radio broadcast. The California Golden Bears were the undefeated champions of college football. The horse named Paul Jones was the Kentucky Derby winner.

1920 Model T:

A new open car body was offered for the 1920 model year. While not dramatically different from previous open car bodies, it did have a rear panel that was an integral part of the side panel. An oval gas tank was introduced and it allowed the Model T seats to be lowered and raked a bit for more comfortable seating angles. Overall, the Model Ts rebounded from sluggish sales and exceeded the one million mark in production during the model year.

1920 MODEL T			
Body Type and Seating	Factory Price	Shipping Weight	Production Totals
3-door Touring-5p	$675*	1,650 lbs.	367,785
3-door Touring-5p	$575	1,500 lbs.	165,929
2-door Runabout-2p	$650*	1,540 lbs.	63,514
2-door Runabout-2p	$550	1,390 lbs.	31,889
2-door sedan-5p	$975	1,875 lbs.	81,616
2-door coupe-2p	$850	1,760 lbs.	60,215
Chassis	$620*	1,210 lbs.	18,173
Chassis	$525	1,060 lbs.	47,125

* Price is indicated before the March 3, 1920, changes.

Engine:

L-head. Four cylinder. Cast-iron block. B & S: 3 ¾ x 4 in. Displacement: 176.7 cid. Compression: 3.98:1 Horsepower: 20 at 1,600 rpm. Three main bearings. Solid valve lifters. Holley NH and Kingston L4 carburetors. Torque: 83 lbs.-ft. @ 900 rpm.

Chassis:

100 in. wheelbase. Length: 11 feet, 2-1/2 in. (car with body). Front and rear tread: 56 in. Tires: 30 x 3 (front) and 30 x 3-1/2 (rear). With demountable rims, tires were 30 x 3 ½ all around.

Standard Equipment:

On open cars, two magneto-powered headlamps plus two oil-fueled side lamps and an oil-fueled taillight were standard along with a magneto-powered horn.

Options:

An electric starter was available for $75 on open cars and included the battery, 6-volt headlights and an electric taillight plus an ammeter inside the car. Speedometers were dealer-installed options. Demountable rims cost $25. Racing parts were becoming popular in the aftermarket.

1920 T-spotting:

—The oval gas tank now could be found under the seats of many Model T Fords. It allowed a lower seat structure. The sedan used a square tank.

—The steering wheel now was increased to 16 inches. The center or spider of the steering wheel now was pressed steel.

—The muffler on the Model T was pressed steel in 1920.

—Electric starting and demountable rims were available on all models throughout 1920.

Technical-i-T:

The 1920 Model T continued to make room for the electric starting components with modifications to the engine block, a starter ring gear and the notch in the magneto field coil ring—all to allow a notch to flywheel to allow it to clear the starter shaft. A new transmission cover also was made.

Trivial-i-T:

Many 1920 hubcaps had black centers with reversed letters. The hubcaps were nickel-plated.

An early 1920s Model T coupe crosses an Iowa bridge during a Model T rally. The front-opening doors were unique to this edition of the Model T in 1920.   *Robin Heil-Kern*

A 1920 Model T roadster was on display near a small old home with a period license plate mounted in front, a sign about its history and a tool kit on display.   *David Lyon*

Following World War I, production and sales of the Model T picked up in England. This is a restored example of a touring car from that period.   *Andrew Morland*

When many people recall the Model T, they often picture a car from this period, such as this roadster photographed in a California parade.   *Tom Myers*

1921 The New Touring Body

Ford Motor Company news:

By 1921, there had been something of a "brain drain" from Ford Motor Co. as several of the top minds in the company went on in new directions. Norval Hawkins, for example, had been involved in marketing and advertising for a decade. John R. Lee had come from the purchase of the Keim Mills. Frank Klingensmith had taken over from original treasurer and business manager James Couzens. William Knudsen had been involved in several assignments for the company including the coordination of the River Rouge plant. Knudsen would move on to General Motors where he took over the Chevrolet Division and made it a strong competitor to the Model T. In 1921, there was one Chevrolet sold for every 13 Model Ts that were taken in delivery. That ratio would soon change.

U. S. news:

Warren G. Harding of Ohio became President and speakeasies became the new rage as Americans coped with the constraints of Prohibition. Comedian Roscoe "Fatty" Arbuckle was arrested on manslaughter charges. After three trials, he was acquitted but his acting career was ruined. Rudolph Valentino debuted in the movie "The Sheik." The first burial was held at the Tomb of the Unknown Soldier at Arlington National Cemetery, near Washington, D. C. The entity that became the National Football League was founded at a Hupmobile dealership in Canton, Ohio.

1921 Model T:

More Ford buyers grew to like their Model Ts with an electric starter. While some had thought the electric starter was an "unmanly" choice, it was OK with many women. The traditional crank-start and magneto-powered Model Ts continued to be offered. The 1921 models included the open touring car and runabout plus the center door sedan and coupe. Many customers, especially businesses, chose the chassis-only version and added bodies from the aftermarket suppliers. The Model TT trucks continued to be popular with more than 118,500 produced in 1921.

Engine:

L-head. Four cylinder. Cast-iron block. B & S: 3 ¾ x 4 in. Displacement: 176.7 cid. Compression: 3.98:1 Horsepower: 20 at 1,600 rpm. Three main bearings. Solid valve lifters. Holley NH and Kingston L4 carburetors. Torque: 83 lbs.-ft. @ 900 rpm.

Chassis:

100 in. wheelbase. Length: 11 feet, 2-1/2 in. (car with body). Front and rear tread: 56 in. Tires: 30 x 3 (front) and 30 x 3-1/2 (rear). With demountable rims, tires were 30 x 3 ½ all around.

Standard Equipment:

On open cars, two magneto-powered headlamps plus two oil-fueled side lamps and an oil-fueled taillight were standard along with a magneto-powered horn.

Options:

An electric starter was available for $75 and included the battery, 6-volt headlights and an electric taillight plus an ammeter inside the car. Speedometers were dealer-installed options.

1921 T-spotting:

—Pressed steel running boards replaced the forged steel units that had been used since 1909.
—Cars with electric starters had dashboards in either metal or leatherette covering wood.
—The oval gas tank under lower seats was in its second model year of production.

Technical-i-T:

Model T headlights briefly came with a green "visor" and then a ribbed lens style was introduced.

Trivial-i-T:

While American Model Ts went to the 30 x 3 ½-inch tire size all around when equipped with demountable rims, the Canadian versions always had all four tires in this size.

1921 MODEL T			
Body Type and Seating	Factory Price	Shipping Weight	Production Totals
3-door Touring-5p	$440/$415*	1,500 lbs.	84,970
(w/ electric start)	$535/$510*	1,650 lbs.	647,300
2-door Runabout-2p	$395/$370*	1,390 lbs.	25,918
(w/ electric start)	$490/$465*	1,540 lbs.	171,745
2-door sedan-5p	$795/$760*	1,875 lbs.	179.734
2-door coupe-2p	$745/$695*	1,760 lbs.	129,159
Chassis	$360/$345*	1,060 lbs.	13,356
(w/ electric start)	$455/$440*	1,210 lbs.	23,436

* Prices show before and after reductions made on June 7, 1921.

The low angle of this image of a 1921 Model T coupe emphasized its high roof line with tall windows and windshield. Doors still opened from the front on the 1921 edition.   David Lyon

A 1921 Model T touring car is on display with its top up. A second Model T is just visible around the corner. By 1921, 60 percent of cars in the United States were Model Ts.   David Lyon

ABOVE: This rather formal-looking 1921 Model T center door sedan was pictured by what appears to be a high school or college building. It seems like the perfect place for this serious-looking Model T.

LEFT: Many people recall early 1920s Model T touring cars in this manner—filled with smiling people, enjoying a ride over a bridge. Is there room for one more?   Robin Heil-Kern

1922 The New Runabout Body

Ford Motor Company news:

On January 4, 1922, the Ford Motor Company purchased the bankrupt Lincoln Motor Car Company from Henry and Wilfred Leland for $8 million. It was an addition that Ford Motor Company had not offered since the troubled Model K—a car that appealed solely to an upper class market. Both Henry Leland and his son, Wilfred, resigned from the Ford-based Lincoln operation by June 10, 1922. More Model Ts were being made than ever before at lower prices as the assembly lines produced cars and trucks at record rates. Work on the experimental X-8 engine began this year. Both water- and air-cooled versions would be produced. The 288-cid X-8 proved to be too heavy for the Model T chassis and also was plagued by oiling and crankshaft problems. 1

U. S. news:

The Lincoln Memorial was dedicated on May 30, 1922. Coal miners in several locations struck, some for as long as six months, to protest wage cuts. A magazine called Reader's Digest was introduced. The New York Giants defeated the New York Yankees to capture the World Series. The Toronto St. Pats were Stanley Cup champions. "Alice Adams" by Booth Tarkington won the Pulitzer Prize for best novel while Eugene O'Neill's "Anna Christie" was named best play.

1922 Model T:

New in the Model T lineup in 1922 was a revised body for the runabout. The new look included a larger turtle deck, a distinctive style that would be a memorable throughout the 1920s. Changes that were made in 1919 and refined over the 1920 and '21 model years continued on the 1922 Model Ts.

1922 MODEL T			
Body Type and Seating	Factory Price	Shipping Weight	Production Totals
3-door Touring-5p	$348/$298*	1,500 lbs.	80,070
(w/ electric start)	$443/$393*	1,650 lbs.	514,333
2-door Runabout-2p	$319/$269*	1,390 lbs.	31,923
(w/ electric start)	$414/$364*	1,540 lbs.	133,433
2-door sedan-5p	$645/$595*	1,875 lbs.	146,060
4-door sedan-5p	$725	1,950 lbs.	4,286
2-door coupe-2p	$580/$530*	1,760 lbs.	198,382
Chassis	$285/$235*	1,060 lbs.	15,228
(w/ electric start)	$380/$330*	1,210 lbs.	23,313

Prices are shown before and after reductions made October 17, 1922.

Engine:

L-head. Four cylinder. Cast-iron block. B & S: 3 ¾ x 4 in. Displacement: 176.7 cid. Compression: 3.98:1 Horsepower: 20 at 1,600 rpm. Three main bearings. Solid valve lifters. Holley NH and Kingston L4 carburetors. Torque: 83 lbs.-ft. @ 900 rpm.

Chassis:

100 in. wheelbase. Length: 11 feet, 2-1/2 in. (car with body). Front and rear tread: 56 in. Tires: 30 x 3 (front) and 30 x 3-1/2 (rear). With demountable rims, tires were 30 x 3 ½ all around.

Standard Equipment:

Two magneto-powered headlamps plus two oil-fired sidelights and an oil-fueled taillight were standard along with a magneto-powered horn.

Options:

An electric starter was available for $75 and included the battery, 6-volt headlights and an electric taillight plus an ammeter inside the car. Speedometers were dealer-installed options.

1922 T-spotting:

—The runabout got a new body and larger turtle deck.
—Look carefully at the windows. They moved up and down with latch pins instead of straps.
—There were some trim and upholstery changes made on the 1922 models.

Technical-i-T:

This was the final year that closed cars came with magneto-powered headlights.

Trivial-i-T:

This was the final year of the lower radiator and "ski slope" style cowl on Model Ts.

1 Spencer Murray, editor, *Ford in the Thirties*, (Los Angeles, 1976), pp. 17-18 and 24.

Late in 1922, something new appeared on the scene. It was a Model T sedan with four opening doors. Ford Motor Co. coined the term Fordor to make its sedan unforgettable.

The "NL" on the windshield and the wide rectangular license plate mean this 1922 Model T touring car has a story to tell. It was registered in the Netherlands. Ts were popular everywhere.   David Lyon

The 1922 Model T center door sedan continued to offer a stately-looking vehicle. It was plush inside with full upholstery and trim, the most luxurious of the Model Ts offered.

A beautiful 1922 Model T coupe shows off its best angles. Coupes were the third most popular choices among Ford buyers in this model year. David Lyon

1923 Two Million Model Ts

Ford Motor Company news:

It was another successful year at Ford Motor Company but competition was coming up quickly. While the Model T was being produced in the millions during the model year, Willys-Overland had introduced a new design that was a dead ringer for the Model T in many ways and Chevrolet advertised itself with the heading "The Awakening" and noted its sudden shift from seventh to second place in sales. "Are you with the tide of trade or against it?" asked the Chevrolet writers, a not-so-veiled reference to the Model T. 1 Meanwhile, Ford Motor Company was marking its 20th anniversary. An article in the June 20th edition of *Motor World* noted the company had made more than 7.75 million cars and trucks over its lifetime. Ford Motor Co. had several automotive plants, coal and iron mines, timber land and a glass factory. Ford also owned a small railroad at the time.

U. S. news:

President Warren G. Harding died of a sudden illness at San Francisco in August 1923. Vice President Calvin Coolidge succeeded him. While the Ku Klux Klan spewed hatred, singer Bessie Smith recorded her first song "Down Hearted Blues" and Harlem's famed Cotton Club opened.

The Fighting Illini of Illinois and Michigan Wolverines were each undefeated in college football.

1923 Model T:

The open cars now had a sloping windshield plus what was called the "one man top." Model Ts kept their previous low radiator style this year. Late in calendar year 1923, the first

1924 models had a higher radiator. A 1923 Ford ad showed a doctor climbing a hill from his parking spot to visit a patient in an isolated cabin. "Dependable as the doctor himself" said the ad. It compared faith and trust in physicians with the bond that existed between drivers and their Model Ts. "Such universal faith is the result of Ford reliability proved over a long period of years..." said the ad.

Engine:

L-head. Four cylinder. Cast-iron block. B & S: 3 ¾ x 4 in. Displacement: 176.7 cid. Compression: 3.98:1 Horsepower: 20 at 1,600 rpm. Three main bearings. Solid valve lifters. Holley NH and Kingston L4 carburetors. Torque: 83 lbs.-ft. @ 900 rpm.

Chassis:

100 in. wheelbase. Length: 11 feet, 2-1/2 in. (car with body). Front and rear tread: 56 in. Tires: 30 x 3 (front) and 30 x 3-1/2 (rear). With demountable rims, tires were 30 x 3 ½ all around.

Standard Equipment:

On open cars, two magneto-powered headlamps plus two oil-fueled side lamps and an oil-fueled taillight were standard along with a magneto-powered horn.

Options:

An electric starter was available for $75 and included the battery, 6-volt headlights and an electric taillight plus an ammeter inside the car. Speedometers were dealer-installed options.

1923 T-spotting:
- A "one man top" was debuted during this model year.
- The windshields on 1923 Model Ts are slightly sloped.
- A battery-powered horn appeared on all cars equipped with electric start.
- All Model Ts have a dashboard beginning with the 1923 models.

Technical-i-T:

American-made Model Ts had a divided front seat for the first time, making refueling easier. Canadian-built Model Ts had used this feature for several years.

Trivial-i-T:

The familiar center door sedan was discontinued during the 1923 model year.

1 *Motor World* Feb. 28, 1923 p. 90

1923 MODEL T			
Body Type and Seating	Factory Price	Shipping Weight	Production Totals
3-door Touring-5p	$295	1,500 lbs.	136,441
(w/ electric start)	$380	1,650 lbs.	792,651
2-door Runabout-2p	$265	1,390 lbs.	56,954
(w/ electric start)	$350	1,540 lbs.	238,638
2-door sedan-5p	$590	1,875 lbs.	96,410
4-door sedan-5p	$685	1,950 lbs.	144,444
2-door coupe-2p	$525	1,760 lbs.	313,273
Chassis	$230	1,060 lbs.	9,433
(w/ electric start)	$295	1,210 lbs.	42,874

The final edition for the Model T center door sedan came with the 1923 version of the spruced up Ford.   David Lyon

A restored 1923 Model T touring car was on display at a quiet moment at a local car show. Touring cars were extremely popular models throughout the Model T years.   David Lyon

A newly designed coupe appeared in the 1923 Model T lineup. Gone were the front opening doors and in was a more conventional looking car.

This photo is rather timeless. If color photography was available at that time, it easily could have been taken sometime in 1923 with a Fordor sedan parked next to a farm field.   David Lyon

A well-preserved 1923 Model T roadster stopped in front of the photographer briefly for a portrait. The roadster was the least expensive Model T with a factory body.   David Lyon

1924 The New Model Fordor and Tudor

Ford Motor Company news:

General Motors introduced plans that went directly against the views of Henry Ford. One was the GM system of installment payments that Ford refused to follow. He also disliked the concept of frequent design changes. "We cannot conceive how to serve the customer unless we make him something...that will last forever," said Henry. 1 Yet the Ford Motor Co. was recognizing trends such as the movement toward buyers who wanted more closed cars in the 1920s. While they didn't follow the GM's installment plan, Ford did come up with an installment savings plan of its own. The Ford Enrollment Plan, introduced in 1924, offered a $5 savings book that encouraged saving for a new Model T. Payments were made to local banks cooperating with the plan and a firm called Motor Buyers Inc. kept track of prospective buyer installments. The payment book had 40 savings installments and when it was completed, the buyer could visit any Ford dealer and order a new Model T, credited with the amount saved in the plan. Ford Motor Co. wasn't involved in the monetary transactions like the General Motors Acceptance Corporation. During the year, the River Rouge plant joined Highland Park to offer more production capabilities. Production was expected to grow to 10,000 units each week according to a Motor World story in August 1924.

U. S. news:

International Business Machines Corp. (IBM) became the new name of an old New York business firm known as the Computer Tabulating Recording Co. Interior Secretary Albert Fall was sentenced to prison for his role in the Teapot Dome scandal that involved oil reserves. The Washington Senators won the World Series. George Gershwin's "Rhapsody in Blue" premiered. Under coach Knute Rockne's guidance, Notre Dame forged a 10-0 season in college football.

1924 Model T:

A new five-passenger Tudor sedan was introduced and replaced the venerable center door sedan in the Model T lineup. The Fordor sedan, introduced late in 1923, continued to be produced. A restyled coupe also premiered. It featured doors that opened from the rear, matching the majority of Ford models. Ford closed cars now had all-metal construction replacing metal over wood framing. A taller radiator and larger hood gave the Model Ts a new appearance.

Engine:

L-head. Four cylinder. Cast-iron block. B & S: 3 ¾ x 4 in. Displacement: 176.7 cid. Compression: 3.98:1 Horsepower: 20 at 1,600 rpm. Three main bearings. Solid valve lifters. Holley NH and Kingston L4 carburetors. Torque: 83 lbs.-ft. @ 900 rpm. The engine featured lighter connecting rods beginning in 1923.

Chassis:

100 in. wheelbase. Length: 11 feet, 2-1/2 in. (car with body). Front and rear tread: 56 in. Tires: 30 x 3 (front) and 30 x 3-1/2 (rear). With demountable rims, tires were 30 x 3 ½ all around.

Standard Equipment:

On open cars, two magneto-powered headlamps plus two oil-fueled side lamps and an oil-fueled taillight were standard along with a magneto-powered horn.

Options:

An electric starter was available for $65 on open cars and included the battery, 6-volt headlights and an electric taillight plus an ammeter. Speedometers were dealer-installed options.

1924 T-spotting:

—Exterior sun visors were installed on closed cars.
—A new taillight and license plate bracket was introduced during the model year production.
—A cowl ventilator was used on closed cars and offered direct air into the car.
—The larger turtle deck on the coupe offered more room for cases and packages.
—A spare tire rim came with cars equipped with demountable rims but not the tire!

Technical-i-T:

A dash light and hand-operated windshield wiper were standard in 1924 on closed-bodied Model Ts. A vacuum-powered wiper was optional.

Trivial-i-T:

Ford Motor Company began national advertising again after a 10-year hiatus. Ford dealers had continued to use company-prepared advertising in local and regional markets during this time.

1 Robert Lacey, Ford: *The Men and the Machine*, (London: 1986), p. 302.

1924 MODEL T			
Body Type and Seating	Factory Price	Shipping Weight	Production Totals
3-door Touring-5p	$290	1,500 lbs.	99,523
(w/ electric start)	$375	1,650 lbs.	673,579
2-door Runabout-2p	$260	1,390 lbs.	43,317
(w/ electric start)	$345	1,540 lbs.	220,955
2-door sedan-5p	$580	1,875 lbs.	223,203
4-door sedan-5p	$660	1,950 lbs.	84,733
2-door coupe-2p	$520	1,760 lbs.	327,584
Chassis	$225	1,060 lbs.	3,921
(w/ electric start)	$290	1,210 lbs.	43,980

The 1924 Model T coupe was captured in a photo that could have been taken when it was new—parked alongside a period brick building. This is a well-preserved example.   David Lyon

A larger rectangular rear window was part of the tasteful design that was offered with the 1924 Model T coupe.   Doug Mitchel

The memorable 1924 Model T coupe. The second most popular car in the Ford lineup, the coupe was in its second model year after some sensible restyling. Doug Mitchel

1925 Balloon Tires and Low, Low Prices

Ford Motor Company news:

Sometime late in the Model T's long and distinguished run, Ford Motor Co. began to experiment with some newer engines. Henry Ford disdained the six-cylinder engine, as he recalled the troubles he'd had with the Ford Model K. Work did begin on a limited basis on some new types of engines to possibly be used in the Model T or a replacement car. Ford engineers studied engines produced by other companies and conceived both a five-cylinder engine and an X-shaped eight-cylinder version. The Model T had reached record production numbers in 1924 and number 10 milion had been built on June 15. The Ford share of the market was dwindling as Chevrolet was gaining, along with others. Roads also were improving and people were expecting more from their automobile.

U. S. news:

The worst tornado on record caused 689 deaths as it streaked across Missouri, Illinois and Indiana. Nellie Taylor Ross of Wyoming became the nation's first woman governor. Tennessee teacher John Scopes was arrested for teaching the theory of evolution to high school students. The Pittsburgh Pirates won the World Series while the Dartmouth Big Green and the Alabama Crimson Tide were colorful champions of college football.

1925 Model T:

For at least 10 years, and possibly since the Model T was introduced for the 1909 model year, owners had been removing the tonneau portion on older touring cars, then the turtle deck on runabouts, despite Ford Motor Company warnings to the contrary. Replacement packages had included crude homemade boxes and aftermarket specialty additions designed to convert dependable Ts into utility vehicles. During the 1925 model year, Ford offered a two-for-one package that converted the roadster, sans turtle deck, into the "pick up box," a simple square box unit. It was both the forerunner of the 1950s Ranchero and the grandfather to today's stylish and tough Ford trucks. Ford also began selling a larger 4.40 x 21-inch tire called the balloon tire.

Engine:

L-head. Four cylinder. Cast-iron block. B & S: 3 ¾ x 4 in. Displacement: 176.7 cid. Compression: 3.98:1 Horsepower: 20 at 1,600 rpm. Three main bearings. Solid valve lifters. Holley NH and Kingston L4 carburetors. Torque: 83 lbs.-ft. @ 900 rpm. The engine featured lighter connecting rods beginning in 1923.

Chassis:

100 in. wheelbase. Length: 11 feet, 2-1/2 in. (car with body). Front and rear tread: 56 in. Tires: 30 x 3 (front) and 30 x 3-1/2 (rear). With demountable rims, tires were 30 x 3 ½ all around. Larger 4.40 x 21 "balloon" tires were optional in 1925 model year.

Standard Equipment:

Two magneto-powered headlamps plus two oil sidelights and an oil-fueled taillight were standard along with a magneto-powered horn, the last year for this standard equipment on Model Ts.

Options:

An electric starter was available for $65 on open cars and included the battery, 6-volt headlights and an electric taillight plus an ammeter inside the car. The "pick up body" was available as an option for Ford roadsters.

1925 T-spotting:

—Many of the same additions as 1924 were carried on such as the new taillight and bracket and the sun visor on closed cars.

—Cars with balloon tires seemed fuller and less upright.

—Model Ts without electric starting equipment had a new "sideways" taillight in 1925. The small red lens on the side of the light faced out and a larger white lens was pointed sideways.

Technical-i-T:

A squarer, slightly wider splash apron and rear fenders were used on the 1925 cars.

Trivial-i-T:

It was the final year for Model Ts with oil lamps.

1925 MODEL T			
Body Type and Seating	Factory Price	Shipping Weight	Production Totals
3-door Touring-5p	$290	1,500 lbs.	64,399
(w/ electric start)	$375	1,650 lbs.	626,813
2-door Runabout-2p	$260	1,390 lbs.	34,206
(w/ electric start)	$345	1,536 lbs.	264,436
2-door sedan-5p	$580	1,875 lbs.	195,001
4-door sedan-5p	$660	1,950 lbs.	81,050
2-door coupe-2p	$520	1,760 lbs.	343,969
2-door pickup-2p	$281	1,471 lbs.	33,795*
(w/ electric start)	$366	1,621 lbs.	
Chassis	$225	1,060 lbs.	6,523
(w/ electric start)	$290	1,210 lbs.	53,450

*Note: Production figures were combined for Model T roadster pickups.

The windshield on the 1925 Model T touring car was angled slightly but kept the traditional simplicity Ford owners expected. Part of that was the hand-operated windshield wiper. Doug Mitchel

Popular in the 1925 model year was the Model T Tudor sedan, a roomy and practical car in keeping with the car's traditions.

The 1925 Model T, like this touring car version, had more rounded fenders and was a clean looking vehicle. Yet in this time, other companies were catching up, especially Chevrolet. Doug Mitchel

1926 Those Colorful Model Ts

Ford Motor Company news:

If you looked carefully at the 1926 Ford Model T, restyled for the first time since 1917, you might have seen the future, with hints of the Model A to come. Ford Motor Co. was officially holding on but also was thinking ahead. A new Ford was in the planning stages, something that would replace the Model. In the 20-plus years since they had perfected the car, the United States and the world had changed. Still Henry Ford resisted change. When his son got up at a company board meeting to talk about hydraulic brakes, Henry thundered: "Edsel, you shut up!" Edsel was often resisted. That was the way things happened at Ford late in the days of the Model T.

U. S. news:

Marine forces were sent to quell problems in Nicaragua and remain on duty there through 1933.

The National Broadcasting Company was formed offering the Red and Blue radio networks to the United States. Martha Graham danced and Robert Goddard showed off rockets. Both would become American legends. It was a great year for those who liked shades of red with the St. Louis Cardinals World Series champs, the Montreal Maroons winners of the Stanley Cup and the Stanford Indians (now Cardinal) and Alabama Crimson Tide college football co-champions.

1926 Model T:

For the first time since 1917, the Model T received a fresh look with different fenders, running boards, hoods and all but the Fordor getting new bodies. The 1926 Model T touring sedans had a driver's door that opened, the first since 1911. It was something Canadian Model T drivers had long enjoyed. Chassis modifications, including some different spindles in front and new springs, meant the T now was an inch lower. Bodies were available in colors for the first time since the teens. Some coupes were dark green while a number of Fordor

models available in dark maroon. Fenders continued to be all black. All Model Ts came with an electric starter and demountable wheels.

Engine:

L-head. Four cylinder. Cast-iron block. B & S: 3 ¾ x 4 in. Displacement: 176.7 cid. Compression: 3.98:1 Horsepower: 20 at 1,600 rpm. Three main bearings. Solid valve lifters. Holley NH and Holley Vaporizer, Kingston L4 and Kingston Regenerator. Torque: 83 lbs.-ft. @ 900 rpm.

Chassis:

100 in. wheelbase. Length: 11 feet, 2-1/2 in. (car with body). Front and rear tread: 56 in. Tires: 30 x 3-1/2 early in production, then early optional 4.40 x 21 "balloon" tires become standard later in production run.

Standard Equipment:

An electric starter with generator and six-volt battery now was standard on all Model Ts.

Options:

The "pick up body" was available as an option for Ford roadsters. Wire wheels become available during the production run, early in 1926. Ford officially sanctioned such aftermarket options as the Ruckstell rear axle this year.

1926 T-spotting:
- —Wire wheels were optional and available in black, green, straw, Casino Red and Vermillion.
- —These Model Ts had nickel-plated headlight rims.
- —Nickel-plated radiator shells came on some models, like the coupe.
- —The carbs used were often called "hot plates" and were made by Holley (Vaporizer) and Kingston. They were able to offer good economy but performance often suffered.
- —The traditional mounting of the coil box ignition now was found to the upper left of the engine.
- —All models but the Fordor had the gas tank mounted in the cowl area.

Technical-i-T:

For 1926 Model Ts, the transmission brake was made about ½-inch wider and the rear wheel brakes were enlarged to 11 inches.

Trivial-i-T:

The Model T grew very sporty during 1926 with the introduction of the Sports Touring and Sports Runabout editions. Each had five wire wheels, a nickel-plated radiator shell, wind wings, a tan top and nickel plated bumpers front and rear.

1926 MODEL T			
Body Type and Seating	Factory Price	Shipping Weight	Production Totals
3-door Touring-5p	$375/$380	1,738 lbs.	364,409
2-door Runabout-2p	$345/$360	1,655 lbs.	342,575
2-door sedan-5p	$495	1,972 lbs.	270,331
4-door sedan-5p	$545	2,004 lbs.	102,732
2-door coupe-2p	$485	1,860 lbs.	288,342
2-door pickup-2p	$281	1,471 lbs.	75,406
Chassis	$290/$300	1,167 lbs.	58,223

Something that was brought back in 1926 was color for the Model T. This touring car heads down a country road showing off its green body and matching lighter green wheels. David Lyon

The upright styling of the 1926 Model T Fordor was falling behind that of its competitors but Ford still was a top seller. This version seems right off the showroom floor.

1927 15 Million Model Ts and a Final Bow

Ford Motor Company news:

For many years, the Model T and Henry Ford had become known all over the globe and the term "Universal Car" was no mere advertising gimmick. From town squares to temple grounds and from remote plains to thick jungles, people who were as diverse as the great continents were familiar with the light, four-cylinder cars. The Model Ts had changed the way people thought about the automobile and how those cars were made. But now it was time to exit the automotive stage. Shortly after the public celebration of Model T number 15 million, Henry Ford announced that Model T production would end on May 26, 1927. "The Model T was one of the largest factors in creating the conditions which now make the new model Ford possible. We are still proud of the Model T Ford car." 1 Like a great Broadway production, the Model Ts had been a smash hit and had set the records for others to follow. "Ford's Flivver," also called the "Tin Lizzie," exited with class.

U. S news:

The Holland Tunnel opened and connected New York City's borough of Manhattan with Jersey City, New Jersey. Charles Lindbergh, an airmail pilot from Minnesota, became an international hero for his solo transatlantic flight from Long Island to Paris. Philo Farnsworth demonstrated the first all-electronic form of television. Jerome Kern's "Show Boat" premiered on Broadway and "The Jazz Singer" introduced sound to silent movies. The Ottawa Senators were Stanley Cup Champions while the New York Yankees won the World Series.

1927 Model T:

Wire wheels became more common on the 1927 Fords as the option now gave the cars a more modern look. The typical Ford changeover was in July from one model year of the Model T to the next but the 1927 version began in August 1926. More colors were available at that time including Phoenix Brown, Gunmetal Blue and Fawn Gray. There were few changes as the "new look" cars introduced for the 1926 continued until their final curtain call on the automotive stage.

Engine:

L-head. Four cylinder. Cast-iron block. B & S: 3 ¾ x 4 in. Displacement: 176.7 cid. Compression: 3.98:1 Horsepower: 20 at 1,600 rpm. Three main bearings. Solid valve lifters. Holley NH and Holley Vaporizer, Kingston L4 and Kingston Regenerator. Torque: 83 lbs.-ft. @ 900 rpm.

Note: The transmission now bolted to the rear of the cylinder. The fan was mounted on the water outlet and later production models used a nickel-plated head and water connection bolts.

Chassis:

100 in. wheelbase. Length: 11 feet, 2-1/2 in. (car with body). Front and rear tread: 56 in. Tires: 30 x 3-1/2 early in production, then early optional 4.40 x 21 "balloon" tires become standard later in the 1926 production run.

Standard Equipment:

Electric starter with generator and six-volt battery now is standard on all Model Ts.

Options:

Wire wheels become standard on some closed models during the 1927 production run, though they still were an option available on other Model Ts this model year.

1927 T-spotting:

(See 1926 for spotting suggestions. The 1927 cars had few or no outward changes.)

Trivial-i-T:

Ford Motor Company began advertising the availability of its parts late in 1927 as dealers assured Model T owners their cars would remain dependable as ever.

Trivial-i-T:

Model T engines continued to be produced on a limited basis until just before World War II.

1 *Automotive Topics* May 28, 1927   p. 205.

1927 MODEL T			
Body Type and Seating	Factory Price	Shipping Weight	Production Totals
3-door Touring-5p	$380	1,738 lbs.	81,181
2-door Runabout-2p	$360	1,655 lbs.	95,778
2-door sedan-5p	$495	1,972 lbs.	78,105
4-door sedan-5p	$545	2,004 lbs.	22,930
2-door coupe-2p	$485	1,860 lbs.	69,939
2-door pickup-2p	$381	1,736 lbs.	28,143
Chassis	$300	1,272 lbs.	19,280

The Model T was put to many uses in business as well as in family life. Here's a 1927 Model T roadster that used a special utility box out back. It carried a side-mounted spare tire.

By the final year the Model T was produced, the roadster pickup by Ford was a popular choice. Earlier roadsters had been converted by owners or aftermarket suppliers. *Mike Mueller*

This colorful Model T Ford coupe for 1927 included a nickel-plated radiator, a cowl vent, a sun visor and complementary-colored wire wheels. *David Lyon*

Ford Motor Co. decided to keep some basic black with their later generation Model Ts. The fenders, running boards and lower bodies were black. The bodies were available in colors. *Don Voelker*

This 1927 Model T touring car seems to be lingering just a little longer on a village street. The Model Ts continued to be popular and driven for many years after production stopped. *David Lyon*

The Model T ended isolation for many people whom the railroads and other means of transporation had missed. With this car, people had a better way to connect to the world.   Tom Myers

"One of the great discoveries a man makes, one of the great surprises, is to find he can do what he was afraid he couldn't do. Most of the bars we beat against are in ourselves—we put them there, and we can take them down."

Henry Ford

Chapter 5

THE MODEL T REVOLUTION IN SOCIETY

Wherever you are in the world of the 21st century, you probably have been influenced in some way by the revolution that was touched off in society by the Model T Ford's introduction to the public after October 1908.

The gangly-looking, four-cylinder car perhaps seems light years away from our world of computers, cell phones, interstates and I Pods as well as a world networked by satellites, but a closer look will show how extensively the Model T, Henry Ford and the golden era of the car influenced the world around us.

One name soon became synonymous with automobiles around the world, thanks to the Model T's popularity. In the far corners of the world, people knew the meaning of the name Ford.   Tom Myers

The Legendary Model T Ford | **107**

Men and women, families and businesses in nations around the world were able to travel as they never had before because of the Model T. Jerry Banks

One only has to examine the working world of 1900 to understand how far we've come. Workers in factories were paid little and had a limited view of the world around them. Hours were long and, before child labor laws were enacted, children joined men and women in toiling six days a week for 10 to 12 hours each day.

Conditions were dirty and dangerous. There was no worker's compensation for injuries either. Factories were quite noisy and factory hands were barely a step away from poverty.

Farm work also was hard, though farm ownership was a definite advantage over toiling for someone else in a factory. Both farms and ranches were subject to constant changes in weather and fluctuations in prices. Farm and ranch families faced distance and isolation. In parts of our nation, tenant farmers who rented their land often were mired in a vicious cycle of debt.

Having grown up on his father's farm, Henry Ford understood the need to find mechanical solutions to the grinding drudgery of some farm chores, especially those involving fieldwork. His earliest goal in life was to find an engine or a vehicle that would help farmers. It was a basic tenet that drove Ford long before he finished his Quadricycle in 1896.

The beginning of Model T production in September 1908 and their introduction to the public on October 1, 1908, may have seemed to be just another event. But the timing, the car and the thinking behind it were perfect for that moment in history. The Model T created a revolution in North America and around the world. It helped Henry Ford become a celebrity business owner, instantly recognizable even in the most remote corners of the globe.

In this chapter, we'll look at the ways the Model T influenced people in at least five general ways including their need for a car, the freedom it brought, the way it changed their lives, the way it changed their locales and the possibilities it offered.

Henry Ford's Model T also had several automotive industry-related effects that included freedom from patent restrictions, the $5 day, mass production, left-side driver controls, the establishment and control of dealerships with regular parts and service, aftermarket choices, a foreign production network, employment culture, unions, consumerism and effects on trucking, farming and the railroad industry.

There probably are more influences we haven't listed. Henry Ford started the car and the Model T took all of us for quite a journey!

Taking the Model T Revolution to the People

The Model T was designed to be a simple, practical, affordable and dependable car. The Ford team saw the possibility of making a car that they correctly thought would reach into an untapped market, even creating that market.

In 1903, when Ford Motor Company was incorporated, and even by 1908 when the first Model T was readied for the public, the automobile was not what we think of it today. Then it was more like a personal jet aircraft would be in our world—something expensive and out of reach for the average worker or farmer.

A man who would soon be President of the United States, Princeton University president Woodrow Wilson, a respected author in 1906, summed up the disgust many had for the early automotive culture with this remark:

"Nothing has spread socialistic feeling in this country more than the use of the automobile," wrote Wilson. "They are a picture of arrogance and wealth, with all its independence and carelessness." [1]

Henry Ford and his associates were working hard in 1906 to turn the prevailing viewpoint of the early automotive industry upside down, pushing aside the notion of making a profitable vehicle for the privileged few and putting their energies into an automobile that would be attainable and practical for the majority of working people. One of the basic concepts of the Model T was rooted in Ford's long-time goal of helping farmers with their chores.

"He planned to have a car whose engine was detachable so the farmer could use it to saw wood, pump water and run farm machinery." [2]

The Ford Model T was more than a machine that would take people from one place to another. It could traverse ruts and potholes, climb hills, cross rushing streams and barren arroyos, follow cow paths and more. For those people who were used to walking from place to place or riding a horse, the Model T was a practical and tough asset.

"These were the conditions for which the Model T was designed, and which it triumphantly overcame with its wobbly, almost double-jointed wheels." [3]

Of course, converting the average person from someone who rode a horse, used a horse-drawn wagon or buggy, or rode a train or trolley did take a short time of seeing and

The Model T brought people together, especially in rural areas. The car often changed their lives and brought them out of isolation.   Robin Heil-Kern

demonstrating the car, but when people were able to drive the Model T, they quickly became believers. The Model T was a simple machine.

And the Ford Motor Company as well as Henry Ford were soon noticed and appreciated for their understanding of what life was like in the real world. One example came in a letter from the wife of a Georgia farmer.

"You know, Henry, your car lifted us out of the mud. It brought joy into our lives. We loved every rattle in its bones." 4

Model Ts were put to work on farms and in urban businesses. They pulled, moved and hauled goods and people. Some owners attached belts and various gadgets that were used to perform all kinds of tasks. Some even removed the front wheels, attached skis and slid over the snow. More and more attention was focused on the possibilities of the Model T and that meant more and more people wanted one.

Because people bought so many Model Ts and wanted to go places with them, the "car culture" was created and better roads were constructed. Many roads were paved for the first time. Robin Heil-Kern

The Model T was a car that made sense to people. One enterprising Iowa farmer calculated that the Model T was cheaper to operate over 1,000 miles than it was to buy a new pair of $10 shoes!

And the Model T supposedly cost just a penny per mile to operate. 5

South Dakota historian Reynold M. Vik recalled the many uses of the Model T on his family's farm.

"In the fields, the Model T pulled hay rakes, mowers, grain binders, harrows and hay loaders," said Vik and also added other chores. "Grinding grain, sawing wood, filling silos, churning butter, shearing sheep, pumping water, elevating grain, shelling corn, turning grindstones and washing clothes." 6

The Model T also brought something new to everyone who owned one. The Model T brought them freedom and possibilities. No longer did the farmer or rancher have to endure the isolation of his or her community. Neither did the small town person or city dweller have to depend on the schedules of a train or other public transport to go somewhere. Day or night, the Model T was available to go wherever it was driven.

"Henry's wonderful Model T was the right car, at the right time, at the right place, at the right price. It provided dependable, fast, economical transportation to a country that was limited in progress because of the dependence upon the horse and buggy," said Mrs. Harry (Emma) Wright, who owned a Model T with her brother Arlen in 1914.

"Until the Ford came along, going to town shopping was not something we did on the spur of the moment. It was an all day event." 7

The Model Ts began to pop up everywhere—from quiet streets to country lanes. Town squares that had recently held horse troughs and shade trees were overtaken by the growing numbers of automobiles, dominated by the Ford Model Ts.

In 21st century terms, it's as if the early IBM computers with their punch card access and jumbo, room-filling sizes suddenly were offered in PC or laptop form and went from the

With the coming of the Model T, people were able to go places more conveniently than they had been able to travel with horses. Their horizons expanded—and Model Ts filled the horizon!
Robin Heil-Kern

outrageously complex to convenient, adaptable simplicity.

The mere ability to go somewhere whenever a person made the decision seemed to fit the popular views of democracy. It was as if the Model T had been extended to them through the Bill of Rights in the United States or the Articles of Confederation in Canada.

"…[the Model T] brought about a revolution…defining the automobile in a practical sense as an efficient and economical means of transport. It must be viewed, historically, as the most important car ever built. It remains the most endearing." [8]

From place to place in North America, then from nation to nation, automobiles, led by the Model T, got people moving. Once they moved, they enjoyed the freedom of traveling when they chose to do so.

Historian Kimes says one example of the Model T's impact was an aging man who thought he'd travel west to die. But he wrote to Henry Ford that when he got behind the wheel of a Model T for a few days, he felt so good his health improved. [9] That was the kind of effect the little Ford had on society.

The Model T appealed to women as well. It was smaller and simpler to operate than many cars and there was nothing complex about it under the hood or behind the wheel. In Canada, the Model T was said to be as easy to operate as the kitchen stove. Ford Motor Company even published a brochure called "The Woman and The Ford."

"It has broadened her horizon, increased her pleasures, given new vigor to her neighbors and faraway friends, and multiplied tremendously her range of activity. It is a real

FORD of CANADA

The fourth Ford car ever made was sold in Canada. Ford of Canada was a strong partner for the Ford Motor Co. and exported many cars, including the Model T, throughout the world.

weapon in the changing order. More than any other—the Ford is a woman's car." 10

Henry Ford's great granddaughters, Anne and Charlotte, did a great deal of research and reported that women, teens and even pre-teens quickly learned to crank the Model T. A 1909 article by Jean Lorimer suggested that any woman could quickly learn the knack of cranking the Model T suggesting it was "...a knack rather than a matter of strength." 11

As early as 1913, the *Ford Times* related the story of writer Helen Gaut who set out from her Pasadena, California, home on a trip to Coachella, Arizona in a 1911 Model T Torpedo roadster. Pictured without a windshield but with its top up to protect her from the sun and both an aftermarket trunk and optional spare tire mounted in back, the story noted that her journey often took her through sand up to the car's

axles and over rock and boulder-strewn trails. 12

In the 1920s, when Ford Motor Company resumed national advertising for the Model T, one series of ads featured color photos of women in various occupations who were driving a number of cars. One memorable ad showed a young woman in boots and pants exploring nature with the headline: "Freedom for the Woman Who Owns a Ford" and the ad's copy promised: "Where a narrow lane invites or a steep hill promises a surprise beyond, Ford will take you there and back in comfort, trouble-free."

Mrs. Emma Wright was a young woman when the Model T was gaining its reputation in places like her home region of rural Ohio. She was thrilled by the choices it offered her and her brother Arlen and they soon convinced their father to join them in buying one.

"We talked about the places we could go, the things we

could do, the fun we could have, if only we owned a Model T Ford," she recalled. "No other car even entered our minds. We made sure our father heard all the good things about owning one." 13

Everyone appreciated the affordability of the Model T. When the car was introduced in 1909, the touring car and runabout were priced at $850 and $825, respectively, in an era when many cars were double and triple that amount. By 1914, the similar touring and runabout versions of the Model T were just $490 and $440. Putting a dependable car in the price range of the average working family or farm family was a major step in putting North America on wheels.

"Some of the owners of more expensive cars kind of looked down their noses at the Model T because their car cost more," said Mrs. Wright. "We were equally proud that our car ran just as good or better and cost less." 14

The Ford Motor Company continued to find ways to get their Model T to the customers. In 1914, when sales began to lag, a creative plan was originated to offer rebates and a price reduction if Ford sold more than 300,000 Model Ts by Aug. 1, 1915.

While some, including the *New York Times*, questioned the timing of the unprecedented offer because World War I had begun in Europe, others praised the idea, especially when the company reached the sales goal and began to send what Ford called "profit-sharing" checks out at $50 each.

"Checks totaling $15,410,650 thus were mailed into virtually every American hamlet, town and city during the next few months," said *Ford Life* in 1973. 15

A letter sent to a man who bought a Model T during this time talked about the profit sharing and also asked Ford owners to help the company with referrals.

"It will be our pleasure some time in August 1915 to redeem the Profit-sharing Rider with our check from $40 to $60, if we sell at retail 300,000 new Fords. You are now the owner of a Ford car, and we are certain it will deliver all your expectations. We speak confidently, because more than 750,000 owners of Ford cars have told us about their own experiences. With your purchase of a Ford car, you become 'one of us,' with every reason to expect a share from the profits of the Company. Yours for the 300,000 and profit-sharing. Ford Motor Company, Sales Department"

Ford Motor Company moved excess stock during a slow period and customers not only received a discount on their car but money back in return. It was another reason they enjoyed owning a Model T.

While Ford never repeated the rebate plan during Henry Ford's lifetime, the company introduced what was called the "Ford Weekly Purchase Plan" in the 1920s. Prospective Model T buyers could deposit $5 per week toward buying the Model T of their choice. It reflected Henry Ford's personal distaste for credit but allowed the company to encourage a version of installment buying.

As people continued to enjoy the freedom the cars brought them, the mushrooming numbers of cars, especially the Model T and the desire to drive them, changed the way North Americans thought of the world around them. They no longer were satisfied with a slower pace of life nor were they prepared to stay put.

Almost immediately, Model T owners explored their neighborhoods, their townships and other portions of the world around them. Ford Motor Company continued to emphasize that advantage in its literature and publications as the "Sunday drive" became a popular part of life. People began to make traveling and exploring part of their leisure time. Such journeys were described and pictured in the *Ford Times*, such as the travels of Ford Motor Company employee E. Roger Stearns who explored some rugged portions of California in 1913.

"...the Model T handled the tricky mountain roads, rocky canyons, and abundant sand without a single hitch." 16

Of course, the more they traveled, the more drivers and passengers were no longer satisfied with roads—or the lack of them. That was fine when only horses were used but soon, automobile owners demanded better roadwork. Roads were planned that had never existed before. Other roads were paved that had been rutted. Townships, counties and states looked for ways to build, maintain and improve their roads. City streets also were re-examined as automobiles became more common than horses and horse-pulled vehicles.

In 1919, ads written by Ford Motor Co. and intended for the local market, showed that they understood the car's impact on the nation, especially on the lives of people in rural areas.

"Out of the more than 3,000,000 Ford cars now in use, about sixty percent have been sold to farmers. Probably no other one thing has brought to the farm so much of comfort and profit as has the Ford car. It has...doubled the facilities for marketing, brought the town next door to the farm, multiplied for the farmer the pleasures of living..." 17

And at least 15 to 20 years before the term was used in Germany, Ford Motor Co. offered a moniker for the Model T.

"The Ford car will be called the 'people's car.' The Ford car [is] so easy to understand, so simple in construction that anybody and everybody can safely drive it. It is everybody's necessity because it doubles the value of time, and is the quick, convenient, comfortable and economical method of transportation." 18

There was something about owning and driving a Model T that brought people together. At first it was probably the common bond of auto owners versus horse owners. But, especially in rural areas, people began to view the Model T as a practical, vital part of bringing them together for church services, picnics, baseball games and meetings. Families could more easily get together to celebrate after chores. Families could go shopping and still get work done. The Model T had, according to the *Ford Times*, "...remodeled the social life of the country." 19

The Model T standardized left-side placement of driver controls in North America and elsewhere but this 1914 Model T shows the ancient right-hand-drive carriage tradition was kept in England.

Taking the Model T Revolution to the World

The Model T Ford was popular and helped change the lives of everyone the car touched. It not only gave people of average income a chance to own a car, it offered them a new way of life. Those changes were multiplied in the tens of thousands, and eventually the millions, in communities across the United States and Canada.

The concepts behind the Model T, their production, marketing, sales and export, the sub industries that supported them, the culture of the automotive industry and the place of the automobile in the world all would be influenced by the coming of the Model Ts.

There were many ways that the Model T brought new thinking to the automotive world. One was quite simple, but no less influential. Early automobiles had been built with right-side driving controls, a vestige of the British tradition of carriages and wagons driving in the left lane so the drivers could shake hands (or in ancient days, draw their swords!)

Driving in the left lane with driving controls on the right side continued in Great Britain, Ireland, various British Colonies and in nations that had opposed Napoleon, like Austria. But in the early American Colonies, teamsters had started the practice of riding the left rear pulling horse, leaving their right hand as their whip hand.

Americans grew to prefer driving in the right lane and having traffic pass on the left. That right lane driving tradition remained, but was awkward with driving controls on the right side. The sheer numbers of Model Ts with left-side controls led the way for making all vehicles that way in North America. Traffic patterns followed suit in the United States and Canada.

The increased demands for Ford Model Ts meant a sea change in the way cars were produced. George Dickert, an early supervisor at Ford of Canada, described for the Ford Archives the older style of making cars that had come from carriage making.

"When we received an order for a car, the first step was to place a frame on two horses. Then you would put your

Motor Block Test

The Ford Motor Co. planned volume production and scaled costs low enough to make a profit and constantly lower the prices of the Model T—a winning formula.

front axle on, then your motor and dashboards and body. We assembled everything right on these horses. We would take these horses out, put the car on the floor, and push it away." [20]

Early assembly line techniques weren't a lot different when the new Model T manufacturing facilities began operation at the Highland Park plant in Detroit. That would soon change but older methods still were used, according to William C. Klann, a veteran Ford employee.

"When we first moved to Highland Park, they assembled the chassis along Woodward Avenue, on the first floor of the A building. They laid the frame on two horses and they assembled the front and the rear axle. Then they would tip it over and put on the four wheels. You pushed it along by hand—it wasn't a conveyor-type thing at all." [21]

Klann also recalled that engines came from building B at Highland Park and were hoisted into place, followed by the radiator, tie rods, steering column and crank.

"You would drive it out there right straight onto John R. Street and Frank Hadas tested...every one of those cars. They put the body on after they tested it." [22]

Henry Ford was convinced there was a better way and had given a great deal of thought to cutting down the time needed to assemble both the final car and the various components that formed the cars. Early in the Model T's

An Assembly Line
- of the
ord Motor Company

Ford Motor Co. workers were the talk of the world when the success of the Model T influenced the company to offer the $5-per-day wage structure. Tom Myers

production, Ford Motor Company hired Frederick "Speedy" Taylor, well known for his industrial time and motion studies.

Intensive studies were done in 1913 on timing the assembly of 100 cars. They began with a figure of 12.5 man hours per chassis, considered a good average in those times. Then the chassis were hooked together forming a continuous, moving assembly line, powered by a motor. That step lowered assembly time down to just under six hours. Refinements and more study continued to bring the times down, first to two hours and 8 minutes, then one hour and 34 minutes. [23]

Assembly time was reduced, short cuts were prepared and time was taken out of the processes, all with a "time is money" manner of thinking. Early assembly areas at the Piquette plant, then later at the new Highland Park facilities, strove for minimal worker movement and maximum component movement. Henry Ford's concept of specialization was increasingly being applied to making cars, as he described.

"The man who places a part does not fasten it. The man who puts in a bolt does not put on the nut; the man who puts on the nut does not tighten it." [24]

Eventually, methods from other businesses, like the

meat packing plant processing lines that had begun during the Civil War, were adapted to making cars. Parts and sub assemblies moved along belts, conveyors and various lines merging where they were needed, from beginning to final car. It was all designed to reduce the time and money needed to produce each car, the cost per unit.

"Save 10 steps a day for each of 12,000 employees and you will have saved 50 miles of wasted motion and misspent energy," Ford claimed. [25]

Model T production had increased from 1911 through 1913. And it continued to rise. In 1914, more than 202,000 Model Ts were made and in 1915, that total rose to more than 308,000 Model Ts assembled. It was the beginning of a new way of making a product, with many people repeating tasks at their stations along the way, each adding something to the moving units that would become a car. The speed and capacity of the operation influenced a new term, something the experts called "mass production."

Of course, profit was the ultimate motive, yet the Ford Motor Company looked at profit from a different angle. Other carmakers simply charged as much as the market would bear but since everyone was doing the same thing, there was a limited marketplace.

The new concept, especially associated with the Model T, was to decrease the price as much as possible to make the car as affordable to many people as they could, a concept described by Henry Ford.

"I hold that it is better to sell a large number of cars at a reasonably small margin than to sell fewer cars at a large margin of profit," Ford explained. "It enables a larger number of people to buy and enjoy the use of a car and because it gives a larger number of men employment at good wages." [26]

People who'd never thought of having more than horses or mules now leapt into the world of automobiles. And that demand continued to be stirred with the consistent lowering of prices.

"Every time I reduce the price of a car by one dollar, I get one thousand new buyers," claimed Henry Ford. [27]

The Ford Motor Company's profit structure continued to increase as buyers swept up the Model Ts. In 1909, it was estimated that the new Model T enabled Ford to dent the automotive market with a 9.4 percent share and made a $2 million profit with a $220 cost per car. By 1914, that cost per car was cut to just $99.34, profits had skyrocketed and the market share for Ford had mushroomed to 48 percent. [28]

Early on, Ford Motor Company had made two decisions. They would set up and control their own network of official Ford dealerships and they would take on the restrictive Selden patent that required automakers to pay an organization fees in order to make their cars. Each step was a marked change in the auto industry.

Taking on the Selden patent holders in the early years of the Ford Motor Company could have meant corporate suicide with restrictive payments and penalties had they lost. A long court battle ended on September 15, 1909, great timing for the auto industry, especially the Model T. Because of winning their legal battle, Ford Motor Company and Henry Ford were praised and respected by both the public and other automakers that no longer had to pay the Association of License Automobile Manufacturers, the establishment and keepers of the Selden interests. [29]

The systematic structuring of dealerships across North America also meant a consistent quality of service and parts availability. Cars had been sold in a rather haphazard manner with dealers going in and out of the business of selling certain brands. For the public, it meant a degree of confidence and reliability in the Ford brand wherever they were. Other carmakers noticed and set up their dealers in a similar fashion or found ways to improve on the Ford lead.

As demand for the Model T increased, Ford Motor Company found it needed more workers to fill their production needs. Lower prices and the popularity of the Model T continued to spur demand.

Yet working in the Ford plant was tough and workers found it was hard to stay with the incessant demands and repetitious work of the assembly areas, especially as Ford

Motor Assembly

Ford plants quickly gained a reputation for their organization, brightness and cleanliness.

Motor Company continued to experiment with processes along the line. At one point, there was a 380 percent turnover that meant it took 963 workers to fill 100 stable producers in the Ford plant. 30

As soon as Ford and his associates had understood the profits they were making and made plans about how they would assemble their cars, the next step was to stabilize the costly worker turnover rate. The company's solution was a bold step. Top wages at that time rose to $2.50 per day for skilled autoworkers. Ford Motor Company sent a resounding clap of thunder to all industries in 1914 when they decided to double that top rate and offer the $5 workday.

Ford and his top associates also decided to reduce the working day to eight hours, from 10, and to add a third shift to their plant. All were new standards for the auto industry and for the business community in general.

There had been troubles and restlessness at other plants and Ford had witnessed men fighting in his own plant. Now he thought he would be able to contain that restlessness by

showing his work force how he could share the profits from their hard work.

The Ford Motor Company was saluted by many who praised the higher rate of pay, for those qualified to earn it, but also was condemned by some business leaders who thought Ford was setting a terrible precedent for worker expectations. An internal Ford calculation at that time showed they could have increased wages to as much as $20 per day under their profit structure. 31

"When you pay men well, you can talk to them," Ford explained about the higher wages. 32

Ford was buying a degree of loyalty and also worker stability as well as some additional control. His workers wouldn't be so compelled to rebel or strike. He thought the $5 per day wage and the steps it took to earn that wage would create groups of dedicated workers. And through Ford Motor Company's social and educational programs, they'd also become good citizens.

"..let me lay my hands on the most shiftless and worthless

A rare shot of the Seattle branch of Ford Motor Co. shows Model T assembly prior to the use of mass production techniques. Older carriage-making assembly styles dominated.

Final Assembly

Studies of several industries convinced Henry Ford and his associates that the moving assembly line would play a key role in limited wasted motion and increasing production.

fellow...and I'll bring him here, give him a job with a wage that offers some hope for the future...and I'll guarantee that I'll make a man out of him," Ford told the Rev. Samuel Marquis, head of the Ford Sociology Department. 33

In Canada, the Ford assembly plant near the Windsor neighborhood known as Walkerville, eventually called Ford City, would also increase wages, though at a lower rate. Yet Ford of Canada workers were enthusiastic about their company, according to veteran Neil Morrison.

"When Ford employees went downtown on Saturday nights, 'they wore their company identification badges proudly on the lapels of their best suits.' Men looked upon their association with the company as a distinction." 34

Ford Motor Company was able to lead the way early on with its $5-day wage structure. It did bring the company thousands of workers looking for a higher income. Grudgingly, other companies were forced to go along with the move and that meant life improved for many workers.

Yet all was not in harmony for long because even higher wages couldn't take away the grueling work required to make the wages. The reason so many had left the Ford assembly lines in the first place had its roots in the drudgery of assembly line work, some of the same reasons that drove Henry Ford away from farming as a young man. A letter from a worker's wife described the problem to Henry Ford soon after the $5-day was enacted. The letter was dated Jan. 23, 1914.

"The chain system you have is a slave driver! My God, Mr. Ford! My husband has come home and thrown himself down and won't eat his supper—so done out! That $5 a day is a blessing—a bigger one than you know—but, oh, they earn it." [35]

Later, a song about assembly line work was quoted by labor organizer Walter Reuther, "You Gotta Fight That Line," by Joe Glazer. The song ended this way:

"Foreman told me the day I was hired, 'You miss one door, Mr. Jones—you're fired.' I slapped those doors on, always on the run, every 14 seconds, never missed a one. And I staggered home from work each night, still slappin' 'em on—front door right." [36]

It was quite a difference from the joyful songs that people sang about the Model T or the humor they used to praise the cars. Assembly line work and the demands it placed on workers would increasingly lead to dissatisfaction, especially when combined with internal Ford practices that gave overwhelming power to foremen and others.

While the Ford production facilities were known for their brightness and cleanliness and also had good safety records, the pressure to produce wore men down over months and years and created a new sense of tension, the constant feeling that people's jobs were threatened.

"Ford was no fun. The place had a tautness about it. Whether you worked in management or whether you worked

One Model T that Ford Motor Co. decided to make was the roadster-based pickup, due to public demand. Think of this 1927 roadster pickup as your grandfather's Ford Ranchero! Mike Mueller

In Canada and the United States, Ford Motor Co.-produced films were popular attractions. Some showed factory assembly. Others were travel films. The finished films often drew crowds.

Shipping Platforms

In an effort to save costs, Ford officials found that more Model Ts could be shipped per box car if bodies and fenders were separated from the chassis. Everything had a stacking procedure.

First Ford English Class

Many Ford Motor Co. workers were immigrants who could speak no English. Others had little formal education. Language classes were required in order to receive the $5-per-day wage.

Part of New Six-Story Building—Showing the Body Chute

The body chute at the Highland Park plant was the final assembly point for Model Ts and became a symbol to many of mass production. Here bodies met the assembled chassis.

Assembling Ford Animated Weekly Motion Picture Films

A rare shot of the Ford Animated Weekly post production and editing crew at work. Note the large barrels and editing stations. Some film didn't make "the cut."

on the line, you could never be sure of anything. Henry liked to boast that he kept executives around him perpetually off balance, and this spirit seeped right down to the factory floor." 37

Charles A. Madison was a line worker from the Dodge Brothers plant who tried to work at Ford for the higher $5 wage, then returned to Dodge for a $3-per-day wage, and wrote that he resented the Ford assembly line methods.

"...the firm exploited its employees more ruthlessly... dominating their lives in ways that deprived them of privacy and individuality..." 38

Along with the promise of the $5-per-day carrot was the stick of the Ford Motor Company's Sociology Department. They carried out the demands from Henry Ford himself that workers uphold strict standards. For example Henry Ford never liked boarding houses and believed the family home was the most stable place for a Ford worker. He disliked smoking and drinking, among other vices. Those who expected the $5 per day wage came under the scrutiny of the Sociology Department at work and in home inspections.

Photos in the 1915 booklet "Factory Facts from Ford" showed before and after images of a family kitchen. The cluttered room was a real mess in the first photo but neat and orderly in the second with dishes sorted in a corner cupboard as well as curtains on the windows, a clean sink

and a spotless tablecloth on the dining table.

In the past, other companies had expectations and controls over employees in company-supplied housing. Ford Motor Company let workers have some degree of independence, yet looked over their shoulders in terms of their personal habits. There were good elements in this company attitude in addition to what we might consider an invasion of family privacy.

Since many Ford Motor Company workers were immigrants and did not speak English, the Ford Sociology Department took steps to help workers and their families take classes, including English, if it was deemed necessary.

A photo in a 1915 Ford Motor Company booklet shows row upon row of what must be over 1,000 workers seated at tables with tutors standing at blackboards outside the plant. The booklet mentioned 2,500 workers enrolled in English classes under the guidance of 150 teachers.

Another image shows Ford workers seated rather uncomfortably in a classroom with the teacher holding up a tea kettle. Lessons included the English language phrases: "I get up from the table" and "I clean my overcoat with a hand broom."

There was other advice for those who were determined to earn the $5 daily wage that was offered by the company's Sociology Department.

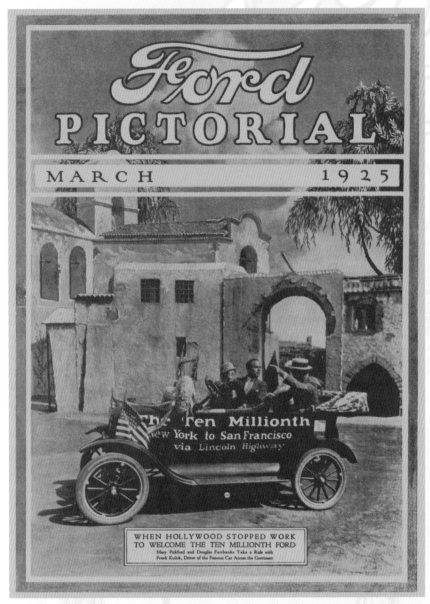

The Ford Pictorial was one of the many ways the company communicated to the public. This printed publication was available in 1925.

The Model T was produced in England, and at one point in Cork, Ireland. British assembly was done at Manchester, then at Dagenham, England. Andrew Morland

"Employees should use plenty of soap and water in the home, and upon the children, bathing frequently. Nothing makes for right living and health so much as cleanliness." [39]

Ford Motor Company set up the $5-per-day wage rate in a manner it called the "Profit Sharing Plan." The $5-per-day wage, for example, was determined by a basic wage of 34 cents per hour plus a 28.5-cent profit sharing addition for a total wage of 62.5 cents an hour. Based on the eight-hour day and what the company called "...a voluntary increase of from 15 percent to 20 percent in production," workers could make as much as $6.25 per day, if they qualified.

1915 FORD WAGE SCALE			
Wage per hour	Profit Sharing	Total per hour	Total per day
.34	.28 ½	.62 ½	$5.00
.43	.25 ¾	.68 ¾	$5.50
.61	.17 1/8	.78 1/8	$6.25

Source: Factory Facts from Ford, 1915

There also was a probationary system that was enforced if a Ford Sociology Dept. official considered the worker unworthy of earning the full $5-per-day wage. In those cases, a portion of the worker's wages was withheld until the deficiency was cleared up and the worker met the standards. The Ford Sociology Dept. looked at marital status, the number and ages of the worker's children, the person's nationality as well as religion and church attendance, the family savings account, debts, cleanliness and any use of alcohol or boarders in the home.

If workers were put on probation at Ford, a sliding scale was used to leverage their progress toward meeting the company standards based on the time it took them to get into compliance.

NUMBER OF DAYS	WAGES REPAID
30 days	All
60 days	75%
90 days	60%
5 months	25%
6 months	Termination

Automotive News, June 16, 2003

1,000 Assembled Chassis—In 1913, this was a Record Daily Output. Since then Ford Production has Mounted as High as 2768 Cars in a Single Day

In 1913, Ford Motor Co. employees made a record 2,768 cars in one day—a record that dazzled the auto industry and showed off mass production.

Over a period of months, the $5 wage and accompanying policies cut down on worker turnover and helped stabilize the Ford work force and within two years, 90 percent of the Ford Motor Company workers still remaining were able to earn the full $5 wage package. [40]

The company hired physically challenged workers and minorities in its assembly plants, including African-Americans. Both were controversial moves at the time but proved to be trendsetting choices. Women also were hired in more limited roles and did not receive the wage advantages that men could get, especially when the $5-day was introduced.

Women worked in such areas as top making, sewing upholstery and assembling magnetos. Their 44-hour work was done on the 7:30 a.m. to 4:45 p.m. first shift with full days on Monday through Friday and a half-day on Saturday. At least in the early years at Highland Park, men and women worked separately, though there is evidence this changed after World War I. The minimum wage for women workers began at 32 cents an hour. [41]

The Ford Motor Company earned a sterling reputation for plant facilities, such as their bright, campus-like Highland Park complex, the first plant designed from the ground up for auto production and not adapted from some other form of manufacturing.

The Ford Highland Park facilities also were displayed in "Factory Facts from Ford." All areas of the factory, from forge areas to assembly and offices were pictured as orderly and clean as possible.

The positive side of the $5-per-hour wage was the beginning of the middle class lifestyle in the United States and elsewhere. Working families that made enough money were able to elevate their lives from a subsistence existence to attain personal dreams such as saving, owning their first car, purchasing a home and perhaps even setting aside some money for a college education for their children.

It did come with a painful price. The early positive records of production increases and satisfaction with the

LEFT: *Ford Motor Co. used both assembly-only plants as well as regional full production plants in many countries. This 1919 Model T was produced at the French plant, near Paris.   Andrew Morland*

ABOVE: *By the time Model T production ended in 1927, the popular cars literally were everywhere. People around the world recognized them and millions of people drove them.   Robin Heil-Kern*

higher wages turned into a long journey toward the end of Model T production.

"...in the early days at Highland Park, with production records getting broken and new techniques being discovered, there seems to have been a genuine excitement. As he had cut the price of the Model T in his desperate attempt to prove that the vehicle was not behind the times, the only area for economy had been in 'speed-up'—more cars per man hour." [42]

Increasing pressure, lack of toleration for union organizing and other pressures unique to Ford production methods would eventually lead to beatings, bloodshed and worker versus management entrenchment at Ford Motor Company, many years after the Model T, but this was also an outgrowth of the Model T period. Henry Ford, who detested organized labor, would fight against it for about two decades at his plant, until the latter part of the 1930s.

"I don't know anything about organized labor," said Ford before the U. S. House of Representatives Commission on Industrial Relations in 1915. "We have never had any of it, to my knowledge, around our place." [43]

Yet for Ford and other automakers, the labor and management struggle that would begin to heat up in

the Model T era and would boil over in the 1930s would eventually bring a new era. Labor peace that came from the hard times gave the North American auto industry a new direction that became even stronger with a more equal understanding between employers and workers. That labor-management cooperation became a model around the world, another journey that began with the revolution in society created by the advent of the Model T.

The large numbers of Model Ts sold and their uniqueness in the automotive marketplace also led to another business revolution. Suppliers, wholesalers and inventors soon found ways to sell products that enhanced or supported the Model T with any number of products.

While this automotive aftermarket had existed before the Model T, the number of Fords sold made many businesses worthwhile and some of the unique aspects of the Ts made new products possible. It was a small business revolution, again spurred on by the Model T Ford. Details of this phenomenon, including some of the unique and memorable products, will be discussed in Chapter 7.

Exporting the Model Ts was another way that Ford Motor Co. influenced the world, sending Model Ts to at least five continents. It was a short but rich history from the founding of the company in 1903 to the final production of the Model T in 1927.

By then, Ford Motor Company and the Model T were players in every corner of the world. History tells us the sixth Ford Model A made in 1903 was sold to a Canadian owner and in 1904, Ford Motor Company reached an agreement to begin making Fords at the former Walkerville Wagon Works, across the river from Detroit at Windsor, Ontario. That arrangement quickly grew into Ford Motor Company of Canada.

Ford of Canada began shipping cars to Calcutta, India and to New Zealand in 1905. The next year, Fords from Windsor were sent to Egypt and the Natal Province of today's South Africa as well as India. And cars also went to Australia, a continent that became a fertile new ground for Ford sales. [44]

Also in 1904, Ford Motor Co. in Detroit organized sales in England and by 1907 had dealers in France, Germany, Belgium, Holland, Spain, Sweden and other European countries as well as contacts with Russia. In just a few short years, Ford's Model T would be a best seller in England and Ford Motor Co. soon was the first auto company with direct sales to South America from Buenos Aires, Argentina. Soon the success of the Model T would foster an assembly plant in Argentina, then assembly plants in both Asia and Africa. [45]

Ford Life reported that 500,000 Model Ts were on the road around the world midway through 1914. Henry Ford went against the prevailing views of the nation once again, at a time when automotive tariffs were 45 percent in the United States. Ford saw plenty of room around the world to sell more cars.

"I don't know what a tariff means except that it means giving one crowd an advantage over another," Ford said. "Free trade is competition and nothing can get large enough if you don't have competition." [46]

Ford Motor Co. in Detroit and Ford of Canada continued to find ways to sell, send, assemble or manufacture Model Ts around the world. By the 1920s, Ford displayed its worldwide sales and assembly operations like a giant oak tree with many branches.

Model T assembly factories, and in some cases full Ford manufacturing facilities, began during the Model T years in these countries beyond North America and England: Argentina, Australia, Belgium, Brazil, Chile, Denmark, France, India, Ireland, Italy, Malaya, Mexico, South Africa, Spain and Uruguay. Ford branch offices also were found in countries like China, Cuba, Egypt, Holland, Japan, Peru, Turkey, Uruguay and Venezuela during the Model T era. [47]

Ford Motor Co. and Ford of Canada overcame a number of problems that included distance and geography in order to have fully equipped dealership in Padang, Sumatra or to deliver a new Model T across the Gobi Desert in China. Wherever they were sold, Model Ts became part of their new homes.

"For Ford, the greatest obstacles occurred in the Australian market where shipping difficulties, chassis-only

While the Model T was the "Universal car," there were some regional nuances, thanks to some factory differences and regional body makers. This 1924 Model T is an example of variation.   Andrew Morland

exports and declining market share continued to burden Ford Canada. Model Ts, nonetheless, remained the leading automobile import into Australia." [48]

The overwhelming success of the Model T in North America, Europe and around the world made both the car and Henry Ford instantly recognizable. Ford became one of the first business personalities and it often meant he was quoted on any number of subjects or was the focus of writers, politicians and stars of the day, including actor, comedian and writer, Will Rogers.

"It will take a hundred years to tell whether he helped us or hurt us, but he certainly didn't leave us where he found us," Rogers quipped about Henry Ford.

Ford's viewpoints were well known about the Model T and auto production inside of Ford Motor Company. And his personal viewpoint was made public in statements in his newspaper, the Dearborn *Independent*. Those views, such as his feelings about Jews, diet, large financial institutions and more, ran the gamut of totally abhorrent to incredibly odd. Yet many considered Henry Ford a folk hero, especially during the Model T era.

In an interview with famed columnist Drew Pearson in 1924, Ford predicted that cities were out of date and that there would have to be a balance between small villages and cities to keep industries going.

"Instead of having the men come to the city, we take the work out to him in the country," said Ford. "Improved transportation methods have made that possible and the

This dramatic image shows how poor roads and bridges were during the Model T era. The car was designed to cope with conditions like this couple was facing.   Tom Myers

process will become steadily more feasible as transportation facilities grow." [49]

Ford's idea was a network of small specialty factories that fed the main Highland Park facility. Examples were at an old mill at Nankin as well as operations at Plymouth, Northville and Flat Rock. The Nankin facility, for example, offered work on Ford engraving projects through World War II.

When Henry Ford absorbed more and more control and influence of his automaking operation, and suffered with the occasional misstep as well as the overwhelmingly successful moves both he and the company made, other automakers were watching.

Under Alfred Sloan's leadership, General Motors became many things that Ford Motor Co. was not including a company that was organized along specific corporate lines and definitely was not personality driven. Sloan, in fact, always referred to any decision he or others made using "GM did such and such." He was intentionally reclusive in terms of personal publicity and very much the opposite of Ford both in personality and the way he operated the company. [50]

Ford Motor Co. was masterful with its public statements, doing much to help craft the modern, well-oiled media and public relations examples that have been followed by other companies. Having someone as popular and prolific as Henry Ford helped as did the popular culture that the Model T engendered.

And when it chose to do so, Ford Motor Co. offered strong advertising campaigns through such popular magazines as the *Saturday Evening Post* where the Model T debuted in October 1908 and brought a clamor for the car. Ads were published regionally or in local newspapers during the years when there were no national advertising campaigns placed by Ford.

Several newspaper ads found in research for this book from the late 1910s told potential customers to "Place Your Order Today" in order to avoid higher prices. Another ad simply listed the six-digit number "320,817." It was the number of Model Ts delivered for sale by Ford since Aug. 1, 1916.

And through local dealers, Ford continued to announce itself as the "people's car" in 1919, a car for farmers that same year and "the family car of class and comfort" in the early 1920s.

Ford's reputation and the popularity of both the Model T and Henry Ford meant there was no national advertising in the United States after 1914, but Ford of Canada continued such advertising and Ford Motor Company advertised in local newspapers and created some media of its own including lantern slides for movies and the ongoing publication *Ford Times*, a publication that was distributed for free to both dealers and owners. Ford also promoted itself and its cars in *Ford Pictorial* beginning in 1925.

Both in Canada and the United States, the popularity of the Model T meant Ford-produced films could be "boffo box office" in some communities.

In 1914, Ford Motor Company established a motion picture department and began releasing one-reeler films under the title "Ford Educational Weekly." While they definitely had an advertising content, the Ford films could draw audiences.

"...the films cost the cinema proprietors nothing; the advertising value for Ford was immense. Audiences were thrilled by films depicting the 'final assembly of a thousand Ford cars in a single day in the Detroit plant and also the making of a Ford piston.'" [51]

In Canada, dealers advertised the Ford films with signs and gave away tickets. They sometimes paraded Model Ts up and down the street. "Ford Nights" were offered in small towns across the Dominion. The films became a small part of the larger industry and were copied by others.

"Something New," for example, was a 1920 silent film witnessed by this author on a national cable TV channel. It was a remarkable tour de force with a cowboy and a Maxwell that was skillfully and slowly balanced on rocky terrain, straddled over arroyos and chasms, and doggedly driven over every kind of desert dry river bed and through sand in pursuit of bandits. Reportedly, the Maxwell went through three transmissions in its perilous journey, but none of that ever made the final movie cut!

Like the Model T, the Ford films were another step in unifying people across North America. Their impact preceded radio and television and they were enjoyed by thousands of viewers. In the United States, the films were called the "Ford Animated Weekly."

"The Ford films had a wide circulation, in theaters, clubs, church groups and industrial cafeterias and auditoriums. Their impact was the same as that of the Model T—reducing distances and class distinctions." [52]

In many places, Ford film crews were ambassadors of good will, filming events and places that people had heard about but hadn't seen. In Canada, the Department of Trade and Commerce saw the Ford films and others that railroads had made and decided to also circulate the films.

In addition to being a unifying factor, through travel and through such mediums as print and films, the Model T Ford also promoted a sense of consumerism. Americans and the people of other countries who had to watch every penny now got some pleasure from finding the money to spend on a Ford Model T.

They began to look at the world around them and realized there were other conveniences that could help improve their lives. It was another unifying force that spurred economies in North America and other nations where the little Fords rolled in. Spending down savings and buying on time for a purpose, such as owning a car or an appliance, became increasingly popular throughout the lifetime of the Model T Ford.

North America enjoyed more freedom after World War I that meant more choices in the marketplace because of such influences as mass production and the good feelings encouraged by advertising. Cereals, toothpaste and cleaner bathrooms all were presented as symbols of a better life. Mainstream society saw spending on new goods as a desire for security and contentment while at the same time, the pleasure seekers of the Gatsby Era were running all out in life.

These also were times when movies and the telephone, invented earlier, became more popular and commonplace. More areas of the country had electricity and were soon tuning into the widely popular phenomenon of radio. All of these factors contributed to people loosening their wallets and spending their money much more freely than in the past.

The Model T influence spread to all forms of transportation. In addition to influencing the importance of the car for mass audiences, the practicality of the Model T encouraged many owners to modify it to adapt to their needs.

Soon the Ts were being transformed into light-duty hauling tasks in construction, delivery, utility, farming, sales and an array of commercial uses. Ford Motor Co. discouraged modification of its cars early on but the availability of its chassis-only versions of the Model T as well as the resourcefulness and creativity of owners produced a number of interesting body styles. Aftermarket body companies also added memorable and creative editions of the Model T.

It wasn't until 1924, probably after thousands had done so with their own resources, that Ford Motor Co. finally worked on the "pick up body" that could be switched with the roadster's turtle deck. The new steel box attachment appeared in 1925, and one might consider it the Model T version of the famed Ford Ranchero. [53]

The Model T became a common sight on farms and ranches throughout North America. Incredibly adaptable, the Model T could actually be used for farm tasks, especially with a conveyor belt added to a rear wheel. The Model T also could take on just about every kind of rough road or geography that rural life could offer.

While some owners had to be broken of their horse riding habits as they learned to drive the Model T, they quickly adapted and found the Model T a trusted resource.

Indirectly, the Model T also influenced other forms of transportation. While railroads had a monopoly over transportation of people, freight and farm goods late in the

19th century, the availability of affordable cars like the Model T meant railroads no longer had a firm hold on the public. People were beginning to enjoy having transportation choices.

Some people also found that their Model Ts could travel well on train tracks with their road wheels and tires removed and with metal wheels added to roll along the rails.

The airplane came into its own almost on the same timeline as the automobile in the early 20th century and Ford Motor Co. looked to the sky with pleasure once they could devote time and resources to get involved.

In 1925, Ford bought the Stout Metal Aircraft Company and began making a single-engine transport plane. Ford also formed an arm called Air Transport Service. One memorable Model T truck was made of a shiny alloy metal called Monel and was used as the Air Transport Service ground vehicle. The next year, an early version of the Ford Tri-Motor was made with an open cockpit and a closed cabin with room for eight passengers. [54]

Famed flyer Charles Lindbergh also had a tie to the Model T. He learned to drive one as a boy in Minnesota and said the family called their car "Maria." [55]

Following its introduction in the fall of 1908, the Model T led the world on a journey of discovery and self-confidence. People began to realize a great deal more about the world around them and their own potential in it. The Model T truly became its advertising nickname, the Universal Car, circling the globe and influencing people. One might say the little Ford helped the world get rolling.

In 1918, President Woodrow Wilson, who had targeted the automobile as a symbol of wealth and arrogance earlier in his career, bought himself a Model T and was supportive of Henry Ford. Rich and poor, famous and obscure, men and women all over the world learned to respect the Model T.

And observations about the Model T ranged from the practical to the poetic.

"No automobile can ever take the place in the hearts of so many motorists that the Model T occupied for the nineteen years it was manufactured," noted Floyd Clymer. "...in the

generations to come, the legend of Henry Ford and his 'Tin Lizzie' will never die." [56]

"Freeing us all from the compulsions and contacts of the railway," wrote Edith Wharton, "the bondage to fixed hours and beaten track, the approach to each town through the area of ugliness created by a railway itself, it has given us back the wonder, the adventure and the novelty which enlivened the way of our posting grandparents." [57]

In its Oct. 18, 1924 issue, the *Wisconsin Agriculturist* published a study of its 3,866 members.

All of them subscribed to newspapers of some sort and all of them owned some type of car or truck. The reader could read the Model T influence between the lines.

"An automobile is no longer a luxury. There is an automobile for every home reported. In fact, the number of automobiles runs quite a little ahead of the number of [farm] homes, frequently showing a small car for strictly farm use and a more expensive one to be taken by the family when on pleasure bent." [58]

WISCONSIN AGRICULTURIST 1924 MEMBER SURVEY							
Item	Car or Truck	Newspaper	Telephone	Running Water	Electricity & Lights	Radio	Washing Machine
Members	3,866	3,866	3,427	1,069	1,191	247	1,158
Percent	100%	100%	89%	28%	64%	6 %	30%

Source: Wisconsin Agriculturist, Member survey, Oct. 18, 1924

On a warm summer day in 1917, Methodist minister Ernest Davidge bought a used Model T touring sedan from a garage at Gleichen, Alberta. Rev. Davidge and his wife reportedly took a week to appreciate the car.

" 'We practiced opening the doors and climbing into the seats and out again.' They soon summoned up the nerve to drive it, and the thrill '...opened up a whole new world with adventure, expense and novel situations...'" [59]

From 1908 through 1927, that scene was repeated at least 15 million times in 15 million different ways around the world. The "universal car" offered a universe of personal experiences. It was quite an adventure!

Chapter 6

DISSECTING THE MODEL T FORD

From 1908, when it was introduced, until the last cars rolled off the assembly line in 1927, there were some constants that stayed with the Model T Ford.

Among these were its four-cylinder engine, the planetary transmission, its vanadium steel frame, and its flywheel magneto.

The importance of good care and proper understanding of the cars meant many Model Ts offered years of good service.   *Robin Heil-Kern*

The Model T Ford could be considered a work of art, especially one in this condition, but it was also a practical vehicle that could adapt to many uses.
Robin Heil-Kern

Body styles would change. Accessories, when available from Ford, would come and go. While the touring body style probably is the most consistent over the lifetime of the Model T, the styles and trends of fashion dictated changes, or at least some cosmetic work to freshen the exterior styling of the cars.

Still it was the inner workings of the Model T that most reflected Henry Ford and the people who worked with him in the earliest days at the Piquette Avenue plant's "think tank," the third floor room that produced a car that was unlike anything ever produced before.

It was certainly reflective of Henry Ford—practical, down to earth and dependable. But it also was part of people like C. Harold Wills, Joseph Galamb, Charles Sorenson, Edward "Spider" Huff, Ed Ver Linden and others—the group that is referred to as the "Ford Motor Co. team" so often in this book.

CRESS FARM
HOME GROWN
PRODUCE

The Model T was popular around the world because it was so versatile and adaptable. It was put to many kinds of uses in North America and elsewhere. *Mike Mueller*

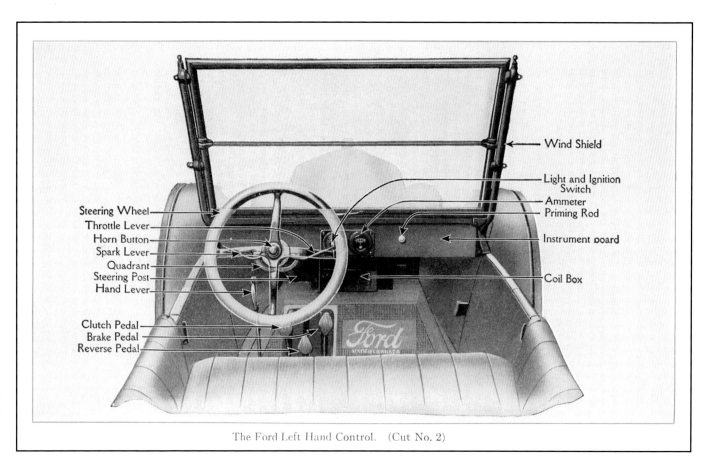

Steering Wheel
Throttle Lever
Horn Button
Spark Lever
Quadrant
Steering Post
Hand Lever

Clutch Pedal
Brake Pedal
Reverse Pedal

Wind Shield

Light and Ignition Switch
Ammeter
Priming Rod

Instrument board

Coil Box

The Ford Left Hand Control.   (Cut No. 2)

The Ford Manual took owners inside their cars and showed them how their cars functioned and what they needed to know. Don Chandler

They were a young, creative group and were concerned with innovation and pushing the concept of what an automobile could be. While the Model T was very progressive—with a fresh, wide-eyed look that said it was ready to explore the world—the Model T also was part of its times, an Edwardian era creation that was somewhat stiff and upright, as if still dressed in a starched collar.

The Model T adapted well wherever it was sold. Owners ran it in the jungles of Sumatra and across the vast Gobi Desert of China. Australians enjoyed its toughness in the outback. The Model T took riders over the Pampas of Argentina and the Velde of South Africa. It ran with the troika sleds in Russia and trekked over the Nile River Delta near the Pyramids in Egypt. Grain farmers in Saskatchewan and Alberta treated Fords like lost friends. And 60-inch wheelbase versions coped with ruts and mud on the back roads of Mississippi, Alabama, Georgia and elsewhere in the Southern United States.

The Model T was many things to many people. They quickly found ways to personalize the Model T with their own tastes in mind and for their own needs. When they weren't driving it, they were attaching something to it or tinkering with it. There were special bodies and accessories as well as owner-inspired inventions. The Model T was made part of their families and their lives.

While other cars and trucks were mere machines, the Model Ts had personalities. It was almost as if the Ford engineers had taken apart the horse and put it back together with a vanadium steel spine, a four-cylinder heart and a magneto-sparked brain—the four-wheeled version of "Old Dobbin."

The Model T was, according to reviewers outside the automobile industry: "…the greatest creation in automobiles ever placed before a people." [1]

Of course, someone trying to start one in cold weather or up to their elbows attempting to replace transmission bands might not have been so eloquent about the Model T.

Model Ts seemed to engender both a feeling of affection and an attitude of tolerance that bordered on frustration. Just as the horse needed hay and attention to the inevitable shoveled leavings, the Ford seemed to need attention in a manner that Cadillac and Packard owners—or even those who got behind the wheel of a Chevrolet, Dort or Dodge Brothers—never expressed.

Writing for *Automobile Dealer and Repairer* in January 1920, Henry Mulenford said the Model T and the mule must have had some kind of connection.

"They have their little eccentricities and traits of character which must be understood before they will accomplish that for which they were designed." 2

The Model Ts weren't really designed for fashionable boulevards or stone-paved circular driveways in front of fashionable mansions. Perhaps one of the endearing qualities was the Model T looked very much at home in some of the worst natural conditions.

"There was an adventuresome, almost exotic quality about Model Ts in deep mud, deep snow and deep dust," wrote David Roberts in his book *In the Shadows of Detroit.*" 3

While many restorers and owners may be thoroughly familiar with the inner workings of the Model T, many younger generations who didn't grow up with the car or have never had a chance to peek under the hood of a Model T might not be aware of what made them run.

In this chapter, we'll briefly look at some of the inner workings, with an assist from Ford literature of the day like "The Model T Instruction Book" of 1913 and the 1922 "Ford Manual." These pages are not intended to be a "how to," but more of a "what was," a snapshot of some of the basic elements that made the car memorable, dependable and popular.

"The simplicity of the Ford car and the ease with which it is operated renders an intimate knowledge of mechanical technicalities unnecessary for its operation," said the foreword to the 1922 "Ford Manual" and added that the existence of 20,000 Ford service providers "…gives to Ford owners a singular freedom from mechanical annoyances which beset owners of cars having limited service facilities."

"The Ford is the simplest car made. It is easy to understand and is not difficult to keep in proper adjustment and repair," the manual added.

The 1922 "Ford Manual" seemed to compare the Model

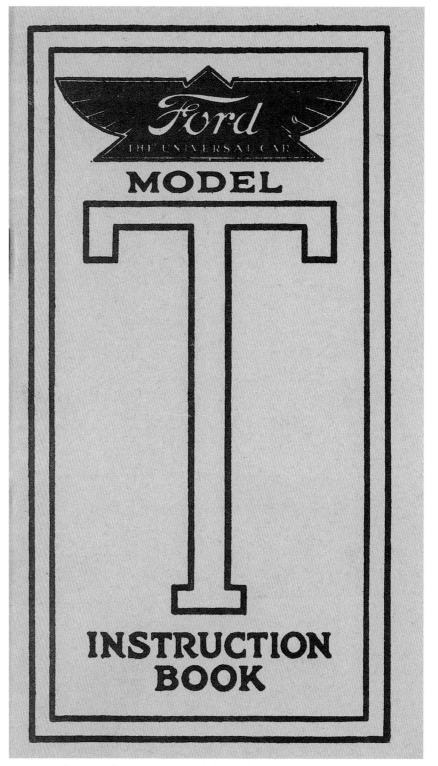

One item that Model T owners around the world shared in common was the car's very important instruction booklet.

T to a fine trotting or racing horse when it said that drivers should be patient and prudent with the Ford, especially when it was new, suggesting the car, in female gender, needed to "find herself" and that all parts needed to be "limbered up and more thoroughly lubricated by running."

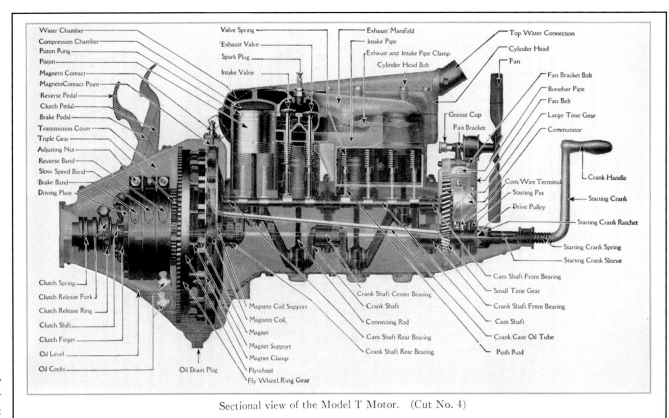

Labels (top to bottom, left side): Water Chamber, Compression Chamber, Piston Ring, Piston, Magneto Contact, Magneto Contact Point, Reverse Pedal, Clutch Pedal, Brake Pedal, Transmission Cover, Triple Gear, Adjusting Nut, Reverse Band, Slow Speed Band, Brake Band, Driving Plate, Clutch Spring, Clutch Release Fork, Clutch Release Ring, Clutch Shift, Clutch Finger, Oil Level, Oil Cocks

Labels (center): Valve Spring, Exhaust Valve, Spark Plug, Intake Valve, Oil Drain Plug, Magneto Coil Support, Magneto Coil, Magnet, Magnet Support, Magnet Clamp, Flywheel, Fly Wheel Ring Gear, Crank Shaft Center Bearing, Crank Shaft, Connecting Rod, Cam Shaft Rear Bearing, Crank Shaft Rear Bearing

Labels (top right): Exhaust Manifold, Intake Pipe, Exhaust and Intake Pipe Clamp, Cylinder Head Bolt, Top Water Connection, Cylinder Head, Fan, Fan Bracket Bolt, Breather Pipe, Fan Belt, Large Time Gear, Commutator, Grease Cup, Fan Bracket

Labels (right side): Com. Wire Terminal, Starting Pin, Drive Pulley, Crank Handle, Starting Crank, Starting Crank Ratchet, Starting Crank Spring, Starting Crank Sleeve, Cam Shaft Front Bearing, Small Time Gear, Crank Shaft Front Bearing, Cam Shaft, Crank Case Oil Tube, Push Rod

Sectional view of the Model T Motor. (Cut No. 4)

A Ford Motor Co. cutaway image showed car owners the inside of their four-cylinder engine with all the parts carefully labeled. Don Chandler

The Ford engine was remarkable on its own. It was a convergence of careful thinking, intelligent design and a desire to produce a power plant that was practical and simple. Mike Mueller

And especially for the new drivers of the Model T came this stern warning for 1913 Ford owners.

"The first rule in motoring is to see that every part has, at all times, plenty of oil. The second is to see that every adjustment is made immediately the necessity of such adjustment is discovered."

So as we take our brief tour of the Model T in this chapter, let's keep our oil cans in hand and be patient and vigilant as we examine some of the unique features of the Model T.

The four-cylinder Model T engine was a marvel in its own right. Cast with the water jackets and cylinders *en bloc*, as opposed to a single cylinder or pairs of cylinders being assembled with others to cobble together an engine, the Model T's power plant was relatively small at 176.7 cubic inches and with its 3-1/4 x 4-inch bore and stroke.

The engine's output was measured at 22 hp in the earliest years and later was estimated at producing 20 hp after the compression was reduced slightly beginning with the 1912 editions. Most literature offers the 20 hp rating for the remaining years of the Model T's production.

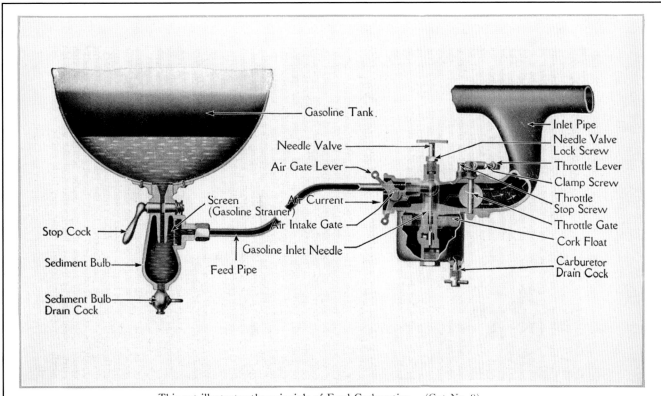

Gasoline Tank.

Needle Valve

Air Gate Lever

Screen (Gasoline Strainer)

Air Current

Stop Cock

Air Intake Gate

Sediment Bulb

Gasoline Inlet Needle

Feed Pipe

Sediment Bulb Drain Cock

Inlet Pipe

Needle Valve Lock Screw

Throttle Lever

Clamp Screw

Throttle Stop Screw

Throttle Gate

Cork Float

Carburetor Drain Cock

This cut illustrates the principle of Ford Carburetion. (Cut No. 9)

Understanding the gravity-fed fuel system was an important part of successful driving with the Model T Ford. Don Chandler

The L-head engine used three main bearings—front, center and rear. The crankshaft symmetry meant that cylinders one and four rose on upstroke of the crankshaft while cylinders two and three were in the down stroke.

The crankshaft, made of vanadium steel, was tested in the extreme. In fact, a Ford brochure of the period displayed the circus contortionist's twists and bends the tough little crankshaft could endure without breaking.

Reliability of crankshafts, axles and other major components was constantly called into question during the early era of auto making, so emphasizing the Model T's internals were tough as well as lightweight was important as the car gained its reputation.

One visible item that changed in the engine were the solid valve lifters, exposed for the first two years of the Model T, they were covered beginning in the 1911 model year.

The design of the Model T engine, from the standpoint of those involved in the fine art of casting metals, was an innovation. It was both sturdy and economical to produce.

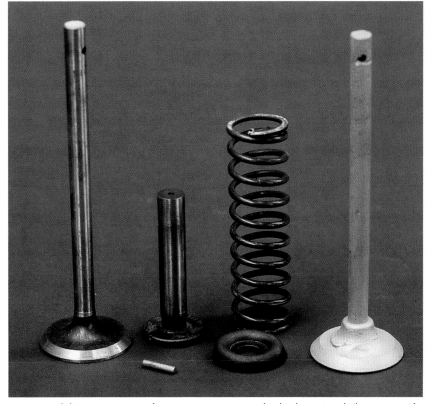

Many Model T owners were first-time car owners who had previously been part of a world dependent on the horse. They learned about engine parts like valves and valve springs. Mike Mueller

The secret of the casting was the concept of its detachable head. It allowed the majority of the engine block to be cast as one piece. It also meant the engine would be potentially easy to service.

Other automakers mistrusted the Ford detachable head concept at first, then adopted the idea. It was dependable and Ford proved their misgivings were groundless.

The removable cylinder head provided easier access to pistons, cylinders and valves. And a plate on the bottom of the crank case offered access as well. "No tearing down of the motor to reach the crank shaft, cam shaft, pistons, connecting rods, etc." said 1912 Ford specifications. 4

Serving fuel to the engine throughout most of its years were carburetors built by Kingston or Holley. Early on a small number of carbs also were supplied by Buffalo.

Originally, some of the carburetors also were supplied by Dodge Brothers, but, as would later happen with the relationship between the Ford Motor Co., Henry Ford and brothers John and Horace Dodge, the dissatisfaction grew quickly.

The Ford team that included Wills and "Spider" Huff from racing, decided to contact George Holley, who'd worked on motorcycles and some cars at that point. That relationship worked well.

"...together, Ford, Wills and Holley worked out a sturdy, reliable and cheap carburetor significantly ahead of any others in the market." 5

Said Ford Motor Co. about its carburetor in 1913: "Unless it has been tampered with, the carburetor adjustment is right, having been set by the head tester, so do not meddle with it until you are certain it needs adjusting."

The little Ford booklet of 1913 advised drivers to watch for too rich or too weak fuel adjustments and cautioned that the cork float in the carburetor needed to be varnished to become waterproof. Drivers were advised to clean the spraying nozzles with pumice or fine emery and to occasionally drain the fuel tanks using the petcock at the bottom to ward off sediment buildup.

When putting fuel into the tanks of their Model Ts, Ford gave drivers these instructions:

"Always strain through chamois skin to prevent water and other foreign matters getting into the carburetor. When filling the gasoline tank, extinguish all lamps; throw away your cigar and be sure there are no naked flames within several feet..."

Model T engines were gravity-fed from fuel tanks that were mounted under the seat. That basic design remained until the 1926 model year when most Model Ts received cowl-mounted fuel tanks. There were some variations, including the early teens runabouts that had a fuel tank behind the driver's seat. The center door sedans briefly had a fuel tank mounted under the rear seat but it caused some fuel feed problems and was moved back under the driver's seat in subsequent model years.

The gravity-fed fuel supply meant no fuel pump was used but also created the occasional problems when Model Ts had to grapple with a steep incline. Of course the ever-resourceful Model T owners found their cars functioned just fine when they backed up those inclines, allowing gravity and the Ford fuel system to work well and dole out fuel to the carburetor. The gravity-fed fuel system remained with the Model T throughout its production years and was another mark of the self-reliance and simplicity of the cars.

Innovation and self reliance often seemed to be reflected in the Model T. In the earlier years of the Model T, hand cranking was the only way to start the engine. By 1919, an optional electric starter was made available for Model T owners. While not without its eccentricities, especially in colder climates, the Ford four-cylinder engine would prove to be extremely reliable over its lifetime. In fact, a number of Model T engines were made and used for industrial purposes up to World War II.

There was nothing complex or hidden, especially when the Ford engine was compared to some much more ornately engineered engines of its time. The intake and exhaust manifolds were placed on the right side of the engine along with the carburetor and the access panel to its valves.

The Ford instruction manual recommended valve timing

maintenance after one year in operation or even sooner if the camshaft was removed. "The valves are accurately timed at the factory," said the 1913 Ford instruction booklet. "The necessity for re-timing usually occurs as a result of wear in the valve seats, valve stems, push rods and time gears, after the car has been in service for a year or more."

Ford Motor Co. literature recommended that valves should have a good grinding periodically "...whether they leak or not." The idea was to prevent uneven wear and leaks in valve stems that caused compression loss.

Excessive wear on valves required the attention of owners or service personnel. Model T valves were to have a space of no less than 1/64th and no more than 1/32nd of an inch between the valve and push rod to function properly. Weak valve springs also led to problems and sometimes needed to be replaced.

A formula for a compound to clean the valves was suggested by the early Ford manual. "Put a small amount of emery in a suitable dish, adding a spoonful or two of kerosene and a few drops of lubricating oil to make a thin paste."

The grinding came with a simple motion, rotating the valve back and forth in quarter turns, lifting it slightly from its seat, continuing the motion until each valve was smooth and bright.

Another problem for Model T engines was carbon deposits "...one of the most fruitful sources of trouble..." according to Ford Motor Company in 1913. Oil deposits left to scale caused knocking and backfiring from premature ignition in the cylinder walls or fouling of the porcelain spark plugs.

One of the best innovations with the Model T was its long oil pan or crankcase, the one piece covering that extended from the rear of the transmission to the front of the engine.

While such a covering seems logical today, it was advanced thinking nearly 100 years ago when transmissions often were exposed to all kinds of elements and lower portions of engines were vulnerable to anything on the road—dust, dirt, rocks, clay, mud, water, snow or ice.

The crankcase covering not only protected the inner workings from exterior elements, it allowed the engine and transmission to share oil. That system also would find its way to other cars in other generations of automotive history.

One reason the Model T became popular was because, like the good football official, it was occasionally cursed in a stressful moment but more often was so dependable it was overlooked and was taken for granted.

Transmission

Irish poet William Butler Yeats wrote a famous comparison of someone learning to drive the Model T with its planetary transmission to St. Vitus dance, the ancient description of nervous disorders.

While exercising with the pedals of the planetary transmission might seem more like a drill for an Irish step dancer, some of the principals of the planetary transmission itself can be found in our modern automatic transmissions.

Coupled to the simple Ford four-cylinder engine was an equally efficient magneto and a planetary transmission.   Mike Mueller

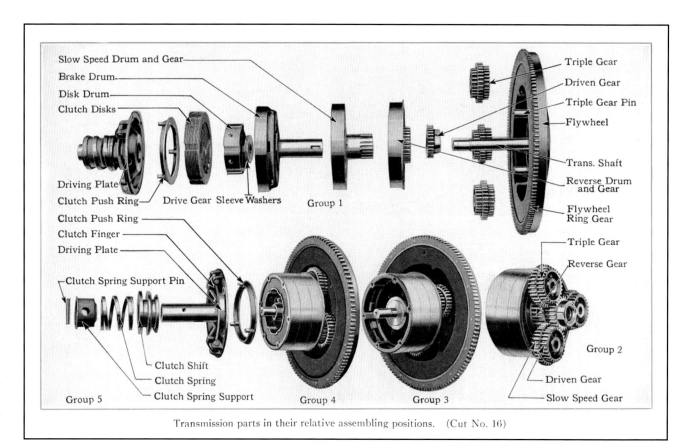

Slow Speed Drum and Gear
Brake Drum
Disk Drum
Clutch Disks

Driving Plate
Clutch Push Ring   Drive Gear Sleeve Washers   Group 1

Triple Gear
Driven Gear
Triple Gear Pin
Flywheel

Trans. Shaft
Reverse Drum and Gear
Flywheel Ring Gear

Clutch Push Ring
Clutch Finger
Driving Plate

Clutch Spring Support Pin

Triple Gear
Reverse Gear

Group 2

Clutch Shift
Clutch Spring
Group 5   Clutch Spring Support   Group 4   Group 3

Driven Gear
Slow Speed Gear

The pieces of the Model T's planetary transmission may have seemed small but it was a tough and durable unit that served owners well if they cared for it properly.   Don Chandler

Transmission parts in their relative assembling positions.   (Cut No. 16)

The planetary transmission was neither new to the Model T nor revolutionary by 1909. Versions of it had been used in some European cars as well as on Ford's Model N, R and S series cars.

"With two speeds forward and a reverse, it was the epitome of the gearbox of the day. If the planetary was cranky and anything but quiet, it still made motoring a sport," wrote auto veteran Floyd Clymer. 6

What made the planetary transmission stand out, in part, was both Henry Ford's insistence on using it rather than the more popular three-speed sliding gears prevalent in the early 1900s. The Ford Model T team, particularly Wills, took the existing planetary transmission and made improvements. The Model T version was encased with the engine and shared its oil, protected from the elements and also well-lubricated.

Even that was not a new idea but the Ford method of encasing the engine and transmission was light and practical, different from boiler-plated, cumbersome versions used on a few early cars.

The transmission received its name from the motion of the triple gears around the transmission shaft. It reminded designers and engineers of the planets revolving around the sun.

"The gears are constantly in motion around the main driving gear," explained the 1922 Ford Manual. It noted that the rotation of gears not being used was stopped and the needed gears were brought into action by bands that stopped and held or freed rotation, depending on the motion needed.

"The planetary transmission is the simplest and most direct means of speed control," added the 1922 driver instruction booklet. "It is a distinct advantage of the Ford car."

The small transmission was located immediately behind the magneto and flywheel. Bands, activated by three foot pedals, governed the motion of the planetary gears and offered low, high or reverse speeds.

From left to right, the left-most foot pedal was for the friction clutch and engaged high or low speeds. Low was engaged when the clutch pedal was pressed all the way forward. The center pedal engaged the reverse drum. The right pedal engaged the brake drum on the transmission driveshaft. A separate brake lever engaged rear wheel-mounted brakes.

The high gear ratio was 3.63 to 1 while low gear was 2.75 to 1. The low gear ratio, combined with the rear axle reduction, was 9.98 (2.75 x 3.63) or nearly 10 to 1.

"In general, owing to frictional losses in the transmission, and other causes, it may be assumed that the car will travel about three times as fast in high gear as in low. But the car will have about twice as much power when low gear is used." [7]

The planetary transmission on the Model T was relatively compact and was accessible for maintenance from a plate mounted over the transmission. The drums and bands could be viewed from the passenger side of the vehicle when the floorboards and inspection plate were removed.

Viewed from left to right, the drums were brake, slow speed and reverse.

Veteran Model T owner Don Chandler, co-founder of the Madison, Wisconsin, Capital T Club and a source for technical advice for this book, said modern drivers often have some confusion with the Model T's clutch pedal action.

"Drivers today, familiar with standard transmission, make the mistake of pushing the Model T clutch all the way forward, engaging low gear as they anticipate slowing down or stopping. This can be a heart-stopping experience for the novice Model T driver!"

One of the reasons the foot pedals were used with the simple but rugged planetary transmission on the Model T was the consideration that the car would encounter rough or nonexistent roads and drivers would need the ability to easily rock back and forth to maneuver the Model T out of mud or snow while still maintaining control of the steering wheel.

With few exceptions, the clutch pedal was in constant use. Drivers used the emergency brake lever and foot pedals to navigate the Model T.

Here's another look at the various components of the Model T's planetary transmission.   Mike Mueller

Model T owners learned the advantages of driving the car using the famed three foot pedals—clutch, reverse and brake—from left to right in this image. Mike Mueller

Releasing the clutch pedal and pushing the lever forward engaged the high-speed gear. A center or vertical position of the hand lever acted as a neutral position. Pulling the lever back engaged the brake bands on the rear wheels.

The 1913 Ford manual instructed drivers this way: "With the hand lever thrown forward in high speed, a light pressure of pedal 'C' released the clutch, while full pressure on the pedal throws in the slow speed. By gradually releasing the pedal, it will come back through neutral into high speed."

The planetary transmission was used on all years of the Model T. People often commented on the silent whir of the Model T transmission gears when they were properly maintained.

In 1912 sales literature, Ford Motor Company offered this explanation of the transmission: "Special Ford spur planetary type, combining ease of operation and smooth, silent running qualities. Clutch is so designed as to grip smoothly and positively and when disengaged to spring clear away from the drums, thus assuring positive action and maximum power."

One condition often described by Model T owners was "nudging" or "Ford creep." While the cars may have seemed as if they were alive, the problem, Ford explained, was a clutch lever screw that needed to be adjusted or replaced to keep the clutch in neutral while the owner started the car.

Chandler says there were practical causes and ways of avoiding this situation.

"The creeping or forward movement occurred as a result of cold and thickened oil in the transmission. The transmission responded as if it was in gear. Experienced Model T drivers learned the condition could largely be avoided by leaving high gear engaged while the car was not in operation. Oil could not get between the clutch discs and thicken.

And Chandler adds a cautionary note.

"It was imperative that the emergency brake be fully engaged or the wheels be blocked before hand cranking. Failure to do so could result in the operator being seriously injured."

The transmission inspection plate cover was removable and owners or trained service personnel used the opening to adjust the brake, low speed and reverse bands as well as the ability to re-line worn bands.

Automotive historian Beverly Rae Kimes said the Model T version of the planetary transmission was praised by early automotive journalists.

"Journalists of the day...noted that the noise in low or reverse of previous planetary transmissions had been eliminated by the T's increased size of the externally driven gears, this producing 'the same quiet purring sound whether the car is running fast or slow, forward or backward.'" [8]

Wrote author David Roberts: "Sales bulletins in February 1914 needed to remind dealers that Ford gears were always smoothly in mesh while sliding-gear transmissions led to grinding and damage." [9]

The venerable planetary transmission was a major reason why the Model T was both memorable and unique—and why the car ran in all kinds of conditions around the world.

Magneto

In the early years of automobiles, dry cell batteries used to provide electricity for ignition systems were both heavy and unreliable. Neither quality would do for the Model T so some other system had to be used. In order to make a car that was lightweight, practical and self-reliant under as many conditions as possible, the team working on the Model T devised a magneto that ran off the car's flywheel.

It was as revolutionary then on a mass-produced car of the early 20th century as fuel-saving hybrid technology is for 21st century cars. Yet it was based on basic principles of generating electricity.

Edward "Spider" Huff, an associate of Henry Ford at the Edison Illuminating Company in Detroit and one of his partners in racing endeavors, was credited with developing the Ford version of the magneto. Huff specialized in electrical projects on the Model T.

Magnetos did not originate with the Model T. They had been used in European cars previously and Bosch was already building versions of a magneto in 1905 in Germany.

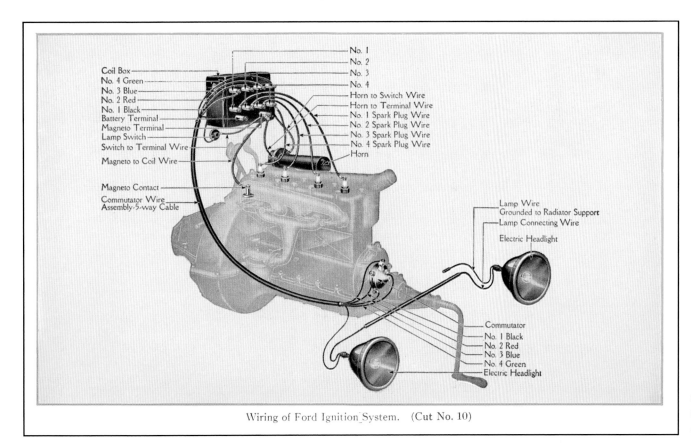

Wiring of Ford Ignition System. (Cut No. 10)

The wiring diagrams were clear on the Model T and this image attempted to show the key components of the ignition system.   Don Chander

The Model T version was practical and innovative.

We've come a long way in terms of electrical equipment and electronics used in modern cars and wouldn't think of using a magneto in our cars today. But in 1908, when the magneto appeared on the flywheel of the 1909 Model T, it offered a reliable, though fluctuating source of electricity.

The Ford system used two basic sections. Sixteen magnets were attached to the flywheel, just 1/32-inch from 16 narrow strips of copper wire that were tightly wrapped in insulating tape and mounted on a metal ring at the rear of the engine block. The wire mountings formed a coil assembly or armature. The revolutions of the engine generated alternating current.

Owner and Dealer described the current production this way in November 1923:

"In each revolution of the flywheel, the magnetism reverses sixteen times (each reversal of direction of magnetic lines of force producing a flow of current), thus producing sixteen electrical impulses which, at ordinary engine speeds, produce a practically continuous flow of alternating

When Model T owners opened the hood, they could recognize that their car's wiring looked just like the diagram portrayed in the Ford Manual.   Mike Mueller

current of a much higher frequency...than is used for house lighting (133 cycles at 500 revolutions). Because of this fact, it is possible to operate lights satisfactorily from the Ford low tension magneto..."

The 1922 Ford Manual for Model T drivers offered this explanation:

"In revolving at the same rate of speed as the motor, the magneto on the flywheel passing the stationary coil spools create an alternating low tension electric current in the coils of wire. [The current] is carried from these coils to the magneto connection (wire) heading to the coil box on the dash..."

Of course, the moving car went slower as well as faster so the magneto's current output varied from as low as 200 rpm to as much as 1,200 rpm or more. The magazine article offered a chart that showed the output, edited slightly here.

RPM	MPH	VOLTS	AMPERES	CYCLES
200	5	5.0	6.1	26.4*
400	10	9.8	7.9	52.8*
600	15	14.4	8.5	80.0*
800	20	18.8	8.8	106.4*
1,000	25	22.8	8.9	146.4*
1,200	30	26.2	9.0	160*

*The cycle was considered one complete reversal of current from negative to positive then back.

Original product literature from the Ford Motor Co. for the 1909 Model T not only proclaimed that its Model T drivers no longer needed dry cell batteries, they promoted the lack of brushes, commutators or moving wires when compared to other cars of the era.

Early Model Ts used carbide gas headlights into the 1915 model year. One way to identify these cars is by their vertical tanks on the running board (or horizontal tanks with the Prest-o-lite aftermarket option.) Dripping water mixed with carbide crystals to form a gas that was fed to the headlights. When lit, the carbide headlights produced a beam considered by Chandler to be a "...relatively bright and constant light source."

Magneto-powered headlights did take some getting used to, according to Chandler.

"Some first-time users of the new magneto light had some frightful experiences as they slowed to turn sharp corners. The slow speed of the engine allowed the lights to become dim, leaving the driver in peril. Drivers soon learned to overcome this situation by using low gear at corners. That permitted a higher engine speed and full lighting."

The current produced by the Model T's magneto, was directed through the coil box mounted in the car, then sent to the timer (or commutator) and to the spark plugs in the engine.

Chandler says the hand-cranked Model Ts that had headlights used a dry cell battery, called the "electric fence battery," to start the engine. This battery was placed under the front seat, to the right of the gas tank.

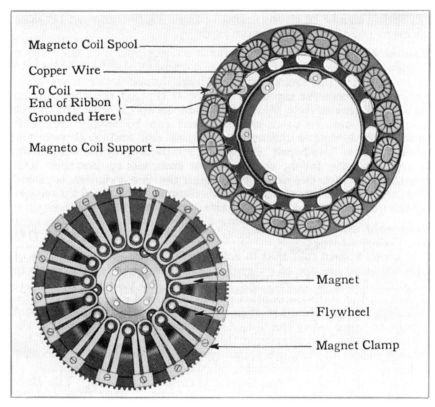

Magneto Coil Spool

Copper Wire

To Coil
End of Ribbon
Grounded Here

Magneto Coil Support

Magnet

Flywheel

Magnet Clamp

The Ford Manual for Model T owners depicted the basics of the magneto used in the Model T.   Don Chandler

"Once the engine was running smoothly, the ignition switch was changed from the 'Bat' to the 'Mag' setting. Generally, an engine would run better on the higher voltage."

From the beginning of Model T assembly in 1908 to 1910 the magnets were 9/16th of an inch thick. Then from 1911 through 1914, magneto magnets were 5/8 inches thick. From 1915 on, they were just ¾ inches thick.

The magneto was the sole component of the Model T that was pictured but lacked instructions in the 1913 owner's manual for repair or maintenance. The 1922 manual did suggest that magnets could be replaced. Chandler says work on the magneto was something left to the skilled mechanics of the Model T owner.

Ironically, drivers had to be careful not to accidentally connect the Model T magneto to a battery or the magneto would lose power or even become demagnetized. Excess force, heat, vibration and age all caused de-magnetism to occur.

And there was this dire warning for later Model Ts with starters:

"…the powerful current of the 6-volt storage battery is ever waiting for a chance to sneak into the windings of the magneto coil assembly and demagnetize the magnets. This may occur by the mixing of the wires on the terminal post or not properly insulating the battery wire on the block by means of extra rubber insulation." [10]

There were problems with the magneto running in oil that lubricated the engine and transmission, sometimes causing short circuits, especially if metallic particles were in the oil. The remedy was to change the oil, clean out the crank case with fresh oil and also to clean the drain plug.

"In addition," says Chandler, "perhaps the most common cause of short circuits—and the easiest to remedy—was that cotton fibers could drop off the band linings and become lodged in the magneto plug. By simply removing the plug, one could remove the offending particle and replace the plug."

Excessive wear on the magneto also occurred when people mistakenly wired the headlights in parallel rather than in a series.

"By taking 8 amperes, instead of the usual 2 amperes, parallel connection of the headlights tends to grossly overload the long suffering magneto," said in 1923. [11]

Service personnel tested the magneto for gap and clearance as well as polarity. Individual magnets could be replaced but it was one of the few jobs encouraged for the professional, not the owner.

Electric spark for the ignition system was and still is the steady pulse of the automobile. The ingenious magneto system was a simple and reliable power generation system.

And it's one more factor that made the Model T Ford such a memorable car.

Chassis

One of the underrated points about the Model T was its chassis, a system designed with symmetry in mind as well as a new combination of strength and lightness.

The frame was a perfect rectangle and the use of three-point mountings offered both degrees of flex and rigidity.

Early cars, even earlier Ford models like the K, often ran into trouble when the rear wheels were elevated at too severe of an angle. Engines could not be cranked, transmissions would not operate properly and they were out of alignment if twisted, even in normal operation.

The team that designed the Model T with Henry Ford, including Hungarian-born engineer Joseph Galamb, Charles Sorenson and Wills, realized these problems and decided they could do something about it, perhaps drawing on experience they'd gained with a car never produced by Ford, but tested.

"…there was a Model G developed but never put in production," recalled early Ford Motor Company veteran Fred Rockelman. "The engine was a four-cylinder having a three-point suspension." [12]

Rear-mounted radius rods offered a triangular mounting of the rear axle to the frame with the rods attached to the rear axle mounting points and angled to the point where the universal joint met the transmission. That made a perfect

The Ford Model T frame and other components were made of the strong but light vanadium steel. Tom Myers

triangle with the torque tube bisecting it.

The engine also was mounted on three forward points in the frame—one centered in front and two on either side of the magneto and flywheel case.

The geometry of the chassis would be an important part of the Model T's overall reliability, though often overlooked because it was so simple.

"This method of suspension insures absolute freedom from strain on the parts and permits the most comfortable riding of the car body," said Ford literature.

In front and back, the Model T had transverse mounted springs, actually one of the oldest forms of technology on the car. Transverse springs were used on horse-drawn wagons and buggies. They offered a firm ride and could cope with the roughest conditions most motorists would find.

The steel used in the Model T was revolutionary for auto making. It was a perfect match for the Ford Motor Co. Model T team's desire to produce a lighter car, yet offered a combination of rigidity and strength that was unmatched.

Vanadium steel had been developed in England after the essential compound called vanadis was discovered in Mexico earlier in the 19th century. The compound was named for a Swedish goddess. The compound drew a large question mark until it was found to be useful as a metal alloy ingredient. The blend meant the vanadium steel mix was three times stronger than regular steel and easier to use.

Once metallurgists learned how it could strengthen iron, it began to be used in several ways. Today, vanadium steel is used in surgical instruments and jets as well as in making cars.

Vanadium steel became a key factor in making the Model T chassis strong and resilient.

Vanadium steel was used by Ford Motor Co. as early as 1907 and was mentioned in their product literature that year. The Ford literature described a search for a better alloy than nickel steel. The vanadium steel became more widely used after a large deposit of the precious vanadium ore was discovered in South America. That brought the price down

and Ford jumped into the technology. They found more uses for it in their manufacturing and by 1907, springs, axles and gears were made with the vanadium steel, according to Ford product literature.

At that time, Ford mentioned their demand for steel was 280 tons per month and they decided vanadium steel would be the future.

"...as rapidly as possible," said at least two 1907 Ford brochures "it will take the place of every other carbon or nickel steel parts in all Ford models, regardless of price. Let others follow as soon as they can. We reckon they are about a year and a half behind at present writing."

At the same time that vanadium steel uses were being explored, Ford Motor Co. reported to their potential customers that Ford parts were all heat treated and said the process improved machining.

Both the increased use of vanadium steel and heat treatment of steel were strong influences for the Model T.

The overall chassis was simple and very durable and could host a number of body styles that it did for the 19 years the Model T was built.

Ignition

The Model T used two basic ignition systems during the life of the Model T Ford. The original system used power from the flywheel magneto through the coil box to the spark plugs. The other system, introduced in 1919, used a storage battery, starter, ammeter and generator as well as battery-powered electric lights. The battery-powered system was optional on open Model Ts and standard on closed cars.

The simple system was wired through a series of coils and also was attached to a front-mounted commutator, commonly known as the timer.

"The commutator (or timer) determines the instant at which the spark plugs must fire," explained the 1922 Ford Manual. "When the commutator roller in revolving touches the four contact points, an electrical current is passed..."

Each spark plug was attached to a post on the coil box and had a connecting point position on the commutator— perhaps black, red, blue and green wires for spark plugs 1,

2, 3 and 4, respectively. That early system was cranked by hand.

Owners often referred to a buzzing—that was inside the coil boxes where the vibrators were working to supply proper current for ignition.

The 1913 Model T instruction manual noted the potential problems with the coils:

"The first symptom of a defective coil is the buzzing of the vibrator with no spark at the plug. A leak in the condensor is often indicated by a 'fat' bluish spark..."

The commutator, or timer, was a simple unit. It was located on the front of the engine, near the crank. It consisted of a spring, brush and contact points with a tiny roller.

Later, the ignition system was attached to a battery that brought power to the headlights and horn as well as the spark plugs. These cars still were cranked to life.

"The location of the ignition switch," he added "changed from being a lever on the coil box to a key-operated switch on the dash except on non-starter equipped cars. Technically speaking, the car equipped with a storage battery allowed headlights to be turned on without the engine running. This was not possible otherwise."

After 1919, the modern starter-equipped Model Ts relied on battery power and a generator to offer current for the lights, horn and gauges. The number of Model Ts with this system increased through the end of the car's production in 1927.

Cooling

Some people might not be aware that the earliest Model Ts had gear-driven water pumps. Throughout the Model T's existence, aftermarket companies offered water pumps for Model Ts. When changes began to be made at about car 2,500, one of the changes was the elimination of the water pump and the use of thermosyphon cooling.

"Much could be written about the pros and cons of using a water pump," said Chandler. "But under all but a few

The coil box was an important part of the early Model T Fords like this 1910 example.   Doug Mitchel

conditions, the thermosyphon system worked adequately well."

The thermosyphon theory was that warm water would rise and circulate back through the radiator where it would be fan-cooled and heat also was drawn off by the water passing through the radiator tubes. The water would complete the cycle by flowing up the connecting pipe to the cylinder areas and surrounding water jackets.

"...hot water seeks a higher level than cold water," explained the Ford owner's manual. "When the water reaches a certain heat, approximately 180 degrees, circulation commences and the water flows from the lower radiator outlet pipe up through the water jackets into the upper radiator water tank."

The system did away with water pumps, though some owners chose to get one in the extensive Model T aftermarket arena.

"Extra large water jackets and a special Ford vertical tube radiator permit a continuous flow of cool water and prevent excessive heating. A belt-driven fan is also used in connection with the cooling system."

Of course, heat could overtax the system and then the radiator produced steam instead of the water cooling! And cold weather offered other problems.

CAUSES FOR ENGINE OVERHEATING:
1. Carbonized cylinders
2. Too much driving at low speed.
3. Spark retarded too far.
4. Poor ignition.
5. Not enough oil or use of a poor grade of oil.
6. Racing the motor.
7. A clogged muffler.
8. Improper carburetor adjustment.
9. A broken or slipping fan belt.
10. Clogged or jammed radiation tubes, leaky connections or low water—all a lack of proper ventilation.

Source: Ford Manual

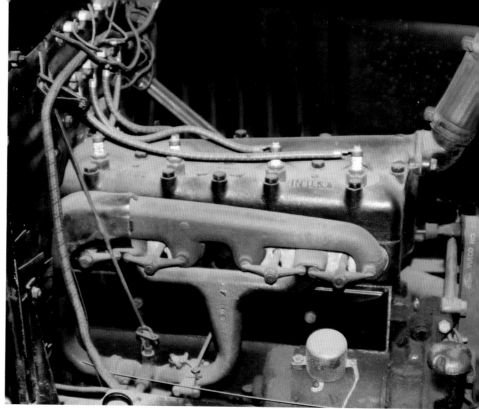

The Model T's cooling system was efficient and practical. It matched the simplicity of the four-cylinder engine.   Tom Myers

Before water became chunks of ice in cold weather, Ford suggested mixing water and "wood alcohol" with glycerine. And frequent flushing of radiators was recommended. At least one of the contributors in this book mentioned draining the radiator when the Model T was parked overnight in cold weather, then pouring hot water into the radiator once the engine was started.

Ford offered a chart of the mixture of wood alcohol with water:

PERCENTAGE	FREEZING POINT
20%	15 degrees
30%	8 degrees
50%	-34 degrees

Source: Ford Manual

"On account of evaporation fresh alcohol must be added frequently in order to main the proper solution," said Ford.

Many Model T owners would have bouts with the thermosyphon cooling system—which often boiled over and caused some owners to do the same! Yet the simplicity of the cooling system was another memorable feature of the Model T.

Spark and Throttle adjustments

Another memorable feature of the Model T was its spark and throttle levers mounted just under the steering wheel. The spark lever was on the left and throttle on the right. Each lever could theoretically be pulled down from a 45-degree angle to a point where they almost touched. Notched half rings were used as guides for the spark and throttle levers.

An old Ford diagram showed several positions, from fully retarded to completely down or open.

Maximum speed was achieved by pulling down spark and throttle levers as far as they could go—at least according to an early Ford Motor Co. diagram.

Chandler cautioned that the practice would not be advised for today's Model T drivers.

"There would be a price to be paid," suggesting such a "full throttle" position as depicted in the early Ford diagrams would possibly destroy a preserved or restored engine today and probably caused some serious problems if practiced with an original Model T.

There were at least a dozen settings in the early diagram. Of course, throughout the car's history, Model T owners of the time and today's Model T restorers know they had to work with the spark and throttle adjustments and learned more from experience than from an artist's rendering of how something was supposed to work.

Owners learned the importance of using the spark and throttle levers mounted on the steering column of the Model T.   *Doug Mitchel*

Many Model T owners may not realize the same spark and throttle arrangement was used on the N and R series Fords during the 1907 model year. "...both can be operated by the index fingers without removing the hands from the steering wheel," said the 1907 Ford R brochure. "...the car may be driven at any speed from four miles per hour to its maximum of about 45 miles per hour by simple throttle and spark control alone..."

Model T drivers often recalled the exercise of retarding the spark (pushing the spark lever) all the way to the horizontal position.

The two small levers on the steering column were unlike putting a gear selector in drive. The positioning of the spark and throttle levers was an inexact science that varied from car to car and, like many components of the Model T, demanded thought and attention to detail.

Like the three floor pedals or the magneto, the spark and throttle levers are something modern drivers wouldn't think about but all were items that Model T drivers used every day.

Coping with the Model T

The Overhauling

In the August 1919 edition of Automobile Dealer and Repairer, a story about thorough maintenance began with this poem, intended for all Model T owners:

"Bill Taylor owned a Ford machine, he used it every day, for hauling wood and carting coal, and taking loads of hay.

And when the cool of evening came and Bill's day's work was done, he'd use that little flivver car for three more hours of fun.

Now, cars, like men, will stand so much, then go upon a strike; Bill's Ford machine was right in style, it failed to work one night!

Bill cranked it thrice and cussed it once, then cranked it still some more; the engine wouldn't make a sound, it wouldn't even snore.

He towed it home and used a wrench and found just why it 'twas stalling; it needed lots of big repairs, in fact an overhauling.

Bill wasn't equal to this task, he worked with hesitation; he had the tools and had the strength, but needed information.

Bill had a friend who worked on cars, and shone at Ford repairing; he wrote at once to him for help 'cause he was near despairing."

The poem was a reminder to all Model T owners that their tough little cars needed attention and caring. Bill's friend wrote back a lengthy letter, recommending a month of teardown and maintenance to what he called "The Nation's Go-Cart."

Troubleshooting

A 1920 article in the January Automobile Dealer and Repairer compared the Model T with mules. It offered some humorous tips about troubleshooting the Model T, with excerpts offered here.

"...a mule can be started—if one knows how to do it...the same statement applies to Ford cars.

Your Ford car just naturally kicks if it is not approached in the proper way. During the cold weather a light grade of oil should be used in both the engine and the gearset.

Mules and Fords are subject to attacks of nerves. I know of no troubles more prevalent than those which arise from the ignition system. It is a good plan for the novice to keep his hands at home when there is trouble of any kind.

The Ford timer has a very peculiar habit of working all right at a walk, but refusing to gallop, just like that mule. After a time, the metal contacts wear and the timer roller makes a poor contact. It is safe to say that the timer will bear investigation...

The coils on the dash board can cause many anxious moments... By holding one of the spark plug wires about ¼ of an inch away from the cylinder head the strength of the spark can be determined. If the spark is strong enough to burn a piece of paper, then it will explode the mixture in the cylinders.

'Lizzy won't work so long as she has the asthma.' The engine compression must be maintained or it won't give power. It's one case where fresh air is no cure, for it is a case of too much air.

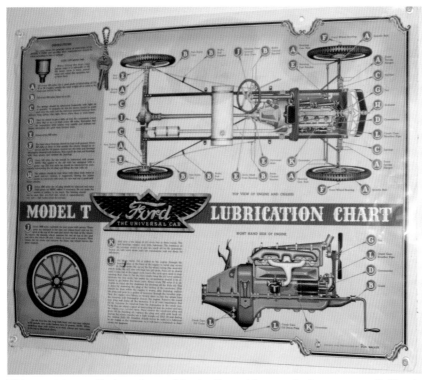

This surviving wall chart, located in the Towe Museum in Sacramento, California, shows how straight forward maintenance and lubrication tasks were on the Model T Ford.   Tom Myers

The Ford car often takes a notion to go where it pleases as regards to its general direction. The driver finds it a difficult matter to keep the car in a straight line. The trouble is usually caused by a sprung axle or king pins out of line.

In general, I would say that the Ford car, though it has its little traits and eccentricities, is…a very willing little beast. It may balk, like the mule, on the road and remain passive for hours at a time, but eventually it will recover from its mood and be its sunny self for a time. Mules and Fords, may they always thrive!"

Henry Mulenford

Cleaning Instructions

In the early 1920s, a Ford service bulletin offered Model T owners, many of whom were car buyers for the first time, instructions about cleaning their vehicles. Here are some excerpts.

1. Dust on top of a closed car should first be removed. A whisk broom can be used to good advantage. Mud spots should be washed off with a slow stream of water flowing from a hose without a nozzle… After a top has been in service approximately six months it is a good plan to apply a brush coat of high grade spar varnish containing 5 percent of black color.

2. The interior of the car is brushed with a whisk broom. If the upholstery is soiled it should be cleaned with gasoline or cleaning fluid. The floor mat should be brushed and, if necessary, cleaned with gasoline. (When using gasoline keep fires away.)

3. The motor may be cleaned with kerosene applied with a water tool brush after which it should be washed with water in linseed oil soap. Any excess water should be taken up with a sponge, and the motor allowed to dry. If any parts are rusty, sand, dust off and touch up with M-165 Black Enamel.

4. Plenty of water should be used when washing the body in order to remove all dust and mud. Avoid the use of soap whenever possible. If a polishing fluid is used only one that is neutral and contains but a small amount of finely ground abrasive should be used.

5. The running gear is washed with water flowing from a hose without nozzle attached, using a sponge to facilitate the operation. If the greasy spots are such that soap and water will not remove them, wash with kerosene and then apply soapy water as directed above. Tires can be cleaned with a rag moistened with gasoline after any mud or dust have been washed off.

6. The windshield and windows should be cleaned last. For this purpose use a sponge that has been well soaked and wrung out in water containing a small amount of ammonia. Dry and polish with soft clean rags…washed free of linters.

It is imperative that in drying and polishing the operation must be carried out in one way strokes only…horizontal or vertical but never crosswise or circular. In drying with a chamois, use only the flesh side which is soft and fluffy."

Tools

"A screwdriver, a monkey wrench, baling wire, fishline, stove pipe, waxed twine; a paper clip might be just the thing, a bent nail would do wonders…" [13]

So wrote historian Beverly Rae Kimes in her story about

the Model T in *Automobile Quarterly* in 1972. It was written with the sense of humor many Model T owners had about fixing their cars.

To many Ford owners, it may have seemed that both real and self-manufactured tools were the answer to Model T maintenance. In fact, Ford Motor Company encouraged and expected many owners to service their own vehicles, especially in the first years of the Model T.

Part of the special allure of the Model T was that owners could park one under a shade tree or in a barn and do some work on it. Tools for the Model T became as important as the car itself and Ford Motor Company did its part by supplying and selling such tools. Companies that were heavily into the Model T aftermarket also added specialty tools.

To the non-Model T owners, some of the quaint gadgets seemed like they were out of a Charles Dickens novel or while more sinister tools seemed like remnants of the Spanish Inquisition. But lay an assortment of tools in front of the knowledgeable Model T man or woman and they would recognize such items as a hub cap wrench, an L socket, a brace wrench, various pullers or even motor lifting tongs.

Common items that have transcended Model T times now have a nostalgic flavor including the long-necked oil can, the hand-power tire pump or the small jack.

Say "5-Z-285" in the right group of people and they'll know you're not calling a football play but talking about a brace wrench.

Model Ts had pouches of small tools available for the do-it-yourself mechanic, far more plentiful in that era than in the 21st century.

According to experts, the tool pouches, called "tool rolls" because they rolled out for use and rolled up for storage, were available beginning in 1913. They were updated at least through the 1924 model year.

In 1913, an oil can and tire pump were standard Ford Motor Company issue along with a small combination or "band" wrench, pliers, a screwdriver, a multi-purpose hub wrench, an adjustable or "monkey" wrench, a spark plug wrench and a tire iron. 14

Ford Motor Co. and the automotive aftermarket each provided an array of tools for working on the Model Ts. Both owners and mechanics found various Model T specialty tools. Tom Myers

Some tools were made by the Model T component makers. For example, a wrench for wheels made by the Pruden Wheel Company. Many Model Ts used the Stewart speedometer and there was a tool for them as well. Tire makers got into the act as well, endorsing tire irons with the logo of their brands.

Tools that were offered changed as the Model T changed but there was something about the car that brought out the best in their owners and other self-made mechanics.

Pyroxylin was a key ingredient that allowed automakers like Ford Motor Co. to use more modern spray painting and drying techniques on the Model T by 1926.

About That Model T Black Paint

There have been two persistent myths about the Model T through the years. One is that all the cars were painted black. The second and most persistent myth is they were painted black because it dried faster than other colors.

Both myths are false, in light of research done by Professor Trent E. Boggess of Plymouth State College in Plymouth, New Hampshire.

We know that the very first years and the very last years of Model Ts were painted in various colors. Of the 15 million plus Model Ts made between 1908 through the end of production in 1927, it is estimated a majority were painted black, about 11,500,000 of them.

The remaining colorful Model Ts were green, gray, red and blue prior to late 1914 and began being painted maroon and green with the 1926 model year. For the final model year, an even wider array of colors was available when pyroxylin paints offered more choices.

Professor Boggess carefully researched both Ford records and paint company information from the period when Ford began painting cars black, late in 1914 or early in 1915.

"One of the often cited reasons for the use of japan black on the Model T was that it allegedly dried faster than any other paint," wrote Boggess. "There is no evidence, in either the Ford engineering records or the contemporary literature on paint, to indicate that this was the case." [15]

In fact, he says the black paint took just as long to dry as any other color that could have been used. Shades of blue, green and maroon all were possibilities. All were darkened by a compound used at that time called Gilsonite that was intended to resist dampness.

Ford Motor Company used 37 different types of black paint in preparing Model Ts, Boggess found in his research. Some had different thinners and pigments. Some were able to be dried in ovens while others had to be air dried.

The term "japanning" was taken from a Japanese varnishing technique. In American paint circles of the day, japan dryers were additives in paint that chemically reduced the time for paints to dry.

It is true that some Model T components were painted japan black and oven dried fairly quickly. The front axles are good examples.

Boggess found that Ford Motor Company used three techniques to paint its cars. Dipping was performed on fenders, hoods, running boards, coil boxes, windshields.

Those items could be baked in drying ovens at temperatures of 400 to 500 degrees. Some items, like wooden wheels, were dipped, spun rapidly, then air-dried. Other parts, like the front axles, were brushed.

The third method, used on Model T bodies, was called paint flowing, as described by J. L. McCloud, a Ford employee of the era.

"The paint was contained in an overhead tank…and it came down in a pipe. [It] came out in the form of slow streams from a comb-like end on the pipe. That was held up alongside of the body and drawn along…as the body moved on a conveyor. In that way it was flooded with paint. The paint ran off and was returned to the tank and reused…" [16]

Boggess discovered that Ford could not oven bake the Model Ts painted black from late in 1914 through 1922 for a very practical reason. They had too much wood to withstand the 400 to 450 degree temperatures that all metallic parts, like fenders, could withstand.

"These [wooden] parts were painted with multiple coats of air drying color varnish," Boggess wrote. [17]

"It took days to really dry the paint finish on the Model T," recalled Ford worker McCloud. "The body plants had a lot of bodies in them at temperatures just slightly above room temperature." [18]

In fact, Boggess wrote, one of the reasons Ford Motor Company built four six-story buildings at the Highland Park plant's Manchester Avenue wing was to have room for all the bodies to air dry.

A 1965 article by George R. Norton Jr. in the *Model T Ford Restoration* Handbook also talks about drying the bodies involved in the painting process, specifically breaking down the painting steps. Along with the application of a blue-black paint, Norton wrote that the bodies had to dry for 24 hours between paint coats. [19]

Norton said the painted bodies, following the drying period, were then rubbed with curled hair, a technique called "mossing." They were given a second coat, traveled 200 feet to partially dry the paint, then workers tilted the bodies to drain off surplus paint. Then they were mossed again.

Norton says the final step was another drying period. [20] "After being stacked for drying, the body was ready for final assembly." [21]

About 2,000 car bodies were produced per day and the bodies took four days to completely air dry. So at any time, Ford needed 8,000 spaces for bodies to air dry.

That practice continued into the early 1920s when assembly lines needed more than the 2,000 per day of dried bodies ready for assembly. Ford Motor Company began to make changes. One was putting more metal into the bodies to allow them to be oven baked for drying, similar to Dodge Brothers bodies of the era. The second was finding a paint compound that could be baked dry.

Between 1922 and 1926, Ford was able to use a low-bake method, still using the paint flowing technique. That, says Boggess, was the reason the dark shades of Channel Green and Windsor Maroon were used late in 1925 for the 1926 model year.

The pyroxylin paints that were introduced late in 1926 changed the color spectrum available and the methods used for painting.

Instead of the gravity-based paint flowing methods that meant thin paint coats toward the top of a body and thicker coats below, more uniform painting techniques were available.

"The Model T was a most practical car," Boggess concluded. "No doubt Henry Ford was convinced that black was simply the most practical color for the job. Model Ts were not painted black because black dried faster. Black was chosen because it was cheap and very durable." [22]

So they weren't all painted black and black was chosen because it was a practical choice. And there you have the story about paint in black and white!

Collectors probably would like to find this 1912 Model T that was converted to use as a utility vehicle with an aftermarket box replacing its factory-made deck

Chapter 7

THE POPULAR MODEL T AFTERMARKET INDUSTRY

> *"The automobile makes prosperity. It gives a momentum and diversity to the people's activity which tends to constantly increase and is almost difficult to stop."*
>
> *Henry Ford*

I f you ever have a chance to look at an historic photo of a Model T Ford, chances are you may see an item on the car that was purchased after the original sale, one that was not an official Ford-issued option.

The Model T was a Spartan car. There can be no doubt about that. The cars were designed to be reliable and adaptable and were never intended to shower the owner with a wide array of accessories, glimmer and gadgets. Many enterprising companies filled the void with accessories and extra items that ranged from the practical to the outlandish.

Henry Ford and his team weren't thinking about a lot of excess when they designed the Model T. They wanted to offer a car that cut out the luxuries and stiff prices found on many cars built when the Model T was introduced in 1908. Glimmer and gadgets were for cars up the price scale.

Here's another version of a cooling system gauge, usually mounted in place of the standard radiator cap. These aftermarket monitors were practical and decorative. Andrew Morland

This version from the Towe Museum in Sacramento, California, even sprouted decorative wings while offering cooling system information! Tom Myers

The hand-operated klaxon-style horn was an option for Model T owners, like this 1914 version.

There were even prow-shaped radiators to replace the standard Model T units. These aftermarket items offered some sculpted styling if the owner chose to go this way.   Andrew Morland

The Model T was for those who wanted something reliable and affordable.

As detective Joe Friday often said in the "Dragnet" radio and television series, the Model T was "just the facts."

The Model T was designed to be for the self-reliant and drivers were expected to monitor what was going on. At least on the earliest version, that meant some work was involved. For example, checking the oil meant opening two pit cocks under the oil pan to see how high or low the level was at a given time. Checking the fuel level in the gas tank meant getting out of the driver's seat and taking any front seat passengers with you to remove the seat cushion and inserting a stick in the filler opening.

Starting the car was a multi-step process, especially in winter in cold weather climates. Owning a Model T was about being patient and resourceful.

If there were contraptions that made life even better with the car or made it easier to repair it, that was even better.

The original position of the Ford Motor Company erred on the side of automotive legend Ettore Bugatti who, when questioned about something an owner thought was wrong with the car, sniffed: "That's the way it should be."

In the case of the Model T it wasn't so much Bugatti's "take it or leave it" modus operandi as it was "that's all there is."

Owners were left to accept the Spartan nature of their cars or do something about it themselves. There was something about a Model T that not only demanded some owner customization but also seemed to create an attitude of caring for the car. It often went beyond practical chores of car ownership and approached a mystical bond between the car and its owner.

Because of the practical and low-price-oriented nature of the Model T, Ford Motor Company left a lot of territory for others to fill as their policy of few or no options, depending on the model year, inadvertently opened up an entire industry of post-production accessories and necessities.

"A $60,000 industry grew up supplying for the Model T what Henry wouldn't," said historian Beverly Rae Kimes. "He made a lot of men very rich." [1]

As sales of the Model T mushroomed, publishers noticed and latched onto the trend.

Entire magazine sections and catalogs in the 1910s were devoted to Model T repair tips and questions. *Automobile Dealer and Repairer* had a regular feature called "Ford Department" with extensive stories about such matters as overhauling the Model T, fixing a cracked block or renovating the engine.

It was possible to rebuild much of a Model T from the ground up with available small parts, large components and various add-ons advertised in the magazines and in catalogs.

"At the height of the Model T's popularity in the early 1920s, the Sears-Roebuck catalog featured no less than 5,000 different items that could be bolted, screwed and strapped to the vehicle." [2]

A sampling of some old magazines from the legendary

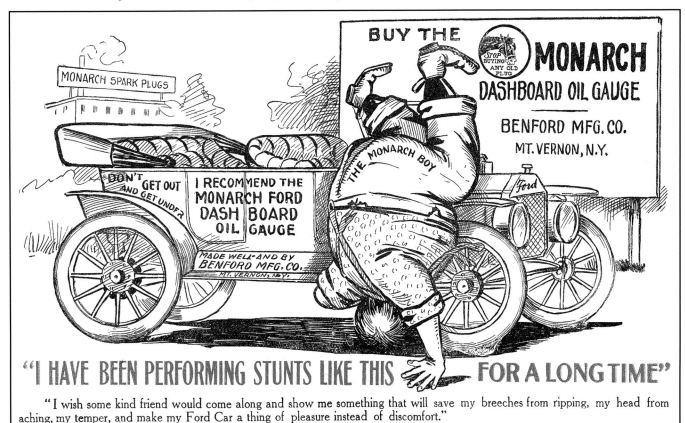

The Monarch dashboard oil gauge poked fun at the way Model T owners were told to check their engine oil levels.

Krause Publications' Archives offered a window into the time period of the Model T, almost from its beginnings.

In 1912, the thick guidebook-style *Automobile Trade Journal* ads relating to the Model T included Badger auto tops, the Hofweber Motor Starter, the Spengler Optical Ford timer and McCord Cellular Radiators. There was something called the Pantasote top. Those who weren't content with the standard bulb horn could select the "Long-Horn" hand-powered klaxon-style horn. A-C, Sharp, Black Eagle and Mossler offered spark plugs for Model Ts. Hayes replacement bodies and fenders were available. There even was something to clean the Model T called Rex Metal Cream and Rex Wood Oil.

By 1915, a check of the *Automotive Trade Journal* showed the Model T's increasing dominance in the automotive world. That guide contained a special aftermarket section that offered dozens of Model T items for sale over 50 pages. The items included everything from a tilting steering wheel to spare fenders. Ford owners could choose valve tools, a visible gas tank gauge, custom lamps, shock absorbers, special radiators, custom windshields and much more.

Just a few years later, a 1919 issue of *Automobile Dealer and Repairer* also included a number of Model T-related ads including Halladay Spring Bar bumpers and shocks, both Gem and Cox gasoline gauges, the Detroit Demountable Top, Brodrib Brothers pistons, Superford Honeycomb and Rockford-Mayo radiators, Hay-Dee frame extension systems, Rudge-Whitworth wire wheels, Thomas Elevator, Rush and Red Star timers, Benford Golden Giant spark plugs and the Veltum pneumatic valve grinder.

Many were companies that burned out like a meteor in the night sky or died away when Model T production was ended, names that have been lost in the past. A few companies still are with us. They all played a part in the aftermarket industry that the Model T's incredible popularity created.

Some companies concentrated solely on creations that helped Model T owners with practical needs like Apco All-Ways Right with its steering column brace, anti-rattling devices, radius rods, a steering wheel-mounted horn button, valve adjusters, timers and more. Gemco sold a tilting steering wheel, bumpers and transmission bands. Johns Manville offered asbestos brake linings and a fancy speedometer. The Spirex radiator offered to keep Model Ts cool "under any circumstances."

Ford itself also was a player, offering a smattering of options early on but increasing those to a small degree as years went by. While buyers never got the pages and pages of options available in living color as car buyers did in the 1950s and beyond, some practical items from Ford or the local Ford dealer offered a small degree of customization.

Ford Motor Co. might have been lean on extras but they knew enough to back up sales of cars with replacement parts. That was one aftermarket they controlled and promoted. Owners were constantly cautioned to use Ford parts available at the Ford dealer.

A series of stories about the Model T parts market showed how economically potent the parts sales world could be. One 1924 story in *Motor World* reported the Model T parts market was a half-billion dollar business. The article showed a pie chart with just 20 percent of that market, or $110 million, going to official Ford dealers but more than $440 million going to repair shops and non-Ford dealers. [3]

In September 1924, Crawford J. Nelson, a major Ford dealer in Clifton Heights, New Jersey, sent Philadelphia cabinet makers Lupton Systems a letter congratulating them for their design of a display case the Nelson dealership used to promote its Ford parts. Nelson Ford, and Lupton Systems, promoted the ability to carry more Ford parts in less floor space.

During July 1924, Filmore Ford of Santa Barbara, California, took the part sales angle one step further and showed how it carried Ford parts in a Model TT truck to repair shops within a 40-mile range of the dealership. Filmore Ford also employed a full-time customer contact person.

"Fillmore carries the stockroom to the wholesale customer rather than forcing the customer to come to the dealer's establishment to make purchases." [4]

And owner E. M. Fillmore suggested the Model T era concept of restraint with Ford accessories and options when dealing with Ford owners.

"If it is apparent to him that you are trying to load him down with as much merchandise as you can, he is not going to have as high an estimation of your sales policy as if you adopted more conservative methods." 5

From the earliest days of the Model T sales, it was the aftermarket that took up the cause of "loading customers down" with as much as they could bear for their Model Ts.

Despite the Ford Motor Company warning about aftermarket additions, buyers made it their own choices from the multitude of pure gimmicks to the array of practical selections available. And there were so many Model Ts on the roads, it was inevitable many would be outfitted to the tastes of their owners.

"...when confronted with the first truly standardized machine for individual conveyance," wrote Robert Lacey, "human nature felt an irresistible need to personalize it."

The venerable auto historian Floyd Clymer, who sold cars in his pre-teen years and later sold aftermarket automotive equipment and books about the auto industry, talked about a product called the Hunter starter, a mechanical device that was intended to eliminate the need for exiting the driver's seat to crank the Model T engine to life.

"The Hunter Starter ($10) was a clever item that looked like a Rube Goldberg invention. It turned the engine over quickly by a chain operating from a combination of levers that finally ended up inside the car with a handle located within reach of the driver. All he needed to do was to pull the handle, as he would that of a slot machine. Sometimes it actually worked." 7

With names that ranged from Aerobelle to Fordezer to Halladay, the aftermarket shock absorber makers promised to remove as much bounce from Model T rides as possible.   Doug Mitchel

One large portion of the aftermarket industry for Model T Fords concentrated on shock absorbers that made many promises of a better ride.   Doug Mitchel

A rugged aftermarket radiator was offered to Model T owners. Spirex appealed to the added cooling capacity available and usually showed real life scenes.

In the midst of all the hokum and the helpful, there quickly arose a hierarchy of major players in the Model T aftermarket, whose creations made so much sense that even Ford Motor Co. put a similar gadget into production or blessed and approved the aftermarket company's product.

Among the major aftermarket players were Ruckstell and its two-speed axle, the Boyce Moto-Meter and the Atwater-Kent and Bosch electronic parts.

Atwater-Kent ignition systems, for example were used in well-known brands of the time including Chalmers,

Hupmobile, Peerless, Thomas and Velie cars. "Tens of thousands of Ford owners…will discover for the first time the flexibility, power, speed and economy of which their motors are capable," suggested the Philadelphia-based Atwater Kent Mfg. Works.

On the other hand, Bosch, then as now a specialist in electronics and ignition parts, attempted to appeal to the no-nonsense attitude of Ford Motor Co. suggesting its offerings were practical choices. "A necessity, not a luxury" said the Bosch headline. "Most Ford accessories now being offered to Ford owners are luxuries—something added for looks or extra comfort. The Bosch-Ford attachment provides efficient and reliable ignition. The weak, irregular spark is no more."

If all that practicality didn't make the customer salivate, Bosch did throw in a little sizzle as well. "You can have the same ignition system that was used by the winners of the 1915 Vanderbilt Cup and Grand Prize Racers…"

Glover E. Ruckstell's two-speed rear axle was one extra that eventually gained the Ford blessing and even was available through dealerships where Model Ts were sold.

It "Makes Your Car Two Cars in One" said the Ruckstell brochure. The company made a differential that created a two-speed rear axle for both Model Ts and a heavier version for the TT truck "cousins."

It replaced the stock left rear axle with a special Ruckstell housing that contained extra gears to work with the standard gears to offer drivers choices including overdrive.

Many drivers considered the Ruckstell two-speed axle a vital part of their Model T car or TT truck and wouldn't have been without one.

The Ruckstell unit offered two extra gear ratios with a secondary version of high and a secondary version of low available to the driver. There was also a second reverse speed available. The multiple speeds were an asset in everything from hill climbing to churning through deteriorated roads.

In its ads, Ruckstell claimed 20 percent more speed potential on the highway or 55 percent more power in unfavorable road conditions. The Ruckstell two-speed axle was built by the Hall-Scott Motor Car Company of Berkeley, California.

The Boyce Moto-Meter was made by the Moto-Meter Company of Long Island City, New York.

"Aside from protecting the Ford owner against overheating and subsequent costly repair bills, it adds an attractive touch to the appearance of any car."

The Moto-Meters made for Model Ts offered a clearly-visible measure of the fluid level in the radiator with marked gradients on the gauge that showed high, low and regular water levels. The $4-device was designed to replace the standard radiator cap, serving the dual function of cap and gauge. The Moto-Meter was a popular add on and was immediately recognizable, a simple but practical form of a radiator ornament.

Even spark plug companies we still rely on today sold their wares to the Model T owners. Champion advertised its X-series for Ford cars. "It has been officially specified to all Ford agents as the best adapted to the requirements of the car's motor," claimed the Champion Spark Plug Company.

One other Ford-sanctioned mainstay in the early days of the Model T was the Highland Body Company of Cincinnati, Ohio. Highland took Model T chassis and made some series of their own offering customized units.

The basic Highland body styles advertised in 1914 were the F panel van, the O open sided canopy delivery, the R with its covered utility box and the D with the "demountable flare board body" (think pickup!). Other versions included the stylish FX delivery van, the OB with its rigid park bench driver's seat and no top, and the RX that looked like a roadster with a two-place "mother-in-law" seat out back.

"They carry any load the Ford car will carry and are built so as not to burden the chassis with unnecessary weight."

A number of companies later used the Model TT chassis for an incredible array of truck and bus modifications.

Highland Body Company also made a special coupe top for roadster owners that was claimed to be interchangeable with the folding top and turned the little roadster "...into

Aftermarket body companies specialized in providing closed bodies for those who owned Model T roadsters and touring cars.

a handsome closed coupe, perfect in lines and finish." The Highland coupe top used the same support irons and windshield as the folding top.

It was left to the Model T aftermarket to offer items that many buyers really desired and needed. Some of the offerings even added style to the plain but practical Model Ts.

The Mandel Limousine Co. of Chicago offered to "Make the Ford a Year Round Car" for $100 to $150. The Mandel Limosette offered closed bodies for the touring car and the runabout styles. The Mandel Limosette claimed easy installation and that it could be detached for summer driving.

The Koupet Auto Top Company of Belleville, Illinois, offered its "California Top" for Fords that included window glass and a slanted windshield.

Sport Factories of America in Aurora, Illinois, was well known for its aftermarket racing bodies, as were a number of other companies. One of their choices for the non-racing crowds was the Chummy Sportster for the Model T chassis.

For just $84.50, the buyer received a sporty slanted windshield, a rugged "Gypsy style" top in military or bow styling and a two-place rumble seat. The Chummy Sportster could be painted in tan and gray or blue and gray for $4.65 extra. Stylish wheel disks also were $7.25 a set.

Some companies offered pumps to do the jobs Ford Motor Company had left to gravity—such as water and fuel pumps in the aftermarket. Others attempted to offer reliable non-Ford sources of linings and fan belts.

Many companies attempted to cushion the ride offered by the stiff transverse wagon-style springs in the Model T. Pacific Leather Works of Oakland, California, offered its Sturges Hydraulic Road Smoothers, an early attempt at shock absorbers. Hartford Suspension Company offered its "Cushion Springs" at just $16 for a set of four promising to "Make your Ford ride easy."

The L. P. Halladay Company of Streator, Illinois, offered its spring-mounted and fully lubricated Halladay shock absorbers—nickname the "Goat" and called the "Greatest

Little Trouble-Taker on the Road." The Halladays were $7.50 per pair or $12.50 for a set of four.

Halladay appealed to the driver's back and joints in its ad. "...there are a hundred devilish jolts waiting to play havoc with your backbone the next time you take a long ride. Every joint means a mashing of cartilage and a yanking of delicate nerves. Let the Halladay Shock Absorber be the 'goat' instead of your backbone."

Resler-Wallace Sales Company of Detroit even played off the Model T's family name when it offered its "4rd" brand of shock absorbers. There was a "Fordezer" brand as well.

K-W "Road Smoothers" promised to "Smooth Out the Roughest Roads" for drivers and even offered to send readers a booklet called "Taking Out the Bumps." K-W also was known for various ignition specialties offered for Model Ts.

In 1914, C. F. Roper and Company of Hopedale, Massachusetts showed a huge cutout of a gasoline can with a woman driving a Model T touring car next to a sign that read "5 miles to anywhere." The Roper Air Feeder, under the commanding headlines "Save Gasoline" and "5 Miles More on One Gallon." If drivers did not get the desired miles per gallon, Roper offered they would get their $2 back.

The Model T repair technician wasn't left out either. Many special tools were available to work on the Model Ts. The Frank Mossberg Company of Attleboro, Massachusetts and the Fawsco brand by the J. H. Faw Tool Company were among a range of companies that offered tool specialties for repairing the Model Ts.

A series of ads by the Benford Manufacturing Company of Mt. Vernon, New York, even poked fun at the way Ford owners had to check their oil. One ad showed a rotund cartoon man labeled "The Monarch Boy" standing on one hand to check his Model T touring car's oil level.

"I've been performing stunts like this for a long time," read the caption. Ad copy worried about his temper, his headache and saving his "breeches from ripping." "Don't get out and get under," read graffiti on the car. "Buy the Monarch Dashboard Oil Gauge" read a sign near the car.

Driver comfort and convenience wasn't overlooked either with all manner of switches, non-slip pedals and even the Burpee-Johnson locking steering wheel. Various tire and baggage carriers also were offered.

Romort Manufacturing Company of Oshkosh, Wisconsin, clarified the fact that their accessory "shock absorber" for Fords actually was a steering wheel lock and device that deflected road shock from weary drivers. They wanted to use a catchier name and offered $100 to anyone who could come up with a better way of identifying their product.

Band Ease was one of the many companies that attempted to deal with wear and tear on the planetary transmission. The company focused on removing "…the jump and clatter out of the Ford Car." The Band Ease brand promised not to leave residue that caused hardening and glazing as other linings did.

Products that helped Model T owners keep their bands properly lubricated included the "Chrystalites" oiler. Grundy Corporation offered its "A-Just," a mechanical valve that regulated fuel distribution.

Other companies that were tied to the Model T success story were Aerobelle shock absorbers, the Bull Dog and Williams accelerator pedals, the Uloy body stamping company, Rose top covers, the Red Star timer, Maxim Silencer mufflers, the Splitdorf magneto and both the Century and Rochester starters.

Even Bib the Michelin man got into the act rising in a hot air balloon to promote balloon tires for Model Ts in the mid 1920s.

Automobile Dealer and Repairer offered its take on what the "well dressed Flivver" should wear or have along in an April 1922 article. The list of items included a tool kit, a hydrometer for checking the battery fluid, a tire gauge, pump, tire chains and a tire patching kit.

"The man who drives without a set of tire chains is a criminal, without repair materials is a thief and without a tire pump is a fool," wrote the unnamed editor, who explained that tire chains avoided sliding and causing an accident in bad weather. He said having tire repair materials avoided

The Highland Body Mfg. Co. of Cincinnati, Ohio, made many aftermarket bodies for Model Ts that people often think were made in Ford factories.

the inevitable borrowing of them. And drivers could not blow tires up with their mouths.

Front and rear bumpers also were recommended as was a jack, a tow rope or tow bar and windshield cleaner.

"I'd rather go without a spare tire and be a fool without a pump than take a chance on summer weather without some sort of a cleaner," the editor noted.

A trouble light with 12 feet of cord was suggested and the article also suggested using a rear view mirror. There was an extra burst of opinion for the Ford system of checking two oil pit cocks.

"Only an expert spirit medium or an improved ouija board could tell when the oil level was correct in height. An oil level gauge, kept clean, is a good investment."

The editor also suggested a humidifier or water vaporizer for the Model T engine manifold to avoid excess carbon. And he said he valued "a set of leather boots for the springs" to help keep the chassis free from squeaks.

Prior to the introduction of Ford's own electrical starting system in the 1919 model year, the Dayton Motor-Dynamo was an interesting choice that promised to end crank-starting drudgery for Model T owners.

The Dayton system did away with chains, clutches and gears and included a small motor where the crank was normally mounted. The system, made by the Dayton Electric Company, still offered the ability to crank the car by hand but also included a floor-mounted starter button, a battery that offered up to 12 volts capacity (two six-volt batteries in parallel wiring) and a battery box that was mounted on the running board. A steering column-mounted switch offered electric headlights with dimming ability as well as an electric horn.

One accessory made certain the Model T earned its living. The Schluter Auto Belt Attachment was made by the E. F. Elmburg Co. of Parkersburg, Iowa, and was reminiscent of horse-powered farm equipment ads that had been so prominent just one generation previously.

Pictured in the Schluter ad was the ever-present Model T with a pulley that was mounted at the end of a shaft that went into the crank hole. The Schluter attachment became a Model T –powered farm hand. One end of the work belt wrapped around the pulley at the front of the Model T and the other portion was attached to whatever gadget needed power.

The industrious Model T was shown mixing concrete, powering a saw, separating cream, milling grain, pumping water, running a conveyor and even washing clothes! All in a day's work in Schluter World! Henry Ford would have been very proud to watch the Schluter Auto Belt-equipped Model T in endless action.

FORD ITEM	PRICE
Piston and pin	$ 1.40
Connecting rod	$ 1.60
Crankshaft	$ 10
Cylinder head	$ 6
Cylinder	$ 20
Time gear	$ .75
Time gear cover	$ 1
Crankcase	$ 12
Magneto coil assembly	$ 5
Fly wheel	$ 13
Transmission gear shaft	$ 1.65
Transmission cover	$ 6
Clutch pedal	$ .65
Steering gear assembly (less wheel and bracket)	$ 8.50
Starter drive	$ 4.25
Generator	$12.50
Battery	$ 8.50
Carburetor	$ 3
Vaporizer assembly (with fittings)	$ 9
Rear axle shaft	$ 1.75
Differential drive gear	$ 3
Universal joint assembly	$ 2.50
Drive shaft pinion	$ 1.50
Front axle	$ 9
Spindle connecting rod	$ 1.75
Front radius rod	$ 1.80
Rear spring	$ 6
Radiator—less shell (1917-'23)	$ 15
Radiator—less shell (1923-'27)	$ 14
Hood (1917-'23)	$ 6.50
Hood (1926-'27) (black)	$ 7
Gasoline tank	$ 6
Front fenders (1917-'25) each	$ 4
Front fenders (1926-'27) each	$ 5
Rear fenders (1922-'25) each	$ 3.75
Rear fenders (1926-'27) each	$ 4
Running board	$ 1.25
Horn (battery type)	$ 1.50
Headlamp assembly (1915-'26) pair	$ 5.50
Touring car top (1915-'25) complete	$ 27
Touring car top (1926-'27) complete, includes curtains and curtain rods	$ 35

The manufacturer claimed it hooked into the crank socket without screws or attachments—both on and off in about 15 seconds. "$22.50 and a Ford gives you 8-horsepower portable gas engine capacity," said the Elmburg Company ad. "Hundreds of Schluters are now used on farms in every state in the corn belt. By actual tests against regular gas engines, the Ford engine with the Schluter does more work on an equal amount of gas." [8]

For the Model T owners, there were any number of possibilities for work and comfort for their cars, an aftermarket that lasted well into the 1930s, as long as Model Ts were active.

Ford Also Chose from a Market of Suppliers

According to original body identification tags found in a well-kept early Model T, Ford Motor Co. chose from a number of interesting vendors and component makers when the cars were produced.

In addition to Ford factory bodies, for example, Fisher— later the bodymaking arm of General Motors—and Monroe made bodies for Ford Motor Co. Tops were made by at least seven companies while body finishing was done by five companies in addition to the Ford plant.

Here is a chart of the relevant suppliers, according to a story in *Vintage Ford* 6-3, from May-June 1971:

BODY MANUFACTURER	BODY FINISHERS	TOP MAKERS
Fisher	American	American Auto Trim
Herbert	Briggs	Am J
Monroe	Detroit	Apple
Pontiac	Herbert	Detroit Motor Co.
Wilson	Pontiac	Iroquois
		Taylor
		Warner

The Model T Market Kept on Going

What some contemporary Model T owners may not realize is how fervently the marketplace remained for parts for at least two years after the Model T ended production.

Ford advertised the parts and service portion of their business to assure owners that their cars would be no orphans.

"The Ford Motor Company will continue to make replacement parts for these cars 'until the last Model T is off the road' said a Ford ad from April 1928. "Millions of Model T Fords are still in active service" read a headline that same month.

"No matter where you live," said the ad, "you can still buy Model T Ford parts with the same assurance…knowing that they will give you the kind of service you have a right to expect, and at the same time protect the money you have invested in your car."

Another ad, from May 1928, reminded Ford owners that the company was making a new car but was still proud of the Model T and suggested more than eight million of them were still in service—available to drive for two, three, five or many more years.

"…a small expenditure may enable you to maintain or increase the value of the car and give you thousands of miles of additional service."

In April 1929, Ford offered a price list for the Model T in local newspaper ads as follows:

"These prices are for parts only," said the Ford Motor Co. ad. "The charge for labor is equally low. It is billed at the flat rate so you may know in advance what the job will cost." [9]

Model Ts that Shattered Stereotypes

So were you among those who thought all Model Ts just came in black? Perhaps you were a secret Chevy-Sixer, a Dort-Nick or had pinups of the Dodge Brothers in your garage. You might have been a Peerless-poobah or a Minerva-maven. So it's time you broaden your perspective and shatter some stereotypes about the Model T Ford!

Some Model Ts were sporty. Some could even be considered plush. Some came in bright colors!

Some Model Ts (cover your eyes Henry Ford) were downright luxurious!

Even if you ever dreamed of being outdoors in an Overland, having life the Gray way or taking a Flint sprint, you know the Model T Fords were extremely adaptable and were put to work in all kinds of ways.

What you may not know is there were special editions of Ford Model Ts.

One key item in the Livingood conversion apparatus was a two-speed or three-speed gearbox that was attached to the unit. Warford units were common while a Spicer, like this one, was rarer.   Jim Allen

The 60-inch

In the American South, as in other parts of the country, the roads were tough, especially in the first five to seven years of the Model T's production. After World War I, more corners of the nation began focusing on building and maintaining roads. But early on, roads that had been considered good enough for horse-drawn wagons were expected to be good enough for the early automobiles.

In trying to meet the needs of rural areas with poor roads, the Ford Motor Company offered a wider track, especially for rural roads in the South where wagons had wider tracks than elsewhere. The 60-inch track, also known as the Dixie Tread or Southern Tread, was offered on the Model T to help cope with the wider ruts.

Talk about wide track—and some 45 to 50 years before the 1959 Pontiac appeared! The Ford 60- inch track added four more inches from the standard 56-inch track. That meant a longer front axle and tie rods plus more room at the end of the axle/spring perches.

On all 60-inch Model Ts, the fenders were two inches wider as well.

After July 31, 1916, there were no more 60-inch versions built by Ford for U. S. markets, though there is evidence Ford of Canada built cars with wider wheelbases. After 1916, Southern Model T buyers were told to ride with one wheel in a rut and one on a ridge.

There probably is a country song that could go with that phrase!

Livingood Four Wheel Drive

Just when you thought your SUV was state of the art, it might be a time to pause for a moment to realize that four-wheel drive was patented by two gentlemen from Clintonville, Wisconsin, in 1909, the first year the Model T was produced. Otto Zachow and William Besserdich applied their concept to their Four Wheel Drive Auto Company cars and trucks that year and beyond, and others had similar ideas.

One was Jesse Livingood, a Pennsylvania native who moved to rural Iowa. Shortly before American involvement in World War I in 1917, the Livingood Motor Truck Company

The Livingood four-wheel-drive conversion unit for Model Ts used an offset Spicer transfer case and a special notch in the front spring.   Jim Allen

Owner Frank Piskur of Grafton, Ohio, puts a 1921 Model T with the Livingood four-wheel-drive conversion unit through some snow.   Jim Allen

was formed but it failed shortly afterward. The Iowa-based company intended to make full-size trucks with chain drives, according to pictures that survived from that time.

After his truck-based four-wheel drive production concept failed, Livingood experimented with the concept of coupling the popular Model T with an all-wheel drive unit.

Thanks to Livingood's persistence, Model T owners were able to take their custom-bodied wooden station cars or even a roadster direct from the factory and get a conversion for all-wheel driving. Of course, in the 1920s, the use of four-wheel drive wasn't intended mostly for show at the mall parking lot and a little bit of snow.

Having a Livingood four-wheel drive system on your

already spry Model T made it even more at home in the wilds of nature.

There were two generations of the Livingood conversion units. While he had experimented with the system in the late teens and early 1920s, the first type appeared on the market just shortly after he received his patent in June 1923.

The Livingood conversion kit came with a special front axle, and spring shackles. The differential was offset to the right side. The Livingood axle ends were tapered and keyed just like the rear axles. And they used rear-wheel hubs on the front wheels.

The original style used a special notch on the right

These are the original Jesse Livingood molds and blueprints used to make the four-wheel-drive conversion system.   Jim Allen

end of the transverse springs to allow room for the four-wheel drive differential housing up front. The transfer case openings matched both the rear end of the standard engine/transmission and the universal joint for the torque tube drive. It coupled into these fittings easily once the original torque tube drive was shortened 10 to 12 inches to make room for the transfer case.

The original Livingood conversion kit used a selector that allowed the driver to engage the front wheels so all four wheels drove the vehicle. The front wheels could be disengaged for two-wheel drive only. With the front wheels engaged, the Model T with Livingood conversion also had four-wheel brakes.

The second generation of the Livingood conversion arrived later in the 1920s. In addition to the items used on the first generation conversion kit, the second generation Livingood unit applied a transmission gearbox, usually made by Warford, though some others were used.

In addition to regular Model T gears from the floor-mounted planetary transmission pedal action the Livingood setup let the driver choose four-wheel drive in high and low or to select neutral for normal T driving.

This version had an abbreviated torque tube drive to the rear with the transfer case immediately behind the engine/transmission case and the secondary gearbox behind the transfer case. In the second version, the front axle was constantly engaged.

Livingood designed other conversion systems but not all were put into production. The second-generation four-wheel drive conversion was produced beyond the life of the Model T, into the late 1930s. A Livingood version was available on Chevrolets at that time.

Radius rods in the front and back as well as a redesigned steering link were other changes made with the Livingood conversion systems.

According to a 1998 article in *Vintage Ford*, Jesse Livingood II was still making the second-generation components using his father's design with an updated transfer case. He lived in Graysville, Pennsylvania, at that time. [10]

A short ride in the Livingood-equipped Model T was described in *Four Wheeler* magazine.

"The Livingood T shows us its stuff in the mud and snow, with a few deep ruts and undulations to stretch the suspension out. A Model T at work …is a combination of the low 'angry bee' buzzing of the engine, the whine of straight-cut bevel gears, creaking wooden spokes, groaning springs and various sheet metal parts clanking and banging against each other. The realization how far ahead the Livingood T would have been over everything else in [the 1920s]." [11]

Jesse Livingood Jr. built this 1915 Model T Speedster and included his dad's conversion unit. This angle is a good one to see the stance of the four-wheel-drive conversion unit.   Jim Allen

Model Ts in Snow and Sand

There was a time in North America, especially where winter conditions set in, when cars—even Model T Fords—were set aside when the weather turned colder and winter conditions set in, just as motorcycles are stored in the colder climates today. Road maintenance—and in several cases the roads themselves—were lacking. Some people even resorted to horse-drawn sledges and cutters to get from place to place as the snowfalls mounted.

Virgil D. White had another idea. He thought the winter lay-up didn't have to continue. A Ford dealer from Ossipie, New Hampshire, White envisioned the sturdy, practical Model T would work well in snow with some practical modifications.

He registered his idea and the name "Snowmobile."

The White version meant the removal of the standard rear axle, driveshaft, transverse rear spring and radius rods. What took their place was a heftier Model TT rear axle with worm drive and attachments to the Model T frame. Heavy-duty wheels also were used.

One pair connected to the driving axle and the two lead wheels were free rolling. The combination looked like a modern dual-bogie truck unit. Tracks with snow-gripping cleats went over the circumference of the dual wheels on each side.

The usual Model T transverse springs were replaced with a pair of elliptical springs mounted parallel to the frame on the left and right sides.

White's Model T "Snowmobile" conversion used five-foot long skis or runners made of spruce and poplar and covered with ½-inch metal shoes. Most were available with the same 56-inch track used in the standard Model T. A 44-inch version was available in areas where that width of horse-drawn bobsleds was used. The standard Canadian 38-inch sleigh tracks also meant that width was available.

In 1926, when new Model Ts were as inexpensive as

The 1921 Model T Depot Hack shows the stance of the Livingood four-wheel-drive conversion unit in a winter scene. Jim Allen

This 1919 Model T was converted by the Snowmobile Co. of West Ossippie, New Hampshire. The name and the vehicle popularized motorized snow travel in North America. Jim Allen

The Snowmobile Co. conversion used one live and one unpowered rear axle with treads ringing sets of tires on each side of the vehicle. Jim Allen

$260 for a runabout and $290 for a touring car, the White Snowmobile conversion cost $395 for cars and $250 for trucks, which needed less reconfiguration.

According to author Jim Rodell, the father of President Calvin Coolidge had a funeral procession led by Model T Snowmobiles when he died in Vermont. The advent of the Model T Snowmobile conversion spurred competition as well when the first recorded race was held at Three Lakes, Wisconsin between two Model T Snowmobiles.

When some observers saw the vehicles cope with snow they thought about its desert potential. Soon a Sandmobile conversion was available using wheels instead of the skis up front. The sand versions were used in Egypt, North and South Africa as well as the Florida Everglades.

The White Snowmobile operations were sold to Farm Supply Specialty Company of New Holstein, Wisconsin, in 1925. That company built them until 1929.

The Langenfeld family began a second company in the same small town, located in eastern Wisconsin's hilly and rich farm country between Lake Winnebago and Lake Michigan. The Langenfelds formerly owned a hardware store in nearby Marytown.

The Langenfeld unit used a bright blue conversion kit and kept the standard Model T driveline.

A coil-spring loaded cross member was attached to the frame and the unit's free-rolling axle, located ahead of the driving axle like the Snowmobile conversion.

Called the "Snow Flyer," the Langenfeld-built unit used a butterfly-shaped drive belt cleat with the center opened so much less snow was trapped. An auxiliary road wheel could be mounted outside the metal ski unit on the Snow Flyer.

One of these units stands in the Towe Auto Museum in Sacramento, California and appears in this book.

Special bodies were built for the Snow Flyer and included a panel unit, a wooden cab and even a small fuel tanker unit. The Snow Flyer conversions were $165. Normally, the conversion kit recommended use of the Ruckstell two-speed axle, a $59 extra.

Snow Flyers gained a degree of fame in Model A form.

The ski units combined elements of aerodynamics, with their sealed surfaces and traditional skis to glide over snow as smoothly as possible.   Jim Allen

At least one was built for Admiral Richard E. Byrd's trip to Antarctica. In 1930, the Langenfelds left the conversion business to raise fur-bearing animals for a living.

About that time the Farm Specialty Co. resumed production of what had been the Snowmobile operation and combined the remains of the former Langenfeld Snow Flyer operation to form the Snow Flyer Corp. Their product was the Snow Bird, a conversion that was briefly available for the remaining Model Ts and also was available for Model As, Chevrolets, Stars, Durants and Whippets.

Tracks were offered in 38-, 44- and 56-inch widths. Hubs brought out driving wheels 1-1/2 inches on either side. Driving tracks were available in 9-, 10- and 12-inch sizes. The runners or skis were much lighter than previous units and used the conventional steering gears of the cars.

Snow Birds were made well into 1939. The company moved into other specialties during World War II, then went on to build posthole diggers, backhoes and similar construction equipment for the postwar world.

"The Snowmobile Can't Be Snowbound" promised the company's advertising. "Whenever it is possible to buy a Ford car in the snow section of the United States, it is generally possible to buy Snowmobile attachments."[12]

A second type of snow vehicle was the Snow Flyer, a company that took up in New Holstein, Wisconsin, from the Snowmobile Co. remnants. Note the skis and wheels together up front. Tom Myers

Model T Ambulances Served "Over There" 13

When wars break out, automobile and truck manufacturers often are called on to contribute their skills. It often becomes a lucrative and emotional endeavor but one that reminds workers of the ultimate costs of lives lost and people injured in war.

In 1914, Europe was enmeshed in World War I. Ford Motor Company's French assembly plant was asked to contribute to the effort. Ford's manager in France donated 10 Model T chassis to help the American Military Hospital in Paris.

The first group of ambulances had only a canvas covering over the rear portion of the chassis with a wooden plank floor. Drivers were exposed to the elements without any kind of a roof, doors or windshield to protect themselves.

The Model Ts earned praises from the French Army for the car's ability to function in terrain that often prevented even horse-drawn vehicles from functioning in those early months of the war.

More companies got involved in the effort as Britain, France and then officially neutral United States pooled more than 19,000 vehicles for the war effort. American drivers became more involved and in 1915, an American banker raised enough to supply 35 more Model T ambulances.

The light Model Ts could only carry three stretchers but offered reliable service and could navigate through muddy conditions that bogged down larger vehicles. Their ground clearance, originally designed to deal with rough or nonexistent North American roads, was perfect for the battlefields in France.

French soldiers called the Model T "le chevre" or "le bouc," a goat or billy goat. British soldiers called it the "mechanical flea."

Drivers like Walt Disney and Ernest Hemingway would become famous after the war but spent time driving American Field Services Model T ambulances in World War I.

By 1916, though Henry Ford officially was opposed to the war effort, Ford in Detroit recorded 20,700 ambulances made, primarily for the war effort. The Ford City plant, Ford of Canada, also made ambulances and other vehicles for the World War I effort. Ford of Canada produced a booklet promoting its efforts in World War I through its exports to various British Commonwealth countries.

In 1917 and 1918, America became involved in World War I and Ford Motor Company production served the military's needs, though production of the Model T continued. More ambulances, as well as some TT trucks, were built for the war cause.

Ford Motor Co. U. S. Military Ambulance Production—WWI Era	
1916	20,700
1917	1,452
1918	399

Source: Standard Catalog of Ford 1903-2003, 3rd Edition

The V-8 Model T That Could Have Been

In a story first written in 1967, then reprinted in 1976, Henry Ford Museum official Kenneth Schwartz related the story of a V-8 engine that could have been a very interesting aftermarket item for Model T owners if it had been put into production.

The V-8 was the creation of Southern California Ford dealer J. Dale Gentry and his sales manager, Martin S. Lewis. The Gentry-Lewis engine was built in their spare time and used a stock Model T crankshaft, timing gears, valves, the planetary transmission and even the stock engine pan.

Their plan was to produce an aftermarket engine block that easily bolted onto the stock Ford four- cylinder pan and transmission to yield more horsepower and torque. The V-8, built in 1915, produced 226 cid and had a 3 x 4 in. bore and stroke. No horsepower was recorded but one can guess it would have been much more than the standard 20 for the Model T.

The Gentry-Lewis V-8 manifold combined intake and exhaust units in one piece and used a Zenith updraft carburetor with air drawn in near the manifold. The left cylinder head was grooved to easily allow the steering column to function.

The Gentry-Lewis V-8 was the victim of all work and no play, in a sense. When B. L. Graves, Los Angeles District Manager of Ford, visited the Gentry dealership and saw the engine, he scolded both Gentry and Lewis for not focusing more of their time on selling and promoting Model Ts.

Since Gentry preferred not to rock the boat, the V-8 became a footnote rather than the next Ruckstell axle or Livingood four-wheel drive.

According to the Schwartz account, published in *Vintage Ford* in 1976, Gentry wished he would have disregarded the nearsightedness of his district manager and manufactured the V-8. In hindsight, so do many Model T lovers! 15

RIGHT: Glover Ruckstell's two-speed axle was a Model T aftermarket choice that proved to be so popular and practical that it became a Ford Motor Co.-endorsed product.

The Aftermarket Created the Model T Truck Market

Citizens of average means influenced Ford Motor Company to begin producing its own brand of trucks.

Ford had waded into the truck market with the early express delivery in 1910 through 1912, but had pulled back when that vehicle's sales were sluggish compared to the

other successful Model Ts. The Ford decision makers left it to the aftermarket.

"Merchants and dealers throughout the country...had constructed delivery wagons and truck bodies of various types on Model T chassis, demonstrating the feasibility of a commercial vehicle." 16

Finally, just before America's involvement in World War I, Ford Motor Company introduced the Model TT truck, yet Ford continued to make only the chassis and running gear.

In 1924, Ford introduced its first body and cab unit, a one-ton truck. The next year, Ford introduced the official conversion that made a Model T roadster into a small pickup.

Commercial conversion of the Model T was one aftermarket with a steady drum-beat that finally changed the Ford Motor Co. tune about making trucks.

Atwater-Kent was a popular choice for Model T owners who sought to improve the performance of their ignition systems.

The Story of a Small Town Model T Component Maker

By 1925, Clintonville, Wisconsin, was used to making a splash on the national and even the international stages. Its Four Wheel Drive Auto Company, formed in 1909, had become an international success story, a company that sold trucks to buyers on at least five of the seven continents.

Menominee Truck Company, a second vehicle maker in the small Waupaca County community, was successful as well, especially with its Hurryton trucks and buses. The Menominee Truck also had a national reputation.

And just before World War I, the heavy-duty tractor maker formed by Clintonville dentist Dr. Charles Topp and his father-in-law, D. S. Stewart, the Topp-Stewart Tractor Company, had gained a well earned reputation among road builders across the country.

So when Arthur Patterson began making mechanical drawings in 1921, his brother, Thomas, began dreaming of the possibilities of what might happen with their efforts. He thought that the Patterson brothers might become the fourth Clintonville business to flex its muscles in the national and international automotive arena.

What interested the Patterson brothers was the idea of connecting a speedometer to the planetary transmission of a Model T Ford.

While their efforts are not well-known or remembered, even by keen-eyed Model T buffs in the United States, the Patterson units were sold between 1926 and 1928 through Ford Motor Company of Canada, especially in their export territories—Australia, New Zealand and portions of Africa—as well as in the Dominion of Canada.

The Clintonville *Tribune* reported in 1928 that 20 men were working for Patterson Brothers and they had moved from space in the Topp-Stewart plant on the northeast end of Clintonville to "more suitable quarters" on Third and Main Streets on the south side of that city.

In their April 23, 1926, issue, Clintonville's other newspaper at the time, the *Dairyman's Gazette*, had reported about the company's prospects:

"The Patterson Manufacturing Company is experiencing a boom in business with the opening of spring and orders for their transmission drive speedometers for Fords are going faster than they can be filled. Orders for some 1,000 have been received from Canada, over 100 from Sydney, Australia, and orders are on the books from Japan, Argentina and many of the larger cities of the United States... A market has been firmly established for the company." [17]

Patterson Manufacturing had not spent much effort on advertising until that time but the *Dairyman's Gazette* mentioned the company had prepared a display for the trade markets. Patterson also was trying to be versatile with its product.

"Though the speedometer drive is made to fit either the A. C. or Stewart head the company is standardizing on the Stewart head in its complete equipment."

But it was not meant to last beyond the Model T and by 1928, Patterson Manufacturing was looking at different markets for its business, premiering a portable brake-testing machine.

From this small shop in Clintonville, Wisconsin, the Patterson Brothers shipped Model T speedometer heads to Ford distributors around the world.   Tom Collins

"Clintonville's Home and Farm Paper," the *Dairyman's Gazette*, summed up the problems of being a Model T component or aftermarket product maker in its July 12, 1928, issue introducing the new Patterson brake testing machine.

"Tom Patterson would have been a rich man and Clintonville would have had a factory employing a hundred men if Henry Ford hadn't changed his car. Tom invented the only successful speedometer which could operate on the planetary transmission of the Model T. It sold by the thousands to Ford dealers in the United States, Canada and foreign countries, and then Henry changed to his new car and threw a good-sized monkey wrench into the machinery of a thriving Clintonville industry." [18]

The brake-testing dream lasted only a few years and Patterson Manufacturing Company was hard hit by the Depression Era by 1931. While its big dreams of success had faded, the Patterson Brothers remained well into the 1960s as a specialty machine shop in Clintonville.

This author remembers well its garage door open in summers on Third Street, watching work in progress at the Patterson shop.

Henry Ford's dream of success brought many people who were happy to follow on his coattails. The story of the Patterson Brothers Company from Clintonville, Wisconsin, was just one that shared a brief moment in the Model T's bright spotlight.

Speedometers were used on the early Model Ts, like this version mounted in a 1910 version of the car. Doug Mitchel

Chapter 8

MODEL T
LORE AND HUMOR

A Model T Prelude

Child of the brass age, grown up in war, coming of age with jazz. They called her Liz and she was part Great Gatsby—the flapper with cloche-knit hat and trim, short dress. And she was part Edwardian with wide brim hats and ankle-length, button-up dress.

Her face was as well-known as Chaplin's and she was as soulful as Bessie Smith's blues.

Liz was equally at home in the Cotton Club and the Grand Ole Opry, the Algonquin Round Table and the World Series.

She became an icon of the silver screen, a scene stealer, who fit into any role.

> *"If money is your hope for independence you will never have it. The only real security that a man can have is a reserve of knowledge, experience and ability."*
>
> *Henry Ford*

Child of the brass age, the Model Ts brought people together everywhere they could go in the cars that lasted until late in the age of jazz. Robin Heil-Kern

The true superstar—as familiar in London, England, as she was in East London, South Africa and New London, Wisconsin.

She was a cartoon character long before Felix the Cat or Mickey Mouse. She was cute before the cupie doll. She was Stan and Ollie all in one.

As madcap at the Keystone Cops and flagpole sitters, she was as classy as "Rhapsody in Blue" at Carnegie Hall, as written about as the prose from the "Lost Generation," as mighty as the Empire State Building.

There were stories about Liz and post cards, too. Jokes were told and songs were sung. She was all over the movie screens, and poems and books were doted on her.

Liz was in her glory in the 1920s but she's never really faded. She is part of us now, almost as much as she was then.

She is the good song we always enjoy singing. She is the friendly face we always like to see.

Henry's Lady, made of tin, became much more than the sum of her parts, more human than machine.

Flapper, flivver, hunk of tin, lovely Liz—always drawing a crowd and a grin.

She is a part of us, wherever we live in the world. Liz has been there helping us grow and explore and work. Liz, the Model T, has been a part of us for some time and will be a part of our world, a star who shuns the spotlight but earns applause whenever she appears.

Tom Collins 2007

Country roads never again meant isolation. When the Model T came along, they took people to new places beyond the visible horizon. Robin Heil-Kern

The Model T became an important part of the world wherever people decided to purchase one of the cars. It was a character that had many parts in many scenes of life.   Robin Heil-Kern

Of Model T Prose and Humor

Whether the form was stories, post cards, joke books and songs, movies, serious literature and poems or just the 15 seconds of fame, the Model T was constantly talked about, pictured or portrayed. There may not be another car that was so uniformly honored in so many forms. This section will look at the rich lode of ways the Model T has been featured in all of these forms. And at the end of the chapter, some special samples from modern writers that have never been published before will be featured.

The Model T was a superstar that engendered hundreds and thousands of jokes and stories, yet the car was always there, dominating entertainment as much as it did sales. Here is a look at some of the ways the Model T made people sit up and notice.

Model T Lore

There are classic memories told about the Model T, as if the car was part of some ancient Viking lore, Native American tradition or Irish ballad. They go beyond a simple story and take on an epic quality, even in simplicity.

One can almost imagine a roaring fire and people who are mesmerized by the tale. Here are some examples, from old books as well as from recent stories submitted for this book.

My First Model T

My first car was purchased when I was a senior in high school in 1946. It was a 1926 Model T coupe. I bought the Model T from an old retired farmer for $50. My father drove it home, as I couldn't operate the three pedals for the transmission.

I brush-painted the car and put on a new top. I remember looking out the back door each morning to see if the tires were full of air. There was no money to buy better tires so I resorted to putting cold patches on the tubes. For winter driving, I put a piece of stovepipe over the manifold and into the car for heat.

Some 40 years later, I saw an ad in the local paper with a 1926 Model T for sale and it whet my appetite for another

Logan Vander Leest bought a 1926 Model T coupe like this one for just $50. It probably wasn't in the shape of this museum car.   Don Voelker

Model T. When I saw the car at a farm sale, it was exactly like the one I owned 40 years earlier.

I had the coupe restored and still have it today. My wife, who I courted in high school, and I have enjoyed it. We have participated in Model T Ford Club of America tours.

There is nothing quite like having a Model T!

Logan Vander Leest
Pella, Iowa

The Sister Was Happy

In one of the small churches in a country town the pastor took for the subject of his sermons "Better Church Attendance."

The parson held forth on the theme that the automobile has taken more people away from the church than any other single invention. He concluded with this exclamation: "The Ford car has taken more people to hell than any other thing I can mention!"

An old woman began to clap her hands and shout: "Glory to God! Praise the Lord!"

"What's the matter, sister?" asked the parson.

"A Ford never went any place that it couldn't come back from, so I reckon all them folks in hell will be comin' back some day. So praise the Lord." [1]

My Dad and the Model T

My dad was born in 1900 and was ordained a Methodist minister in 1925. He always had a dry sense of humor. He purchased his first Ford, a 1926 Model T touring car, shortly after their introduction. He had fun pulling into a filling station and telling the attendant to "fill it up." Up until then, the gas tank was under the seat cushion and had to be removed to fill the tank. The new 1926 had the tank in the cowl and the filler was in front of the windshield. It must have been fun for him, as I heard the story many times.

Another T story he liked to tell was about the young couple walking into town carrying a back seat cushion and saying someone stole the car.

(I didn't understand the story the first time I heard it!)

Melvin Duling
Watseka, Illinois

Name that Car

In a large garage a man wagered with the owner that he could name any car merely by the sound of its engine. An attendant was instructed to crank the different machines, the boastful one was blindfolded and the test began.

"Overland" he called for the first one.

"Correct, try the next one," said the owner.

"Studebaker."

"Right! Crank another," said the owner.

Just then a load of coal was shot into the alley from a wagon.

"Ford," said the guesser. [2]

This pretty 1926 Model T touring car was decorated like a member of the wedding. It is owned by Richard Wieden of Wisconsin. Andrew Morland

Model T touring cars were popular choices among Ford buyers over the entire time the cars were sold around the world.   Tom Myers

Texas T Tale

My father and grandfather each bought their first cars in 1925—brand new 1925 Model Ts. My dad got a new starter on his for an extra $25 but my grandpa said he could do a lot of cranking for $25!

My mother and dad were married sitting in the 1925 Model T while the preacher stood outside and read the vows.

This took place on July 11, 1925 in Stephenville, Texas. The marriage lasted 63 years until my dad passed away in 1988.

Jimmie Clark
Pampa, Texas

Empty Cans

A thrifty housewife saved all her empty cans and, after a quantity had accumulated, shipped them to Detroit. After a few weeks she was delighted to receive the following letter: "Dear Madam: In accordance with your instructions we have made up and are shipping you today one Ford. We are also returning eight cans which were left over." 3

Curios-i-T

Back in 1914, my dad, a young farm lad, and my grandfather had a Model T experience that they often would tell with a hearty laugh!

Grandfather purchased a new Model T from the local Ford garage. The Ford salesman brought it to the farm, parking it in the straw shed next to the barn. He suggested that the father-son duo not tinker with it until he returned in several days to teach them how to operate it.

Curiosity got the best of Dad and Grandpa. With a little trial and error, they got the Model T running and made several trips around the barnyard.

Now the fun became panic. They wanted the car back in the shed exactly as the salesman had placed it but neither knew how to put the Model T in reverse!

Fearful that their joy ride would be discovered, they hitched the farm team of horses to the new Ford and pulled it backwards into the shed. The Ford salesman never suspected a thing when he arrived at the farm several days later!

Robert C. Antram
Somerset, Pennsylvania

In America or Canada, this Model T touring car might be considered a curiosity with some of its top and body differences.   Andrew Morland

The Model T—the world's popular little flivver—became everyone's economical means of transportation.   Tom Myers

Keep Her in Congress

In the 1920s, Ford Motor Company actively pursued women as prospective customers. One loyal Model T owner was a VIP in Washington, D. C.

"One of the numerous women who responded to this sales pitch was Alice Robertson of Oklahoma, the second woman elected to the House of Representatives. In 1922, *Ford News* reported that Robertson drove her Ford center-door to and from the Capitol daily and found it invaluable, especially during the rainy winter seasons…"

Peter Winnewisser
Old Cars Weekly Oct. 3, 1991

The Legend of the Flivver

Should you ask me whence this flivver, whence this noisy, flimsy road-louse, with its lack of paint and varnish and its crazy, dented mud guards, with its curtains all in tatters, and its tires a mass of patches, I should answer, I should tell you:

Forth into the barn or woodshed, in the early hours of morning, in the early Sunday morning, comes the owner bent on travel. First he pumps his tires and tests them, then he fills the radiator, tries his oil and cleans his timer, fills the gas tank, oils the bearings, pounds the wheels to knock the mud off. Fusses 'round till called to breakfast, when the house is put in order.

Dad gets out and cranks the flivver. First he lifts it, then he spins it; by and by, with snorts and splutters and explosions in the muffler. Off she starts and keeps on running. Dad gets in and works the levers, makes her jazz and smoke and rattle. Puts his feet upon the pedals; first he starts her, then he backs her, turns her 'round and then on second, out she goes upon the highway.

Down the street and o'er the crossing bucking, kicking, popping, snorting, down the cross streets, up the main street to the road into the country. When she's warmed up she goes better, better still as she goes further, till she settles down to business. Purrs and hums as though contented.

Miles and miles along the highway runs the flivver without effort. Passing those who do not hurry, keeping up with all the others; till the hot and sultry noon time, till they reach a grove of pine trees; Dad then backs her down a cart path, Ma and Sue unpack the basket.

By and by the lunch is eaten, Dad is smoking, Mother's reading; Willie's found a nest of hornets and been stung upon the forehead; and the dog, with John and Henry, are down to the creek and in swimming. Thus they pass the hours of leisure, till it's time to start homeward.

Dad looks in the radiator, says it leaks and needs more water; Willie ducks behind a pine tree, Fred is missing, John is hunting for the dog who's chasing squirrels.

By and by they all get settled, all in their respective places; after that there came the cranking, came the priming and the spitting, just the same as when they started, in the early hours of morning; but at length, when this was over, back they trundled to the city.

So they sat and blessed the flivver, for their cool and pleasant Sunday. And they blessed the name of Henry, and they said that in the future, when they heard the funny stories, from the owners of the high-priced ones, they would grin and just say nothing."

Automobile Dealer and Repairer   April 1922

Mules and Fords

"They have their little eccentricities and traits of character which must be understood before they will accomplish that for which they were designed.

...a mule can be started—if one knows how to do it. In my article I endeavor to prove that the same statement applies to Ford cars.

They both kick. A simple sentence but fraught with meaning. Take a cold and cantankerous Ford car and try to twist its tail in an endeavor to start it and it rears right up on its wheels. Usually a surgeon and three weeks of time mends the broken wrist, but the scar remains. Once kicked, always shy.

Your Ford car just naturally kicks if it is not approached in the proper way. Of course, we all know enough to retard its spark, but when the oil is congealed in its crank case and gear box and when the gasoline stays liquid and does not vaporize, then is the time to be careful.

Mules and Fords are subject to attacks of nerves. I know of no troubles more prevalent than those which arise from the ignition system. It is a good plan for the novice to keep his hands at home when there is trouble of this kind. Indiscriminate 'puttering' is all foolishness. There is always a reason for trouble.

The Ford car often takes a notion to go where it pleases as regards to its general direction. The driver finds it a difficult matter to keep the car in a straight line. The trouble is usually caused by a sprung axle or king pins out of line.

In general, I would say the Ford car, though it has its little traits and eccentricities, is as a whole a very willing little beast. It may balk, like the mule, on the road and remain passive for hours at a time, but eventually it will recover from its mood and be its sunny self for a time.

So it is with the mule and that's why I've entitled my article 'Mules and Fords, May They Always Thrive.'"

Automobile Dealer and Repairer   January 1920

Model T Post Cards:

There was a tradition that began long before the Model T was introduced to the public in October 1908. It was popular to send family pictures, favorite scenes and outrageous comedy in the form of post cards to friends and loved ones.

The overwhelming popularity of the Model T made it the perfect candidate to be butt or hero, depending on the card creator's viewpoint. Post cards were a popular medium. With the Model T, they both promoted the car's advantages and protested the car's foibles. The cards showed everyone a sense of pride in what the little cars from Ford could overcome.

In hindsight, both the foibles and the praise were quaint ways of showing just how deeply the loyalty and love ran when it came to the Model T. It was much like rooting for the favorite college eleven or baseball team. Win or lose, experiencing the ups and downs, it was your favorite team.

In many ways, the post cards reflected the person reading the humor. We looked in the mirror and saw a part of ourselves.

Writer Gordon Gee broke down the various Model T-based cards in a 1999 article. 4 There were novelty cards, usually from A. S. Johnson Company, that pictured a 1915 touring car in unbelievable situations like being run over by a steam traction engine. Sometimes the novelties were

The popular Model T post cards offered humor with the advantages of the car emphasized, like this vignette with the car and a talking rabbit.   Dave Nolting

embossed with the name of a city.

Poetry cards had a 1922 Model T on a country road with the same passengers plus two unique dogs, one on each fender. The poetry was either folksy or somewhat poignant, depending on the cards. An example of the finer poetry was this one with the picture described earlier in this paragraph:

"Once she was straight and full of pep,

Had a fast gait and kept her step.

Now she is faded and beginning to wrinkle,

Her eyes look jaded and refuse to twinkle.

My eyes they fill when I'm tempted to part, Because she still holds a place in my heart.

She carried me to hunt, she carried me to marry, Without a single grunt or suggestion to tarry.

Along the countryside or down by the river, I've enjoyed every ride in that dear old 'flivver.'" [5]

King A. Woodburn

Tourist cards were another style, with their "wish you were here" style message. One of the most famous versions was a Model T pulling a fish out of a lake.

Some of the rarest Model T cards, according to Gee, are from World War I showing Model T ambulances. And there was a style of cards that were very popular before the Model T called reality post cards—basically black and white family or business photos memorialized in a post card that reflected a "slice of life" situation.

The comic cards in the Model T era were by Witt or Cobb and Shimm. They were fun and colorful and portrayed the advantages of the Model Ts as well as some of their foibles, depending on the card's style.

A classic example of the humor cards showed a farmer talking to his wife, in the driver's seat of a multi-tasking Model T connected to a network of pulleys. She was giving the car more gas to power a washing machine, a dish washer, a butter churn and a mechanism that rocked a cradle. "Give her more gas," said her husband. "I want to cultivate the back 40." [6]

Many times, Ford positives were encouraged. One famous card showed a tiny Model T pulling a huge touring car with the caption: "A Ford is A Handy Thing to Carry in Your Tool Box."

Thanks to David Nolting, some of the more famous comedic post card images were made available for this book and show the classic humor—such as the "10 miles straight and 60 miles up and down," the displaced horse and dogs barking at the rattling Ford. The cards supporting the Model T's advantages included the frustrated rabbit chasing a Model T and the dog that wanted to be owned by a Model T driver.

Dogs were barking at the Model T in this early post card. Did the little Ford really bother anyone this much?   *Dave Nolting*

This famous post card showed a sad dog standing by a road watching a Model T go by. The pensive dog wishes he was riding in the car with its owner.   Dave Nolting

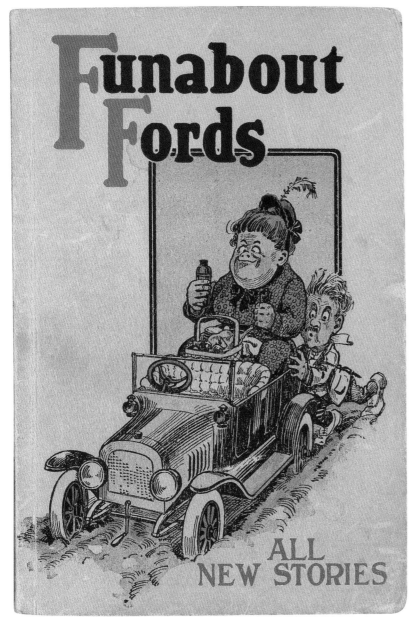

"Funabout Fords" was an example of the many stories that were told about the Model Ts. The stories made people laugh and shake their heads. *Don Chandler*

Joke Books and Songs

Perhaps it was an element of a simpler time—long before television, the computer, the Internet and so much "busy-ness" of life in our modern era. People seemed to enjoy telling involved jokes or standing around the parlor piano and singing the latest songs they learned from sheet music.

People had time for one another and the songs and jokes reflected their lifestyles. Perhaps they didn't have so much but they had one another and one thing they understood was the Model T Ford. It was everywhere—in cities, small

towns and rural areas. It had changed their lives in many ways and it was fun to make fun of or to sing about.

Here are some examples of Model T jokes from *Funabout Fords*, a booklet first printed in the late 1910s and reprinted, in this case, in 1921. It was contributed by Don Chandler, a Model T owner and president of the Model T Ford Club of America's Wisconsin chapter.

"The man who claims that he never gets rattled has evidently never ridden in a Ford."

"Beat it, beat it, little car.

How I wonder what you are, Climbing up the hills on high, Passing all the others by."

"Why does a one-year-old Ford look twice as old as a 10-year-old horse?"

"An enterprising garage uses the following sign: 'Automobiles Repaired and Fords Mended.'"

"A man has given up driving on Sunday because flivvers pop out at every corner.

He thinks that every standard car should be equipped with a Ford swatter."

"The Bible says that 'Elijah went up to Heaven on high.' What other 'chariot' than a Ford could have done this?"

As the 20th century dawned, one of the popular family traditions was buying and singing sheet music. It was the way songs were circulated throughout the country in an era before the radio became a household item, for at least the first two decades of the century, much of the production life of the Model T.

According to the June 1978 edition of the *Ford Times*, Henry Ford understood that both music and jokes could promote his Model T and he encouraged both mediums.

In 1908, Ford commissioned composer Harry H. Zickel to write some music about the car and he penned "The Ford March and Two Step." [7]

"Love is seen in the many songs tying the Ford car to a girl, a kiss, a honeymoon" noted the *Ford Times* adding that the Model T was like a popular movie character.

"The Model T was looked on by several songwriters as a sort of Charlie Chaplin of combustion." [8]

People who bought songs were used to music about cars by the time the Model T appeared. The famous "Merry Oldsmobile" was a hit several years before the T appeared and Billy Murray was known for his songs "He'd Have to Get Under, Get Out and Get Under" and "Gasoline Gus and His Jitney Bus," all before 1915 but the Model T took songwriters to new levels.

Among the popular titles were: "I Didn't Raise My Ford to Be a Jitney*," "Let's Take a Ride in the Jitney* Bus," "On the Old Back Seat of the Henry Ford," "Flivver King," the latter about Henry Ford, and two popular 1914 songs, "You Can't Afford to Marry If You Can't Afford a Ford" and "The Little Ford Rumbled Right Along."

The latter song included the lyrics: "The car kicked up and the engine wouldn't crank," said the lyrics. "There wasn't any gas in the gasoline tank" and ended with the chorus "His little Ford just rambled right along." 9

Other songs included "It's a Rumbling Flivver" with the memorable line "…when I time her for a block, both the hands flew off the clock." "The Packard and the Ford" was a song that suggested that if the Packard married the Ford, the union would have a "little Buick." 10

The *Funabout Ford* booklet added its own twist with Ford-inspired lyrics to "My Country Tis of Thee." The song was written by J. C. Davenport in *News About Fords* and began: "My Fordie t'is of thee, short cut to poverty, of thee I chant." It continued with the relationship between owner and car concluding with: "Thy motor has the grippe, Thy spark plug has the pip, and woe is thine, But we climb any hill, Nor know a repair bill, To give out pocketbook a chill, Hurrah, Hurrah." 11

In 1928, as the Model T was ending its long run and the Model A was beginning, several songs commemorated the event including "Poor Lizzie" by Abner Silver and Jack Meskill and Walter O' Keefe's popular "Henry's Little Lady Made Out of Lizzie."

Another memorable tune was "I'll Be Ready to Marry When You Buy Me a Ford" written by Lawrence Lewis, a love song that cautioned the suitor that rings, bankrolls and

"Henry's Made a Lady Out of Lizzie" marked the transition from the Model T to the Model A in the late 1920s. Don Chandler

bungalows were fine, but real love meant the bride expected her own Model T Ford!

Model Ts weren't forgotten as the years went on. In 1947, famed songwriter Sammy Cahn wrote the memorial tune "There's Nothing Like a Model T" for the Broadway production "High Button Shoes."

It seemed there always was something to sing about when it came to the Model T.

* A jitney was a small bus and it was often used as slang for the Model T as well.

Model Ts and Movies

Like two friends from the same neighborhood, the Model T and the movies grew up in a similar era. Edison's "flickers" were gaining audiences beyond the penny arcades when the automobile was beginning to change from a curiosity to a possibility.

The Model T would make the automobile a necessity and the movies would become the most favored method of public entertainment.

Ford Motor Co. in the United States and the Ford Motor Company of Canada each made their car a star in company-produced movies about the Model Ts that, in some cases,

One of the most famous Laurel and Hardy scenes with a Model T included this special collapsing car—caught between street cars. It's now a museum piece in California.   Bruce McCalley

grew to be beloved features. Filmmaking began in 1914 in the United States and in 1915 in Canada. "Ford Educational Weekly" film features were popular in the United States while, in Canada, "Ford Nights" were popular attractions and Canada's Department of Trade picked up the features along with private films and railway travelogues. 12

Many Ford Motor Company film features highlighted life and popular locations in each country and they also showed viewers what it took to put together a Model T.

"The Ford films had wide circulation, in theaters, clubs, church groups and industrial cafeterias and auditoriums," noted *In the Shadows of Detroit* author David Roberts. 13

Ford features in both countries promoted travel and they often created interest in places with the United States and Canada that the average citizens had not seen before.

When Hollywood became the place to make movies, the ever-present Model T was a natural—a stand in for street scenes and a scene stealer for the one-reeler dramas and comedies. As the movies grew in plot and complexity, the Model T's roles increased.

Lizzie was a natural in the silent movie days. She was available at less than scale and always seemed to have a way to fit in. She was like the cross-eyed character actor Ben Turpin or the woeful "Little Tramp" of Charlie Chaplin. Even in a crowd or next to the prettiest ingénue, audiences were riveted to their screen presence. Lizzie, the Model T, began appearing in all sorts of scenarios.

"Just seeing a Ben Turpin, Spud Pollard, Will Rogers or any heavily mustachioed silent movie clown ride up in a Model T prepared one for a session of belly laughs," wrote Bob Raitch in a 1992 *Skinned Knuckles* magazine retrospective. 14

The best directors noticed that the car was more than a bit player. She became a vehicle of choice in several of the popular Keystone Cops movies and in various Mack Sennett comedies. One of the Keystone Cops vehicles was a Model T that could fold almost to the width of two tires. The Model Ts were almost as famous in silent movie chase scenes as the stars themselves.

If there was one lesson to be learned from "Hog Wild" in 1930, it was don't use a Model T touring car to steady a ladder when you work on the roof of your home! Bruce McCalley

"...a wild chase of Model T Fords going everywhere madly just missing cliff edges and trains was a logical transition," Raitch recalled. "Someone was forever losing the nut that held on the old Ford's steering wheel and as it would go through several lines of laundry, muscles would be ruptured...laughing hysterically." 15

Producer Hal Roach was behind many popular comedies in the Model T era including the work of Harold Lloyd, the various casts of the "Our Gang" and "The Boyfriends" series as well as period comedians who are not as well known today like Charley Chase and Max Davidson and early female comedians Priscilla Dean, Mabel Normand and Mae Busch.

Who else would cram some Christmas trees in a Model T touring car and begin a sales trip in summer as Laurel and Hardy did in "Big Business," made in 1929. Bruce McCalley

Roach also produced the famed supporting character actor Jimmy Finlayson, the mustachioed Scot with the "you're fooling me, aren't you?" look. And he teamed the beautiful Thelma Todd with the gangly Zasu Pitts in other comedies.

Under Roach's guidance and the work of many others on his team, the Model T really reached long-lasting movie star fame when it joined the wildly popular pair known around the world as the fat man and the skinny one, Stan Laurel and Oliver "Babe" Hardy. When Ollie demanded that Laurel give him the wheel or "throw out the clutch," Laurel complied,

then cried and the mishaps with the Model T often began.

Laurel and Hardy had played in various movies separately into the 1920s. Ironically, they first appeared together in 1917 in "Lucky Dog," with Hardy a crook with a gun and Laurel with the desired handful of cash.

Somehow, the Model T was the perfect foil for the hapless twosome who never really fit in whatever job they were working or whatever home situation they were taking part. The Model T was almost as hapless as Stan and Ollie who squeezed together in the front seat to form a trio of weathered characters—the two comedians and the car.

Model Ts of Laurel and Hardy

"Leave 'Em Laughing"	1928	The boys inhaled too much laughing gas at the dentist. They laugh as a tough policeman writes out a ticket.
"Two Tars"	1928	Stan and Ollie are sailors who rent a Model T runabout. There is a wild chase scene with many cars and a train. Their car and many others are ripped apart.
"Bug Business"	1929	The two try to sell Christmas trees in July in California. Jimmy Finlayson works to destroy their Model T touring.
"A Perfect Day"	1929	Laurel, Hardy, their wives, an uncle with gout, "helpful" neighbors and car that won't start make a memorable scene.
"Blotto"	1930	Mrs. Hardy blows the poor Model T away with a shotgun after the boys have spent a night of drinking.
"Hog Wild"	1930	Attempting to steady a ladder to fix a radio antenna on the roof of a house, the boys use their Model T touring car. In the mayhem, with the ladder still firmly attached in the back seat, they go on a wild chase and end up getting hit by a street car.
"One Good Turn"	1931	The Model T plays a funny bit role, falling apart immediately after Stan and Ollie sell it to pay for their travels in the Great Depression.
"County Hospital"	1931	Hardy, recovering from an accident, is taken home by Laurel, with several wild moments of chase scenes in Los Angeles.
"Midnight Patrol"	1933	Laurel and Hardy are policemen patrolling in an old Model T sedan.
"Busy Bodies"	1933	Working in a lumber yard, their Model T is sawed in half.
"Going Bye Bye"	1934	Stan and Ollie leave town in a Model T when a murderer is released from jail.
"Them Thar Hills"	1934	Laurel and Hardy go to the mountains for some relaxation. They travel there in a Model T touring car.
"Blockheads"	1938	Hardy picks up friend Laurel in a Model T touring car. Laurel accidentally dumps a truckload of dirt on the car, then wrecks it in the Hardy garage. Laurel and Hardy were famous for their Model T devices, some of which are described above, cars that were rigged to accordion or collapse. The famed "accordion car," a Model T squeezed between two trolley cars, is displayed at the Peterson Museum in Los Angeles and commemorates one of their most memorable scenes.

One of the scenes in "Two Tars" involved tearing apart some cars, including a Model T.
Bruce McCalley

The Legendary Model T Ford | **191**

Model Ts on DVD

The Model T continued to appear in movies for decades after, even into our time. Here is a short list of movies that featured Model Ts. Perhaps you have movie favorites of your own to add to the Model T credit list:

1961   "The Absent Minded Professor" Fred McMurray flies in a Model T touring car.

1982   "Ragtime" Racist fire fighters, jealous that Coalhouse Walker has a brand new Model T, impound the car and fill it with manure.

1991   "Reds" Many street scenes show beautiful brass era Model Ts.

1992   "Chaplin" Robert Downey Jr. drives a 1915 Model T roadster. Many other cars including more Model Ts, are seen in this movie.

2000   "The Color Purple" The mayor's wife tries to destroy a Model A roadster with her bad driving but Model Ts also are present in other parts of the movie. Decade after decade, "Lizzie the T" has been stand in and bit player, sidekick, walk on (or is it roll in?) and character actor with the stars of the silver screen—and an irrepressible star in its own right.

"The boys" rented a car—a Model T, of course—and then ran into trouble on shore leave from the Navy in "Two Tars," made in 1928. Bruce McCalley

Laurel, Hardy, a tough cop and a Model T were center stage in "Leave 'Em Laughing," originally made in the silent movie days of 1928.

The Literature and poetry

Some of the best writers of the 20th century have tried to analyze the Model T or have offered some retrospective thoughts, adoring phrases or simply mixed the car in with the people in gritty real life scenarios. The Model T became a device, like the skull that drew out the conscience of William Shakespeare's Macbeth.

Featured here are excerpts from writers E. B. White and John Steinbeck as well as poet Edgar Guest.

The Model T Named "It"

I guess Model Ts would run forever, if you would let them. I was well gone in adolescence before I came by one at a price I could afford to pay—fifty dollars. It was almost as old as I was.

It had intelligence not exactly malicious, but it did love a practical joke. It knew, for instance, exactly how long it could keep me spinning the crank and cursing it before I would start kicking the radiator in. It ran perfectly when I was in blue jeans, but let me put on my best suit and a white shirt, and maybe a girl beside me, and that car invariably broke down in the greasiest possible manner.

I never gave it a name. I called it—IT.

When I consider how much time it took to keep IT running, I wonder if there was time for anything else, and maybe there wasn't. The Model T was not a car as we know them now—it was a person—crotchety and mean, frolicsome and full of jokes—just when you were ready to kill yourself, it would run five miles with no gasoline whatever. I understood IT, but as I said before, IT understood me, too.

In the years I had IT, no mechanic ever touched it, no shadow of a garage ever passed over it. I do not recall any new part every being bought for it.

Just perhaps, in the corner of some field, the grass and the yellow mustard may grow taller and greener than elsewhere and, if you were to dig down, you might find the red of rust under the roots, and that might be IT, enriching the soil, going home to its mother, earth.

John Steinbeck, 1953

RIGHT: John Steinbeck's famed ode to the Model T called "It" mentioned a Model T with personality. Was it like this 1927 coupe?

Farewell My Lovely

"…[The Model T] engine almost always responded—first with a few scattered explosions, then with a tumultuous gunfire, which you checked by racing around to the driver's seat and retarding the throttle. Often, if the emergency brake hadn't been pulled all the way back, the car advanced on you the instant the first explosion occurred, and you would hold it back by leaning your weight against it. I can still feel my old Ford nuzzling me at the curb, as though looking for an apple in my pocket.

"Farewell My Lovely" could have been written about a Model T like this 1911 touring car in an ideal rustic scene in England.
Andrew Morland

Mechanically uncanny, it was like nothing that had ever come to the world before. Flourishing industries rose and fell with it. As a vehicle, it was hard working, commonplace, heroic.

Springtime in the heyday of the Model T was a delirious season. Owning a car was still a major excitement, roads were still wonderful and bad. The Fords were obviously conceived in madness: any car which was capable of going from forward into reverse without any perceptible mechanical hiatus was bound to be a mighty challenging thing to the human spirit.

The days were golden, the nights were dim and strange. I still recall with trembling those loud, nocturnal crises when you drew up to a signpost and raced the engine so the lights would be bright enough to read destinations by. I have never been really planetary since. I suppose it's time to say goodbye. Farewell, my lovely!"

From the book *Farewell to the Model T*
by E. B. White, 1936

(Ironically, long-time Christian Science Monitor reporter Richard Strout, a friend and working associate of White's, claimed co-authorship to the book this excerpt was from, *Farewell to the Model T*.) 17

There was no holiday that escaped a chance to market the Model T, including Valentine's Day.

Vintage Ford Prose

Even the Ford Motor Company promoted its own lore about Model Ts. Here are two samples from the earliest days of the Model T:

Christmas 1911

If every Model T today could spread our thoughts afar, wherever Christmas trees are gay or shines the Christmas star,

A Christmas passes with its bells, and clasping hands and jovial hearts, into that silent past which spells too oft the oblivion of earth's art.

But we could fain believe, who delve in retrospection's firelight lore and hard the chimes of 1912 resounding at our very door, that we not thinkless are, nor dumb to all the kindly aids and true this bygone year have come from you, and you and YOU!

Accept our greetings most sincere, where'er you live, who'er you are—associates, friends of all the year, and sterling patrons of our car!

To each of you nay richest gifts in terms of purse and soul descend, love and good fortune that uplifts and lightens to the end!

To you for numerous debts and dear, incurred, yet past all coin to pay, we owe these sentiments sincere—the brightness of our common way!

Then take these feeble lines to mean our genuine gratitude and just, and find within them or between full measure of our trust!

A Merry Christmas! 18

Mr. Tightwad's Christmas

Mr. Tightwad had more money than any man in his town. But he was very poor. He lived in the finest house on his street. But the curtains were always drawn. He was afraid of fading the rugs.

He was sitting there Christmas Eve, the poorest man in the town, figuring up how many thousand dollars he had made that day, when he heard the soft chug, chug of a Ford automobile. The next moment Santa Claus, all glistening with frost, blew into the room.

"Where did you come from?" asked Mr. Tightwad, looking at his visitor disapprovingly.

"From the North Pole," replied Santa Claus, good cheer emanating from his rotund, fur-clad body, his beamish face.

"You never come from the North Pole in a Ford automobile or anything else that runs on wheels. You have to have a sled," Mr. Tightwad scowled over his glasses.

"I used to, before Fords came into existence. But you see, they skim over the ice crust as though it was macadam, and when they come to a snow drift, they're regular little snowbirds."

"Well, you needn't have bothered to come here. We never celebrate Christmas," said Mr. Tightwad.

Santa Claus chortled.

"You've got lots of money," Santa continued, "and a fine house to live in, but You Don't Live! You have made a beaten path from your house to the office, and you travel back and forth each day with your eyes to the ground. You never see the sun shining, the blue sky overhead, the flowers blossoming on each side of the path. You never hear the songs of the birds, or breathe in the rare sweetness of the meadowlands in springtime. You're making money. That's all. But they don't cash traveler's checks over on the other side."

Mr. Tightwad looked shocked. This was the second time that day he had been reminded of such things. Only that morning the doctor had told him he must get out into the air, or he would not promise him a return of health.

Perhaps it was not too late. He wondered. He wandered back in memory to the days when he was a barefooted boy, he had followed the trail through the woods, or chased fireflies as they flashed their lights along the hedges. He could almost hear the call of the whippoorwill as it stole from the purple shadows…and what joyous times the winter brought forth, with its ice and snow, and its health-giving, biting air. His eyes sparkled.

"I'll buy a Ford tomorrow," said Mr. Tightwad, with boyish enthusiasm. "I know a place where we boys used to wallow waist deep in the drifts. Do you suppose she'll make it?"

But Santa Claus was gone. He had other work to do.
Stella M. Champney
Ford Times, December 1913

Oddi-Ts and Model Ts

Like the Volkswagen that came later, the Model T seemed to engender a sense of artistic expression. Many of our readers have commented that they painted the car

The Model T has always brought out creativity from its varied owners, like this special version. Ray Kruse

with graffiti and various colors or invited friends to do the same.

For some unexplainable reason, the Model T became their canvas for expression. And as if the car wasn't unique enough, they had to find ways to make it even more unique. Of course, some of the movie tricks added to their desire to be original.

And they probably could look around on any street or country highway and see a Model T being modified and used in hundreds of different ways. Here's an account from the author's hometown, Clintonville, Wisconsin, circa 1920.

Novel Vehicle Here
Family Travels in Home on Wheels and Enjoys Many Comforts Enroute Through State

A novel and unique traveling vehicle passed through this city last week enroute to northern Wisconsin, and attracted many spectators on account of its shape.

It was virtually a house on wheels, in which Mr. and Mrs. Galloway and two children are migrating from Indianapolis to Los Angeles, Calif.

The outfit consists of an enclosed body mounted on a Ford chassis and is about 14 feet long, six and a half feet wide and six feet high. There are windows on the sides, and it is equipped with lace curtains and screens. The rear end may be opened so that it is entirely a screened enclosure. It is lighted by electricity supplied by storage batteries.

Beds are provided in the car, two sleeping on the floor level and two in an upper berth. There are four upholstered seats in front, upon which the family rides during the day time. It is also furnished with a complete cooking outfit, making it possible to keep house any where at any time. The family seemed to be thoroughly enjoying the trip.

Clintonville, WI, *Tribune*   July 9, 1920

On Dec. 20, 1923, *Motor World* pictured a young boy at the barber shop sitting in the comfort of a Model T mockup. The Brooklyn, New York, barber was trying to offer "cryless hair trimming."

Model Ts often were cut, lengthened, sectioned and painted in all manner of ways.

A contemporary photo showed how some clever body shop had put the front halves of two Model Ts together, so the conjoined twin Ts seemed to be going in opposite directions at once.

The Mack Sennett movie production company players were loaded into a super-stretched Model T for a publicity photo, another way the little Ford was exaggerated.

And for some reason, people didn't just make unusual Model Ts, they felt compelled to do odd things with them as well. One of the fads that began in 1913 was playing a version of polo with Model Ts instead of horses. Invented by a Wichita, Kansas, Ford dealer, auto polo gained sudden popularity, as described by historian Douglas Brinkley.

"...stripped-down Model Ts took the place of polo ponies, their drivers circling one another while mallet-wielding strikers mounted on their running boards attempted to whack a large ball through a goal post." [20]

The versatile Model T polo vehicles were not as athletic as the horses they replaced. Brinkley says that rollovers occurred and deaths followed. As rapidly as auto polo gained popularity, it waned, often the victim of states such as New York that outlawed it.

"Ford dealers," said Brinkley, "were urged to discourage it...and the sport pretty much disappeared after 1915." [21]

While Model T polo may have been officially discouraged, there still were pockets of interest regionally. In the Oct. 8, 1992, edition of *Old Car News and Marketplace*, writer Sylvia Hendricks interviewed Selby "Buck" House, then age 84, who was a veteran Model T polo driver in the 1920s.

He drove a T "polo pony" in the Hoosier Auto Polo Club in London, Indiana. The circuit included medium-sized towns in Ohio as well as Indiana.

"The driver had the more important job," House recalled. "He had to get the car to where the mallet man [who rode on a special running board on the side of the car-made-for-polo] could hit the ball."

He recalled the cars, more frame, engine and roll bar than anything else, were driven from one appearance to another. After the official disapproval, auto polo continued on the fair circuits and in smaller communities all over the United States and Canada at least as long as the Model T was produced. While some saw danger in the wild action of the pseudo-sport, House saw some fun.

"We knew what we were doin'," he recalled, "We were puttin' on a show!"

Auto polo was one more oddity not often recalled as time has put distance between it and the game. But it was just one example of people having fun with the cars and playing out their tame or wild ideas with the cars.

The Model T flaws and foibles begged for changes and modifications and often people were all too willing to find ways to try to make lemonade to the best of their abilities with the Ford Motor Company-supplied raw materials.

Author Bob Raitch noted the following foibles that begged change and brought out the odd side of Ford owners.

The planetary transmission offered extremely low and often too high gearing for steep hills. The front wheels "flopped," he wrote and made backing or moving in a straight line difficult. The brakes were a "built in humor device" and he noted that drivers had to "pull of the parking brake and pray." Model T radiators for the first 17 years of production were inadequate while the thermosyphon cooling system invited modifications. [22]

Phil Niemeyer, who wrote "A Modern T Tale," works on one of his Fords.
Phil Niemeyer

Working Ts took on all shapes and sizes from milk bottles to mobile chapels and everything in between.

Whether it was accentuating their flaws or creating something new from their basic form, the Model Ts offered an incredible pallet that offered no end of creativity—from the kid with the jalopy to the customizer with an endless array of tools.

There was an oddity about the Model T in any case. It stood out with its simple looks in any case. In the hands of someone with a taste for the unusual, it could be shaped and changed in many ways.

The Model T often underlined creativi-T.

Modern Prose

Several readers went beyond telling stories and sharing memories about the Model T. They used the car as the protagonists in their 21st century stories. Long after the Model T production was halted, the car lives on with us in spirit. These special stories enrich that spirit. Here are some excerpts from these talented writers who have offered some of their memories and insight. Each deserves more space but we're limited and are highlighting some of their work in this chapter.

Phil Niemeyer shares his special memories in this brief excerpt from his childhood in Minnesota.

A Model T Tale

My grandfather's farm was a short three miles from our home in town and I spent every waking hour I could out there playing out a hundred adventures in the grove and fields. In the chicken yard was a strange beast of a machine that I was told was once the family's 1924 Ford Model T touring.

Dad and his friend from the next farm dismantled the old T and re-birthed it as a sawmill. It was really quite ingenious, with a steam governor grafted to the carburetor.

Granddad decided one fine day it was time for me to see the insides of an engine, and how it operated. We tore it down and after the lesson was over, left parts strewn around the yard. I began to assemble the car parts into something that vaguely resembled a car. The body parts lay underneath an evergreen windbreak, but only two doors were usable. I had an old car!

Hour after pleasurable hour were spent behind the wheel of my beauty as imaginary scenery rushed by and equally imaginable sounds belched from the engine.

At the ripe old age of 13, summer came to an abrupt halt as I collided with Old Man Polio, a sojourn in the hospital for nine months in 1954. During the stay, I began to read everything I could regarding the famous Tin Lizzie. Even though temporarily in a wheel chair, I searched out a "barn fresh" 1923 Fordor. Sixty bucks and she was mine. Soon my feet were able to do the Fred Astaire dance moves required to drive the thing.

Just a few years ago, I heard again the siren call of the little vixen's howling planetary, and purchased a delightfully original 1927 touring. Only the fenders had been refinished and the top replaced about 40 years before I owned it. What a thrill to look out from the seat and know I was looking at the exact scene the original owner experienced on his trip home from the dealership!

My collection now consists of a 1928 A roadster and a 1955 Crown Victoria with glass top. Nice cars; fun to drive, but every so often I find myself daydreaming my way back to my peach crate seat in that old pile of T bones. The scenery once again rushes by and I am a boy again.

Phil Niemeyer
Rochester, Minnesota

Bob Frey's wry sense of humor and memory is featured in a local club newsletter called "Behind the Motometer" in New Jersey. Here is a sample of his talents.

Lloyd's Model T

Lloyd was a most precocious kid. After high school he got a city job with a large Ford agency and eventually the dealer would send him with cash money (Henry Ford wanted cash)

Writer Bob Frey poses with his grandsons Caleb (middle) and Abe (at the wheel).
Bob Frey

and four other guys to bring back a batch of new Model Ts from the New Jersey assembly plant.

Ford made police specials and he was able to persuade them to save him a Ford that the Bayonne Police Department had rejected due to an ill-fitting top.

Now on weekends, Lloyd could visit the country cousins and get to see the local country girls. He became a bit of a hero after rescuing a team of runaway horses and later, single handedly pushing a tractor out of a burning barn.

Before long, he got to going steady with a fair farmer's daughter who lived way out in Warren County. He would make the trip in an hour and one half. He made up for [a mountain] going down hill with both gas and spark levers all the way back. Magneto headlights do get brighter the faster you go.

One Saturday afternoon young Esther persuaded Lloyd to teach her to drive, and she happened to get a little too close to the edge and over they went into an open ditch with the Model T on its side.

They picked up the Model T and the fenders all sprung right back in place.

Lloyd and Esther have now passed on but living proof exists in two children, nine grandchildren and lots of nice great grandchildren with more on the way.

From "Behind the Motometer"
Bob Frey Phillipsburg, New Jersey

Esther poses with the Model T from "Lloyd's Story" by Bob Frey.

Jack Pledger's writing samples the wealth of memory and sensitivity that our nation has been blessed with through its rich vein of Southern-born writers. Jack is from Georgia. Here is a condensation of his reflections on the Model T.

My Model T Ford Story

Fifty-four years have passed since that spring morning in 1952 when my dad and uncle asked if I would like to go with them to get an old car. Cars were my link to my dad and the anticipation that I might be able to help do anything automotive was all I needed to hear.

My dad just kept telling me we were going to get a Model T touring car—a term I wasn't familiar with and with his Georgia drawl, I thought he was saying "Model turn car."

Most people in the old car hobby have heard countless stories of having to cut down trees to recover old cars from their resting places and, sure enough, this one is true.

What finally emerged…was a complete and unmolested

A photo of the Pledger family from the 1950s. Mom, Mildred, is on the left with Debbie and dad, Fay, is on the right with young Jack, the writer of this story.
Jack Pledger

1916 Model T touring car. Amazingly, the old dry and cracked tires held air pressure. My dad soon announced that the engine was "stuck," whatever that meant. Nothing appeared to be missing and…the wooden body frame was sound so we would take it home.

In 1952 rural Georgia there were no new or reproduction Model T parts and accumulating original parts was essential to restore these old cars.

For the rest of that summer, I would wait impatiently for my dad to come home in the evenings so we could work on the Model T. My dad revered mechanical perfection above all else. He tried to explain to me what everything was and what it did.

My job, of course, was cleaning parts. I was given a little pan of kerosene and an old paint brush, an old putty knife and a bag of cotton waste from the knitting mill we used for rags—and an endless pile of old, greasy parts. I would scrub and scrape and wipe until my dad indicated his approval.

The only things that measured up to working with my dad on the Model T were the trips we made searching for those elusive antique parts. An eccentric old black gentleman in Lafayette, Georgia, had several salvaged Model T and Model A cars on the grounds of his tumbled down home.

Then there was the retired postman just outside Rome, Georgia, near Russell Field airport who had a collection of old cars and equipment spread over acres behind his house. He would buy them for little or nothing over the years when he came upon them on his rural postal route.

He had a 1916 Model T with the rear half of the body removed and made into a truck that finally donated some engine parts to our Model T.

After the frozen engine was rebuilt and my dad tuned it to his satisfaction, the way it ran was a tremendous source of pride for him. When driving through our little town on a Saturday afternoon, nothing pleased him more than to push the spark up and set the throttle just above an idle in high gear. The Model T would chug along at a walk and you could practically count the cylinders firing.

Some years ago a museum was opened at Berry College and one of the displays is a 1916 Model T Ford touring car. Before my uncle J. D. passed away, he told me of his visit to the museum. The curator assured him that it was not [our] car but Martha Berry's personal car.

My uncle asked him to lift the back seat and look in the lower left corner of the body for an old Georgia license plate patch. The curator looked up from the back seat of the old Ford with a bewildered expression as J. D. just smiled and walked on through the displays.

Jack Pledger
Arlington Heights, Illinois

Jesse Ball's efforts carry a folk-like tradition found in music and stories. Jesse submitted several quality chapters for consideration. Here is a sample of his talents.

The 1921 Model T Ford

Late in 1921, my father purchased a '21 Model T Ford car. It cost $268. It would have been less but we wanted lights on it. It had all the basics including headlights but that was all. No horn, no starter, no top and no back seat. Only a platform back there with two chairs bolted on the floor.

The roads were terrible. The main ones in town were brick but the side roads were dirt and mud. When we got out of town in any direction it was ruts, dirt or mud. Nearly every time we went for a "spin" it rained and we came home wet as could be.

Jesse Ball sits at the wheel of his Model T touring car. He wrote the "1921 Model T Story" in this chapter.   *Jesse Ball*

We lived in Bluefield, West Virginia, but my parents were from Richlands, Virginia, which was about 50 miles away by the old roads. We went to see [the kin] about once a month.

When we went through a certain bottom we had to open gates and go through fields of grass, corn and cattle. We had to go through the creeks and we had to get a start to go through some creeks or we would get stuck. We carried a bucket so we could put some water in the radiator anytime we found water.

By the time we got to Richlands the motor was so hot my father had to put the car up against the barn and with the clutch in low gear he finally would "kill" the motor. Simply turning the ignition key to the off position made no difference. It kept on running.

Many times when the motor was warm he would turn the ignition key to magneto (or left) before he cranked it and it would start running on its own. No cranking, no "nuthin."

On April 11, 1925 my father and I rode our beloved '21 T up town and walked into the Ford showroom. There sat a 1925 Ford touring car. It was black and shiny. The most beautiful thing I had ever seen. It had everything. It was loaded. It had a starter, top, curtains, horn and beautiful seats. My father peeled off two-hundred and ninety bucks and bought the car.

We bounced out over the sidewalk and curb and started down the avenue on those old brick streets and everyone knew the Balls had a new car. I don't know what happened to the '21 Model T. I never saw it again.

Jesse Ball
Bluefield, West Virginia

FORD GOES RACING

For nearly 105 years, there has been a Ford Motor Company, and in most of those years, people who have enjoyed speed have taken the raw material, the cars produced by Ford, and created something faster, more enduring and more powerful from them.

It is as if there has been one more step or ritual not available at the factory that has bestowed on the cars the mantle of a fighter versus a non-competitor.

When Ford Motor Company jumped into the automotive fray with its early cars, especially when the versatile, lightweight Model T began to be produced, the Ford name was firmly associated with racing. Henry Ford sought to prove himself and his cars in the tests of speed and reliability.

Racing was a jump start for the early Ford venture to make a name for itself and to follow the early reputation Henry Ford had forged in the heat of competition.

The early automotive world already had taken up manufacturing and racing when Henry Ford knocked through the walls of his rented shed in Detroit to bring the Quadricycle to light.

Karl Benz, Gottlieb Daimler and Wilhelm Maybach had been busy in Germany moving from engine-powered bicycles and wagons to four wheeled vehicles. By 1893, the Daimler venture was selling licenses to its engines to French enthusiasts. In France, people from the former bell maker Amadée Bollée to the Comte de Dion were becoming automakers.

Two years before the Ford's automotive birth, in 1894, a competition was held in France to offer the public some choices about reliability. Author Peter Roberts says the

Sometimes the car that was taken into racing competition was closer to the standard Model T chassis than anything else, like this example.   Bob Harrington

French trial provided important evidence for early car buyers, starting from square one.

"That petrol was more reliable than steam—half the steamers broke down. It proved that the car could be of use for serious transport. And it proved a sharp boost for French manufacturers..." 1

France and Germany were the early crucibles the world was observing, where thought about self-propelled vehicles was taking shape in form and action. Proving the new vehicles was all part of sorting out the automobile in its infancy.

In 1895, the Paris to Bordeaux race established a measure that others would compare themselves against. Emile Levassor's Panhard-Levassor rumbled 732 miles in 48 hours and 42 minutes, a steady 15 mph. And that competition also offered the first racing use of Michelin pneumatic tires, shod on a Peugeot.

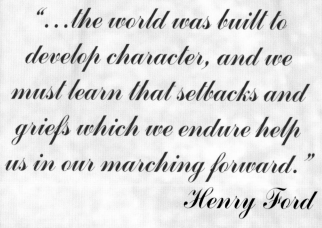

"...the world was built to develop character, and we must learn that setbacks and griefs which we endure help us in our marching forward."

Henry Ford

Stripped of all its non-essential components, such as the fenders, the Model Ts were extremely light and could be made to go fast. Mike Mueller

RIGHT: *Road competitions in Europe proved the worthiness of the early automobiles, including this Panhard racer from France.*

BELOW: *A young Henry Ford (right) poses with his driver and one of the most famous early Ford-built race cars, the 999. The success of this car drew investors to Ford's side.*

The first ten finishers were powered by gasoline engines. The automobile was proving more practical and reliable. Competitions showed that engineer's drawings or the manufacturer's best promises were only as good as the results.

On Thanksgiving Day 1895, just months before Henry Ford took his Quadricycle for a test drive, competition came to America with the Chicago to Evanston, Illinois, event. Frank Duryea finished first on the 54-mile course. The news spread across the nation.

Many inventors saw racing success as a laboratory to prove or disprove their theories about engines, transmissions and automotive components. Attention from competition also drew speculators, with visions of quick bucks before their eyes. A few incredibly wealthy Americans saw racing as a diversion and the early cars as their toys.

So was born the Vanderbilt Cup in the United States, a competitive environment that promoted the cars as well as ego-driven status. On Oct. 8, 1904, a Vanderbilt Cup race was observed on Long Island, one person recording what more than 300,000 saw.

"Cars that were traveling 60 mph rattled over washboard level crossings, tipping out their drivers. Other competitors dodged chickens and children in dramatic slaloms, buckled their vehicles on corners or lost their engines over rutted sections." [2]

By 1901, the average racing speeds had climbed through the 50s and even approached 80 mph. But deaths and accidents caused by focusing on lightness and horsepower to weight ratios began proving that a balance was needed between speed, reliability and durability.

Not everyone enjoyed racing—or even the seemingly helter-skelter disruption of quiet rural lives by the automobile.

"We can't keep our doors or windows open for dust and nuisance is the greatest on Sunday," complained one member of the Canadian Grange. "Why should we pay for good roads when we are driven from them by the automobile?" [3]

But the pendulum was shifting and those opinions, so dominant just a few years earlier, now were changing. In country after country, time trials, hill climbs, match races and other forms of competition were proving that the automobile was something substantial with uses waiting to be tapped.

There were many Americans who entered automotive competitions but it was Henry Ford who was in the right place at the right time—and had the moxie to not only design and tinker with his automotive concepts but to put his ideas in practice in competitions.

Before there was a glimmer that there would be a Ford Motor Co., a Ford racer was turning heads. In fact, Henry Ford seemed to gravitate from the experimental stage of the Quadricycle to the racing arena, despite those who were trying to help him establish himself as a car builder.

It was racing that consumed Ford and his aids like Edward "Spider" Huff, C. Harold Wills and others as they focused on competition instead of the fledgling Detroit Automobile Company in 1899, the remnants of that company brought back from the ashes in 1900 and the Henry Ford Company, begun on the coattails of racing success in 1901.

Wills, for example, was a talented young man who took a giant leap into racing in an era when there was no compensation for his talents.

"...Wills jumped at the chance to become Ford's unpaid helper," wrote author Jack Woodward.

His glory was being a part of successful challenges to famed racers of the era. [4]

The greater Detroit area had been exposed to racing before Henry Ford at places like Belle Isle and Grosse Pointe. Both bicycle racing and various horseracing competitions had interested people in Michigan and Ontario for at least 20 to 30 years.

But Ford was a local man who was beginning to get more and more attention. Racing against the powerful and well-known American automaker and competitor Alexander Winton really established Ford.

A 1915 Model T racer shows its special radiator and body as it leans into a corner.
Bob Harrington

On Oct. 10, 1901, Winton was scheduled to appear in a 25-lap race against any competitors. But problems cut the field and Winton insisted the race be shortened to just 10 laps—the sooner the better to claim the prized cut-glass punch bowl Winton sales manager Charles Shanks had selected for the winner. Shanks' assumed his boss would win.

Author Robert Lacey wrote that early auto competitions were like one of the early ventures to outer space.

"They combined drama, real human courage and danger with the demonstration of technical progress, a chance for ordinary mortals to witness man expanding the limits of his day." [5]

The 40-hp Winton seemed to have the power edge over the upstart created by the locals, Henry Ford and his crew. The Winton ads bragged about racing successes and used the ad slogan: "Always ready for use. Never gets winded."

The Ford team's vehicle had a very low carriage, not much higher than its tires. The long wedge was tapered and sleek but still as massive looking as a modern truck chassis.

The driver's seat was the highest point which meant the driver had to lean over, much like a jockey on a race horse.

Four large elliptical springs supported thin tires mounted on wire wheels. At just 1,600 pounds, the "Sweepstakes" was lighter than many racers and had a 540-cid, two-cylinder opposed engine with a healthy 7 x 7-inch bore and stroke. The Ford achieved 26 noisy horsepower. It used a porcelain spark plug coil wrapping, made by a Detroit dentist. It was the predecessor to the modern spark plug casing.

One source said the Olds Works was closed so that workers could take in the race. [6]

Predictably, the Winton screamed out in front and held the lead for seven laps until oil problems and destiny overtook the veteran racer. The steady Ford overtook the Winton and won the race.

Like a scene from Hollywood, the local boy thrilled the crowd.

"The people went wild," wrote Clara Ford later. "One man threw his hat up and when it came down he stomped on it, he was so excited. [7]

There is something about Fords and racing that have always gone together well. This is a 1924 Ames-bodied Model 814 Model T Speedster on the track.
Bob Harrington

In its 2003 retrospective on the Ford Motor Company, *Automotive News* reported the race had lasted just over 13 minutes with approximately 8,000 people present. But it was a landmark event.

The result was a major upset that sent shock waves around the automotive world and inspired new investors to boost the winner. On Nov. 30, 1901, a little more than one month after the racing victory, the Henry Ford Company was formed.

Yet the company's namesake was still intent on racing, as focused as a milk horse on a crowded city street. With presence of mind based on her years of marriage to the compulsive Henry, Clara Ford felt the tidal wave of success following the race would be a "hard struggle." [8]

Other American companies had their eyes on racing. Packard offered its majestic Grey Wolf racer in sales literature. A car called the Pirate was in the making at the same time the small curved dash cars were being assembled at the Olds Motor Works. Winton continued his racing efforts.

"Every early carmaker raced," Ford recalled years later. "How else to prove their product?" [9]

Of course, Ford and his associate race car builders envisioned a car that combined speed and power with lighter weight and more agility. They wanted to use lessons from the track to eventually produce a popular vehicle.

As the Henry Ford Company supporters were anticipating car making successes, the embodiment of the company name had forged a partnership with a bicycle racer/raconteur named Tom Cooper. Ford's backers demanded he make a choice between the plant or the race track. Ford took to the track, where his heart was at that time.

"If I can bring [French racing champion Henri] Fournier in line there is a barrel of money in this business," Ford wrote to his brother-in-law. "I don't see why he won't fall in line and if he don't I will challenge him…" [10]

With Cooper, Ford and his associates prepared two cars for racing, both named after fireballing New York Central Railroad trains, the "Arrow" and the "999."

In 21st century hindsight, grandson Edsel Ford II offered some perspective on what spurred Henry Ford to be such an intense player in the early racing scene.

"The auto industry…was growing up without him," said Edsel III in 2003. "Companies were already making automobiles and most of them were produced in the Northeast and Europe, not in Detroit. Henry Ford might well have slipped into obscurity as just another dreamer. He needed to get the world's attention. Henry Ford built a race car." [11]

Actually two race cars—and what cars they were! Both were so powerful that Ford and Cooper thought the better of trying to drive them. They brought in Barney Oldfield, an early automotive legend. It was a real coup for the team.

"…this chariot may kill me," said Oldfield, "but they will say afterwards that I was going like hell when she took me over the bank!" [12]

On Oct. 25, 1902, one of the twin beasts won the Challenge Cup at Grosse Pointe, Michigan, withering the Winton Bullet in the process. The Ford-Cooper cars set records almost every time they took to the tracks. And Oldfield would become the first to break the one-minute mile in the Ford team-prepared racers.

This 1919 Champion-bodied racer shows a few clues to its Model T underpinnings in this profile image. Bob Harrington

Ford expressed nothing but respect for the Arrow and 999. It was as if he had breathed life into a monster that he couldn't quite control. He respected it just as he had respected the old Nichols-Shepard steam traction engine of his boyhood. This creation was the product of his hands.

"There was only one seat," Ford recalled. "One life to a car was enough. I tried out the cars. Cooper tried out the cars. We let them out at full speed—going over Niagara Falls would have been a pastime after a ride in one of them." 13

The victory against the Winton rocketed Ford and Oldfield into national stardom. Now Ford was ready to get back to manufacturing, with enthusiasm. By the time of the Oldfield win in 999, and while still officially linked with Cooper, Ford had entered a manufacturing partnership with coal seller Alexander Malcomson. Ford-Malcomson Ltd. was set to make the "Fordmobile."

Financial reality would soon hit both men and wiser and deeper pockets had to come to the rescue. The venture was re-formed with a much more solid foundation after just a few months of debt and became the Ford Motor Co. in the summer of 1903.

Racing-experienced associates now joined Ford in a new automotive venture. The Ford Motor Co. would last as would, for at least a short time, Cooper's racing endeavors with Barney Oldfield.

Late in 1903, Henry Ford bought the Arrow and rechristened it the 999. This time, it was a Ford factory team racing car, trying to break the French Mors' land speed record.

On New Year's Day 1904, a route was cleared over ice and the 999 tried to break the record. It wasn't exactly a smooth course, according to automotive historian Beverly Rae Kimes.

Ford cars, including Model Ts like this 1923 racer, have always taken to speed and curves well. There's something about competition that is in their genes.   Bob Harrington

"At every fissure the car leaped into the air. When it wasn't in the air, it was sliding." 14

A record of 100 mph at 36 seconds was set. Unfortunately, no official timekeepers caught the record. When the trial was run again, three days later, watches were set in timekeeper's hands. The Ford 999 ran at 91.37 mph in 39.4 seconds officially setting a new world speed record.

The success underlined the arrival of the young Ford Motor Company and focused attention on its cars, including the Model B and the more popular, lighter C and AC. Lighter cars were the future that Henry Ford wanted to pursue and their success underlined what he'd learned from racing.

One might say Henry Ford and his new company were the automotive world's version of the fast new gunslinger on the block in an Old West movie. They took on all comers in every dusty street as they worked their way up the scale of reputations and attention.

An observer of the Ford Motor Company once reflected that Henry didn't care what humor, publicity or racing success he received, just so he received it.

Even the troubled Model K, that unwanted step-child pushed so hard by Malcomson, proved to have some racing provenance.

With either biblical understanding or irony, the K-based racer was named the 666 by Henry Ford. First it cracked a crankshaft in competition. Then in Florida, the 666 was beaten by a French Darracq in one heat and was stuck in the sand in another beach race heat.

At a Michigan State Fair racing event, the ill-fated 666 went out of control with Ford driver Frank Kulick at the wheel.

"...it ended its competition life over an embankment, upside down. Henry wanted to bury it right there." 15

Ford would wait a long time before he approved of any car with a six-cylinder engine or a car that massive and expensive.

The former Ford racing team now was preparing a new car. The Model T was the sum of both the racing experiences and the Ford's team's desire to offer a car to a wider audience.

The Model T Gives Birth to a New Racing Era

By the autumn of 1908, American prowess had produced a new generation of racing cars.

Gone or soon leaving were predominantly heavy, power-laden behemoths. What Ford and others understood was that light cars meant more speed per horsepower and less stress on components.

Racing also taught American car makers what perfection was possible. Many, again like Ford, knew that if interchangeable parts and components could be made for racing, those processes could be expanded in production. More cars at a decent price meant more demand and more sales.

Ford's vision of a light, practical, affordable car became a reality in the Model T and that success story meant more and more people had much more to work with. People who never had a chance to own an automobile, much less something they could race, now cast their eyes on the humble Model T—a malleable ball of clay in their racing hands.

From roadsters to racers

Cross country competitions and various racing successes were the icing on the cake for the Ford Motor Company with the Model T. Almost from its beginning, people were thinking about ways to race the lightweight T or to find challenges for it. Ford Motor Co. led the way.

By 1910, Frank Kulick was racing a Model T against an ice boat on Lake St. Clair, near Detroit.

That year, a Model T went up the steps of the YMCA in Columbus, Ohio.

In 1911, a fresh racer called the 999 II or "Super T" beat the world famous "Blitzen Benz" from Germany and also took checkered flags in New Orleans, Chicago, Milwaukee and Detroit.

Model Ts literally went up in the world as well as in the eyes of potential buyers with their climbing exploits. Model Ts went stair climbing—up three flights of stairs in the St. Louis County court house in Duluth, Minnesota, and scaling all 66 steps at the Tennessee State Capitol.

And Ts headed up mountains as well including the rocky slopes of Ben Neven, at 4,406 feet, the tallest point in the

British Isles. An American team climbed all 14,108 feet of Pike's Peak in their Model T. Even more successes followed in 1912.

In Toronto, Ontario, Ford sales manager Fred Fox raced an open, body-less Model T prepared for speed and won against an ice boat in Toronto Harbor.

By 1913, the young and successful Ford Motor Co. was ready to compete in the All-American event, the Indianapolis 500. But race officials gave the Ford team an ultimatum that was unpalatable. They wanted 1,000 pounds added to the Model T before it could compete.

As always when he was rebuffed, Henry Ford stiffened his back, brushing off the Indianapolis crowd with a memorable remark.

"We're building race cars, not trucks," Ford hissed. [17]

And with that remark, Ford Motor Co. backed away from leading competitions. The racing baton was handed over to a much broader field of racing innovators and racing dreamers, giving them permission to create something for competition—and they did.

Passing the baton

By 1915, the Model T Ford had firmly established itself as the leader in the automotive world. People were learning to drive on Model Ts all over the world. Many people were able to own an automobile because there was a Model T.

It was symbolic that Henry Ford, so successful in the early portion of the 1900s, had set racing aside as his primary interest. Then he'd turned his back on establishment racing when rebuffed for having too light a racer for the Indianapolis 500.

The Model T was used in hundreds of ways on the road and on farms, and now people were taking the baton hand off and adapting the universal car to new ways of racing.

The people who led the way took the Model T and their creativity and produced something faster, more fuel efficient, more race ready, sleeker, tougher—it was as if Ford and his early racing associates had set up think tanks across the nation to come up with new ideas.

Henry Ford posed in the driver's seat of the Barber-Warnock Fronty-Ford racer in 1924.

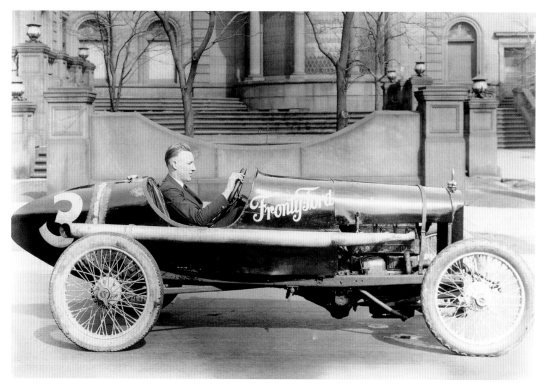

Here's a 1921 Fronty-Ford with both the company's famed bullet-shaped body and the typical Fronty engine prep with exhaust pipe streaking along the right side of the body.

Carl "Pop" Green and Green Engineering

There were several component makers who focused on racing. One of the earliest, Green Engineering of Dayton, Ohio, was led by the venerable Carl "Pop" Green.

The Green components included engine parts such as an early form of supercharging. They also promoted Alumite pistons and connecting rods for racing.

One Green ad claimed the pistons and connecting rods were "...used in 90 percent of the successful dirt track racing cars throughout the country and thousands of fast touring cars."

The Green Power-Plus cylinder head was said: "...to fill the Ford owner's long felt need of something to increase the power, pep, speed and getaway...to make driving the Ford car more of a pleasure. Buy one today. Enjoy your Ford more tomorrow," said the Green ad.

Green Engineering also produced a racing chassis and other parts for the Model T, including the Green Engineering Special Super-Charger. One of Green's products was a head with nearly hemispherical combustion chambers, at least 35 years before the early Chrysler Corporation Hemi engines of the early 1950s.

The Green Special Racing Car and Green Racing Chassis were built for the tracks of the era—whether they were dirt, brick or board. A complete Green car, with the supercharger cost $2,200. The chassis only was just $750.

Craig-Hunt and Speedway

Another early component maker was Craig-Hunt of Indianapolis, Indiana. Fittingly, at the home of America's most famous race, the Indianapolis 500, the Craig-Hunt firm specialized in racing-only parts in the pre-World War I era.

One of their specialties was a 16-valve cylinder head for Model Ts, following the lead of the Peugeot and Stutz-Wisconsin racing heads. The Craig-Hunt unit featured four valves per cylinder and was "...for use on racing, speedster and sport cars, where maximum speed and power is the chief requirement."

"Super-Ford" Racing Chassis

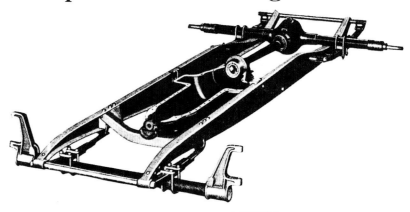

Racing Car
—and—
Parts List

Green Engineering Company
Dayton, Ohio, U. S. A.

ALUMINITE

Pistons and Connecting Rods for All Cars

Special Speed and Race Car Parts for All Cars

Everything for Racing Fords

Famous "Super-Ford" Racing Cars

ABOVE: *Green Engineering produced the "Super-Ford" racing chassis for those who wanted to get an edge on the competition.*

LEFT: *Pop Green Engineering of Dayton, Ohio, was famous for his Aluminite pistons and similar racing components.*

Craig-Hunt 16-Valve Peugeot Type Racing Head for Fords
FASTEST IN THE WORLD : FOR SPEED ONLY

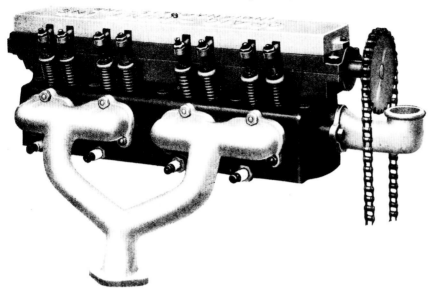

The Craig-Hunt 16-valve racing head brought the successful racing technology developed by Peugeot in France to the reliable Ford Model T engine.

The Craig-Hunt head was available for $150 and featured a large open chain connected to a large sprocket at the front of the head. Later, Craig-Hunt brought out an eight-valve head that offered two valves per Model T cylinder.

When Craig-Hunt succumbed to the temptations of making their own auto in the heady post World War I era, they fell flat in the tough recession of 1920 that leveled many automotive newcomers. Craig-Hunt went out of business and a new enterprise called Speedway Engineering rose from the ashes.

Speedway entered the racing and specialty body segment of the Model T business offering products "Making the Ford Fleet-Footed." Eventually they expanded offerings that Craig-Hunt had supplied and also offered a $1,500 to $1,700 version of a Model T-based racing car.

The Speedway racing body was a cigar-shaped unit made of 21-gauge steel.

"The flared cowl, a feature found only on the highest priced custom built racing bodies, has a tendency to direct air currents up and over the driver's head," said Speedway advertising.

Speedway also offered Maluminum racing pistons at $32.50 a set and Su-Dig spark plugs for racing at $1.75 per plug. Speedway offered Underslung components to lower the Model T for racing, Splitdorf High Tension magnetos, Pasco Quick Change wire wheels and racing gears.

Note: Green, Craig-Hunt and Speedway information was compiled from ads printed in *Vintage Ford*, 16-4, published in July-August 1981.

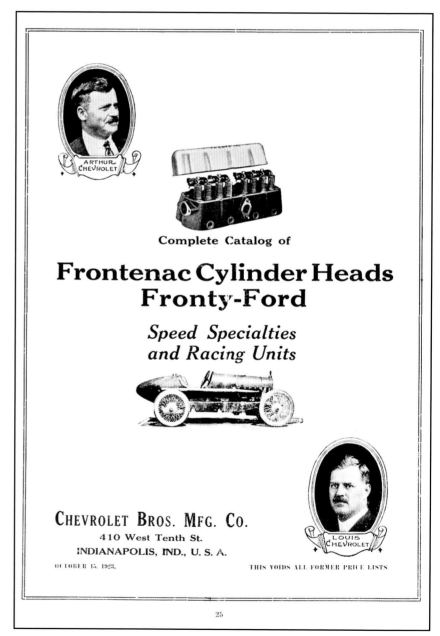

The famed Frontenac cylinder head and Fronty-Ford racing components were produced by the famous Chevrolet Brothers.

Joseph Jagersberger's Famed Rajo

Racer Joe Jagersberger also was one of the many who made something special from the raw material of the Model T.

The Austrian native had an impressive resume from his work in Europe. He'd apprenticed at the Daimler Motor Works in Stuttgart before he turned 14. He was a mechanic for early racing champion Camille Jenatzy of Belgium and Jagersberger drove in the extremely competitive Paris to Madrid race of 1903. He stepped away from race driving, became a chauffeur to wealthy American John Jacob Astor, then came to Racine, Wisconsin, to work for the J. I. Case Company.

Case was intent on racing in the 1910 and 1911 Indianapolis 500 races. Jagersberger lost his right leg and right eye in a racing accident. He decided to become a component maker for Model Ts about 1918. Since he lived in Racine, a city south of Milwaukee, he combined the first letters of his home town with his first name to create the memorable "Rajo" products.

Rajo heads became popular because of their adaptability to stock Model T engines. Jagersberger used standard exhaust valves and manifolds adding overhead intake valves. The Rajo head could be added without cutting into the Model T's firewall.

Advertising claimed that the Rajo equipment would help the Model T perform: "…as wonderfully as any $3,000 automobile."

The eight-valve Rajo head was a common sight on competitive Model Ts by the late 1920s. Rajo heads came in a number of variations but always were serious about speed and performance.

Jagersberger and his Rajo products also were popular in the Model A era. At one point, Rajo heads were shipped at the rate of 500 per month. Jagersberger died in 1952, but not before showing a new Rajo head for the venerable Chevrolet six-cylinder engine in an early *Motor Trend* magazine.

Note: Material for the Rajo section courtesy of writer Chad Elmore and Old Cars Weekly.

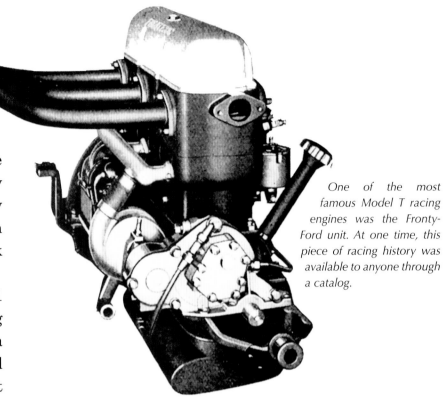

One of the most famous Model T racing engines was the Fronty-Ford unit. At one time, this piece of racing history was available to anyone through a catalog.

The Chevrolet Brothers and Frontenac

The Swiss-born Chevrolet brothers—Louis, Arthur and Gaston—gave their name to a famous automotive product but their second endeavor, the Chevrolet Brothers' Frontenac Motor Corporation endeared them to Ford followers.

Louis, the eldest, had designed bicycles, worked for automakers Darracq and Dion-Bouton on engines in France, then worked in New York City where he and younger brother Arthur were hired by Billy Durant to work for the new General Motors.

The brothers Chevrolet devoted their time to racing, keeping the youthful GM in the headlines in 1910 and 1911. By 1914, they created their Frontenac enterprise, the name of the French bicycles Louis had designed and the name of the French governor-general of Canada in the 18th century.

Several designers joined the Frontenac group including Etienne Planche, who worked with Louis to bring out the early "iron engine" dual-overhead-cam Frontenac-built racing cars with their aluminum alloy bodies.

Former Duesenberg associate Cornelius Van Rant also contributed with single and dual overhead cam designs. Frontenac made a racing-style camshaft for Model T engines.

After World War I, dirt track racing became more popular and independent sponsors and mechanics alike prepared cars for racing in all corners of the country. The Chevrolets and Van Rant decided that Frontenac speed parts would be a good idea.

They knew they had something special when they tested a Frontenac overhead-valve head on the stock Model T of shop foreman Skinny Clemons. Suddenly Skinny's T was one of the fastest around!

When the Frontenac head went into production, orders came rolling in. They decided to segment the heads, which quickly were nicknamed "Fronty." The R series was dedicated to racing, the T was a lower compression model for cars and trucks. The S was a high compression version for the Model T Speedster crowd.

"The Fronty greatly increases power and gasoline mileage and eliminates vibration and overheating," read a busy ad for the Chevrolet Brothers' Frontenac equipment. "The Fronty-equipped motor can easily be throttled to 5 miles an hour—then accelerated to 40 miles an hour in 16 seconds."

"Will Win for You" was the Fronty ad slogan and they set out to prove it in 1922 when the Fronty Ford racer was entered in the Indianapolis 500. While it didn't earn the checkered flag, the car endeared itself to Model T owners everywhere who understood they could have a Fronty unit for $115. That was pretty solid advertising.

Other Fronty-Ford parts included a radiator for $75 or $85 for a nickel-plated version. The One-Man Racing Body was tagged at $125 while the Speedster body was just $100. It was designed, the ad said, for "fast road cars."

Fronty Fords were led by the famed Barber-Warnock racer, named for a Ford dealership and driven by Lora L. Corum. The car became the star of the Model T crowd with its strong fifth place finish at Indianapolis.

"When Corum…dashed across the finish line he drew the loudest and longest applause ever heard at the Speedway. Arthur Chevrolet had prepared car number 23 and its truly remarkable performance made him one of the heroes of the year." [18]

Drivers who relished speed yet still needed their Model Ts for civilian uses realized the Fronty-Ford cylinder head offered the best of both worlds. With it, their Model Ts had increased power and performance, and could reach speeds of over 100 mph while still using the engine and transmission the factory had supplied.

Then Frontenac offered something the speed-minded just had to have, the D-O Fronty Head was said to "satisfy the insistent demands for something still faster." If that wasn't enough, the new head came with a hands-on Chevrolet Brothers promise.

"Each order receives the personal attention of Arthur Chevrolet, both during the course of construction and testing."

Dual camshafts were mounted overhead and were available with or without the intake/exhaust manifold and carburetors. Those choosing the whole works had a bonus. They were offered two Zenith carbs for the same full price of $600. Fronty-Fords were also built to order for those who really wanted to achieve a personal level of satisfaction and speed.

Note: Material for the Frontenac section was gathered from ads and story information including *Vintage Ford* 6:4 July-August 1971 and 11:4 July-August 1976 and *Model T Times* #232 Nov.-Dec. 1987.

Joseph Gallivan and the Gallivan components

One of the latecomers to the racing specialty group was Joseph Gallivan of Rantoul, Illinois, who had worked for Curtis Wright Corp. on their WWI aircraft engines. The Gallivan components were produced rather late in the Model T era, from about 1925 through 1929.

Yet in this short time, they gained positive reputations, especially on race tracks. The Gallivan engines included oval exhaust ports, a single stage wet sump oil pump, large 5/8-inch valves and Miller racing carbs.

One of the unique features of the Gallivan engines was the timing tower, a series of circular, interconnected and stacked gears that replaced timing chains found on other racing products, including Frontenac.

And There Were Many Others

Robert Roof of Anderson, Indiana, began experimenting with engine components for the Model T in 1917. By 1919, he was offering a range of racing products including manifolds and valves. Roof would become a legend for his contributions to Model T racing designs.

Other component makers included the George Riley lever system for valves and stems and a company that copied his work, the Auxiliary Valve Action Co (AVACO).

All of these companies led the way for the Model T to be turned from a practical family car to a screaming racing success, thanks to their ingenuity.

Note: Information on Gallivan Company was gathered from ads and stories including *Vintage Ford* 12:4 July-August 1977 and 9:4 July-August 1974.

The Amazing Ed Winfield

One man stood out in the annals of Model T racing and for many years among racing car enthusiasts. Ed Winfield grew up around cars and engines and his observations and tinkering became legendary.

Cams, crankshafts, fuel injection and racing heads were just some of the notable inventions created by Winfield.

Born on Oct. 4, 1901, in La Canada, California, he had

The famed Ed Winfield is at the wheel of one of his legendary racing efforts, the Kant-Skore Special from 1924.
Johnny Klann Collection

Another Ed Winfield-prepared racer. Note the lowered front suspension. Hot rodders would copy this technique some 25 years later. Johnny Klann Collection

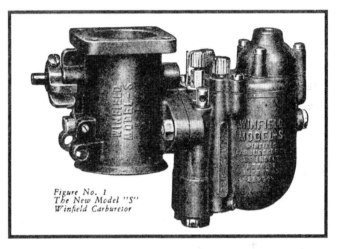

A rare Winfield carburetor is portrayed in an equally hard-to-find pieced of Winfield advertising literature.

several jobs early in life including work with a blacksmith at age 7 and at age 8, he rode a bicycle to pick up parts for a YMCA school. There he was taught about electrical and mechanical skills.

Author H. C. Egsgaard said Winfield was:

"...designer, architect, pattern maker, machinist, metallurgist, research engineer, developer and salesman." [19]

His future might have been predicted in 1913, at age 12, when he stripped the family's 1910 touring sedan to see if it could go faster.

After World War I, Winfield took a job with Harry Miller's firm in Los Angeles. Miller had established his business making carburetors and engines for the American war effort. After the Armistice was declared, the Miller firm turned to preparing racing cars, engines and carburetors.

It was a fertile training ground for young Winfield, who had prepped at the Flintridge Garage in La Canada and elsewhere. Now he was learning from Miller as well as his crew that included draftsman Leo Goosen and the talented machinist Fred Offenhauser.

The intrepid Winfield got involved as a racing driver preparing cars for other drivers before finally putting time into his own race car. He built carburetors, tooled with camshafts and prepared various Model Ts.

Egsgaard said it was a thorough education in what was needed for racing. And the more Winfield got involved, the more he innovated, especially with the Model T engines. He worked on their valve timing, spark gap, carburetor and various fuels.

"He became deeply involved with the technology of the racing car – tire pressure, wheel stiffness, balanced steering and differential ratios, oil and fuel locations and pressures." [20]

Winfield got behind the wheel of his own racer on April 10, 1921, at Banning, California. Ironically, so many competitors were using his equipment on their cars, he recalled having to adjust their cars before he worked on his own engine.

"Some of them came over and said their cars were running better," recalled Winfield. "We got the green flag and I left the hooligans behind. They thought I fixed their carburetors so I would win! I offered to trade any of them any carburetor. I told them I'd beat them anyhow!" [21]

Winfield perfected a famed series of performance carburetors in the Model T era. The H and V series (for horizontal and vertical) and the M updraft carb with its barrel throttle and hourglass shape. And the S series had a plate-like device instead of the barrel.

The Winfield cam for the Model T was also a famous innovation. Winfield noticed the normal firing order of the Model T, 1-2-4-3, caused some fuel starvation. He decided the solution was altering the crankshaft to create even fuel distribution and more balanced performance.

"By changing the crankshaft and camshaft design on the Winfield engine the firing order is 1-3-2-4. The famed "Two Up and Two Down" arrangement solidified the Winfield racing legend." [22]

Winfield's Model T racer, the famed #1, was a terror, especially with the "Two Up and Two Down" crankshaft. Racing for Ed ended when he married in the late 1920s. But he continued working on Winfield racing parts.

Ed continued to craft cams and other parts into the 1970s, and died in the early 1980s. Just as others had helped Winfield grow in his knowledge, so too did Winfield pass on his knowledge to many others. The official biography of Ed Iskenderian, famed for his own Isky cams and other racing parts, credited Winfield as major influence.

When Model T racing is mentioned, Ed Winfield must be honored for his competitive and inventive nature. He could make Henry Ford's little flivvers fly and inspired a generation of men and women to do the same.

Racing in the blood

"I stripped off the fenders, and then came the lights,
away with it all, down to the frame.
My need was for lightness, my desire was speed,
From roadster to race car was my burning need.
Now build it back up, sleek and slender,
Tin Lizzie to track terror, the faster the better.
Just me and the car, racing as one,
A new body, a new role, we'll get it done.
Some carry people, some work at hauling,
My T is a champion, racing is her calling.
Around the tracks of bricks and board and clay,
Through dust clouds and mud, we'll have our day.
Onward we roar with our Frontys and Rajos,
The Greens and Speedways, saying "There she goes!"

These are our cars, the pride of our families, and whole towns, it seems, Model Ts in our hands, our new creations, from flivvers to flyers were our dreams.

Over the hill, around the bend, lap upon lap and mile after mile, Hear them roar, the little T racers, how they make us all smile.

There's something about a dynamic, race-prepared engine—Model T style or modern racing prep—it's all about answering the call of racing in the blood. Mike Mueller

Henry Ford took the wheel and made his family name famous, We, too, wanted to succeed and be champions, all of us.

The men and the women of Model T racing, With speed in our blood, oil in our hearts, pumping dreams worth chasing."

By Tom Collins. 2007

I Raced

Many men and women took Model Ts and made them into racing cars. Whether their race was from the Atlantic to Pacific or around in circles on a dust-choked track, they bonded with their Model T race cars, modified Ts and Speedsters to pursue dreams of competition and glory, of pride and pursuit. Here are four stories about Ford racers. Together, they speak, in their own words, for thousands of men and women who went racing and who built the Ford tradition of racing begun by Henry Ford even before there was a Ford Motor Company or a Model T.

Pop Green Remembers

"Fools rush in where angels fear to tread." Imagine anyone being dumb enough to take a 91-inch Model T flathead-motored race car to Indianapolis to compete in the 500? Well, yours truly will have to confess that he was guilty with Sam Rose of Ann Arbor, Michigan, as chief accomplice in the role of driver. This happened in 1926.

The motor was supercharged with our special Roots type blower built for the job. We were able to get 100 miles per hour out of the flivver, but owing to the weakness in construction of the cylinder block, the head bolts were drawn down tight enough to hold the supercharged pressure. The head gasket would last for only one fast lap and then wear out.

Sam installed one head gasket after another—all kinds of head gaskets—and tried again and again, but one fast lap was all he could get. It was customary in those days to hold a 100 mile championship race, about the middle of June following the 500, on the State Fairground track at Detroit, and only 91-inch cars were allowed to compete.

We lowered our compression a little, figured the motor was good for 100 miles on a dirt track where it would have a chance to breathe occasionally, loaded up and went to Detroit.

Twelve cars started in the race and we lined up about two-thirds of the way back and the race was finally started with 20,000 fans watching. When the checkered flag dropped on Sam, he was in sixth place and sixth place in a championship race in those days was not to be laughed at. It paid us $800—more than the total purse for most dirt track races in those days. Sixty-nine miles-per-hour average for the 100 miles was not so bad either, for a Ford Model T.

Later, Pop added another thought about the Model T in his column.

These Model T rods were made from exceptionally good steel, had to be to carry the four-pound pistons used in the stock car. When pulled on a testing machine, a pull of seven tons was required to break the rod, and then the rod bolts failed first.

Carl "Pop" Green
Green Engineering   Feb. 16, 1939 and Mar. 30, 1939

A President of the United States Went Racing

"One driver of a Stafford recalled his come-from-behind duel with a Model T. 'He had a half mile start on me, and just when I got within about a hundred yards of him one of my lights jarred out and I had to stop. He'll never get done blowing about beating my Stafford with his little Ford.' " 23

Harry S. Truman
Independence, Missouri
Future President of the United States

New York to Seattle, 1909: Excerpts from A Model T Diary

On June 1, 1909, President William Howard Taft touched a key that opened the Alaska-Yukon-Pacific Exposition in Seattle, Washington and signaled the start of a cross country race from New York City to Seattle. The competitors were:

#1	*Ford Model T*	*Frank Kulick and H.B. Harper*		
#2	*Ford Model T*	*Bert Scott and C. J. Smith*		
#3	*Stearns Model 30-60*	*4 cylinder*	*46 hp*	*4,600 lbs.*
#4	*Acme*	*6 cylinder*	*48 hp*	*3,500 lbs.*
#5	*Shawmut*	*4 cylinder*	*45 hp*	*4,500 lbs.*
#6	*Itala*	*4 cylinder*	*60 hp*	*4,000 lbs.*

"The tenacity of the little Ford contestants was an eye-opener to me," said John Gerrie, who was the official Pacemaker for the race. " I found it impossible ever to get away from the midget competitors," he told the New York Herald. Here are excerpts from H. B. Harper of Model T #1, first published by Ford Motor Co. in 1910 to recount the incredible journey.

"Leaving Kansas City in the rain, we encountered an almost continuous spell of wet weather for several days. Every day we wore rubber coats and hip boots and pushed through mile after mile of mud. The monotony of this was frequently varied by having to ford a stream where the unusual rainfall had washed away the bridge. Often these

The Story of the Race

How the Ford Car Won the Transcontinental Contest *for the* Guggenheim Trophy *Told by* one of the Crew on Ford Car No. 1

The Winning Car and Crew

Ford Motor Company
Detroit, U. S. A.

swollen streams had beds of quicksand and the car striking them would instantly sink until the body resting on the sand prevented further settling. We thanked our lucky stars that we of the Ford cars were driving light cars.

[Harper noted that torrential rains continued as they proceeded west through Kansas.]

"The fields provided better going than the highways. Mile after mile cross country made fast time impossible. In 15 hours on June 11th the two Fords covered 90 miles."

[At one point they had to use the roof of a deserted pig pen to get the cars out of a jam in heavy water near Denver, Colorado, but they pushed on.]

"To get to Rawlins [Wyoming] necessitated using the railroad ties for a mile, including the approach to and the railroad bridge over the Platte River at Fort Steele. Our 30-inch wheels hit every separate tie a distinct and separate bump and each car came into Rawlins with a broken wheel. It delayed us 12 hours making repairs…we left the old trail at Granger [Wyoming] and started on that part of the trip which no automobile had before made without railroad aid.

By continuous riding, Ford car No. 1 made Pocatello, Idaho, on June 17th at 2:30 a. m. There are downgrades… several of them up to 1,000 feet in length averaging 30 percent where the roadway in places is six inches wider than the car tread and a slip means dashing hundreds of feet onto the rocks below.

Ford No. 2 made Boise [Idaho] first and received $100 for that. It made North Yakima [Washingon] still further in the lead, crossed the dreaded snow covered Snoqualmie Pass and landed in Seattle at noon on June 23rd, 1909, the winner by 17 hours, having covered 4,106 miles in 20 days, 52 minutes official time."

[Harper wrote that Ford No. 1 continued to have setbacks.]

"We picked up another bone-headed specimen for a pilot. This road juggler lost us in what is known as Horse Heaven Country. Any jury in the land would have brought in a verdict of justifiable homicide if we had followed our inclination.

We had pushed through the snow with less trouble than we had expected. A rock hidden in the mud and snow sprang up to give us one last foul blow. For seven hours we worked on top of the mountain, up among the clouds, remedying the trouble that rock had caused.

The winner…had forcibly demonstrated the superiority of the light weight Ford for all sorts of road conditions."

W. B. Harper
"The Story of the Race" Ford Motor Company, 1910

Racing My T

Somewhere in the mid-1930s, my buddy, Bill Pratt, and I came across a 1924 or 1925 Model T abandoned in a berry patch near our home in Curtis, Washington. Our minds churned with the possibilities this abandoned vehicle offered us.

A Model T race was slated in a few weeks to be held at the Southwest Washington Fairgrounds between Chehalis and Centralia. We aimed to collect us a trophy and some cash, too. A few minor problems and the sky was the limit.

[The "problems" involved such details as getting the car home, getting it started and getting it rehabilitated! Work was done on the engine—but the body had been cut in half and even the upholstery was gone—leaving basic seat springs.]

By the time the race drew near…our 'gem in the rough' was ready. I was to drive and Bill was to ride by my side. And he did—at least until the first turn when he baled out with spring marks on his backside.

Deserted and alone, I reached underneath and discarded the back portion of the seat spring, unknowingly ripping my trousers. There I was, precariously perched on a rusty spring, inside the ugliest race car you ever saw, speeding around a very bumpy and rugged race course.

The car behind us rear-ended us and ended up with his front tire over our rear tire. People jumped in from everywhere, got the cars untangled and we were back on track, having only dropped back a few places. We crossed the finish line in second place and we knew we were in the money.

First place was $50 and second place was $25. We thought we were rolling in hog heaven for sure. Alas, it was to be only a fleeting fancy. We did attain the fame that was our due, having come in second place and all. But the fortune eluded us. We got bilked out of it.

One of the entrants rolled his car and broke his ankle (or so they claimed). Without so much as a "by-your-leave" the $25 purse was cruelly ripped out of our grasp and given to him.

Life can be so bittersweet. We drove 14 miles home to Curtis, still perched on bare springs and in my ripped trousers, we returned home. We drove the 14 miles without a license. I don't know what happened to our beloved race car and I'm not sure I really care!

Buck Owen
Tacoma Model T Club Tacoma, Washington

Saskatchewan's Model T Racer

Canadian Bob Rogers came from a racing family. His dad, his brother and at least one of his uncles were involved in Model T racing and the Rogers family owned machine shop in Regina, Saskatchewan. Bob later raced there and in the neighboring province of Alberta. Eventually, he opened a

The racing heritage enjoyed by Bob Rogers came from his father, Billy Rogers, seated in the Model T racer.   Don Radbruch

custom speed shop in Calgary, Alberta. In 1992 he was retired and planning to write a book on his experiences. He shared some with Vintage Ford that year. Here are some excerpts.

"During the early years of [World War II] the Regina Lions Club decided to hold Model T races on Labor Day... to raise money to help the children of England by having T races with parimutuel betting. They called it 'Milk for Britain.'

The cars had to be strictly stock, with no full bodies or fenders. All cars were taken to the local Ford dealer and were checked to be sure they were stock. We were paid $100 for winning the heats and $300 for winning the main.

My dad raised all kinds of hell over me racing but I went ahead with my plans. I took every nut and bolt apart on the T and started to build it back up. [Older brother]Louie showed me how to balance the engine and make rods and mains hold together under racing conditions.

Some of the guys I raced against in Regina were Harry Bell, Tom Strickland, Johnny Nestor, Ken Ganshore and George Le May.

In 1943 they had two races for Ts—one in May at Moose Jaw and the championship race in Regina on Labor Day. I won the race in Moose Jaw and could hardly wait for Labor Day.

It rained in the morning but the sun finally came out and the race was started. I won my heat and started in the fifth row. By 15 laps I had passed six cars. I won the race. I was one happy guy!

I sold my car for $600 in 1945; a lot of money then. By this time I was destined to become a race car driver. In 1949 they stopped racing in Saskatchewan and I moved to Calgary, Alberta, to continue racing. In 1949 we quit racing the Model Ts and went into 'big cars' [sprint cars].

Racing has been good to me as I have met many good people and have made many good friends.

I wouldn't have missed it for anything!"

Bob Rogers
Tahlequah, Oklahoma *Vintage Ford* 27:6 Nov.-Dec. 1992

Model Ts built for speed were stripped or had custom bodies added to their chassis. Today they are reminders of the focus on speed, even in the heyday of the practical Model T Ford. Andrew Morland

The Model T Racing Afterglow

Model T racing didn't stop when the production of the cars ended in 1927. In fact some of the most competitive Model T racing occurred in the decades after the T was merely a memory. Especially in the time just before and just after World War II, used Model Ts were still plentiful and it was relatively easy and inexpensive to find parts and components.

Many professional racers who had cut their teeth with Model Ts moved on to other types of cars in the 1930s including Indy racers, sprint cars, Ford Model A, B and V-8-powered racers. In Southern California, they continued a new kind of racing that had begun in the Model T era, speed trial racing on the dry lake beds like Muroc Lake. It was the forerunner of modern drag racing.

The Tin Lizzie was not forgotten. In fact, in some of the more remote corners of the United States and Canada, Model T racing was just beginning a new era in the 1930s. It was ironic that racing had moved Henry Ford to compete and make a name for himself and his cars in the early 1900s. That same competition had taught Ford and his associates valuable lessons they could use to develop the Model T.

Now many Model Ts would get a second life on local tracks and fairgrounds, cars that were stripped of most essentials and lightly prepared for competition. The Model Ts were still quite prevalent, though most were now parked as owners had moved on to newer cars.

"There were not too many Ts on the road in the late 1930s," commented author Don Radbruch, "but there were lots of them sitting around unloved and unwanted in back yards, farm yards and even in junk yards." [24]

Basically, old Model Ts were to be stripped of fenders, glass, running boards and as much of their bodies as was feasible. They were to be put in competition with all other elements of the cars left stock. Unlike earlier Model T-based race cars, there were no competition accessories or engine parts allowed.

The Model Ts, stripped of much of their style and identity, would be raced by eager and often young and inexperienced drivers at county fairgrounds and exposition grounds. Many of the tracks were more suitable to horse racing or sulky racing.

A series of circuits were developed, often in areas that had little organized racing to speak of. Pockets like Wisconsin,

TIN LIZZIES

TIN LIZZIE DERBIES

THE HISTORY OF MODEL T FORD RACING 1937-1940

BY
DON RADBRUCH

Writer Don Radbruch told the sotry of Tin Lizzie Derbies, one of the moments in the afterglow of Model T racing history.   Don Radbruch

Alberta, Saskatchewan and Texas became hotbeds of this type of aged Model T racing.

Radbruch says Wisconsin was particularly busy with racing in the state capitol, Madison, as well as mid-sized cities around the state including Beaver Dam, Fond du Lac, Janesville, Jefferson, La Crosse, Monroe and Sparta. Each was a county seat and had a fairground with some type of racing track. In 1938, Wisconsin even had a state-wide Model T championship race at the prestigious Milwaukee Mile, a big time race track at State Fair Park in West Allis. [25]

Alberta was a province that enjoyed the Model T races. The large and small cities in Wild Rose Country that hosted Model T races included Calgary, Edmonton, Innisfail, Lethbridge, Olds, Red Deer and Vegreville.

"The Ts were the stars of the show," wrote Radbruch. "They would boil over, spout smoke and flames. Parts would work loose…but most Model Ts would keep right on going."[26]

But because the cars themselves had not been reconditioned for racing—they basically were tired old well-used models—and because the race drivers were non-professionals, the number of accidents and deaths mounted and the powers that be turned a cold eye on the spectacle.

In Wisconsin, the Appleton *Post-Crescent* weighed in with an editorial against Model T racing published in the late 1930s.

"Auto racing is at best perilous even with cars designed for the strains of high-speed operation and with drivers trained for the job. The exact opposite prevails in the 'Tin Lizzie Derby.' It draws only because the chances of a crash are great." [27]

The overall attention of the United States and Canada on World War II gradually ended such efforts as Model T Derby racing. By 1950, the sport was waning even in the most remote corners of North America.

Something new was taking its place. A younger generation that had seen the dry lakes racing, speed trials and other types of competition now was learning from Ed Winfield and the Chevrolet brothers but were applying new interpretations of speed and custom body work with their cars.

They produced technically sound, racing worthy cars that were intended for visual competition even more than speed. Their *hot rods* were a combination of eras, car parts and engines.

One freshly built car was featured in the May 1951 issue

of the young *Hot Rod* magazine and proclaimed the "Rajo 4-Banger: Modernized and T-Modified." Owner and builder Art Gerrick had taken a Model T roadster body and portions of the T frame and assembled a new roadster.

The name came from the BB Rajo head with dual spark plugs on each cylinder. The Rajo was mounted on an original Model T engine with Winfield carburetors and a Winfield camshaft added. The T block was bored to 3-15/16 inches. The car used a three-speed Model A transmission and differential and a Model T rear spring. Front suspension parts were from a Franklin, a Chevrolet and a Model A Ford. 28

While some, like Gerrick, were seeking new hybrid creations that expressed their enjoyment of Model Ts, others were seeking to bring back the Model Ts.

Restoration and Model T-based associations grew and with them came various competitions that respected the originality of the cars. Hill climbs were one form of competition in the afterglow era of the Model T. Another was begun by Ed Towe, who established the Towe Museum honoring the Model T.

In 1961, Towe began the Cross Country Model T Drivers, a 500 mile endurance meet on a course in Montana. It became a traditional event. And there are other ongoing competitions and events that celebrated the Model T, Model T Speedsters and Model T-era racers.

While the Model T was not bred to race, as many cars have been and still are today, it was born to serve the business and pleasure uses of people—a car that was adaptable to whatever purpose it was prepared to do.

It was fitting that racing and competition, which had been part of the innovations that made the car possible, preserved and elevated the Model T in its afterlife. The Model T has never been forgotten nor will it ever be. It may not look like a racing car at first glance, but it is one car that has racing in its very bloodlines.

Competition with Model T-based racing cars has never really stopped. Today, the racing cars are prized by collectors, like this 1919 Champion Model T racing conversion. *Bob Harrington*

Chapter 10

MODEL T MEMORIES AND STORIES

*T*his chapter was made possible by readers of Old Cars Weekly magazine. When asked, they submitted dozens of letters from a majority of the 50 states. The words and phrases are their own, edited for length. Each person who contributed to the section is noted and some have one of their own photos with their articles. We sincerely thank them. We've also added a dash of news stories from the Model T era. You can find more reader contributions in chapters 8 and 11.

Model Ts were often the first cars people experienced growing up in the 1910s or 1920. Some picked up an inexpensive used Model T for their first cars. Robin Heil-Kern

There is something about the Model T Ford that enocourages stories and memories. Robin Heil-Kern

My Model T Ford and How It Lasted a Lifetime

"My brother and I grew up on a farm in Yates Center, Kansas. My father left before I was born, and in my best efforts to find out who he was, anyone who knew him would say he was the best Model T mechanic in the state of Kansas.

He was also a drunk.

In 1935, at the height of the Depression, my brother and I worked in the hayfield all season. When we had hauled the last load of hay, the farmer said: "Now boys, I just don't have the money. But there is a 1922 Model T touring car. You can have it for the eight dollars I owe you."

We were elated—our very first car! I was 13 and my brother was 15. We cranked it up and it finally started. It was running on three cylinders. We drove it three miles home and immediately started working on it.

My brother had helped our neighbor overhaul his Fordson tractor the previous winter. We started in. I was the "gopher" and trusted my brother to do the technical work. I remember grinding the valves with a suction cup

Some of the Morin family of Osier, Michigan, gathered in front of a Model T coupe in about 1920. Lucille Morin, left front, was married to Ralph Becker for more than 67 years.   Kathy Collins.

at the end of a wooden handle. The following day my palms were so stiff and sore, I had trouble milking our cows.

We sold eggs, milk, cream and butter for spending money. We were making money and every penny went for the Model T. We had wheels, something every teenager dreams of.

[In 1971] I was persuaded to apply for an automotive instructor job in the Los Angeles Community College district. I had to go back and achieve my teaching credential. I attended UCLA—one of the best two moves I made in my lifetime.

The other was becoming acquainted with the Model T transmission while a teenager. That is what transmissions are today—bands, clutches and planetary units.

Small world. Wonderful life. Even though my father didn't wait for me, he must have instilled some mechanical abilities in me.

Thanks, Dad!"

Dr. Alphonse Bachhuber of Mayville, Wisconsin (left front) with his family and friends in their 1911 Model T touring car. Two sons also became doctors. His grandson still drives a Ford truck.   Mark Bachhuber

Harold E. (Gene) Johnston
Yates Center, Kansas

Going a Few Miles Backward before Going Forward

"I was born on Feb. 12, 1913 and my daddy bought our first Model T in 1918, a 1913 Model T. I had five brothers and two sisters. We lived in Center County, Pennsylvania.

We had a total of 13 Model Ts in our family and that included two of the large trucks with worm drive. One of the trucks had a Ruxtell rear end and it also had pneumatic rear tires on it.

The first Model T I owned was a 1926 model and I paid $25 for it. I learned to drive in a Model T and took my driver's test in a Model T.

One of the Model Ts that we had was made into a farm tractor. Daddy bought a tractor kit someplace and we had a large steel wheel on the back.

One day my daddy overhauled the tractor motor and the rear end. The motor was too tight to crank so we got our horse out to pull it to try to get it started. There was such spitting and puttering like you never heard in your life! And it would not start.

My daddy got up on the tractor and put it in gear. Instead of going forward, it went backward!

What happened was when my daddy overhauled the rear end, he got the ring gear on the wrong side of the pinion gear and all morning the engine was turning backward and we didn't know it!

He had to take the rear end apart and fix it the right way!

They were the good old days!"

Clarence Beckwith
Cincinnati, Ohio

A Little Ford Tackles a Big Bus

"Ben Strong of Manawa ran his Ford car into the Schenick bus yesterday morning marking up the rear end of that vehicle and putting the step out of business. The little old Ford came out of the scrap without a mark."

Clintonville, WI, *Tribune*   Friday July 7, 1916

For many people, a Model T might be a distant memory, part of a colorful dream, like this interesting reflection.   David Lyon

Model T Magic

"The Labor Day parade in Lowell still is the oldest one of its kind in Indiana. The parade route came right past our home so we always had friends or relation sit in the front yard to watch.

My plan was to enter a 1924 T coupe with "fatman" steering wheel and spot light in the windshield. When I got to our yard, pull in, get a cold drink, and watch the rest of the parade.

Shortly after the end of the parade, a variety of traffic would be unleashed, causing a commotion. Evidently this commotion caused the ignition on my T to make contact.

Those who know Model Ts have had the experience of turning the key on and the engine starting without cranking it. That is exactly what happened on that Labor Day. There was nobody within 15 feet of the car!

There it was, just idling away, pretty as you please! Of course, I was accused of trickery. To this day my only explanation is—Model T Magic!"

Jim Springsteen
Lowell, Indiana

My Story

"I am 82 now and I do remember...the Model T was a fun car! My poem is about the good times we had with the Model T.

A New, Used Ford Model T

I walked home from school one day,
It was foggy and gray.
As I came over the hill,
I sure got a thrill.
As I looked down our muddy driveway,
There stood a new, used Ford Model T!
My father had a big smile as he turned the key,
Up and down hills we went with glee.
The battery went dead and the tires went flat,
But my father could fix all that.
And I didn't have to walk to school after that!"

Ruby Hendrickson
Cambria, Wisconsin

Johnson's Ford Feels Thrill of Life

"Mail courier Asa F. Johnson, whose car conveys the mail each week day...is delighted with the great improvements made in the roads on the mail routes he serves daily in [Waupaca County, Town of Matteson]. His little old 'Hank Ford' seems to feel the thrill of life...and hums merrily along the public ways on Mr. Johnson's route..."

Clintonville, WI, *Tribune* 1918

A Model T Mugging

"When I was about 16, another boy and I bought a 1923 Model T touring car for $20. It ran, was complete, except it had no top.

The only time we seemed to use it was on weekends. One Sunday afternoon, a friend and I drove out to another friend's farm to shoot pigeons on his barn. We were getting close to the farm when a pickup with five older boys—about age 18—forced our T into a ditch.

There ne'er-do-wells immediately started to disable the T by trying to tip it over, draining the radiator, pouring beer into it, removing the valve cores, etc. At the same time, a teacher of my friend stopped to help. My friend got in her car to go get help. I was alone with the vandals!

One guy was firing my .22 rifle into the engine while another jumped out of the rear section of the car with my dad's 12 gauge shotgun and pointed it at me. (Both barrels were loaded.)

I ran at top speed down the road, zig-zagging with .22 bullets zinging past me. I probably ran a half-mile and met a sheriff's car. He was coming to meet me! I almost collapsed with relief!

My mom said I was white as a ghost when I arrived home.

The sheriff said the bad boys had broken into a country store that Sunday morning and stolen several cases of beer. I don't know what happened to them but I sold the Model T for $50, then later bought a '34 Chevy roadster for $100.

Today I have a 1914 Model T Speedster in my classic car collection."

Dale Underwood
Kennewick, Washington

One Special One-Ton Model TT Truck Tale

"This story refers to a 1923 Ford one-ton truck that was sold at the Kirk-McKern Motor Company in Albany, Oregon, on March 15, 1923 for the sum of $573.66.

It was sold to a man named F. A. Diestelkamp with a down payment of $386 and payments of $35 per week. F. A. Diestelkampf was a railroad telegrapher and moved from station to station working on his job.

On this new Ford chassis, complete with a Ruckstell two-speed axle, he built his living quarters in which, as far as I can tell, he lived until after World War II.

The body was constructed of a wooden framework with canvas covering the sides and top. He was very conscious of its weight. It was constructed with one big room in which the bed folded down for sleeping and folded up for storage. There was also a "shipmate" stove for heating and cooking.

Fast forward to 1971 in Pacific, Missouri, where F. A. Diestelkampf succumbed to the cold in the house he constructed. The last registration I have for the "house truck" was during World War II with an address in Kirkwood, Missouri.

My mother, his first cousin, was elected executor of this estate. I was only 15 at the time but I sure wanted that Model TT!

During the estate auction, my Uncle Harold bought it for me for the grand sum of $100. I had it trailered to my home. The amount of care F. A. took in preserving documents and pictures of the vehicle was astounding!

Today I still have it, less the house chassis and with the sheet metal only as I couldn't store it inside until until the "house" was removed. With all the plans and drawings I have from F. A., it could be rebuilt!"

Mike Riefer
Owensville, Missouri

The Twins and their Model Ts

"Back in the late 1940s, twin brothers were told by their sister, a newspaper carrier, of an old car up the road at a neighbor's house. So they bought it for $50 and pushed it down the road home.

It was a 1919 Model T touring car and they got it working. They were 16 years old. It was their first car and they drove it to school every day.

Then they found a 1919 coupe at auction for $19 and called it a "china closet." It was on blocks so they came home, got the wheels from the touring car and pulled the coupe home.

When the brothers married, they each chose a car. One took the 1919 "china cabinet." His son used it for his wedding and now uses it with the family in the Fourth of July parade.

Twin Louis Hujber kept the 1919 Model T touring car. His brother kept another Model T.   Mrs. Louis Hujber

My husband chose the 1919 Model T touring car. It's the family's favorite Ford car. We use it in parades and for family fun. Our Model T has no self-starter or working headlights, no seat belts or windshield wiper and no air conditioner or heater!

We have a lot of fun! We see the road through the floorboards and water often comes out of the radiator. Someone once said we look like the Keystone Cops in action!"

Mrs. Louis Hujber
Titusville, New Jersey

The Model T Gang

"In 1948, I was a junior in high school. A friend had a 1925 Model T Fordor. Body wise it was in very good shape except the front doors had no glass and we had new transmission bands—but they were not in the car!

The radiator leaked so we carried water and in the winter we had to drain the water at night. Fifty-cents worth of gas and a quart of used oil kept us going for the night!

A friend of my dad was a car buff and checked the progress as we changed motors. The big day arrived, I dumped gas in and off we went. It sounded like it wasn't getting gas. The needle on the end of the choke rod was missing so a machinist brazed on a new tip. We were back on the road.

One night my mother said that the car or I had to go. It could not be in front of the house. Saturday morning I drove it to two junkyards. Best offer was $7.50.

Years later I asked my mom if she knew how much it would be worth. She reminded me if I still owned it, the Model T it would still be parked out front! It was the most fun car I ever owned!"

Fred England
Grinnell, Iowa

Jack Fahs drove his 1923 Model T coupe during his high school years in Illinois.   Jack Fahs

Ford Car Demolishes Plate Glass Window

"Monday night about ten o'clock a Ford car belonging to Stanley Johnson of this city, which had been left standing on the curb near the Peterson Store, started to coast down hill. It crossed the street and jumped the curb in front of L. A. Heuer's Furniture Store, crossed the walk, smashing one of the big plate glass windows before it came to a stop. The Ford was a Model T and its unguided excursion will necessitate a new window in the Heuer Store."

Dairyman's Gazette
Clintonville, Wisconsin   Oct. 29, 1929

High School T

"My Model T days go back to 1947 when I was a junior in high school. I remember I wanted a Model A coupe so bad I could almost taste it but my dad found a 1923 Model T coupe and bought it for me for $50.

I sure wasn't going to complain about it because that was right after World War II and cars were still hard to get. I was just happy to "have some wheels." Even in 1947, that was a 24-year-old car and all the kids would rather ride in it.

The car had to sit outside and with the cold Illinois winters, I would jack up the right rear wheel every night and hope it would start in the morning.

When I came out of the house, there would be my buddy sitting in the car waiting for a ride to school. There weren't any mornings when it would fail us.

The car is long gone. I sold it in 1948 for $75 after I graduated from high school.

I'm still a Model T man. I have a 1924 touring car, a 1925 roadster and a 1920 racer, all restored.

My brother-in-law and I still take our wives for a three- or four-day trip with the roadsters over the back roads to Iowa, Wisconsin and even to Minnesota. Hope we can do it for many years!"

Jack Fahs
Walnut, Illinois

Riding the Model T Chassis

"As a young man of 14, I was a friend of the neighborhood Ford dealer in my boyhood home of Hillsdale, Michigan. I would ride the train from Hillsdale to Detroit and drive new Fords back for $5 per car. I would earn an extra buck if I drove back a truck.

Imagine that distance, 96 miles, sitting on a crate and eating dust from the dirt roads. The 10.5-hour work day included a stop at a greasy spoon, and was done Monday, Wednesday and Friday all through the summer.

When questioned if I had a driver's license at the time… well, let's just say it's a little too late to be worried about that now!

Coming down what is now US 12, then known as the Chicago Road, many of the Fords would overheat and seize. We frequently had to wait around Saline, Clinton or elsewhere along the way for the Ford to cool off—then we were on our way again."

The late Hilton Kiebler, as told to Rick Mills

"Hilton mentioned there was a traffic cop on a main intersection outside the Ford plant. Whenever he saw a group of Model Ts drive away, the cop would stop traffic for the Fords to pass. Hilton also mentioned that on one of the main routes away from the plant a push truck was parked and waiting right about where the Model Ts would be getting hot. If one of the Fords seized, the push truck was there to give it a push or haul it back."

Rick Mills
Secretary/ treasurer, Buick Club of Central Michigan
Lansing, Michigan

Authors note:

Mr. Kiebler's story reminds us that Ralph Becker, for whom this book is dedicated and my wife Kathy's grandfather, also drove Model T chassis. Sitting on a crate above the gas tank, he drove 110 miles from the Milwaukee,

Wisconsin, assembly plant to De Pere, Wisconsin where Ralph, and his step-dad, John Becker, sold and serviced Model Ts. Some of the Model T chassis went to a Green Bay body maker. By the way, Ralph drove the chassis in winter as well as summer!

Yellow Canary and the Red Speedster

"On December 5, 1927, my father bought a 1926 Ford Model T roadster with a cracked block and wheels missing for $7. The car was customized in 1930 by adding side mount red wire wheels and a rumble seat.

The car was in storage from 1939 until 1961 when dad built a new garage called the "T House." A restoration was started but dad passed away in June 1963. I restored the car in 1965.

The car was used for shows, parades and other functions for 32 years. In 1998, a second restoration was started and completed in 2000. I hope I can get another 30 years out of it!

A period photo of the "Yellow Canary" shows the car as it looked in 1930, near the time when Jim Crawford's dad bought the car. Jim Crawford

The "Yellow Canary" 1926 Model T roadster as it looks today, well-preserved at its Maryland home. Jim Crawford

In 1960, dad and I were walking around a car show and flea market in York, Pennsylvania, when dad spotted a brass radiator for an early Model T. The man asked for $20 and dad nearly broke his arm going for his wallet.

Dad had a lot of spare parts to build a brass era Speedster. The parts included an American LaFrance fire truck seat, a round gas tank and some 1913 Model T parts.

I started to build the Speedster in 1968. The entire car was rough-built except the engine and transmission. It was finished in 1996. Both cars have a Frontenac valve head, a Warford transmission and a Ruckstell two-speed rear axle plus Rocky Mountain rear wheel brakes."

Jim Crawford
Rising Sun, Maryland

Mom and the Model T Tudor

"Here is a picture of my mother in a 1926 Model T Tudor sedan. Mother is in the background and her friend is in the driver's seat. My mother's name was Nellie Stoner.

The picture was taken on July 4, 1926, at a park in South Lyons, Michigan.

My folks were married in 1929 in Michigan. Dad died in 1987 at age 89 while mom died in 2003, just three months before her 101st birthday."

Don Dennis
Lakeland, Florida

One "Hot" Model T

"My Model T was a 1925 Fordor with an aluminum body. I bought it for $30 in the summer of 1953. Our gang would ride up and down Main Street having a good time. One Saturday the tail pipe fell off but we kept on cruising. All at once we smelled smoke and we could see the footboards on the passenger side burning. It happened in front of a shoe repair shop and ran in to ask for a bucket of water. I ran out and dumped it on the fire to save the Model T.

Erv Niebuhr and his 1925 Model T Fordor that he owned for 40 years. This is the day that he sold it to a newcomer.   *Erv Niebuhr*

After that summer I parked it and jacked it up until 1993, then ran an ad in *Old Cars Weekly*. A fellow from Eagle Nest, Missouri, was sure tickled to get it. He said he was going to restore it.

I'm in my 70s and still drive a car and a truck and enjoy going on new roads all over the country."

Erv Niebuhr
Fremont, Nebraska

Tipsy T Totaling

"When I was about 18 years old, a buddy bought a "doctor's coupe" Model T Ford. He had a brother who was known for tipping the bottle once in awhile. One Sunday afternoon, he was tipping the bottle and he decided to take the Model T for a ride.

My buddy and I climbed in with him and he decided to see how fast he could come down the hill and then swing into the driveway of the family's home.

The first time he tried, there was a car coming so he had to go past the driveway. On the second trip, he swung in. There was a small spruce tree that he hit head on. It was about two inches in diameter and by swinging in at that speed he snapped one of the spokes off the right front wheel.

My buddy just about cried at the time and he could have killed his brother."

Walter T. LaRue
Okeechobee, Florida
Formerly from Pennsylvania

This 1915 Model T runabout seems to radiate an aura of the past. What kind of memories surround this car?   David Lyon

Two "brass era" Model T Fords—a 1914 touring car with its top down (left) and a 1915 Model T touring car (right). What stories could they tell us?   David Lyon

The elegant, by Model T standards, 1923 center door sedan. Sitting all alone with no people or cars around on this early morning, one can imagine tales surrounding a car like this one.   David Lyon

A 1911 Model T touring car seems almost ghost-like hin this image. Does it hold stories of interesting journeys and the people who bought the car when it was new? David Lyon

Going Up the Mountain...

"Once or twice each summer, back when our 1915 Model T was relatively new, we would pack her up and take the 20-mile trip to Suffield, Connecticut. The trip might include changing a tire or getting water for the steaming radiator, but the most memorable part of the journey was going up a mountain that lay smack dab between Avon and Suffield. This one had an occasional "rest ponies" strategically placed to give teams of horses a place to rest as they hauled their loads up the mountain.

Near the top where the road grew steeper, a well-located rest pony was used to turn Lizzy around and back her up the rest of the way!

Even on level ground the gas tank wasn't that much higher than the carburetor. So when the going got steep, backing up the Model T—getting the back end higher than the front—kept the gas flowing into the carburetor.

We always cheered Lizzy on trying to help her make it all the way to the top going forward, but it never happened. Out little Model T could only reach the crest of that mountain in reverse!"

...and Winter Driving

"The good years for most farmers temporarily ended about the time my father purchased our place, shortly after he came back from World War I. I'd like to think it was the reason, as late as the early 1930s, our family car was still our trusty old 1915 Model T Ford.

To save money, we used the same oil year around—a summer weight that became impossibly thick in cold weather. Hand cranking the engine through that "molasses in January" was virtually impossible so we employed another procedure.

We would block the front wheels, jack up one rear wheel, put Lizzy in high and start turning the rear wheel forward. With my father and I working as a team, we would eventually get her fired up. The next step was to bring hot water from the kitchen stove. We couldn't afford alcohol, the most common anti-freeze back then.

Our farmstead was a quarter mile off the road. We simply inspected the fields flanking our driveway and picked the path of least resistance. Then off we'd go across the field and toward the road. (We always plowed the furrows in the fall parallel with the driveway so we would drive with the furrow as we head toward the road.)

Lizzy could go through quite a bit thanks to her tall, skinny tires and low gearing. We always made it to the highway and back home again.

When Old Henry designed the Model T Ford, he sure had the farmers in mind, especially the poor farmers. The Model T served us for the better part of two decades."

The late Graham Coulter
Avon, Connecticut
As told to David Coulter, Round Lake, Illinois

Model T Groundskeeper

"Back in the 1940s, I lived across from Kriegbaum Field, a football stadium, track, baseball diamond and practice fields for the local Huntington High School Vikings. It was a vast area and needed to be mowed quite frequently in the summer.

One summer morning when [the maintenance man] came and opened the gates, I went in and was running around the track. He came over and asked me if I would like to mow for him.

We headed for an old shed and inside was this odd-looking piece of an automobile. It was the front end of a Model T, intact with the crank included. The hood, windshield, engine, front wheels and axle were all there. Under the seat and frame were three reel-type mowers and behind that was a big roller with sprockets on both sides driven by a chain.

I ended up mowing a number of summers before I left town. As I look back, I wish I would have taken some pictures of this Model T. When I got out of service, they had replaced it.

I never saw anything quite like my old Model T before or after."

Don Stoltz
Zanesville, Indiana

Grandpa Joe's 1915 Model T Coupe

"I was sitting on the front porch on a hot summer day, sipping some lemonade when a young man in a suit, carrying a briefcase, walked by, nodded to me and asked permission to talk with me. The man asked me if I had an automobile. I said I wanted to have one. I poured a glass of lemonade for him and he pulled out pictures and literature about the car.

I told him I didn't owe anybody anything and wouldn't buy a car until it was paid for. He set me up with an account and I paid the Ford Motor Company every month for a year, until the car was paid for. I received a post card from the dealer telling me to come down and pick up my car.

I walked to town and there it was. I wanted a closed car due to the bad winters here in Akron, so I bought a coupe. It sure was pretty.

They gave me some papers and the salesman drove me around the block twice to show me how to drive it. I then drove it home. I was a proud man! I decided that I would drive the car to Toledo to show my parents. I left early Saturday morning. It took me six hours to get there because I took the wrong turn and ended up in Findlay!

You follow the roads west and then headed north. It was a great adventure. I carried an extra gasoline can. It was a real treat to find a set of streetcar tracks because you could follow them until you came to a town. The little Ford ran like a Swiss watch.

I ran across a man late in the afternoon. Unlike me, he didn't bother to get any real instructions nor did he read his owners book. He was driving with his foot holding the transmission down in low range. I showed him and he laughed. We followed each other for several hours. I got to Toledo, showed my parents and then had a wonderful supper."

Joe Sommers, who lived to age 100
Akron, Ohio
As told to Richard Bailey, grandson and Proud owner of Grandpa Joe's Ford Manual

Model T Used Car Caper

"I grew up in Southern California and have always loved cars. I used to cut out cars from magazines—Packards, Hupmobiles and more. At 14, I got my driver's license and [my] paper route caused me to ride past the Podalar Car Company's used car lot.

I spotted an old Ford Model T touring car in their back lot. The car was for sale for $20. I said I only had $17 the man said "sold" and showed me how to start it—how to handle the crank and the spark and throttle. He gave me the pink slip and a receipt for $17.

My dad saw me drive up. I showed him the pink slip and told him I'd bought it at Podolar Motors. We went back and my dad told the salesman he couldn't sell a 14-year-old boy a car. Dad said the salesman had charged too much—that a junk car was only worth $12.

He handed my dad $5 and dad kept it. I didn't have the nerve to ask him for it. There were many incidents with my '27 T touring car!"

Bob Simon
Vista, California

A Model T Escapade in Florida

"At the ages of 18 and 19, my mom and her sister drove what she called her "Tin Lizzie runabout" from New York City to Palm Beach, Florida, in 1927.

Mom was a seamstress and her sister was a beautician in New York City. They both lined up jobs in Palm Beach, despite the objections of their strict German father.

They left New York and the only problem they had was while driving through Georgia in a rainstorm they became stuck in a muddy road. A gentleman came along and simply picked the car up and out of the mud! They went on their way and had no more problems.

After arriving in Palm Beach and getting settled, they [went] to a movie. When the movie was over, they found their "Tin Lizzie" was gone. The police couldn't help.

Like all resourceful young people they simply wired a

sister back in New York for a loan and in no time, they had another "Tin Lizzie," only this time it was enclosed.

When I was growing up and mom would question my sanity, I would remind her of her trip to Florida in the Model T. Needless to say, that stopped her objection."

Bob Howell
Trinidad, Colorado

Model Ts in the Neighborhood

"In 1948 or 1949, we moved to Elmira, New York. Across the street was a young man who had two Model Ts—a red touring car and a black center-door sedan. I remember going with my brother and a friend to have a look and being invited to sit behind the wheel.

I was to advance the spark immediately after the engine fired, but I didn't catch on and the engine stalled. The cars were for sale, I think at $75 or $100 each. The owner said it was more money than I could imagine. I was about seven years old!

In 1955, when it was my father's 40th birthday, my mother found a 1918 touring car for sale. I remember being disappointed that she was going to buy the car for him rather than for me!

She gave my father a great birthday gift. My three brothers and I, and the family dog, were sitting in the decorated car when my father arrived home to see the surprise present. Over the next years, the family had much fun with the Model T.

After my father bought a 1936 La Salle convertible coupe with a rumble seat, the Ford moved on to a new owner. I hope it continues to give someone much pleasure."

Geoffrey Stein
Clarksville, New York

Grandpa's Model T

"My grandfather farmed near Sinai, South Dakota, for many years. In the summer, I would always go and spend my vacation with him. He had a 1927 Model T coupe and had taken the trunk door off to make it a pickup. He would haul the cream to town in the Model T every Saturday. I would ride along and over time, learned to drive the car.

By the fall of 1949, my grandfather retired from farming and had a sale. My older brother drove me to the sale, 70 miles from home, so I could buy the Model T.

I bid $15 and nobody else bid against me. We drove down side roads until I felt at ease driving in traffic. (In 1949 it was possible for me to drive in South Dakota at age 13.)

The car started getting very hot and I pulled into a farmer's yard next to a livestock watering hole and put some water in the radiator. When I started out the yard, the car went right instead of left and hit a picket fence. We jacked the car up. The stops on the steering arm broke off so the pitman arm would go 360 degrees.

It was a long, careful drive the rest of the way home. I had a job at a drive-in movie theater and would drive my Model T to work. There was a big hill on my way and the car wouldn't go up going forward so half way up, I would turn it around and back up the rest of the hill.

Later on I sold the Model T for scrap iron for $21. How I wish I had grandpa's Model T today."

Curtis Keenan
Brandon, South Dakota

Stowe, Vermont, and the Model T Oiling System

"A few years back, my dad, friend Eric and I decided to drive my '24 Model T touring car 200 miles to Stowe, Vermont. Stowe is the location of New England's largest old car meet held annually in August.

When we crossed the Vermont border, the rain began. We snapped in the side curtains, the rain was light and it was quite pleasant in our humid, mobile tent.

We looked at our map and it appeared that Route 17 was a shortcut. Vermont Route 17 was a formidable piece of road. The T had been in low gear for a long time. Suddenly, there was a knock from the engine.

A turnout materialized and I pulled in, shut off the engine and opened the hood. The raindrops hissed as they hit the engine. I noticed a rainbow in the pavement that followed us to the turnout.

I had forgotten how a Model T oiling system works. The flywheel's 16 magnets act as paddles that fling oil from the sump to the transmission parts and into a little funnel. The funnel is attached to a tube that carries oil to the front of the engine.

When connecting rods dip into the oil, the rod bearing is lubricated. This works fine as long as the oil sump has some oil in it and the tube is not clogged.

The hill we were ascending was so steep that oil leaked out the back of the engine at the drive shaft connection. We were three quarts down...we had a burned out rod.

At Stowe the next morning we found T supplier Don Lang at the flea market and he sold me a re-babbitted rod and a head gasket. Since we lacked a piston ring compressor, each of us took a short piece of hardwood flooring and we pressed on the piston rings while my wife sent the piston home with a rubber mallet.

I owned the car for years after that and never did another thing to the engine. I learned that a well maintained Model T is expected to leak oil on upgrades, a lesson I learned the hard way."

David Hagberg
Sterling, Massachusetts

Depression Era Model T Story

"My first Model T was a 1915 touring car. In the small town of Eagle Bend, Minnesota, we had several dealerships including Ford, Chevrolet and Durant.

They hauled their trash to the city dump and at that time you could buy a good running Model T for $15. Often they would take off good tires and a few spare parts and haul the rest to the dump.

I didn't have $15 for a car, so I rescued parts from the dump and soon had a running Model T. My dad decided to move from our home in Eagle Bend to a small farm, about 20 acres. He needed a tractor so he persuaded me to donate the Model T.

We took the body off and added two grain binder bull wheels to the frame. The small sprockets on the rear axle drove the big wheels through a chain drive.

I built another Model T and added a Chevrolet transmission and attached a semi trailer to the back. It would haul a cord of wood.

I still have three Model Ts including a 1917 roadster that I paid $75 for in 1950. My other Model Ts are a 1914 touring car and a 1925 Fordor sedan."

Royce D. Peterson
Dallas, Texas

The Model T Driving Lesson

"I am 80 years old and remember the Model T very clearly. My grandfather had a Tudor sedan and I can still see him jacking up the right rear wheel and cranking it to start it. The choke wire through the radiator was pulled until it started.

Some friends of mine, three brothers, bought this old Model T for $15 and they were going to give me a driving lesson. They put me up in the seat and without any explanation told me to drive. I finally figured out all the pedals and levers and we were off.

The brothers cracked up as we went down through the ditch and hit a fence into a barnyard. They fixed the steering and we went into town. It was easy after that except when I came to a steep hill.

A push on the left pedal shifted the car into low and we went up the hill. Other than the floorboards catching on fire and a final wreck that resulted in a lot of glass cuts, I don't remember which junk yard they took it to."

Charles W. Adams
Valparaiso, Indiana and Sanibel, Florida

A Short but Glorious Model T Adventure

"I had a Milwaukee *Journal* paper route yielding $5 a week when I was 12 years old, in 1947. We lived on Sugar Creek Road, on the edge of town, near Delavan, Wisconsin. My friend, Mike, lived on a farm a mile down the road where his grandpa had a 1925 Model T coupe stored in the barn.

He sold the car to Mike, me and five others for $5 each—a $35 purchase. We drove the Model T out in the cow pasture and around the farm yard—three on the seat, two in the trunk and one on each running board.

One day we drove it to town to get gas. Mom saw us drive past our home and Dad got the whole story after some interrogation and then gave us a stern lecture about driving without a license or insurance. He also talked about what might happen if we had an accident.

So ended our Model T adventure!"

Ron Tilley
Madison, Wisconsin

The 1926 Model T

"The subject of my Model T story was originally purchased from Trio Motors of Pitman, New Jersey, in 1926. In the 1960s, the car was found and purchased from a gentleman in Vineland, New Jersey. It was stored in a barn piled high with old chicken crates, farm baskets, burlap bags and more.

The Model T was purchased and delivery was arranged. The truck unloaded the T, then the work started. I removed the fenders, then…all the doors, door panels, seats and top were removed. All the rust was removed from the body, sprayed with filler, sanded and primed. The wheels were taken apart, scraped and sanded, then refinished by my wife. The fenders and rims were removed, sanded and primed.

Work on the frame meant quite a job to scrape and remove all the grease and grime. After sanding and priming, two coats of finish were applied. The engine was replaced with an engine taken from a "Depression tractor," a car or truck made into a tractor.

The engine was installed. We reassembled the body and fenders on the frame, then the running boards were set in place. Then we prepared the seats and door panels for the upholstery shop.

We went to the Hershey auto show and bought five new tires and tubes. The upholstery shop did a beautiful job and after getting the seats and door panels home, we installed it all, mounted the wheels, checked the oil and filled the tank with gas.

We have enjoyed many Sunday afternoon drives on country roads, entered local shows and parades and we've enjoyed several prizes. The Model T has been used in several weddings. In 2005, the T was filmed for a centennial because of its origin at the dealership in Pitman."

Frank N. Stubbins Jr.
Monroeville, New Jersey

The Hired Hand Buys a Model T

"In the Depression of the 1930s, I was about 10 years old. My dad had hired a man as a day laborer during the harvest season for extra help shocking the oats and wheat and to haul the shocks of grain into the threshing machine. The pay was well below $1 a day.

One day it had rained pretty hard the night before, too wet to work. The hired hand asked my dad if he could have the day off. The man hitchhiked into town, about 10 miles away.

About 5 o' clock in the afternoon, he drove into the farm yard in a Model T Ford. It was a Tudor sedan, complete and in excellent condition, including tax, license and gas in the tank—for a total cost of $5! I was really proud to climb up in the Model T for a ride around the farm."

Cal Frye
Clearwater, Florida

Enthusias-T-ic for a Long Time

"This story of a Model T enthusiast started in Kansas City, Missouri, 63 years ago. It sparked an antique Ford business that last more than 30 years in Martinez, California—Mal's A Sales, Model A and T parts from 1960 through 1995.

I found a 1924 T coupe for $50...it seemed top dollar, even in 1943 prices! A T was all I was interested in for my first car. Model As were priced way too high at $400—way out of reach for my paper route budget!

Gas was rationed at four gallons a week, but on several occasions, the cheap "white" gas was not rationed. The white or stove gas was just 10 cents a gallon.

A paint job with a brush was next—black with yellow wheels and a home-style upholstery job made it very presentable. I got a lot of unusual glances on my daily trips.

My source for parts in those days was Leo's Model T Repair near 18th and Vine Streets in Kansas City. Leo drove his '27 Model T touring car—with a Model A engine. The only new parts were available from Western Auto or Montgomery Ward.

I kept the Model T until 1945 when I joined the Navy. Now, 64 years later, I'm on my sixth Model T—a 1922 coupe—and I drive it once a week!"

Mal Staley
Oakdale, California

Mal Staley, a long-time owner of Mal's Sales Model A and T Parts in Martinez, California, built a rumble seat in his 1924 Model T.   Mal Staley

Money Back Guaran-T

"My first car was a 1925 Model T roadster with a canvas top and side curtains. The year was 1936 and I was 16 years old, attending high school. I paid $12 for it and received no bill of sale or title.

The car would only go in reverse.

My mother saw the car first when I arrived home. She wondered what my father would say when he arrived home from work. He told me to return the car and get my money back.

My mother went with me for support. The seller said he already had spent the money for a hair cut and some food, but would return it—and he did at a later date."

Mitchell Bartold
St. Clair Shores, Michigan

One Guy's Junk Becomes Another's Treasure

"Early in the 1970s, I found a 1923 touring and, a year later, a 1917 touring—both in running condition.

Once recognized as the guy in town with the Model Ts, I was regularly informed of Model T remnants on farms, in the woods and also various parts here and there just for the taking.

Thirty years ago there were a lot of them to be had. I even had three conversion T heads with overhead valves—a Rajo, a Frontenac and a rare Roof.

One day, a friend told me of a T body from his uncle's farm. It was a frame, a couple of fenders and the bucket—the body proper. I wondered what I might have to pay for the rusty bulk.

When I said I was interested in the Model T parts, [his wife] said: "I hope you get that junk out of my yard." (Collectors like that kind of response!)

I became a back yard restorer and felt I had enough parts to make a car from this hulk. My restoration took nearly five years but I'm proud to say I have a classy, restored 1915 Model T roadster to this day. Old guys like me still love the Model T!"

Al Omarzu
Virginia, Minnesota

Florida Model T Story

"I was born in 1927 and raised on a dairy farm. I had the opportunity to learn to drive at an early age. When I was seven years old, the two hired men that worked for my dad taught me how to drive a 1929 Model A truck.

After I turned 16 and could drive alone, I found a man across town that had a 1927 Model T roadster with no top, windshield or lid on the trunk compartment. I bought the Model T for $75. When I drove the T home, I thought my dad would run me and the T both off. He didn't because he still needed a milk truck driver.

One summer, I took two of my teenage pals and the T on a 10-day trip around Florida. I had put a trailer hitch on the T, borrowed a two-wheel trailer and put a tent on it. We slid a 10-foot plywood boat in under the tent with our camping gear in the boat.

Once, coming down a hill in our town, I saw the left rear wheel pass me and run about 100 feet into a lake. I walked back and found the bearings and a washer and everything except the nut that held the wheel on. I replaced the wheel, bearings, etc., and took the nut off the steering wheel that just happened to fit the axle.

I drove without a nut on the steering wheel for months and had lots of fun slipping the wheel off and handing it to whomever was riding next to me.

When I joined the Navy in 1946, I left the T at home and told my dad to sell it. I never knew who got my T or how much it was sold for.

I never thought that now that I am 72 years old and driving my dad's old 1921 Model T touring car, that I'd ever be sorry I let the old roadster get away. I got dad's old car and I guess I'll have it until I'm gone."

James D. Watts
Haines City, Florida

Red's Model T Stories

"My father, Roy C. Burke, was a fine mechanic and worked for years for the local Ford agency, Davies and Morrow, in Buffalo, Missouri. The Model Ts would come to the neighboring town of Bolivar in box cars and a crew of mechanics would put them together just enough that they could be driven the 20 miles to Buffalo.

The dealer would let me drive a car back without fenders, windshield or top. The parts were carried in a truck and the cars were assembled in the shop at Buffalo.

When the Model A Ford came out, dealers took Ts in trade so fast they couldn't sell them. Mr. Davies had a big yard full of Model Ts. One day he told me to take a Fordson tractor and haul the old Model Ts down to a ravine below town and push them over the bank.

My best friend, Bob Parker, and I got to choose the best one, a 1925 touring car that had belonged to a farmer who had hardly driven it. We took every accessory that we could find from the other cars and put them on our car. We spent the next several days towing the rest of the Model Ts to the ravine and pushing them over the edge.

Bob's father was an engineer on the Highway 65 construction job through this area and the state of Missouri gave him a new 1929 Model A touring car to drive, along with a 15-gallon can of Quaker State oil and four extra new tires and tubes. Some of the extra tires ended up on "Hulda."

One day he needed a tire for his state car and there were none left. I think that is when we stopped driving the Model T!

I am past 91 years old now. I spent my long life with cars, airplanes, boats, motorcycles and motor scooters. I truly feel that I lived in the best period in our history."

M. E. "Red" (Rusty) Burke
Fort Bragg, California

$10 and My First Model T Ford

"In 1935, we were living in the Great Depression and money was scarce. Christmas Eve my parents handed me a large envelope. Inside was a large ink drawing of an old Model T with a steaming radiator, leaking oil, a ragged top, a tow-headed kid at the wheel and a pack of ugly dogs barking.

Taped to the picture was a $10 bill and, in my artist-father's beautiful handwriting, 'Merry Christmas Bob. Here's a little money toward your first car.' I was thrilled to my eyeballs.

In 10 more days, on January 4, 1936, I awakened my dear mother to prepare to drive me to the DMV for my written and driving tests. I passed both tests, drove my mother home, borrowed her car and went to look at cars.

An acquaintance had a stripped Model T for $10. It wasn't worth that much but I had the cash plus $1.50 I had made raking leaves…which gave me enough pocket money to buy some gas at 11 cents per gallon and a used clincher 30 x 3 1/2-inch tire at the wrecking yard.

This car—I use the term loosely—had no body, no windshield, no floor boards and a dead battery. The magneto didn't work. I sat on the gas tank.

There was an old Model T touring car body in back of the shop at Modesto High School and I was able to get it. Sometimes after school I'd pick up a car load of girls and drive into dry canals, up and down levies, under orchard trees, laughing 'til I ached as the girls screamed.

After a few months I sold it to another friend. We haggled over the price until we finally agreed on a deal for $7. Just as I got within sight of his house to deliver the car, the primary battery cable shorted and all the lights burned out. We agreed to knock off 25 cents. He paid $6.75 for the car.

My friend Bob Bomberger and a couple of friends drove that car over 450 miles to Tijuana, Mexico and back with no major problems. Then Bob and his cousin Lee went camping and fishing in Yosemite National Park.

On their way home, something in the drive line broke—no brakes! He could neither stop nor slow the car and the canyon was 1,000 feet down. A Standard Oil Company tank driver driving up the grade saw the T gaining speed, heading toward the cliff.

He turned the tanker tractor in front of the out-of-control Model T and let it crash into the back dual rear wheels of his truck. He saved the boys from a tragic fall into the deep canyon.

The boys unloaded their gear, pushed the Model T "Eleanor" over the cliff, watched her crash in the Jawbone Canyon Wilderness and hitchhiked home.

Bob was George Lucas' uncle. Could it be that George Lucas inherited some of Bob's old car genes that inspired him to write, produce and direct "American Graffiti?" I wonder if George Lucas ever heard of that ragged Model T and his uncle and cousin who pushed it over the cliff at the Jawbone Canyon Wilderness."

Robert H. (Bob) Smith
Modesto, California

Another First Car Story

"The odyssey of my first car started in the early spring of 1945. A friend had purchased what was left of a 1917 Model T. He paid about $35 for it and towed it to the field behind his home.

My friend had neglected to install the exhaust pipe that ran from the engine underneath the car. He managed to produce several large backfires—great flames shot out of the exhaust manifold back along side of the engine. Without the pipes, the flames shot almost directly under the floorboards—well soaked with oil from Model T engine leaks. The floorboards caught fire.

My friend asked if he'd sell it and whipped out my wallet and showed him $7, then I added two quarters. After school, I borrowed my father's car and towed the T home.

When I approached my father about having my own car, it was pretty obvious the interest was OK but ownership was not in the cards. With great trepidation I approached him, blurting out…that I had bought a car. He was out of

his chair like a shot asking where it was.

We spent the rest of the evening out there with the car, looking it over, tinkering and talking. He'd had Model Ts when he was young and rapidly filled me in on all the idiosyncrasies.

The rest of the summer, he was often with me lending a helping hand or advice—and more colorful Model T stories. The owner of an inactive farm was good enough to give permission to run the car out on the unused land. I spent many happy hours tinkering with that old car."

Morton M. Boyd
Ames, Iowa

My 1925 Model T Coupe

"In January 1931, I bought a 1925 Model T coupe—the last of the high body models and the first with factory balloon tires. I bought it for $35. It was clean and ran well.

I bought this car because I knew how to start the Model T in cold, winter weather. Our family sedan was difficult to start when the temperature was below 20 degrees.

I used the Model T to travel 14 miles from my home to classes at Syracuse University. In this cold, wintry weather, it was my practice to back in the barn at night and jack up one rear wheel. To start it the next morning, I had a wire connection to close the choke and turn the engine over about three times with the crank.

Then getting inside, putting it in high gear so the jacked up wheel could revolve, I'd turn on the switch, hit the starter and on the first turn, the engine would start with the jacked wheel revolving.

I would put on the brake, push the car off the jack, throw the jack inside and drive away.

After parking on the street all day while I was in classes, I used the same procedure to start the car for the trip home. I often watched "high class" cars grinding down their batteries to get their cold engines started. This vehicle continued to give me trusted and reliable service."

Carlton M. Edwards, age 95
Kalamazoo, Michigan

The Reverend's Model T Adventures

"I have been driving Model T Fords for 63 years, having learned on my older brothers 1925—cut down, topless and cushionless touring car.

He purchased a very nice 1926 touring car for $35. Shortly after that he joined the Navy V-5 officers training program in World War II. I drove the touring car to high school and then to an after school grocery delivery truck job. The head of the rationing board was a customer. I was given a "B" card for two extra gallons of gas a week so I could get to work on time and get his grocery order on the truck, a 1937 Plymouth panel delivery.

Several years later, a Kiwanis friend sold me his very nice 1921 runabout. One day, good friends Bob and Beth Bachtel, who have a smooth running 1925 Model T touring car, undertook several adventures with my wife and I. One was to get on the old "National Road," Route 40 in Ohio and Indiana, and drive west to the Indianapolis Speedway.

A second adventure was to drive around most of Lake Erie. We left Akron, Ohio, in heavy rain. It was very windy on the bridge from Buffalo, New York, to Fort Erie, Ontario. We raised some eyebrows and smiles at Canadian Customs.

Taking back roads and stopping in little villages, we drew many inquisitive viewers. At Kingsville, Ontario, we boarded the ferry to Pelee Island, then a ferry to Sandusky,

The 1921 Model T runabout of Rev. James and Mary Lee Wolf (front) and their friends' 1925 touring car (back) visited Grissom Air Force Base in Kokomo, Indiana.
Rev. James and Mary Lee Wolf

Ohio and American Customs. We chose not to tackle Detroit and Toledo traffic. We arrived home with all eight tires still holding original Ohio air. Both cars behaved as Henry designed and built them."

Rev. James and Mary Lee Wolf
Cuyahoga Falls, Ohio

Me and My Buddies

Note: Florian Schweller, a former resident of Ohio, said when he was 13 and helping his dad with his 1909 Model T, he asked about getting his own Model T.

"Father set out on a search...and found one on March 3, 1945, a 1915 Model T Ford ¼ ton roadster pickup with a huckster or produce delivery removable top and roll-down side curtains. It was owned by an apple orchard merchant in Amherst, Ohio, who had purchased it new in 1915. His name was John M. Geissendorfer.

The rules were that I could only drive the 1915 on our acreage. One very hot day, my best friend, Jimmie Irish, and I went out the back gate and drove the back roads to the swimming hole, about eight miles on the Boy Scout Reservation.

We were heading home when an Ohio State Patrol officer spotted two young boys driving a Model T with no vehicle plates and no driver's license. We were taken to city hall, and the town mayor and my father were called. The mayor fined my father $25, the exact amount he paid Mr. Geissendorfer. Needless to say, I was grounded!

I sure was a "big man on campus" with that T! During my junior and senior year, 1946 and 1947, I was taking cheerleaders to the Friday night football games as far away as New London and Fairview Park, Ohio, a suburb of Cleveland, a distance of 45 miles at a top speed of 35 mph!

I would drive out on the football field with the cheerleaders in that T and the crowd cheering "Here comes Florian and the girls!"

Many fond memories of trips—I even drove it to Kent State in Kent, Ohio, a round trip of 160 miles. Never once did that Model T break down!

I still own that 1915 Model T! It is all original, except for the paint. The original title is all there.

'How about them apples?' From Mr. Geissendorfer, his apple orchards and Henry Ford up to today! It was a great life experience!"

R. Florian Schweller
Former Ohio resident

The Zahorik Family Photo

"This is a picture of my grandfather and his in-laws at my grandmother's parents' farm near Two Rivers, Wisconsin. My grandfather, Art, is standing next to the car. My grandmother's older brother, Uncle Bob, is standing behind the car. The older girl in front is my grandmother's younger sister, Aunt Mabel. The child is Ernestine, whom my grandparents adopted. My grandmother, Emily, was behind the Kodak Brownie camera. The picture was taken on July 4, 1922.

My grandparents lived in Sheboygan, about 35 miles from Two Rivers. My grandfather told me the trip would take more than two hours when my grandmother was in the car.

Few roads were paved. Most of the roads were not marked—you had to know what farm to turn at or had to ask. My grandfather said 'Why would you need [speed limits]?'

My grandfather was the last to die, in 1986 at age 92."

Mike Zahorik
Milwaukee, Wisconsin

The Model T touring car owned by the Zahorik family served as a focal point for this period image taken on a farm near Two Rivers, Wisconsin.
Mike Zahorik

A Model TT Story

"My grandfather owned a Ford Model TT truck in the late 1930s and early 1940s. The truck transported vegetables to sell to various stores, took the family to church on Sundays and doubled as a tractor pulling a single furrow plow. The Model TT was the first multipurpose vehicle!

In 1932, my uncle was able to buy a 1932 Model B Ford car. My grandfather took the steel wheels with bolt on cleats from a discarded tractor that a neighbor had given him and put them on the rear of the truck. He had a tractor that had better traction in the fields and it could still be used on dirt roads in the area and continue to serve as a truck.

My grandfather doubled as a carpenter and handy man for some of the neighbors. One time he took me with him to do some carpentry. At the end of the day he gathered his tools and put them in the truck-tractor to head home.

When he cranked the truck to start the engine, it backfired and split his hand open between the thumb and index finger. This was a terrible sight for a youngster. After the neighbor cleaned and bandaged the hand, my grandfather used his other hand to start the truck and we headed home."

Leland Bonneville
Fruitland, Maryland

Carl Larson's 1926 Model T Ford coupe, now at its new home in North Dakota. Carl nicknamed the car "Henry." *Carl F. W. Larson*

The A-1 Model T Coupe

"In April 1955, when I was a sophomore in high school, we made our regular 25-mile Sunday afternoon drive to Alexandria, Minnesota, to visit my grandmother in a nursing home there.

After an hour in my grandmother's room I would…walk six blocks to downtown Alexandria to visit Traveler's Inn which had a large newsstand and often had more car magazines than were available in Parkers Prairie, my home town.

On Sunday afternoon, I took a half-block jog to see a Model T coupe in the line of used cars. It had an 'A-1' sticker on the window…for cars that were considered to be in good condition.

A salesman came out and explained the Model T coupe was for sale for $75. I pleaded with my father…to buy the Model T.

My father agreed to my pleading and the deal was made. [The Model T] had been owned by a bachelor farmer west of Alexandria… and was part of an estate settlement. I became the second owner and have owned it for 52 years.

At age 15, I became the owner of my first car, a 29-year-old…named 'Henry.' It was driven sparingly—its usual trips were up and down our driveway, then the one-mile length of our farm.

I went off to college and graduate school and became a college English teacher, living 400 miles away in Dickinson, North Dakota. The Model T remained at the farm. After my dad died and my mother moved to town, our renter allowed the car to stay on the farm.

In 1996, after 18 years, the Model T was started and I gave numerous rides at a family birthday party. I showed our son how to drive it. He thought he was probably the only Harvard senior to have driven a Model T that summer.

In October 2006, after being at the farm for 51 years, [the Model T] was trailered to Dickinson and now resides in my garage. The tires have never been changed and three of them still hold air!

(And I still have all the car magazines I have ever purchased!)"

Carl F. W. Larson
Dickinson, North Dakota

Abe Becker's '27 Sweet T

"I was raised in a small upstate New York hamlet called Clermont, famous for Robert Fulton's steamboat that sailed the might Hudson River.

My Model T was driven occasionally by a 90-year-old gentleman, Abraham Becker. A few people wanted to buy the car, but he would not sell it. He bought the car new in 1927 from the local Ford dealer, in Red Hook, New York. He only knew how to drive a Model T.

One day I saw Abe walking by my house. I asked him if he wanted to sell his Model T. He said his eyes were failing. We struck a deal for $60 cash. That evening I brought the car home and I taught myself how to drive the Model T. That was in 1954 and I was 14 years old.

The Model T is a gray and black coupe in very good condition. The upholstery and top are very good as is the headliner and the glass. Even the roll-up shade for the rear window works. The body is so tight you can close the doors with one finger.

When I bought the car it came with seven tires—Ward's Riverside Knobbys all the way around! Under the seat I found several coils, an inner tube in its original Wards box and a connecting rod in a Federal Mogul box postmarked 1947. I had to use the rod in 1973.

Abe upgraded the car with a push button starter on the dash.

I didn't have a repair manual, but I decided to change the transmission bands—also found under the front seat. I didn't know the bands were spring loaded and when I unscrewed the first band adjuster the band popped open. Fortunately the nut was caught between the band and the transmission case and I was lucky to retrieve it.

In 1973, I was coming back from a car show with my wife and two young daughters all snug in the front seat. We were doing about 35 mph when all of a sudden the engine started knocking from a very loose connecting rod. Later, I took the engine apart and used that 1947 connecting rod. The crankshaft wasn't damaged."

Karl Vucich
Mystic, Connecticut

Note: Those Beckers come prepared! Our grandfather, Ralph Becker, long time mechanic who was trained on Model Ts, kept the trunk of his car and his garage stocked with parts and tools. Ralph's cars, like Abe's, were clean, solid and closed with a pleasing thump!

California Dreamin'

"My parents, Neil and Madeline Ensch, were married in October 1923 at Coffeyville, Kansas. They left for Long Beach, California, on their wedding day in a 1923 Model T Ford coupe.

It took eleven days to make the 1,540-mile trip. They averaged 140 miles per day. They told us of the few paved roads of that day—three years before Route 66 was constructed.

About 40 years before there were singing groups like the "Beach Boys" or "Jan and Dean," Neil Ensch was headed to the California surf with his kayak and Model T near Long Beach.   Don Ensch

The roads were mostly just worn pathways through the sand, brush and scrub. When they came to a stream or a creek, they would wait until several cars arrived and then they helped each other across the water.

My father kept the 1923 Model T until 1928 when he purchased a new Model A Tudor."

[Note: Neil Ensch often tied a kayak to the side of his Model T coupe and headed to Long Beach to enjoy the ocean waves.]

Don Ensch
Ventura, California

A Pickup Portrait

"As I'm getting older I'm realizing there aren't too many left who lived in the day of the Model T.

I was born during the Depression. Our car was a 1926 Model T roadster pickup.

We were poor. My folks did not drive the T around town, they walked. The T was mostly used for serious jobs. We often went to the farmers and they would load up the T with potatoes. We filled the T with logs in the fall from nearby forests.

Harold Hancock's mother poses near her home. The family often made long trips in their Model T, just visible in the background.
Harold Hancock

We often took the T up a canyon called "Cold Creek." We would pick choke cherries for pies and take home lots of water cress from the creek. On those canyon trips the T was loaded with small trees and pretty, red flat rocks for landscaping.

A thrilling picture of gassing the pickup is engrained in my mind. The pump was located on the sidewalk in front of a garage. I loved watching the gas bubble up and fill the glass bowl.

When it came time to sell the T, many fond memories went through my mind. We took trips to Twin Falls, Idaho, to see my sister—over 100 miles across the Idaho Desert. It took us about five hours and I sat in the middle between my dad and mom. My view was of the radiator cap in line with the road.

I quietly snuck outside during the negotiation and unscrewed the radiator cap. I have it to this day, almost 70 years later.

What a thrill it is today for me to own two Model Ts—a 1921 touring and a 1909 touring. Every time I start them, the smell of the exhaust, the sound of the engine shifting from low to high gives me a beautiful remembrance of my childhood with my wonderful parents—and our wonderful Model T pickup."

Harold Hancock
Auburn, Washington

More T Tales from Texas

"One Saturday my younger sister and I decided we wanted to see the show. It was dark when we came out of the theater and got in the old T. I fired it right up and we started for home. We did not get far when the lights went out. I had a two-cell flashlight with me and 20 more miles to go. Luckily, we had a little moon light!

One Sunday someone suggested we go to the swimming hole about five miles away. By the time I got the T fired up, there were eleven kids on it. We made the trip OK, but I did not enjoy the swim because my mind was on the ride back and those thin tires!

I believe the good Lord takes care of kids. Some time later it come a big rain and the road from our house to Flora was something else. I got to a long gumbo hill and the old jitney spun out. I…set her up for spinning in high gear and jumped out an pushed her on up the hill. Then I jumped on over in the front seat. There was no danger of the old T getting out of the deep ruts!

I own a 1922 Model T touring car now and my wife and I drive it up to Wal Mart on pretty days and enjoy all the people stopping and talking. My wife of 59 years says she is going to bury me in that thing. What a way to go!"

Clyde S. Hathcoat
Brashear, Texas

The '27 Texas T and High School Memories

"In the spring of 1947, I was 14 years old and wanted a car of my own. Changing oil and adjusting the mechanical brakes of the 1934 Chevrolet family sedan, plus taking care of my father's wood saw engine gave me an inflated sense of mechanical expertise.

I heard about a 1927 Model T Ford roadster for sale. The asking price was $25. Dad said to pay no more than $20 for the Ford. I paid the cowboy $25 and got the title.

We cranked it, towed it, kicked it and prayed for it. After a month of fiddling, and with the help of my buddies, we got it to run. I got rid of the trunk lid and built a pickup box. Twice a day I took buckets of slop out to the hogs.

I drove my '27 Model T Ford to school with a big smile. It was always a hit with the kids and teachers.

On a bet, I drove the T up to the school auditorium on concrete steps. School chums held the doors open while I drove into the lobby. I retarded the spark [and] gave out a few backfires, turned around, collected the bet and drove back down the street.

I collected a $2 bet [and] with gas at 35 cents a gallon, the money helped further my antics."

Tony Setera
Hico, Texas

Chapter 11

PRESERVING THE MODEL T FORD

F or some, it is a matter of polish and tinkering. For others it becomes a ground-up and body-off effort, finding parts, scraping off layers of old paint and rust, then sanding, priming—working on something that becomes as good or better than new.

That is what preservation is all about. It is attention to the old automobile in one's midst, doing one's best to keep it up, have it running, make it a museum display or to restore it in top condition.

"Anyone who stops learning is old, whether at 20 or 80. Anyone who keeps learning stays young. The greatest thing in life is to keep your mind young."
Henry Ford

There is something special about seeing a restored Model T, like this early roadster. Robin Heil-Kern

And it's often not a solitary pursuit. Brothers, family members, friends, husband and wives, multiple couples, generations of people, community members, club members, the devotees come from all types of backgrounds and find common ground when they're sitting in or talking about their Model T Fords.

That's probably the way Henry Ford would have liked it. That was the kind of community spirit that brought the original small group of Ford Motor Co. employees, some of whom had raced together and some who had joined later, to think about the car that became the Model T Ford.

We all know the story, that millions were made and found their way to places all over the world. And now thousands are left from that incredibly large group of cars that transformed our planet.

Preserving and caring for them is the task that falls on owners, clubs, societies and museums today. In this chapter, you'll read about a cross section of people and groups dedicated to the special work of keeping Model Ts whole, running and as new as possible.

The chapter also will look at something old and something new in the world of Model T preservation. Whatever the car or truck, and whatever condition it's in, every day is a great day when people are involved with a Model T!

There's More Than One Way to Preserve a Model T

Some of the best places to see a Model T, next to your own garage if you're fortunate enough to own one, are in some of the great museums of our nation. And two of the very best Model T locations are near one another in the Detroit area, the Henry Ford and the T-Plex.

The Henry Ford

What better way to commemorate the "founder of the feast," Henry Ford, than with a great museum in his name.

Early Model Ts had plenty of brass and color. If you look at them a certair become works of art that please the eye. Robin Heil-Kern

Actually, the Henry Ford Museum and Greenfield Village were opened in Ford's lifetime. Greenfield Village, in particular, was a passion of Henry Ford's with its preserved buildings and historic exhibits.

Henry Ford often is misquoted—that he said all history was bunk. It is an example of people condensing broader thoughts into a bumper sticker-type phrase that is misleading. Actually, Ford respected history but wanted it in what he felt was the proper context.

"History as it is taught in the schools deals largely with the unusual phases of our national life—wars, major political controversies, territorial extensions and the like. When I went to our American history books to learn how our forefathers harrowed the land, I discovered that the historians knew nothing about harrows. Yet, our country has depended more on harrows than on guns and speeches. I thought that a history which excluded harrows, and all the rest of daily life, was bunk." [1]

Ford was so adamant about his views about history that he went to great lengths to show how people lived and worked on farms and in villages. He showed the tools they used and their ways of life. His Greenfield Village was an effort to make the past come alive, thoroughly respecting history.

He further clarified his view of history in 1937.

"History doesn't mean dates and wars and textbooks to me; it means the unconquerable pioneer spirit of man." [2]

The complex now called simply The Henry Ford lies in Dearborn, Michigan and offers at least five major ways that history can come alive for visitors, through five centers of learning.

The Henry Ford Museum has long been a mecca for cars collectors and anyone interested in automotive history. Major automotive exhibits in the Henry Ford Museum include many cars in the Automobile in American Life section, with such prizes as the 999 racer, the first Mustang, the 15-millionth Model T, and the 1908 Locomobile "Old 16," that year's winner of the Vanderbilt Cup. The author remembers it was the first place he ever saw a Tucker back in 1962.

A Presidential Limousine exhibit includes everything from Theodore Roosevelt's horse drawn wagon to Franklin Roosevelt's "Sunshine Special" Lincoln and similar limousines of the Eisenhower, Kennedy and Reagan presidencies.

The Ford Museum also has exhibits of America that include Heroes of the Sky, with the famed DC-3 airplane and a replica of the Wright Flyer. The ongoing revolution in American life is not forgotten in such displays as a chair that belonged to President Abraham Lincoln and the Birmingham, Alabama city bus on which the legendary Rosa Parks was determined to stay seated and sparked the Civil Rights Movement that changed American life.

Nearby is Greenfield Village with its famous seven historical districts that include Ford's farm home, his Bagley Avenue workshop and a replica of the Mack Avenue factory. There is Main Street with an incredible array of stores including the Wright Cycle Shop and a general store.

Greenfield Village also has working farms including a cider mill and a soybean experimental lab.

Henry Ford respected his mentor and friend, Thomas A. Edison, and there is ample tribute to him in several areas that recreate Menlo Park.

The history of the people, their lives and work is on display through old American farm homes from as far back as 1650 to craft areas like the carding mill, pottery shop and sawmill.

Today, an 84-by-62-foot IMAX theater also is part of The Henry Ford with room for more than 400 viewers to see incredible 70-millimeter films and hear them in six-channel sound. Visitors also can tour the Ford Rouge plant, legendary factory from the latter Model T era through the Model A, Mustang and more.

The Benson Ford Research Center also is an historic treasure, especially for anyone interested in automobiles. It contains Ford Motor Company historical archives, product literature, photos, films, post cards, catalogs, maps and much more.

Visiting the T Plex gives people a chance to return to the Piquette Ave. Ford Motor Co. plant that was the site of the company's early success and where the Model T was created. Tom Collins.

The T-Plex (The Model T Automotive Heritage Complex)

Honoring the Old Ford Piquette Avenue Plant

While you're in the Detroit area, you can now take advantage of a second facility that is very d Complex (or T-Plex) is based at the historic Ford plant at the corner of Piquette and Beaubien Avenues.

It is part of the Motor Cities National Heritage area, designated by Congress as an affiliate of the National Park Service. The Piquette Avenue Plant was the formation center where Henry Ford and his energetic associates conceived, planned, tested and finally introduced the Model T Ford.

The Piquette facility was the first one constructed by the early Ford Motor Co. The early Ford leadership soon determined that larger facilities were needed than the Mack Avenue plant. Built in 1904, the Piquette assembly plant became the hub of the growth of Ford and was the site where the Model T was conceived, tested and early versions were built.

Today the Model T Automotive Heritage Complex Inc. is dedicated to the preservation of the Ford Piquette Avenue Plant, the birthplace of the T and the site where at least the first 12,000 Model Ts were made.

Some of the first experiments surrounding the use of the assembly line in automotive production were applied at Piquette. An early production record was set there as well.

The Piquette Avenue Ford Plant was part of what was the early Detroit automotive dynamo, a neighborhood that included assembly plants for Brush, Cadillac, Dodge, Hupp,

Packard, Regal and Everitt-Metzgers-Flanders (EMF). Today, it is the final preserve of the earliest days of the automotive industry.

The general area was nicknamed Milwaukee Junction because the neighborhood was the intersection of two major railroads in Detroit. It was natural, in hindsight, that the area evolved from a carriage-making center to metal fabricating facilities to become the early auto assembly center of Detroit.

The T-Plex, the Ford Piquette Plant, is a National Historic Landmark, on the National Register of Historic Places, a State of Michigan Historic Site and a part of the City of Detroit Historic District.

The facilities are open from May through October and the T-Plex should be considered a "must-see" for Model T owners and owners of other early Ford Motor Co. cars. It is a mecca for anyone interested in automotive history.

State Museums

Of course, Model Ts and other early cars are sprinkled throughout at least 44 of the United States that have auto museums as well as three auto museums in Canada.

One of those famous museums is the Smithsonian in Washington, D. C., a fountain of knowledge on many subjects, including the Model T and the early Model T era.

From Alabama, Alaska and Arizona to Washington, West Virginia and Wisconsin, there are many regional and state museums that highlight the Model T and early automotive history as well as other focuses like race cars, muscle cars and special interest cars.

A visitor can't get much closer to Model T history than the special room where Henry Ford and the hand-picked team of Ford employees worked to create the Model T.
Model T Automotive Heritage Complex

Cars like the 1907 Model R were made at the Piquette Ave. Ford plant before the Model T.   Tom Collins.

Some of the well-known historical museums include:

Arizona	Franklin Automobile Museum, Tucson
California	Blackhawk Museum, Danville
	Museum of Transportation and Peterson Automotive Museum, Los Angeles
Colorado	Forney Museum of Transportation, Denver
Florida	Sarasota Classic Car Museum, Sarasota
Idaho	Vintage Wheel Museum, Sandpoint
Illinois	Museum of Science and Industry, Chicago Volo Auto Museum, Volo
Indiana	Auburn-Cord-Duesenberg Museum, Auburn
	Studebaker National Museum, South Bend
Iowa	Antique Museum of Iowa, Coralville
	Hemken Collection, Williams
Michigan	Gilmore Car Museum, Hickory Corners
Nevada	National Automobile Club of America (Harrah Collection), Reno
	St. Jude's Ranch for Children, Boulder City
Ohio	National Packard Museum, Warren
Pennsylvania	Antique Automobile Club of America Museum, Hershey
South Dakota	Pioneer Auto Show, Murdo
Tennessee	Lane Motor Museum, Nashville
Texas	Pate Museum of Transportation, Fort Worth
Wisconsin	Wisconsin Automotive Museum, Hartford

Sources: *Car Collector*, March 2007 and *Old Cars Weekly*, March 22, 2007.

The museum scenes, like this one at the Sacramento, California, Towe Museum, show how work was done. This Model T is in a farm scene.   Tom Myers

These are just some of the many important automotive centers that keep the Model T and the history of automaking alive and vibrant. There are many public museums that have dedicated some of their community, regional or state history to early automobiles. Wherever you turn, there will be at least some references to the Model T, the cars that changed automotive history.

Regional Museums

Some of the regional museums and local collections are particularly interesting.

For many years, one of the leading Model T collections was owned by Ed Towe in Deer Lodge, Montana. In 1984, the Towe Collection listed 20 Model Ts between 1917 and

MIRACLE OF AMERICA MUSEUM
POLSON, MONTANA

* Americana
* Homesteader
* Wooden Boats
* Dolls & Toys
* Clothing
* Music

Smaller, regional museums often include Model Ts in their exhibits. The Miracle of America Museum in Polson, Montana, sometimes offers visitors rides in the cars. Miracle of America Museum

1927 and examples of Model Ts in the Brass Era, from an early Model T built in 1908 to a 1916 touring car.

In addition to having all years of Model Ts, Mr. Towe had the early "alphabet" Ford cars from A through S—from the company's beginnings in 1903 through 1908.

After Mr. Towe's death, the collection was broken up, but at least a portion of it now is in the Towe Museum in Sacramento, California. Some pictures from that museum are in this book, thanks to photographer Tom Myers.

Another collection that is as popular, and a special friend to Model T Fords and other cars, is the Door Prairie Auto Museum of La Porte, Indiana, a three-level assortment of cars that is the love of Dr. Peter and Charlene Kesling. Dr. Kesling owned his first Model T when he was 15 years old and hasn't stopped collecting them, and other cars, since then.

The range of cars at the Door Prairie Museum includes the beloved Model T, but also cars as varied as an 1886 Benz Motor Wagon, a Duryea, a Duesenberg, a Winton, a Mitchell and a Velie. The Door Prairie Museum is open from April 1 through December 23 each year.

The Miracle of America Museum was founded by Gil and Joanne Mangels. That museum is located at the foot of beautiful Flathead Lake in Montana and houses a variety of toys, armored vehicles, motorcycles, farm equipment, early homes, shops, stores and more. And, of course, both a Model T and a one-ton Model TT truck are among the favorite vehicles.

The museum is a great teaching resource for school groups in the area, among many other visitors. A highlight for children and other selected visitors is a ride in a Model T Ford!

Private Collections

Many of our contributors to Chapter 10 listed the Model Ts and other cars they have owned previously or own now. One remarkable collection was worthy to be highlighted in this chapter, owned by Dr. Herb Bloom.

Among the special cars in the Bloom personal Ford collection are a 1903 Model A, a 1906 Model N, a 1906 Model K, a 1907 Model R roadster, a 1909 Model T touring car and a 1909 Model T town car.

Dr. Bloom explained the perils of getting his first Model T back in shape. It's something many who attempt to preserve Model Ts can understand.

A prized restoration project, like this 1909 Model T touring car, can be a work of art as well as a matter of pride and a piece of automotive history.   *Dr. Herb Bloom*

"I have had several Model T Fords. The first one I bought in 1959. It was sitting outside a Texaco station in North Dallas, Texas. I had never seen a Model T before and it looked like it was in really good shape. Little did I know!

I got it home to Arlington, Texas, about 40 miles west of Dallas. First I wanted to get the starter and generator restored.

Montgomery-Ward had an engine rebuilding service at the time. My brother-in-law was an executive with them and he arranged for me to ship it to Montgomery-Ward to be rebuilt. This proved to be a very big problem because they sent back a 1927 engine painted fire engine red! My engine was a 1924. They didn't know my engine from any other engine.

Later, when I was in Chicago, I scrounged around various junkyards looking for Model T engines and finally found one. Needless to say, I didn't send it back to Montgomery-Ward! I had it rebuilt by a local engine rebuilder who could pour the babbit bearings.

I discovered the wood framework had started rotting out so I completely built the body from the old patterns. I repainted everything and replaced everything that was bad on it. It was a pretty good car to begin with but I simply couldn't leave it alone."

Today Dr. Bloom keeps his collection near his Texas home.

The joy of collecting and restoring cars of any age often is the passion that drives the collector to the point where the pursuit of the cars or particular parts often is as much fun as driving and maintaining the proud possessions.

In the case of the Model T, and its earlier Ford Motor Co. siblings, the cars are just plain fun to drive!

Car Shows and Rallies

In addition to museums, personal collections, restorations and more, you can often see Model Ts in parades or at car shows and rallies. Be sure to follow the calendar of events in your state or province in the pages of Old Cars Weekly and also read about or listen for information in your local news sources that mention such events.

It's a great way to get up close and personal to a Model T. (But don't touch it unless the owner says you can!)

This beautiful 1922 Model T Speedster was on display at a car show in England. What a nice profile!   Andrew Morland

ABOVE: *A well-tended and preserved 1927 Model T engine compartment deserves the attention it receives from appreciative car show attendees.*   Mike Mueller

LEFT: *Car shows often bring out area Model Ts for display. Visitors get a chance to see these beautiful and interesting cars up close and from many angles, like this 1909 touring car.*   Mike Mueller

There's more than one way to preserve a T
The 2003 Ford Model T Story

Henry Ford might have had to sit down.

Certainly Joseph Couzens would have jumped across the closest desk for an adding machine. The costs for making a new Model T had jumped a bit in 2003 when the Ford Motor Company decided to make six Model Ts, based on a 1914 touring sedan, but all new for 2003, complete with new serial numbers.

First of all, Henry Ford might have grown impatient with the time it took to get the cars made—11 months from scratch beginnings to final cars. (Didn't they solve that problem back in 1914—something called the assembly line?)

And the Model T originators like Ford, C. Harold Wills, Joseph Galamb and others might have laughed at all the heavy-hitting technical might Ford Motor Company brought to bear to get the job done. That included the Ford Advanced Mfg. Technology and Development Unit and even the U. S. Air Force. (One of their labs in Ogden, Utah, did a CAT scan of a flivver engine.)

Imagine the water cooler at the Piquette or Highland Avenue plants when that subject was brought up—a fancy X ray of the innards of a Model T engine!

But the Model T project people were bringing every resource to bear in order to make the best Model T they could, long after the assembly lines had stopped to change over from the Model T to the Model A in 1927. It was a long time between Model Ts.

"There were no blueprints, drawings or specifications," explained Guy Zaninovich, a broker and multiple Model T owner who was one of the key people on the project, told Diana Kurylko of the *Automotive News*. "No one had made the engines since Henry Ford stopped making them." [3]

The team replicating the Model T brought in a 1914 T as a model, then tried their best to study, acquire, fabricate and purchase every inch of parts and materials for the version.

"We didn't do anything to improve the car," said Zaninovich. "To test if we made a part right, we often bolted the new part onto one of the original parts." [4]

While the idea of a CAT scan for a Model T engine seems odd, there was a practical reason. It showed exactly what needed to be done in terms of various internal passages. They were able to access some original prints of the engine casting and then pool their information.

Model T collectors were another valuable source of information and filled a lot of needs. And there were some original and many replacement parts available to buy for the 2003 Model T project.

Another way of supplying the Model T was by picking up contemporary catalogs for parts. *Car and Driver* reported in its August 2001 "Up Front" column review that Lang's Old Car Parts of Winchendon, Massachusetts, provided approximately 550 pieces for the new Model Ts.

The 2003 Model T team also burned the telephone wires contacting foreign sources to unearth the parts needed.

For example, some engine cranks were found in one of the earliest centers of Model T export, New Zealand. And the team found a wooden body frame for a Model T in Sweden. [5]

The *Automotive News* article claimed that only 30 percent of many Model T parts were made in the Ford factory. In 2003, that changed, something Henry Ford would have enjoyed. Some 60 percent of the 2003 Model T came from Ford factory sources. The remaining 40 percent, or more than 500 parts, came from vendors and other sources. [6]

The 2003 Model T project began in 1999 and the team tried to replicate everything, from the overall dimensions to the lack of any new pumps or add-ons.

Some changes had to be made. For example, foam replaced horse hair in the seat cushions. And the paint was as modern as any car of the late 2000s, with clear coat and base paint done in a spray booth. Aluminum pistons were used instead of the original cast-iron versions and the valves were made of stainless steel.

Wooden spokes and rims were crafted by an Amish wheelwright. A transmission vendor did the chassis components. Ford Powertrain Operations Engineering and Tower Automotive also made important contributions.

"Thanks to the torque characteristics of this long-stroke four—83 lbs.-ft. at 900 rpm—it lugs along in high at very low speeds and is quite forgiving of beginners," noted the *Car and Driver* road test. "Top speed, with all 22.5 hp pulling, is about 50 mph. We took their word for this..." [7]

The result—the original Ford Motor Company Model T team would have to be sitting for this one—was a few cars costing $40,000 to $50,000 each. Their serial numbers were 2003001 through 2003006.

It was well worth it as the Model Ts celebrated Ford Motor Company's 2003 anniversary.

2003 MODEL T FORD TOURING CAR	
Engine:	2.9 liter inline, 4 cylinder
Horsepower:	22.5
Compression:	4.0:1
Transmission:	Two-speed planetary
Brakes:	Handbrake, rear wheels Foot-brake to transmission
Length:	148 in.
Wheelbase:	100 in.
Weight:	1,200 lbs.
Top speed:	55 mph (estimated)
Price:	$40,000-$50,000

Duane Matson's Model Ts

Duane Matson taught automotive restoration at the famed McPherson College program in the 1990s. That background helped him with several experiences he had with Model T Fords. That kind of Model T "street cred" deserves some space in a section about preserving the Model Ts. We hope you and other car collectors enjoy his humorous exploits.

Lee (left) and Duane Matson (right) pose in front of their 1927 Model T coupe. Duane Matson

Safely Loading Your Model T on a Trailer

"In the early 1990s, when I was still new and somewhat inexperienced in my career as a teacher, I had a job at McPherson College in McPherson, Kansas. I taught in the Auto Restoration program, the only degree program of its type in the country.

The faculty felt it was good experience for students and faculty to attend a few car shows and to display the work of the program.

On Friday evening after classes, a group of two or three students and I were cleaning a beautifully restored Model T coupe, getting ready for the next day's car show. Literally hundreds of hours had gone into the restoration of the car, and everyone was rightfully proud of it.

We were using my personal trailer and pickup as the tow vehicle. My brother and I had built the trailer large enough to haul full size 1960s Chryslers. The trailer was much heavier and larger than necessary for a Model T.

Over time, a small section of wood from one ramp had fallen out, leaving a three-inch gap.

Anyone who has loaded vehicles onto a sitting trailer knows that vehicles like to stall or die part way up the ramps. You often have to give them just a little gas to get them up but quickly let up once you are up to prevent running off the front of the trailer.

As the front wheels approached the top of the ramps, the right tire dropped into the small gap caused by the missing planking. The Model T tires literally 'fell in.' It caused both wheels to cram to the right. In the process, I moved the throttle wide open.

My heart was racing as I instinctively pulled hard left to correct the path of the swiftly moving T. I also managed to drag the throttle lever back up and tromped down hard on two peddles to keep the car from driving off the edge of the trailer. When the car stopped, miraculously, it was centered on the trailer.

Duane Matson has been active in automotive restoration, including work as a teacher at the prestigious McPherson College. Here he shows some of his Model T projects.
Duane Matson

As I crawled out of the Model T, my heart was still racing and my legs were rubbery. I did my best to act as if it was all part of the plan."

If that wasn't enough, Duane and his brother, Lee, had a second experience with a Model T and a trailer. And they almost drove a T into their grandfather Otto's home—but back to the trailer...

"My brother and I were trying to load one of our Model Ts onto a trailer to haul it to a local community's Vaudeville Days event.

We had backed the pickup and trailer close to the overhead door where the 1924 touring car had been parked for at least nine months. After filling the radiator and gas tank, we proceeded to attempt to start it. After much fooling around, it finally roared to life.

When everything was clear, I revved her up...and much to my amazement, the touring car climbed right up the ramps the way it was supposed to. Unfortunately, it kept right on going. Knowing that I was rapidly running out of trailer, I began tromping down on two peddles at the same time. Well it worked, sort of. It stopped with such momentum that for a few seconds I was standing upright as the rear wheels and back of the body lifted up, then dropped back down.

Dust was flying and roofing nails hiding in the crevasses of the body were everywhere.

My brother came up and said 'Well, Ollie, that is another fine mess you have gotten us into.'

It was the perfect line to follow what had just occurred! Our touring car certainly was reminiscent of the Model Ts of Laurel and Hardy from the movies."

America's Oldest Ford Dealers

One of the most modern repair garages of the era. The year is 1914...and Frank Campbell, foreground, Louis Wesselman and Percy Talcott, right, were all working to repair the motoring vehicles of the day.

1903-1928

1903 receipt to balance account.

In the days of the Model T, Steve Tenvoorde invented this jack to move automobiles around in the garage. It was marketed throughout the Midwest. Patented and purchased by Ford assembly plants in 1921.

Steve & Rose Tenvoorde with a 1911 Model T Dinky. Customized by Frank Campbell by installing a built-up cowl and customizing the dash & windshield.

A montage of images shows many points in Model T sales history at the Tenvoorde Ford dealership in St. Cloud, Minnesota.   *Tenvoorde Ford*

Sometimes the best way to preserve something is to just keep it going. That way, each year becomes another chapter in a book that still is being written.

Tenvoorde Ford of St. Cloud, Minnesota, was around before the Model T and the dealership still is selling Fords. That's quite a track record.

The Model T and the demand for it by people all across the U. S., Canada and the rest of the world influenced many dealers to come into the business. But Steve Tenvoorde experienced selling Fords from the beginning. So when the popular Model T was a hit, Steve was ready to increase his business.

The Tenvoorde Garage had been a one-story brick building beginning in 1903. During the Model T era, that changed.

Diehl Ford of Bellingham, Washington, was begun by Hugh Diehl in 1908. It now is the third longest, continuous dealership in the United States.   *Bob Diehl*

This 1907 Model R roadster was taken in trade on a Model T by Hugh Diehl and now has been part of all four generations of the Diehl family involved in the business.
Bob Diehl

"WORLD'S OLDEST FORD DEALERSHIP"

Tenvoorde Ford of St. Cloud, Minnesota, is recognized by Ford Motor Co. as the oldest continuous dealership. The business began in 1903. Tenvoorde Ford

"He remodeled in 1916, adding a five-car showroom and service area on the lower level and a body shop upstairs." [8]

Steve Tenvoorde opened a bicycle shop in St. Cloud in 1895 and sold some of the leading makes during that time including Columbia and Dayton bicycles.

Along the way, he gained a positive reputation as a mechanic. Like many men of the 1890s, he easily added the horseless carriage to his focus in addition to bicycles. In 1899, he brought the first automobile to St. Cloud, a Milwaukee Steamer, complete with its 28-inch wheels and a four-hp output.

On March 21, 1903, he signed on to what became the Ford Motor Co.—forming itself from the Ford-Malcomson Ltd. shaky venture that June. Actually, Ford was just one of the cars available at the Tenvoorde dealership—an all-star array that included Buick, Chandler, Oakland, Oldsmobile and Saxon, all from St. Cloud's favorite bicycle shop.

According to the Tenvoorde dealership's official history, just one car was sold in their first year.

"Buying a car was considered a risky venture. There were no mechanics or garages to repair them. People who had cars even drove them in packs just in case one of them broke down…"

When Steve wasn't driving a mile a minute, selling and servicing cars or leading early car rallies and tours known as Sociability Runs, he was inventing something. His dolly and garage jack brought a lot of attention in the infant stages of the automobile in America.

By 1915, autos were becoming more commonplace and the Tenvoorde business expanded with a five-car showroom and service area plus a body and engine repair shop on a second story.

Today, the business has expanded a few times but the philosophy of sound customer service, wise use of savings and credit in terms of reinvesting in the company and timely diversification into other areas has helped. Tenvoorde has been a leader through both tough and good times. And there are signs that a fifth generation will be leading Tenvoorde Ford well into its second century.

Another veteran dealership is Diehl Ford of Bellingham,

Washington, considered to be the third oldest Ford dealership in the United States. Bob Diehl is the third generation to run the family Ford sales business begun by his great grandfather, Hugh Diehl, in 1908.

"Hugh liked to race and sail," said Bob. "He was the winner of the first Mt. Baker Marathon with a modified Model T."

Bob explained the cars would race up a dirt trail against other cars as well as a train! The driver or a climber had to climb to the mountain peak after exiting the car. During one race, the train was derailed after an encounter with an unfortunate bull.

A trademark of the Diehl Ford dealership is the 1907 Model R runabout. It's been part of the Diehl family for 90 years. Talk about Ford tough!

Bob said records weren't well kept on used cars back then but the story came down from Hugh that the Model R was owned by someone from Tacoma who traded it in, probably on a Model T.

The Model R survived a fire in 1948 when the building housing Diehl Ford collapsed on the car, stored in the basement. Then it spent more than 40 years in pieces until Bob offered to get it restored, acquiring it back from a former Diehl Ford employee.

"The car was originally black. They came in black and green. But everyone likes red," said Bob. The Model R now is a trademark/mascot of the Diehl franchise. A venerable Ford for a very loyal dealer family.

Tenvoorde Ford and Diehl Ford are just two of the many veteran Ford dealerships in the country. Many were brought into the world of automobiles and made their early successes selling Model Ts.

Today they continue that sales tradition, serving customers with 21st century Fords.

The Original Ford Dealer was a Pioneer

William "Billy" Hughson ran into Henry Ford at a bicycle show in Chicago back in 1902. A San Francisco, California, machinery parts supply owner, Hughson was interested in bicycles. Ford, the intrepid car builder and inventor, was at the show to demonstrate his lightweight horseless carriage—heavily influenced by bicycle design.

The two men were a match made in car sales heaven! Hughson quickly fell head over heels for what Ford was trying to produce. It was even better than a bicycle!

According to author Robert Genat, Ford and Hughson agreed on a deal for $5,000 worth of cars. 9 At that time, it was the Ford-Malcomson Ltd. "Fordmobile" that would have been the proposed car of interest to Hughson.

Hughson went back home to raise the money. Ford, fresh from several years of racing success, returned to Detroit to get the automaking venture off the ground.

Hughson traveled east in the summer of 1903 with $5,000 he'd gathered. Unfortunately, there were still no cars. Yet Hughson trusted that Henry Ford would deliver them. Ford even offered Hughson an invitation. Things were looking up. New people were involved in Ford-Malcomson and the picture was changing. Ford wanted Hughson to invest in the ground floor of the new Ford Motor Co. Hughson was interested but his partners were not.

"You went there to buy automobiles," they wired back. "Now buy automobiles!" 10

Hughson declined the investment opportunity and put in his order for 12 Ford cars. In 1919, Ford Motor Co. associate James Couzens received $29.3 million on his original investment in company stock. By doubling the Couzens investment, Hughson and his partners would have made twice that amount. 11

While Hughson became the first Ford dealer, that might not have seemed such a prize at the time. The new Fords sat unsold in San Francisco until 1906. During the aftermath of the San Francisco Earthquake that year, the Hughson Ford cars were used as ambulances.

Like most early Ford dealers, the Model T became the key to their sales success and solvency. And Hughson's Ford franchise became the seed for 120 dealerships on the West Coast. It was long credited as the oldest Ford dealership in the United States. 12

Hughson lived through many generations of Fords. He saw the overwhelming success of the Model T, the followup of that car in the Model A, the innovative Ford V-8, the incredible Thunderbird, the beautiful Skyliner, the sensational Mustang and the luxurious LTD, among many other Ford products.

At age 100 in 1969, Hughson died and his original Hughson Ford dealership closed in 1979.

The early Ford Motor Co. worked hard to create a network of dealers to offer solid sales and service across the nation and throughout the world. Hughson was the first of that long line who believed in Ford cars like the Model T and made believers out of thousands of satisfied customers.

Model T Originals

A dealership can change and grow with the times. Yet an automobile must be of its time to be considered "original" in the purest sense. "Original" is a touchy term in the automotive world. Many cars have been restored or reconditioned in at least some way that has taken away their originality.

Yet, even in the Model T world, there are cars that are "barn finds," vehicles that have aged but have been parked and left over the years. When new and interested parties found them, they felt much like archeologists uncovering some special treasure. The patina of an original Model T was their Holy Grail.

Billy Hughson was the first Ford dealer and sold many Model Ts. He wanted to sell Ford-made cars before the Ford Motor Co. was created. Robin Heil-Kern

Several articles have treated Model T enthusiasts to "originals." In 1996, Kirk Hill of Pinola, Mississippi, talked about a Model T purchased by Dan Mashburn of Bolton, Mississippi. The touring car had been owned by Sally Talbert Thompson of Liberty, Mississippi and was driven by her step-son, Lee, until a second owner bought the car in 1941.

The second owner was going to fix a problem with the rear axle but after 45 years, he still hadn't found the time. When Dan Mashburn bought the car, it had become a nesting and storage place for various critters.

An original car, even if it has deteriorated to a degree, offers us some information that might not be available with a restored example. Materials, or what is left of them, show the owner or enthusiastic witness, how the Model T was constructed.

There was a time when Model T Fords were available in excellent condition on used car lots for a very reasonable price.

Some owners created their own interpretation of an "original," taking a Model T and making it an unusual showpiece.
Robin Heil-Kern

The Mashburn car, for example, had a metal rain gutter that was put on Model Ts beginning in 1919. Inside on the firewall was a round metal plate by the mixture adjustment rod, an ID/patent plate, an instrument panel of the type used from 1919 to 1922, original floorboards front and rear, and even an original steel choke wire.

Originals are case studies for Model T scholars but some people never have a chance to see a "barn find" type of original. They have to see an unrestored Model T at a car show or perhaps find an original car at a museum.

Writer Don Black experienced the joy of finding an original, unrestored Model T at the former Towe Antique Ford Collection in 1991.

"You come around a corner and there before you, standing almost in lonely majesty, is a beautiful, original and unrestored 1914 Model T touring with a sign leaning against the front fender. It reads 'Do it!' It offers the beholder a personal and friendly invitation to…get in and sit behind the wooden steering wheel…" 13

And black was able to experience some other sensory pleasures allowed only by an original car, of Model T vintage or almost any decade.

"What a thrill it is to poke your head into one of these grand old masters, especially a coupe or sedan, and take a big whiff or two…a must for the avid enthusiast—an original car!" 14

Everyone in the automotive world enjoys stories of Southern California cars—often saved from damaging salt and other problems associated with winters in the Midwest or Northeastern United States.

In 1981, owner Bill Hensey was profiled with two original, unrestored Model Ts. One was a family car, a well-used 1914 runabout that was originally purchased by his father and endured a long trip north to the University of California at Berkeley one summer.

At times, the turtledeck would be removed and set aside to make a platform for family camping gear.

The second car, a 1911 Model T touring car, played a bit role in a Hollywood movie, then was unceremoniously sent

In the end, whether they are originals or carefully restored, Model Ts become a vehicle where all creatures large and small can enjoy themselves.   Robin Heil-Kern

for an unlimited engagement on the landfill circuit—it was send to a dump!

Hensey rescued the bruised and battered movie bit player, which had fallen on hard times, and got it going again.

Said *Vintage Ford* in 1981: "The 1911 is a rolling miniature museum of accessories and alterations typical of the Model T age. It has Hassler shocks, an extra front wishbone, a steel truss under the pan…a front seat cut out and hinged to make a sleeper and other items." 15

Cars like the Hensey vehicles or the Mashburn Model Ts and also those on display in various museums are rolling textbooks of Model T life.

The Model T Ford Club of America is an international organization that shows beautiful Model Ts on its Vintage Ford cover and offers valuable information and history in its pages.
Courtesy: Vintage Ford

They educate us in many ways answering questions about assembly techniques. The unrestored cars show what materials were used and how standard components were arranged in the cars. They might show how features were added during a production run, offering clues that confirm someone's theory or some type of historical benchmark.

For example, the unrestored Hensey 1914 Model T runabout had its original engine. The engine number was 375,600 with an engine block casting date of Oct. 16, 1913. The engine was manufactured on Nov. 18, 1913.

Model T hobbyists studying the history of the cars can find a lot of that kind of information from an unrestored car, lovingly preserved to become something that has come down to us through the years, with both its warts of wear and its provenance of pieces that make it something special.

Sometimes, preservation means that the owner has chosen to leave the car alone, other than the important job of keeping the car well maintained.

He or she has decided not to find ways of restoring the car to an idealistic or contemporary image or shrug off history for some personal reason. Rather, this car is something special—it has been left as an historical timepiece—perhaps faded, certainly used and maybe even a bit more frail than some—but radiating the life that has been lived for its many years.

These originals are important and irreplaceable timepieces of the Model T era—or of any auto or truck line.

Clubs and Groups Keep Model Ts Going

If you're interested in Model T Fords and attempting to find out more information about the cars, one direction that is always recommended is tapping into the closest Model T club or organization in your area.

There are at least two major Model T Ford clubs that have affiliates in the United States and elsewhere.

Model T Ford Club of America (MTFCA)

The Model T Ford Club of America is the largest in the world with affiliated chapters in 42 U. S. States. One of the chapters was very helpful in work on this book, the Wisconsin Capital Model T Ford Club of Madison and one of its co-founders, Don Chandler.

Many of the MTFCA affiliates have e-mails and/or addresses that are available and the organization has a wonderful Web site with even more valuable information. They publish a treasure trove of information that was mined for this book in their magazine, *Vintage Ford*.

If you live outside the U. S., you'll find MTFCA affiliates in Argentina, Australia, Austria, Belgium, Canada, Germany, Holland and New Zealand—many important places where Model Ts were manufactured, assembled or imported.

A wealth of information awaits you at www.mtfca.com

Official Publication of the Antique Automobile Club of America

Aantique**AUTO**MOBILE

Volume 70   Number 5   September / October   2006

Antique Automobile, published by the Antique Automobile Club of America, used a 1926 Model T touring car on a 2006 edition magazine cover.
Courtesy: Antique Automobile

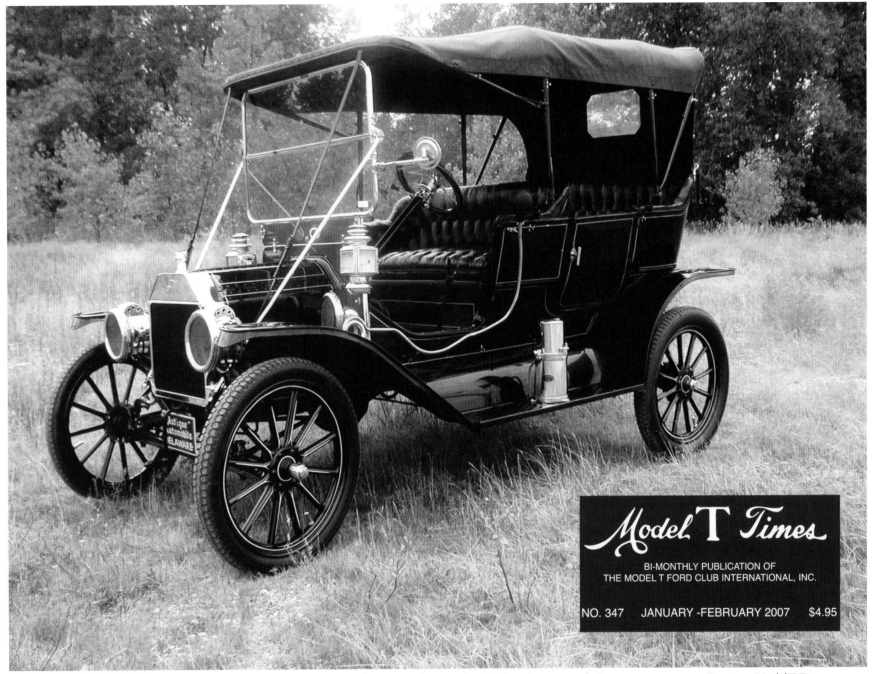

The Model T Times is published by the Model T Ford Club International. In 2007, they put this 1911 touring car on their cover.   *Courtesy: Model T Times*

MODEL T TIMES

BI-MONTHLY PUBLICATION OF
THE MODEL T FORD CLUB INTERNATIONAL, INC.

NO. 347   JANUARY -FEBRUARY 2007 $4.95

Model T Ford Club International (MTFCI)

Founded in Chicago, Illinois, in 1952, the Model T Ford Club International has grown from a regional club into something that reaches out around the world. The MTFCI sponsors tours and events in many member nations and also publishes its own magazine, also used for research in this book, *The Model T Times*.

There are chapters of the Model T Ford Club International in 32 states and the District of Columbia. There also are chapters in Argentina, Australia, Bulgaria, Canada, Ireland and Sweden.

To learn more about the MTFCI, access their site at www.modelt.org

This Horseless Carriage Gazette cover from 1995 showed best friends ice fishing at Cloverleaf Lakes, near my hometown of Clintonville, Wisconsin. Courtesy: Horseless Carriage Gazette

Model T Ford Register of Great Britain

One of the original strongholds for Ford Motor Co. product exports from the United States and later, the manufacture of Model Ts, was Great Britain. Eventually Ford built a plant at Dagenham, England, part of the long history of bonds associated with Fords across the Atlantic.

In September 1959, Lord Montagu invited Model T owners to gather and the concept of the Model T Register of Great Britain was formed the next year. Early "alphabet" Fords from 1903 through 1908, as well as all years of the Model T are eligible and there are more than 400 members in England and elsewhere.

The group holds rallies and autojumbles, has a parts service and even publishes their own magazine, *T Topics*. You can learn more about them at www.t-ford.co.uk

The Model T Ford Register is affiliated with both the MTFCA and the Model T Ford Club International.

The Frontenac Motor Company

One interesting connection for Model T aficionados who aren't affiliated with a club is available online. It is The Frontenac Motor Company of Brockville, Ontario, both a private collection dedicated to brass era automobiles, particularly the Model T, as well as being a virtual Model T club. You can check out this interesting Canadian site at www.modelt.ca

Preserving Model T Memories

A Second Owner's Model T Ford Story

Bud Ring of Combined Locks, near Appleton, Wisconsin, owns a 1922 Model T Ford touring car that has been part of his life for 50 years. That might not sound too unusual to Model T enthusiasts. The fact that Bud bought the car from its original owner might be of interest.

"Art drove it from Appleton to Little Chute where my parents lived," recalled Bud, who still lived with his parents at that time.

Rohm was the original owner of the 1922 Model T and when he handed the car over to Bud he said it was in good condition.

When Bud and Elizabeth Ring were married in June 1961, Bud's Model T served as the bridal car for the newlyweds, a very important part of the ceremony.
Bud Ring

Bud and his father did make sure the T touring car got a fresh coat of paint at Henry's Auto Body by Henry Vanden Heuvel.

Inside, Bud found the Model T needed some new valve springs for the engine and the leather interior was badly aged and needed replacement. The touring car's top also was in bad shape.

"The side curtains, they were shot," Bud recalled. "You couldn't do anything with them!"

Bud and his father also decided to put some new bands in the transmission. While a set of four new tires also seemed in order, Bud's father thought that one was still good enough to drive so Bud bought three new ones.

"The old tire looked great but it started to leak," Bud recalled. "I should have bought the full set."

Yet, now in its 85th year, the Model T is in relatively good shape with its original engine, transmission and rear differential that were installed when Warren G. Harding of Ohio was in the White House.

The '22 Model T has been used in parades through the years and Bud is thinking about some work on the car again—even 50 years of the best of care doesn't prevent all problems, especially when a car is driven, and not totally pampered.

Bud looks ahead and hopes his sons, Tim and Bob, will enjoyed the Model T legacy.

"Cars should be driven and they get scratches and all," says Bud. "I thought I'd be lucky if I owned it as long as Art did—35 years. But now it is 50 years! That's really something!"

The family of Dr. David O' Donnell of Detroit posed in the family's Model T. Dr. O' Donnell was an important person who served the needs of the Ford family. *Tom Payette*

The Doctor's Family in the Model T Ford

Sometimes a picture can preserve a memory—both of the people and the car.

In 1911, a family photo was taken of the O'Donnell family of Detroit. Dr. David O' Donnell was the clan chieftain, ironically, a native of Fordville, Ontario.

He studied pharmacy in Ontario, then went on to medical school at the Michigan College of Medicine and Surgery.

Then in April 1892, he began his practice at Sixteenth and Grand River in Detroit. Later he built an office and home on Breckenridge St.—later Forest Avenue.

In 1896, the doctor married Alice Blanche Parent and they had 10 children. One of them, Dayton O'Donnell, followed his dad into medicine.

We know about all this because a caring grandson saw

the doctor's family photo in the Model T as a child, in his grandparent's home in Detroit. After they died, he didn't see it again until the Michigan Historical Society published it, not knowing who all of those people were and what they were doing in the Model T Ford.

Especially vexing was why the photo had been kept at the Henry Ford Museum.

Grandson Tom Payette of Louisville, Kentucky, answered all of their questions.

He identified the good doctor, wearing the hat and sporting the large mustache in the photo, second from left. He told the Michigan Historical Society all of the other names in the photo, including his mother, Ruth, one of the twins to the far right in the picture. She married Joseph Payette as a young woman.

Tom Payette told them about all the notable things the good Dr. O'Donnell had been involved in—including his service as chief of staff at Providence Hospital and his work on the staff at St. Joseph Retreat House. He mentioned Dr. Dan's work as a trustee of the Wayne County Medical Society. He even talked about all the golfing trophies the doctor prized.

But that still didn't answer the question about why the good doctor and his family were part of the Ford Museum—all of them spilling out of that Model T touring car.

Then Tom told them why.

Among the more than 4,000 mothers and babies that Dr. O'Donnell assisted in delivering was one that happened early in his practice. A young mother to be from the neighborhood liked visiting with the young doctor.

When that woman, Mrs. Clara Ford, gave birth to a son in 1893 named Edsel Bryant Ford, she and her husband, Henry, continued their trust and appreciation of the good doctor. Mrs. Ford kept Dr. O'Donnell as her family physician.

That's why the Ford Museum kept a picture of Dr. O'Donnell and his large family in the Model T Ford.

The U. S. Postal Service honored the Model T Ford with a stamp issued in 1998.

Preserved by the Postal Service

Another way to honor the Model T was done in 1998 when the U. S. Postal Service commemorated an early Model T touring car with its top up with full frontal view, including the brass radiator. The red Model T was right there with stamps honoring other Americans past and present as well as American events. The Model T stamp was a limited and well-deserved honor for the car that changed the country and the world.

"FIRSTS OF THE MODEL T ERA"		
1908	Model T engine	Cast cylinder liners and removable head. Stronger, lighter, less expensive and more durable than other engines.
1913	Moving assembly line	Model T production brings work to the worker, reduces assembly time, increases production, lowers costs.
1925	Aviation	Ford Triplane is the first airplane built on a production line.
1926	Navigation radio beam	Helps pilots fly in low visibility and bad weather.
1927	Laminated glass	Windshield glass is safer and prevents shattering.

Source: Ford 100, Automotive News, June 16, 2003

My old, dear friend

What stories do you have inside your wood and metal framework bones?

What people did you serve when you were new?

Did you take people for their first trip to some distant place?

Were you a city car or did you belong to a farm family?

Some Model Ts hauled squirming children down country lanes, some were loaded with wood and straw and bricks.

Some delivered bread and cakes, others newspaper and milk. some brought meat or mail, others took busy couples to shop.

This 1915 Model T touring car certainly must have been a "dear friend" for some individual or family in its history.   David Lyon

What stories do you have inside your wood and framework bones?

What did you look like when your fabric was fresh and your paint was bright?

Did you bring teachers to their schools?

Did you bring carpenters to build new homes?

Did you carry policemen or a fire chief?

Was your job bringing the country doctor to the sick?

Or did you take an engineer to a city where he dreamed of skyscrapers?

Were you in the wedding with rice flying and tin cans clanging, speeding newlyweds away on their first great adventure?

Did you take a young woman from her hometown to her first new job?

Were you the college boy's prized set of wheels?

Some drove you in the darkness of night, sitting on a gas-tank box, to a distant body maker.

Some picked you from a showroom, fresh and new and complete.

Some chose you from a used car lot, when you were faded and worn.

Maybe you were the "first car," pleasing generations of young drivers, tussled and frayed but a jewel in those eyes that dreamed of the freedom of motion.

Today someone else has rescued you, from the scrap heap of history and a rusty grave, Today someone has decided to dress you up, to make you whole and new again.

Today someone will start you up and make your body and engine whole again.

Someone has a vision for you, not as you are today, all weathered and weary, but preserved and shiny, honored and cared for, driven and praised, a prized treasure saved in photos and a twinkle in the eye of those who remember you, an old, dear friend, the Model T made new again.

by Tom Collins.

Henry Ford and the Model T were brought together for this 1920 photograph. The man and the car succeeded in changing the way the world drives and lives.

Chapter 12

MODEL T ERA PRICES

Prices in this section are a combination of the Krause Publications Collector Car Prices current database and original prices taken from information found in the Standard Catalog of Ford, 3rd edition as well as the Model T Encyclopedia by Bruce McCalley and pricing information from the Model T Ford Club International.

The center door sedan was a Model T offering for several years during the late teens and early 1920s.   Robin Heil-Kern

Pre-T Fords:

Model A 1903

Two-cylinder, Serial numbers: 671-1708, 10 hp

ORIGINAL PRICE:
$850
$950 with tonneau

2007 PRICE	6	5	4	3	2	1
Runabout	$1,840	$5,520	$9,200	$20,700	$32,200	$46,000
Runabout with tonneau	$1,880	$5,640	$9,400	$21,150	$32,900	$47,000

Note: In 2007, one of the three original Model As ordered in July 1903, and the only known survivor, was sold at the R/M Auction for $630,000 plus 10 percent commission. This Model A was reportedly ordered by butter-maker Herbert L. McNary of Britt, Iowa, according to Car Collector, April 2007.

Model A   1904

Two-cylinder, Serial Numbers 671-1708, 10 hp
(Model AC was also made this year.)

ORIGINAL PRICES:
$850
$950 with tonneau

2007 PRICES:	6	5	4	3	2	1
Runabout	$1,840	$5,520	$9,200	$20,700	$32,200	$46,000
Runabout with tonneau	$1,880	$5,640	$9,400	$21,150	$32,900	$47,000

Model B   1904-1905

Four-cylinder, 10 hp

ORIGINAL PRICES:
$2,000

2007 PRICE:	VALUE INESTIMABLE.
Touring	

Model C   1904-1905

Two-cylinder, 10 hp, Serial numbers: 1709-2700

ORIGINAL PRICES:
$850
$950 with tonneau

2007 PRICES:	6	5	4	3	2	1
Runabout	$1,840	$5,520	$9,200	$20,700	$32,200	$46,000
Runabout	$1,880	$5,640	$9,400	$21,150	$32,900	$47,000
Doctor's Model	$1,920	$5,760	$9,600	$21,600	$33,600	$48,000

Model F   1904-1906

Two-cylinder, 16 hp.

ORIGINAL PRICES:
$1,100-$1,250

2007 PRICES:	6	5	4	3	2	1
Touring	$1,920	$5,760	$9,600	$21,600	$33,600	$48,000

Model K   1905-1908

Six-cylinder, 40 hp.

ORIGINAL PRICES:
$2,500-$2,800

2007 PRICES:	6	5	4	3	2	1
Touring	$2,960	$8,880	$14,800	$33,300	$51,800	$74,000
Runabout	$2,960	$8,880	$14,800	$33,300	$51,800	$74,000

THE FAMOUS FORD

FORD MODEL C,
FOR THE DOCTOR.

THE CAR OF SATISFACTION

The 1905 Ford Model C was known as a car for the doctor!   *Tom Collins.*

Ford 4-cylinder—15-18 H. P. Runabout—Model "R

In some ways, the Model R runabout of 1907 foreshadowed the Model T. Tom Collins.

Model N   1906-1908
Four-cylinder, 18 hp.

ORIGINAL PRICE:
$600

2007 PRICES:	6	5	4	3	2	1
Runabout	$1,760	$5,280	$8,800	$19,800	$30,800	$44,000

Model R   1907-1908
Four-cylinder, 18 hp.

ORIGINAL PRICE:
$750

2007 PRICES:	6	5	4	3	2	1
Runabout	$1,760	$5,280	$8,800	$19,800	$30,800	$44,000

Model S   1907-1908
Four-cylinder, 18 hp.

ORIGINAL PRICE:
$700

2007 PRICES:	6	5	4	3	2	1
Runabout	$1,800	$5,400	$9,000	$20,250	$31,500	$45,000

The Model T Era:

"1908" Model T

(One of approximately 2,500 1909 Model Ts built in 1908.)

Four-cylinder, with two levers and two foot-pedals.

ORIGINAL PRICE:
$850

2007 PRICES:	6	5	4	3	2	1
Touring	$1,840	$5,520	$9,200	$20,700	$32,200	$46,000

1909 Model T

Four-cylinder, cars more standardized after first 2,500 produced.

ORIGINAL PRICES:	
Runabout	$825
Touring	$850
Coupe	$950
Town Car	$1,000
Landaulet	n/a

2007 PRICES	6	5	4	3	2	1
Runabout	$1,160	$3,480	$5,800	$13,050	$20,300	$29,000
Touring	$1,200	$3,600	$6,000	$13,500	$21,000	$30,000
Coupe	$1,040	$3,120	$5,200	$11,700	$18,200	$26,000
Town Car	$1,240	$3,720	$6,200	$13,950	$21,700	$31,000
Landaulet	$1,120	$3,360	$5,600	$12,600	$19,600	$28,000

1910 Model T

Four-cylinder

ORIGINAL PRICES:	
Runabout	$900
Touring	$950
Coupe	$1,050
Town Car	$1,200
Commercial	n/a

2007 PRICES	6	5	4	3	2	1
Runabout	$1,120	$3,360	$5,600	$12,600	$19,600	$28,000
Touring	$1,160	$3,480	$5,800	$13,050	$20,300	$29,000
Coupe	$1,000	$3,000	$5,000	$11,250	$17,500	$25,000
Town Car	$1,040	$3,120	$5,200	$11,700	$18,200	$26,000
Commercial	$1,000	$3,000	$5,000	$11,250	$17,500	$25,000

1907 Ford, Model "K" six-cylinder 40 H.P. Touring Car.

Large and long, the six-cylinder Ford Model K was the top of the line car available from Ford Motor Co. in 1907. Tom Collins.

The 1911 Model T touring car in profile. It was restored with wire wheels.
David Lyon

1911 Model T
Four-cylinder

ORIGINAL PRICES:	
Runabout	$680
Touring	$780
Coupe	$1,050
Town Car	$1,200
Commercial	n/a
Delivery car	$ 700

2007 PRICES	6	5	4	3	2	1
Runabout	$1,080	$3,360	$5,400	$12,150	$18,900	$27,000
Torpedo roadster	$1,120	$3,360	$5,800	$12,600	$19,600	$28,000
Touring	$1,120	$3,360	$5,600	$12,600	$19,600	$28,000
Tourabout	$1,080	$3,240	$5,400	$12,150	$18,900	$27,000
Coupe	$ 920	$2,760	$4,600	$10,350	$16,100	$23,000
Town Car	$1,080	$3,240	$5,400	$12,150	$18,900	$27,000
Commercial roadster	$ 960	$2,880	$4,800	$10,800	$16,800	$24,000
Delivery car	$ 880	$2,640	$4,400	$9,900	$15,400	$22,000

1912 Model T
Four-cylinder

ORIGINAL PRICES:	
Runabout	$590
Touring	$690
Torpedo roadster	n/a
Town Car	$900
Commercial	n/a
Delivery car	$700

2007 PRICES	6	5	4	3	2	1
Runabout	$1,040	$3,120	$5,200	$11,700	$18,200	$26,000
Torpedo roadster	$1,080	$3,240	$5,400	$12,150	$18,900	$27,000
Touring	$1,120	$3,360	$5,600	$12,600	$19,600	$28,000
Town Car	$1,080	$3,240	$5,400	$12,150	$18,900	$27,000
Commercial roadster	$1,000	$3,000	$5,000	$11,250	$17,500	$25,000
Delivery car	$ 920	$2,760	$4,600	$10,350	$16,100	$23,000

Robin Heil-Kern

1913 Model T

Four-cylinder

ORIGINAL PRICES:	
Runabout	$525
Touring	$600
Town Car	$740

2007 PRICES	6	5	4	3	2	1
Roadster	$1,040	$3,120	$5,200	$11,700	$18,200	$26,000
Touring	$1,120	$3,360	$5,600	$12,600	$19,600	$28,000
Town Car	$1,000	$3,000	$5,000	$11,250	$17,500	$25,000

1914 Model T

Four-cylinder

ORIGINAL PRICES:	
Roadster	$440
Touring	$490
Coupe	$750
Town Car	$690

2007 PRICES	6	5	4	3	2	1
Roadster	$1,040	$3,120	$5,200	$11,700	$18,200	$26,000
Touring	$1,120	$3,360	$5,600	$12,600	$19,600	$28,000
Coupe	$ 800	$2,400	$4,000	$9,000	$14,000	$20,000
Town Car	$1,040	$3,120	$5,200	$11,700	$18,200	$26,000

The 1912 Model T commercial roadster with the famous "mother in law" sea out back. David Lyon

As Ford Value Goes Up
Ford Prices Come Down

-1904-
$950

-1908-
$850

-1910-
$750

-1912-
$600

1919
$525

1926

$380
WITH STARTER AND
BALLOON TIRES~

The Savings in manufacture due to mass production have been passed on to the consumer in lower prices and better quality.

BEHIND THE PRODUCT

11

A Ford Motor Co. sales basic. As more cars were produced and sold, the prices came down during the Model T era.

Model T number 10,000,000 toured the United States in 1924, celebrating the Lincoln Highway, a major East-West artery.

1915 and Early 1916 Model T
Four-cylinder (brass radiator models)

ORIGINAL PRICES:	
Roadster	$390
Touring	$440
Center Door Sedan	$740
Coupelet	$1,590
Town Car	$640

2007 PRICES	6	5	4	3	2	1
Roadster	$1,040	$3,120	$5,200	$11,700	$18,200	$26,000
Touring	$1,080	$3,240	$5,400	$12,150	$18,900	$27,000
Center Door Sedan	$840	$2,520	$4,200	$9,450	$14,700	$21,000
Coupelet	$1,120	$3,360	$5,600	$12,600	$19,600	$28,000
Town Car	$1,000	$3,000	$5,000	$11,250	$17,500	$25,000

1917 Model T
Four-cylinder

ORIGINAL PRICES:	
Roadster	$345
Touring	$360
Center Door Sedan	$645
Coupelet	$505
Town Car	$595

2007 PRICES	6	5	4	3	2	1
Roadster	$760	$2,280	$3,800	$8,500	$13,300	$19,000
Touring	$800	$2,400	$4,000	$9,000	$14,000	$20,000
Center Door Sedan	$520	$1,560	$2,600	$5,850	$9,100	$13,000
Coupelet	$680	$2,040	$3,400	$7,650	$11,900	$17,000
Town Car	$600	$1,800	$3,000	$6,750	$10,500	$18,000
Coupe	$560	$1,680	$2,800	$6,300	$9,800	$14,000

1916 Model T
Four-cylinder (steel radiator models)

ORIGINAL PRICES:	
Roadster	$390
Touring	$360
Center Door Sedan	$640
Coupelet	$540
Town Car	$595

2007 PRICES	6	5	4	3	2	1
Roadster	$880	$2,640	$4,400	$9,900	$15,400	$22,000
Touring	$840	$2,520	$4,200	$9,450	$14,700	$21,000
Center Door Sedan	$640	$1,920	$3,200	$7,200	$11,200	$16,000
Coupelet	$880	$2,640	$4,400	$9,900	$15,400	$22,000
Town Car	$720	$2,160	$3,600	$8,100	$12,600	$18,000

1918 Model T
Four-cylinder

ORIGINAL PRICES:	
Roadster	$500
Touring	$525
Center Door Sedan	$775
Coupelet	$650

2007 PRICES	6	5	4	3	2	1
Roadster	$760	$2,280	$3,800	$8,500	$13,300	$19,000
Touring	$800	$2,400	$4,000	$9,000	$14,000	$20,000
Center Door Sedan	$560	$1,680	$2,600	$6,300	$9,800	$14,000
Coupelet	$680	$2,040	$3,400	$7,650	$11,900	$17,000

AMONG women, especially, the popularity of the improved Ford Tudor Sedan continues to grow. The low price enables them to own an attractive, convenient enclosed car for their own use, without undue burden on the family income. Many women are buying on the Ford Weekly Purchase Plan —paying out of savings from the household budget. Ask any Authorized Ford Dealer to give you full particulars.

FORD MOTOR COMPANY, DETROIT, MICHIGAN

Runabout $290, Touring $310, Coupe $500, Tudor Sedan $520, Fordor Sedan $565
Special equipment shown on car, bumpers and natural wood wheels, extra. All prices f. o. b. Detroit

Ford

The 1926 Model T Tudor sedan was positioned as a car for women and families in this colorful Ford Motor Co. ad.
Jerry Banks

1919 Model T
Four-cylinder

Original prices:	
Roadster	$500
Touring	$525
Center Door Sedan	$775
Coupe	$650

2007 Prices	6	5	4	3	2	1
Roadster	$ 800	$2,400	$4,000	$9,000	$14,000	$19,000
Touring	$ 840	$2,520	$4,200	$9,450	$14,700	$20,000
Center Door Sedan	$ 560	$1,680	$2,800	$6,300	$ 9,800	$14,000
Coupe	$ 560	$1,680	$2,800	$6,300	$ 9,800	$14,000

1920 Model T
Four-cylinder

Original prices:	March
Roadster	$500
Touring	$525
Center Door Sedan	$775
Coupe	$650

Original prices:	September
Roadster	$500
Touring	$525
Center Door Sedan	$775
Coupe	$650

2007 Prices	6	5	4	3	2	1
Roadster	$ 800	$2,400	$4,000	$9,000	$14,000	$20,000
Touring	$ 840	$2,520	$4,200	$9,450	$14,700	$21,000
Center Door Sedan	$ 520	$1,560	$2,600	$5,850	$ 9,100	$13,000
Coupe	$ 520	$1,560	$2,600	$5,850	$ 9,100	$13,000

1921 Model T
Four-cylinder

Original prices:	June
Roadster	$370
Touring	$415
Center Door Sedan	$760
Coupe	$695

Original prices:	September
Roadster	$325
Touring	$355
Center Door Sedan	$660
Coupe	$595

2007 Prices	6	5	4	3	2	1
Roadster	$ 800	$2,400	$4,000	$9,000	$14,000	$20,000
Touring	$ 840	$2,520	$4,200	$9,450	$14,700	$21,000
Center Door Sedan	$ 520	$1,560	$2,600	$5,850	$ 9,100	$13,000
Coupe	$ 520	$1,560	$2,600	$5,850	$ 9,100	$13,000

1922 Model T
Four-cylinder

Original prices:	
Roadster	$ 319
Touring	$ 348
Center Door Sedan	$ 645
Coupe	$ 580
Fordor Sedan	n/a
Tudor Sedan	n/a

2007 Prices	6	5	4	3	2	1
Roadster	$ 720	$2,160	$3,600	$8,100	$12,600	$18,000
Touring	$ 760	$2,280	$3,800	$8,550	$13,300	$19,000
Center Door Sedan	$ 520	$1,560	$2,600	$5,850	$ 9,100	$13,000
Coupe	$ 520	$1,560	$2,600	$5,850	$ 9,100	$13,000
Fordor Sedan	$ 420	$1,260	$2,100	$4,730	$ 7,350	$10,500
Tudor Sedan	$ 410	$1,260	$2,060	$4,640	$ 7,210	$10.300

The Story of
1925 Registration

Ford

8,120,600
Registrations

Chevrolet

1,439,100
Registrations

Dodge

997,000
Registrations

Overland

654,900
Registrations

Star

227,000
Registrations

FORD 8,120,600

CHEVROLET 1,439,100
DODGE 997,000

OVERLAND 654,900

STAR 227,000

Popularity depends on service. 50% of all cars registered in 1925 were Fords. Every other car a Ford!

COMPARISONS

137

The dominance of the Model T over other cars was shown dramatically in this 1925 Ford Motor Co. sales aid image.

1923 Model T
Four-cylinder

ORIGINAL PRICES:	
Roadster	$ 364
Touring	$ 393
Coupe	$ 530
Fordor Sedan	$ 725
Tudor Sedan	$ 595

2007 PRICES	6	5	4	3	2	1
Roadster	$ 720	$2,160	$3,600	$8,100	$12,600	$18,000
Touring	$ 780	$2,340	$3,900	$8,780	$13,650	$19,500
Center Door Sedan	$ 520	$1,560	$2,600	$5,850	$ 9,100	$13,000
Coupe	$ 520	$1,560	$2,600	$5,850	$ 9,100	$13,000
Fordor Sedan	$ 420	$1,260	$2,100	$4,730	$ 7,350	$10,500
Tudor Sedan	$ 410	$1,260	$2,060	$4,640	$ 7,210	$10,300

1924 Model T
Four-cylinder

ORIGINAL PRICES:	
Roadster	$ 265
Touring	$ 295
Coupe	$ 525
Fordor Sedan	$ 685
Tudor Sedan	$ 590

2007 PRICES	6	5	4	3	2	1
Roadster	$ 720	$2,160	$3,600	$8,100	$12,600	$18,000
Touring	$ 780	$2,340	$3,900	$8,780	$13,650	$19,500
Coupe	$ 560	$1,680	$2,800	$6,300	$ 9,800	$14,000
Fordor Sedan	$ 420	$1,260	$2,100	$4,730	$ 7,350	$10,500
Tudor Sedan	$ 430	$1,280	$2,140	$4,820	$ 7,490	$10,700

1925 Model T

Four-cylinder

ORIGINAL PRICES:	
Roadster	$ 260
Touring	$ 290
Coupe	$ 520
Fordor Sedan	$ 660
Tudor Sedan	$ 580

2007 PRICES	6	5	4	3	2	1
Roadster	$ 720	$2,160	$3,600	$8,100	$12,600	$18,000
Touring	$ 780	$2,280	$3,800	$8,550	$13,300	$19,000
Coupe	$ 560	$1,680	$2,800	$6,300	$ 9,800	$14,000
Fordor Sedan	$ 440	$1,260	$2,100	$4,730	$ 7,350	$10,500
Tudor Sedan	$ 420	$1,320	$2,200	$4,950	$ 7,700	$11,000

1926 Model T

Four-cylinder

ORIGINAL PRICES:	
Roadster	$ 360
Touring	$ 380
Coupe	$ 485
Fordor Sedan	$ 545
Tudor Sedan	$ 495

2007 PRICES	6	5	4	3	2	1
Roadster	$ 760	$2,280	$3,800	$8,550	$13,300	$19,000
Touring	$ 800	$2,400	$4,000	$9,000	$14,000	$20,000
Coupe	$ 560	$1,680	$2,800	$6,300	$ 9,800	$14,000
Fordor Sedan	$ 440	$1,330	$2,220	$5,000	$ 7,700	$11,000
Tudor Sedan	$ 440	$1,320	$2,200	$4,950	$ 7,700	$11,000

1927 Model T

Four-cylinder

ORIGINAL PRICES:	
Roadster	$ 360
Touring	$ 380
Coupe	$ 485
Fordor Sedan	$ 545
Tudor Sedan	$ 495

2007 PRICES	6	5	4	3	2	1
Roadster	$ 800	$2,400	$4,000	$9,000	$14,000	$20,000
Touring	$ 840	$2,520	$4,200	$9,450	$14,700	$21,000
Coupe	$ 580	$1,740	$2,900	$6,530	$10,150	$14,500
Fordor Sedan	$ 450	$1,360	$2,260	$5,090	$ 7,910	$11,300
Tudor Sedan	$ 460	$1,380	$2,300	$5,180	$ 8,050	$11,500

A 1926 Model T touring car in basic black. This Ford was the pride of many car owners. David Lyon

In the end, the Model T was a colorful car that millions enjoyed owning. The car always maintained its traditional value and practicality.   Robin Heil-Kern

One of the final cars in the T series was the 1926 coupe, like this well-restored version. David Lyon

The Model T Times put this landmark Model T on its cover— a 1927 touring car that became number 15,000,000.

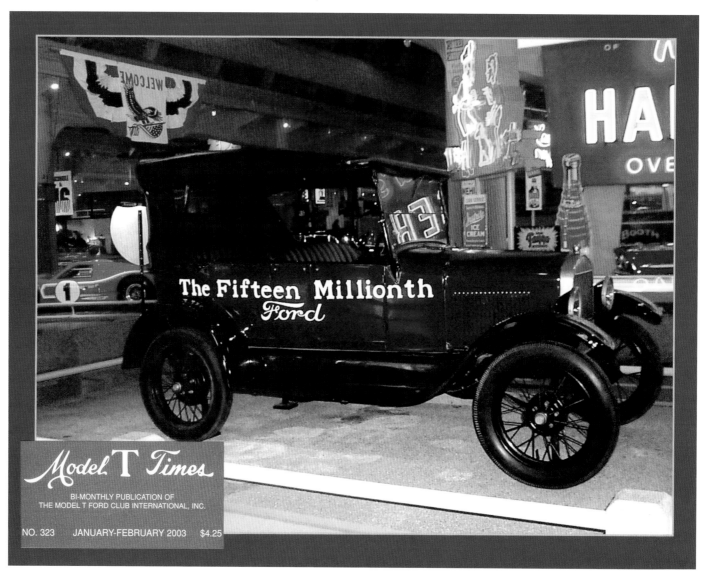

The Fifteen Millionth Ford

Model T Times

BI-MONTHLY PUBLICATION OF THE MODEL T FORD CLUB INTERNATIONAL, INC.

NO. 323   JANUARY-FEBRUARY 2003 $4.25

Car of the Century

It was fitting that in 2000, *Motor Trend* magazine made an announcement that a "Car of the Century" had been chosen. The choice was the result of polls of both members of the public and journalists as well as a panel of 126 judges. The Model T beat all competitors to become the "Car of the Century," leaving in its wake such cars as the British Austin and Morris Mini, the French Citroen DS and the German Volkswagen Beetle and Porsche 911. In tandem with the Model T honor, Henry Ford was chosen as "Entrepreneur of the Century."

Ford and his Model T always were thought of in the same sentence. It's appropriate that people of the 21st century honored them in tandem. The car and the man have never been forgotten and probably never will be.

Source: "Trends and Top News," *Motor Trend*, April 2000, p. 34.

David Lyon

Robin Heil-Kern

Bibliography

Chapter 1

1   David Halberstam, *The Reckoning*, (New York, 1986), p. 60.

2   Fred Smith, "Principles of Leadership," Leadership Journal, Fall 1996, p. 30.

3   Op cit., p. 30.

4   Ibid., p. 86.

5   Profile of Thomas Jeffery, *Hemming's Classic Car*, February 2007, p. 84.

6   Robert Lacey, *Ford: The Men and The Machine*, (London, 1986), pp. 8-86.

7   Terry B. Dunham and Lawrence Gustin, *The Buick: A Complete History, 5th Editio*n, (Kutztown, Pennsylvania, 1997), p. 10.

8   David Nolting Collection, Model T Post Cards, 2007.

9   David Halberstam, *The Reckoning*, (New York, 1986), p. 59.

10   Ibid., p. 69.

11   Beverly Rae Kimes, "Young Henry Ford," *Automobile Quarterly* 10:2, 1972, p. 198.

12   David Halberstam, *The Reckoning*, (New York, 1986), p. 64.

13   Robert Lacey, *Ford: The Men and The Machine*, (London, 1986), p. 15.

14   Ibid., p. 12.

15   Op cit., pp. 12-13.

16   Beverly Rae Kimes, "Young Henry Ford," *Automobile Quarterly* 10:2, 1972, p. 198.

17   Ibid., p. 196.

18   Robert Lacey, *Ford: The Men and The Machine*, (London, 1986), p. 24.

19   Ibid., p. 25.

20   David Halberstam, *The Reckoning*, (New York, 1986), p. 67.

21   Robert Lacey, *Ford: The Men and The Machine*, (London, 1986), p. 27.

22   Ibid., p. 27.

23   Op cit., pp. 29-30.

24   Beverly Rae Kimes, "Young Henry Ford," *Automobile Quarterly* 10:2, 1972, p. 198.

25   Robert Lacey, *Ford: The Men and The Machine*, (London, 1986), p. 35.

26   Ibid., p. 38.

27   Op cit., p. 36.

28   Beverly Rae Kimes, "Young Henry Ford," *Automobile Quarterly* 10:2, 1972, p. 199.

29   David Halberstam, *The Reckoning*, (New York, 1986), p. 67.

30   Beverly Rae Kimes, "Young Henry Ford," *Automobile Quarterly* 10:2, 1972, p. 199.

31   Ibid., p. 199.

32   Robert Lacey, *Ford: The Men and The Machine*, (London, 1986), p. 41.

33   Beverly Rae Kimes, "Young Henry Ford," *Automobile Quarterly* 10:2, 1972, p. 199.

34   Ibid., p. 199.

35   Robert Lacey, *Ford: The Men and The Machine*, (London, 1986), p. 51.

36   Beverly Rae Kimes, "Young Henry Ford," *Automobile Quarterly* 10:2, 1972, p. 212.

37   Robert Lacey, *Ford: The Men and The Machine*, (London, 1986), p. 64.

38   John Anderson's Letter to His Father, *Vintage Ford* 24:5, Sept.-Oct. 1989, p. 44.

39   Op cit., p. 44.

40   David Halberstam, *The Reckoning*, (New York, 1986), p. 70.

41   Beverly Rae Kimes, "Young Henry Ford," *Automobile Quarterly* 10:2, 1972, p. 199.

42   Robert Lacey, *Ford: The Men and The Machine*, (London, 1986), p. 114.

43   Op cit., p. 213.

44   David Halberstam, *The Reckoning*, (New York, 1986), p. 72.

45   Robert Lacey, *Ford: The Men and The Machine*, (London, 1986), pp. 60-61.

46   David Roberts, *In the Shadow of Detroit*, (Detroit, 2006), p. 24.

47   Henry Ford interview, *Ford News*, Jan. 15, 1924.

48   David Halberstam, *The Reckoning*, (New York, 1986), p. 70.

Chapter 2

1   Beverly Rae Kimes, "Young Henry Ford," *Automobile Quarterly* 10:2, 1972, p. 199.

2   David Roberts, *In the Shadow of Detroit*, (Detroit, 2006), p. 18.

3   Beverly Rae Kimes, "Henry Ford's Model T," *Automobile Quarterly* 10:4, 1972, p. 374.

4   Op cit., p. 47.

5   Publisher's advertisement, *Motor World*, 1924.

6   Robert Lacey, *Ford: The Men and The Machine*, (London, 1986), p. 43.

7   Beverly Rae Kimes, "Young Henry Ford," *Automobile Quarterly* 10:2, 1972, p. 199.

8   Ibid., p. 199 and Op cit., pp. 44-45.

9   Beverly Rae Kimes, "Young Henry Ford," *Automobile Quarterly* 10:2, 1972, p. 199.

10 Robert Lacey, *Ford: The Men and The Machine*, (London, 1986), p. 56.

11 Beverly Rae Kimes, "Young Henry Ford," *Automobile Quarterly* 10:2, 1972, p. 201.

12 Ibid., p. 201.

13 Op cit., p. 205.

14 Ibid., p. 205.

15 David Halberstam, *The Reckoning*, (New York, 1986), p. 69.

16 Beverly Rae Kimes, "Young Henry Ford," *Automobile Quarterly* 10:2, 1972, p. 204.

17 Ibid., p. 205.

18 Robert Lacey, *Ford: The Men and The Machine*, (London, 1986), p. 62.

19 Ibid., p. 64.

20 Op cit., pp. 64-65 and Beverly Rae Kimes, "Young Henry Ford," *Automobile Quarterly* 10:2, 1972, p. 212.

21 Robert Lacey, *Ford: The Men and The Machine*, (London, 1986), p. 71.

22 Beverly Rae Kimes, "Young Henry Ford," *Automobile Quarterly* 10:2, 1972, p. 212.

23 Op cit., p. 71.

24 John Anderson's Letter to His Father, *Vintage Ford* 24:5, Sept.-Oct. 1989, p. 35.

25 Robert Lacey, *Ford: The Men and The Machine*, (London, 1986), p. 75.

26 Op cit., p. 35.

27 Beverly Rae Kimes, "Young Henry Ford," *Automobile Quarterly* 10:2, 1972, p. 212.

28 John Anderson's Letter to His Father, *Vintage Ford* 24:5, Sept.-Oct. 1989, p. 35.

29 Ibid., p. 35.

30 David Roberts, *In the Shadow of Detroit*, (Detroit, 2006), p. 24.

31 John Anderson's Letter to His Father, *Vintage Ford* 24:5, Sept.-Oct. 1989, p. 36.

32 Robert Lacey, *Ford: The Men and The Machine*, (London, 1986), pp. 71-76.

33 Ibid., pp. 71-76.

34 David Roberts, *In the Shadow of Detroit*, (Detroit, 2006), p. 21.

35 Beverly Rae Kimes, "Young Henry Ford," *Automobile Quarterly* 10:2, 1972, p. 213.

36 Ibid., p. 213.

37 "Fred Rockelman's Life with Henry Ford," *Model T Times #211,* May-June 1984, p. 33. (Originally published in Springfield, Mass., *Republican*, 1964)

38 Robert Lacey, *Ford: The Men and The Machine*, (London, 1986), p. 106.

39 Beverly Rae Kimes, "Young Henry Ford," *Automobile Quarterly* 10:2, 1972, p. 213.

40   David Roberts, *In the Shadow of Detroit*, (Detroit, 2006), p. 37.

41   Ibid., p. 35.

42   Robert Lacey, *Ford: The Men and The Machine*, (London, 1986), p. 88.

43   David Roberts, *In the Shadow of Detroit*, (Detroit, 2006), p. 41.

44   Robert Lacey, *Ford: The Men and The Machine*, (London, 1986), p. 82.

45   Ibid., pp. 82-83.

46   "Fred Rockelman's Life with Henry Ford," *Model T Times #211*, May-June 1984, p. 34. (Originally published in Springfield, Mass., *Republican*, 1964)

47   Ibid., p. 34.

48   Robert Lacey, *Ford: The Men and The Machine*, (London, 1986), p. 85.

49   "Fred Rockelman's Life with Henry Ford," *Model T Times #211*, May-June 1984, p. 34. (Originally published in Springfield, Mass., *Republican*, 1964)

50   Op cit., p. 86.

51   Robert Lacey, *Ford: The Men and The Machine*, (London, 1986), p. 86.

52   Ibid., p. 94.

53   David Roberts, *In the Shadow of Detroit*, (Detroit, 2006), p. 41.

54   Beverly Rae Kimes, "Young Henry Ford," *Automobile Quarterly* 10:2, 1972, p. 221.

55   *Model T Ford Comprehensive Encyclopedia,* Bruce McCalley, 2007.

56   Robert Lacey, *Ford: The Men and The Machine*, (London, 1986), p. 97.

57   David Roberts, *In the Shadow of Detroit*, (Detroit, 2006), p. 41.

Chapter 3

1   "Fred Rockelman's Life with Henry Ford," *Model T Times #211*, May-June 1984, p. 33. (Originally published in Springfield, Mass., *Republican*, 1964)

2   David Halberstam, *The Reckoning*, (New York, 1986), p. 74 and Beverly Rae Kimes, "Henry Ford's Model T," *Automobile Quarterly* 10:4, 1972, p. 380.

3   William Pelfry, *Billy, Alfred and General Motors*, (New York, 2006). From a transcript of a television interview, Book TV, Dec. 26, 2006.

4   Beverly Rae Kimes, "Henry Ford's Model T," *Automobile Quarterly* 10:4, 1972, p. 374.

5   Ibid., p. 375.

6   Op cit., p. 374.

7   Bruce McCalley, "The All New Ford Model T," *Vintage Ford* 22:2, Mar.-Apr. 1987, p. 17.

8   Jack Woodward, "Childe Harold Wills," *Special Interest Autos*, Aug.-Oct. 1977, p. 32.

9   Robert Lacey, *Ford: The Men and The Machine*, (London, 1986), p. 94.

10   Ibid., p. 94.

11   Beverly Rae Kimes, "Henry Ford's Model T," *Automobile Quarterly* 10:4, 1972, p. 374.

12   Bruce Balough, "Grandfather's Role in the Development of the Model T," *Model T Times* #347, Jan.-Feb. 2007, pp. 3-4.

13   Jack Woodward, "Childe Harold Wills," *Special Interest Autos*, Aug.-Oct. 1977, p. 32.

14   Bruce Balough, "Grandfather's Role in the Development of the Model T," *Model T Times* #347, Jan.-Feb. 2007, pp. 3-4.

15   Ibid., pp. 3-4.

16   Op cit., pp. 3-4.

17   Bruce McCalley, "Developing the Model T," *Vintage Ford* 36:3, May-June 2001, p. 33.

18   "Fred Rockelman's Life with Henry Ford," *Model T Times #212*, May-June 1984, p. 6. (Originally published in Springfield, Mass., *Republican*, 1964).

19   Beverly Rae Kimes, "Henry Ford's Model T," *Automobile Quarterly* 10:4, 1972, p. 376.

20   Robert Lacey, *Ford: The Men and The Machine*, (London, 1986), p. 99.

21   Bruce McCalley, "Developing the Model T," *Vintage Ford* 36:3, May-June 2001, p. 34.

22   Beverly Rae Kimes, "Henry Ford's Model T," *Automobile Quarterly* 10:4, 1972, p. 380.

23   Bruce McCalley, "The All New Ford Model T," *Vintage Ford* 22:2, Mar.-Apr. 1987, p. 14.

24   "Fred Rockelman's Life with Henry Ford," *Model T Times #211*, May-June 1984, p. 34. (Originally published in Springfield, Mass., *Republican*, 1964).

25   1909 Ford Model T Introductory brochure, KP Archives.

26   Bruce McCalley, "The All New Ford Model T," *Vintage Ford* 22:2, Mar.-Apr. 1987, p. 14.

27   Beverly Rae Kimes, "Henry Ford's Model T," *Automobile Quarterly* 10:4, 1972, p. 387.

28   Ibid., p. 387.

29   David Roberts, *In the Shadow of Detroit*, (Detroit, 2006), p. 56.

30   Trent Boggess, "This Little Ford Went to Market," *Vintage Ford* 37:2, Mar.-Apr. 2002, p. 33.

31   Ibid., p. 28.

32   David Roberts, *In the Shadow of Detroit*, (Detroit, 2006), p. 55.

33   Beverly Rae Kimes, "Henry Ford's Model T," *Automobile Quarterly* 10:4, 1972, p. 383.

34-35   1909 Model T Introductory brochure, KP Archives.

36   Robert Lacey, *Ford: The Men and The Machine*, (London, 1986), p. 104.

37   Beverly Rae Kimes, "Henry Ford's Model T," *Automobile Quarterly* 10:4, 1972, p. 387.

38   Floyd Clymer, *Henry Ford's Wonderful Model T*, (New York: 1965), p.13.

39   Ibid., p. 20

40   Beverly Rae Kimes, "Henry Ford's Model T," *Automobile Quarterly* 10:4, 1972, p. 387.

41   Floyd Clymer, *Henry Ford's Wonderful Model T*, (New York: 1965), p.19.

42   Robert Lacey, *Ford: The Men and The Machine*, (London, 1986), p. 102.

43   Op cit., p. 19.

44   David Roberts, *In the Shadow of Detroit*, (Detroit, 2006), p. 60.

45   Ibid., p. 89.

46   David Halberstam, *The Reckoning*, (New York, 1986), p. 71.

47   Ibid., 71.

48   Beverly Rae Kimes, "Henry Ford's Model T," *Automobile Quarterly* 10:4, 1972, p. 384.

49   David Halberstam, *The Reckoning*, (New York, 1986), p. 83 and Robert Lacey, *Ford: The Men and The Machine*, (London, 1986), p. 307.

50   Robert Lacey, *Ford: The Men and The Machine*, (London, 1986), p. 288.

51   Ibid., p. 302.

52   *Automotive Topics*, May 28, 1927, p. 205.

53   Bruce Balough, "Grandfather's Role in the Development of the Model T," *Model T Times* #347, Jan.-Feb. 2007, pp. 3-4.

54   Floyd Clymer, *Henry Ford's Wonderful Model T*, (New York: 1965), p.103.

Chapter 4

Bibliography is noted in the chapter.

Chapter 5

1   Douglas Brinkley, "Prime Mover," *American Heritage Magazine*, June-July 2003.

2   David Halberstam, *The Reckoning*, (New York, 1986), p. 71.

3   Robert Lacey, *Ford: The Men and The Machine*, (London, 1986), p. 103.

4   Ibid., p. 103.

5   Douglas Brinkley, "Prime Mover," *American Heritage Magazine*, June-July 2003.

6   Ibid.

7   Mrs. Harry (Emma) Wright, "Reminiscing: How the Wonderful Model T Changed Our Lives," *Vintage Ford* 7:6, Nov.-Dec. 1972, p. 47.

8   Beverly Rae Kimes, "Henry Ford's Model T," *Automobile Quarterly* 10:4, 1972, pp. 374-375.

9   Ibid., p. 399.

10   Douglas Brinkley, "Prime Mover," *American Heritage Magazine*, June-July 2003.

11   John and LuAnnette Butler, "Women and the Model T," *Vintage Ford* 27:4, July-Aug. 1992, p.16.

12   Ibid., p. 18.

13   Mrs. Harry (Emma) Wright, "Reminiscing: How the Wonderful Model T Changed Our Lives," *Vintage Ford* 7:6, Nov.-Dec. 1972, p. 48.

14   Ibid., p. 49.

15   David Lewis, "Ford Overseas," Ford Life, Nov.-Dec. 1973, p. 23.

16   Douglas Brinkley, "Prime Mover," *American Heritage Magazine*, June-July 2003.

17   Clintonville, Wisconsin, *Tribune*, 1919, Clintonville Public Library.

18   Ibid.

19   Douglas Brinkley, "Prime Mover," *American Heritage Magazine*, June-July 2003.

20   David Roberts, *In the Shadow of Detroit*, (Detroit, 2006), p. 43.

21   Mrs. Harry (Emma) Wright, "Reminiscing: How the Wonderful Model T Changed Our Lives," *Vintage Ford* 7:6, Nov.-Dec. 1972, p. 48.

22   Ibid., p. 17.

23   Op cit., p. 17.

24   Robert Lacey, *Ford: The Men and The Machine*, (London, 1986), p. 116.

25   Ibid., p. 117.

26   Op cit., p. 179

27   David Halberstam, *The Reckoning*, (New York, 1986), p. 60.

28   Ibid., p. 60.

29   Beverly Rae Kimes, "Henry Ford's Model T," *Automobile Quarterly* 10:4, 1972, pp. 383, and other sources.

30   Robert Lacey, *Ford: The Men and The Machine*, (London, 1986), p. 130.

31   Ibid., 129.

32   Beverly Rae Kimes, "Henry Ford's Model T," *Automobile Quarterly* 10:4, 1972, pp. 391.

33   Robert Lacey, *Ford: The Men and The Machine*, (London, 1986), p. 136.

34   David Roberts, *In the Shadow of Detroit*, (Detroit, 2006), p. 7.

35   Robert Lacey, *Ford: The Men and The Machine*, (London, 1986), p. 138.

36   Ibid., p. 358.

37   Op cit., p. 368.

38   Robert Lacey, *Ford: The Men and The Machine*, (London, 1986), p. 137.

39   Ibid., p. 133.

40   Ford 100, *Automotive News*, July 16, 2003, p. 44.

41   John and LuAnnette Butler, "Women and the Model T," *Vintage Ford* 27:4, July-Aug. 1992, p. 27.

42   Robert Lacey, *Ford: The Men and The Machine*, (London, 1986), p. 368.

43   David Roberts, *In the Shadow of Detroit*, (Detroit, 2006), p. 120.

44   Ibid., p. 45.

45   David Lewis, "Ford Overseas," Ford Life, Mar.-Apr. 1973, p. 19.

46   Ibid., pp. 20-21.

47   Op cit., p. 40.

48   David Roberts, *In the Shadow of Detroit*, (Detroit, 2006), p. 205.

49   "Ford Predicts the Passing of Cities," *Motor World*, Aug. 24, 1924, p. 9.

50   William Pelfry, Billy, Alfred and General Motors, (New York, 2006) From a transcript of a television interview, Book TV, Dec. 26, 2006.

51   David Roberts, *In the Shadow of Detroit*, (Detroit, 2006), p. 146.

52   Ibid., 247.

53   Lorin Sorenson, Ford Life, July-August 1973, pp. 4-5.

54   George Damman, Illustrated History of Ford, (Chicago, 1973), pp. 70-71.

55   Douglas Brinkley, "Prime Mover," *American Heritage Magazine*, June-July 2003.

56   Floyd Clymer, *Henry Ford's Wonderful Model T*, (New York: 1965), pp. 41-43.

57   Op cit.

58   "Survey of Our Members," Wisconsin Agriculturist, Oct. 18, 1924, p. 1.

59   David Roberts, *In the Shadow of Detroit*, (Detroit, 2006), p. 154.

Chapter 6

1   David Roberts, *In the Shadow of Detroit*, (Detroit, 2006), p. 56.

2   Henry Mulenford, "Mules and Fords," Automobile Dealer and Repairer, Jan. 1920, p. 27.

3   Op cit., p. 147.

4   Floyd Clymer, *Henry Ford's Wonderful Model T*, (New York: 1965), p. 122.

5   Robert Lacey, *Ford: The Men and The Machine*, (London, 1986), p. 80.

6   Op cit., p. 16.

7   Name/ title, *Model T Times* #250, Nov.-Dec. 1990, p. 15.

8   Beverly Rae Kimes, "Henry Ford's Model T," *Automobile Quarterly* 10:4, 1972, pp. 376.

9   David Roberts, *In the Shadow of Detroit*, (Detroit, 2006), p. 113.

10   "Principles of the Model T Transmission" (brochure reprint), *Model T Times* #250, Nov.-Dec. 1990, p. 16.

11   Ibid., p. 16.

12   "Fred Rockelman's Life with Henry Ford," *Model T Times #211*, May-June 1984, p.34. (Originally published in Springfield, Mass., *Republican*, 1964).

13   Beverly Rae Kimes, "Henry Ford's Model T," *Automobile Quarterly* 10:4, 1972, pp. 387.

14   Larry Smith, "Tools," *Vintage Ford* 33:3, May-June 1998, pp. 36-37.

15   Trent Boggess, "The Customer Can Have Any Color He Wants—So Long as It's Black," *Vintage Ford* 32:6, Nov.-Dec. 1997, p. 30.

16   Ibid., p. 35.

17   Op cit., p. 30.

18   Trent Boggess, "The Customer Can Have Any Color He Wants—So Long as It's Black," *Vintage Ford* 32:6, Nov.-Dec. 1997, p. 36.

19   George R. Norton, Jr.   "Henry Ford's Model T and How They Grew," *Model T Ford Restoration Handbook*, (Los Angeles, 1965), p. 22.

20   Ibid., p. 22.

21   Op cit., p. 22.

22   Trent Boggess, "The Customer Can Have Any Color He Wants—So Long as It's Black," *Vintage Ford* 32:6, Nov.-Dec. 1997, p. 30.

Chapter 7

1   Beverly Rae Kimes, "Henry Ford's Model T," *Automobile Quarterly* 10:4, 1972, pp. 399.

2   Robert Lacey, *Ford: The Men and The Machine*, (London, 1986), p. 102.

3   *Motor World*, Mar. 6, 1924, p. 17

4   *Motor World*, July 3, 1924, pp. 12-13.

5   Ibid., pp. 12-13.

6   Robert Lacey, *Ford: The Men and The Machine*, (London, 1986), p. 103.

7   Floyd Clymer, *Henry Ford's Wonderful Model T*, (New York: 1965), p. 34.

8   "The Schluter Autobelt Attachment," *Model T Times* #307, May-June 2000.

9   *Dairyman's Gazette*, Clintonville, Wisconsin, Apr. 18, 1929, Clintonville Public Library

10   Peter Kable, "The Livingood Four Wheel Drive for Model Ts," *Vintage Ford* 33:5, Nov.-Dec. 1998, pp. 33-39.

11   Jim Allen, *Four Wheeler Magazine*, May 2002.

12   Snowmobile Catalog reprint, *Vintage Ford* 35:3, May-June 2000, pp. 28-29.

13   Harry Jensen, "The Model T in World War I," *Model T Times*, Nov.-Dec. 1999, pp. 20-21.

14   Ibid., pp. 21-22.

15   Kenneth Schwartz, "The Model T Ford V-8," *Vintage Ford* 11:4, July-August, 1976, pp. 41-43.

16   Ford 100, "Ford Trucks," *Automotive News*, June 13, 2003, p. 52.

Chapter 8

1   Floyd Clymer, *Henry Ford's Wonderful Model T*, (New York: 1965), p. 169.

2   Ibid., p. 174.

3   Op cit., p. 173.

4   Gordon Gee, "Why Collect Model T Postcards?" *Model T Times*, May-June 1999, p. 19.

5   (Name/ title), *Vintage Ford 6:6*, Nov.-Dec. 1971, pp. 21-22.

6   "Post Card Memorabilia," *Model T Times*, July-Aug. 1985, p. 17.

7   "They Sang About Fords," *Ford Times*, June 1978, p. 14.

8   Ibid., p. 14.

9   Op cit., p. 15.

10   Floyd Clymer, *Henry Ford's Wonderful Model T*, (New York: 1965), p. 184.

11   *Funabout Fords*, (New York, 1917), pp. 36-37.

12   David Roberts, *In the Shadow of Detroit*, (Detroit, 2006), p. 186.

13   Ibid., p. 247.

14   Bob Raitch, "Model T Ford Music," *Skinned Knuckles*, Aug. 1992, p. 22.

15   Ibid., p. 23.

16   William K. Eversen, editor, The Films of Laurel and Hardy, (New York, 1974)

17   Tim Noah, "Who Wrote the Farewell to the Model T?" 2003.

18   Ford ad reprint, *Vintage Ford 6:6*, Nov.-Dec. 1971, back cover.

19   Ibid., pp. 21-22.

20   Douglas Brinkley, "Prime Mover," *American Heritage Magazine*, June-July 2003.

21   Ibid.

22   Bob Raitch, "Model T Ford Music," *Skinned Knuckles*, Aug. 1992, p. 22.-23.

Chapter 9

1   Peter Roberts, Veteran and Vintage Cars, (London, 1974), p. 44.

2   Ibid., p. 46.

3   David Roberts, *In the Shadow of Detroit*, (Detroit, 2006), pp. 51-52.

4   Jack Woodward, "Childe Harold Wills," *Special Interest Autos*, Aug.-Oct. 1977, p. 32.

5   Robert Lacey, *Ford: The Men and The Machine*, (London, 1986), p. 55.

6   "Ford vs. Winton 1901," *Automotive News*, June 16, 2003, p. 13.

7   Robert Lacey, *Ford: The Men and The Machine*, (London, 1986), p. 59.

8   Ibid., p. 62.

9   Op cit., p. 55.

10   David Lewis, "Ford in Racing," *Vintage Ford 11:2*, Mar.-Apr. 1976, p. 9.

11   "Edsel Ford II Interview," *Automotive News*, June 16, 2003, p. 192.

12   Beverly Rae Kimes, "Young Henry Ford," *Automobile Quarterly* 10:2, 1972, pp. 212.

13   David Lewis, "Ford in Racing," *Vintage Ford 11:2*, Mar.-Apr. 1976, p. 9.

14   Beverly Rae Kimes, "Young Henry Ford," *Automobile Quarterly* 10:2, 1972, pp. 212.

15   Ibid., p. 214.

16   "Ford's 1909 Cross Country Race," *Vintage Ford 11:2*, Mar.-Apr. 1976, p. 12.

17   Beverly Rae Kimes, "Henry Ford's Model T," *Automobile Quarterly* 10:4, 1972, p. 384.

18   John Pete Schmauch, "Metamorphosis of the Model T Ford," *Vintage Ford 9:4*, July-Aug. 1974, p. 17.

19   H. C. Egsgaard, "Ed Winfield," *Vintage Ford 21:4*, July-Aug. 1986, p. 18.

20   Ibid., p. 19.

21   Op cit., p. 25.

22   "The Winfield Cam," *Vintage Ford 21:4*, July-Aug. 1986, p. 26.

23   Douglas Brinkley, "Prime Mover," *American Heritage Magazine*, June-July 2003.

24   Don Radbruch, "Tin Lizzies and Tin Lizzie Derbies: The History of Model T Ford Racing 1937-1940," (Sagle, Idaho, 2005), p. 13.

25   Ibid., p. 34.

26   Op cit., p. 36.

27   Don Radbruch, "Tin Lizzies and Tin Lizzie Derbies: The History of Model T Ford Racing 1937-1940," (Sagle, Idaho, 2005), p. 36.

28   "*Hot Rod* of the Month," *Hot Rod*, May 1951, pp. 25-27.

Chapter 10

No bibliography in Chapter 10.

Chapter 11

1   Henry Ford interview, *American Legion Magazine*, Oct. 1932.

2   Henry Ford interview, *Ford News*, June 1937.

3   Diana Kurylko, "The 2003 Model T," *Automotive News*, June 16, 2003, p. 25.

4   Ibid., p. 25.

5   Ken Juran, "Everything Old is New Again," The Automotive, 2003.

6   Diana Kurylko, "The 2003 Model T," *Automotive News*, June 16, 2003, p. 25.

7   Daniel Pund, editor, "Up Front," Car and Driver, August 2001, p. 31.

8   "The Oldest Ford Dealership," *Automotive News*, June 16, 2003, p. 304.

9   Steven Finlay, "Ford's First Dealer Met Henry At A Bike Show," *Ward's Business*, June 1, 2003.

10   Ibid.

11   Robert Lacey, *Ford: The Men and The Machine*, (London, 1986), pp. 85-86.

12   Steven Finlay, "Ford's First Dealer Met Henry At A Bike Show," *Ward's Business*, June 1, 2003.

13   Don J. Black, "A Visit to the Towe Antique Ford Collection," *Vintage Ford* 16:5, Sept.-Oct. 1981, p. 29.

14   Ibid., p. 31

15   "Two Original Model T Fords," *Vintage Ford* 16:4, July-Aug. 1981, p. 13.

Chapter 12

No bibliography in Chapter 12.

LOSE YOURSELF IN FANTASTIC FORDS

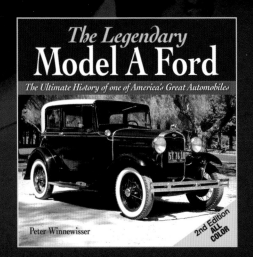

Hardcover • 10-3/4 x 10-3/4
304 pages • 225+ color photos
Item# FMA02 • $39.99

THE LEGENDARY MODEL A FORD
The Ultimate History of One of America's Great Automobiles
2nd Edition
by Peter Winnewisser

Explore the evolution of the Model A from its humble beginnings, through its heyday, into the final years of production and straight into the history books. This new edition of *The Legendary Model A Ford* showcases all the craftsmanship, style and innovation that helped shape the automobile industry.

With sales data, production details, promotional materials-including photos of vintage sales slips, newspaper advertisements, specification sheets, cartoons, brochures and more, this bold and beautiful car book takes you beyond the role of mere observer, straight into aficionado. Plus, a special section containing letters to dealers gives readers a unique peek behind the scenes of Ford ownership.

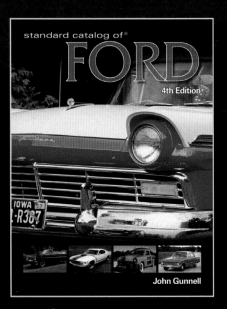

Softcover • 8-1/4 x 10-7/8
416 pages • 1,100 b&w photos
8-page color section
Item# Z1786 • $24.99

STANDARD CATALOG OF ® FORD
4th Edition
by John Gunnell

Ford fans of every persuasion will find that this unique, technically detailed reference delivers the facts you need to properly identify, buy, restore and invest in a collectible Ford. Still one of the most popular car choice of restorers, this catalyst of the old car hobby brings an energy you won't soon find anywhere else.

Inside the pages of this guide you'll find listings with serial number information — essential for legally registering a vehicle, plus:
- Original pricing
- Available models
- Weight and production history
- Collector market values for Fords of 1903-2001

Order directly from the publisher by calling 800-258-0929 M-F 8 am — 5 pm
Online at www.krausebooks.com or from booksellers nationwide, and auto parts shops where available.
Please reference offer AUB7 with all direct-to-publisher orders.
P.O. Box 5009, Iola, WI   54945-5009 • www.krausebooks.com

kp krause publications
An imprint of F+W Publications, Inc.
www.krausebooks.com